SHANGHAI GRAND

Also by Taras Grescoe

Sacré Blues:
An Unsentimental Journey Through Quebec

The End of Elsewhere:
Travels Among the Tourists

The Devil's Picnic:
Travels Through the Underworld of Food and Drink

Bottomfeeder:
How to Eat Ethically in a World of Vanishing Seafood

Straphanger:
Saving Our Cities and Ourselves from the Automobile

TARAS GRESCOE

SHANGHAI GRAND

Forbidden Love and International Intrigue
in a Doomed World

St. Martin's Press ✹ New York

SHANGHAI GRAND. Copyright © 2016 by Taras Grescoe. All rights reserved.
Printed in the United States of America. For information,
address St. Martin's Press, 175 Fifth Avenue, New York, N.Y. 10010.

The permissions acknowledgements on page 457
constitute an extension of this copyright page.

www.stmartins.com

Map artwork by Hemesh Alles

Library of Congress Cataloging-in-Publication Data

Names: Grescoe, Taras.
Title: Shanghai grand : forbidden love and international intrigue in a doomed
  world / Taras Grescoe.
Description: First U.S. edition. | New York : St. Martin's Press, 2016. |
  "First published in the United Kingdom by Macmillan, an imprint of
  Pan Macmillan"—Title page verso.
Identifiers: LCCN 2016001124| ISBN 9781250049711 (hardcover) |
  ISBN 9781466850675 (e-book)
Subjects: LCSH: Shanghai (China)—Social life and customs—20th century. |
  Shanghai (China)—Biography. | Hahn, Emily, 1905–1997—Travel—China—
  Shanghai. | Hahn, Emily, 1905–1997—Relations with men. | Americans—
  China—Shanghai—Biography. | Adventure and adventurers—China—
  Shanghai—Biography. | Aliens—China—Shanghai—Biography. | Sassoon, Elias
  Victor, 1881–1961—Friends and associates. | Cathay Hotel (Shanghai, China)—
  History. | Sino-Japanese War, 1937–1945—Social aspects—China—Shangahi. |
  BISAC: HISTORY / Asia / China. | BIOGRAPHY & AUTOBIOGRAPHY /
  Historical.
Classification: LCC DS796.S25 G74 2016 | DDC 951./132042092—dc23
LC record available at http://lccn.loc.gov/2016001124

Our books may be purchased in bulk for promotional, educational,
or business use. Please contact your local bookseller or the Macmillan Corporate
and Premium Sales Department at 1-800-221-7945, extension 5442,
or by e-mail at MacmillanSpecialMarkets@macmillan.com.

First published in the United Kingdom by Macmillan,
an imprint of Pan Macmillan

First U.S. Edition: June 2016

10 9 8 7 6 5 4 3 2 1

To admirable Erin, intrepid Desmond,
and the noble, newborn Victor:
our future together is grand.

Contents

List of Illustrations

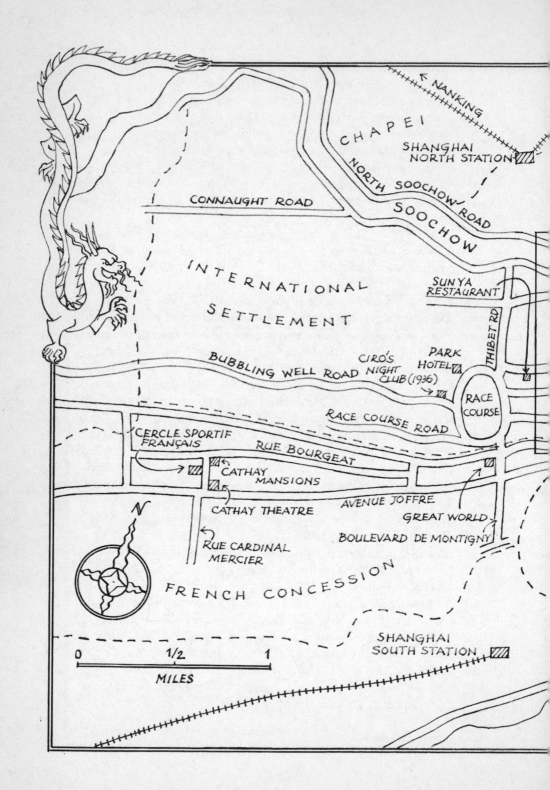

← NANKING

CHAPEI

SHANGHAI
NORTH STATION

CONNAUGHT ROAD

NORTH SOOCHOW ROAD

SOOCHOW

INTERNATIONAL

SETTLEMENT

SUN YA
RESTAURANT

THIBET RD

BUBBLING WELL ROAD

CIRO'S
NIGHT
CLUB (1936)

PARK
HOTEL

RACE
COURSE

RACE COURSE ROAD

CERCLE SPORTIF
FRANÇAIS

RUE BOURGEAT

CATHAY
MANSIONS

AVENUE JOFFRE

CATHAY THEATRE

GREAT WORLD

N

BOULEVARD DE MONTIGNY

RUE CARDINAL
MERCIER

FRENCH CONCESSION

SHANGHAI
SOUTH STATION

0   1/2   1

MILES

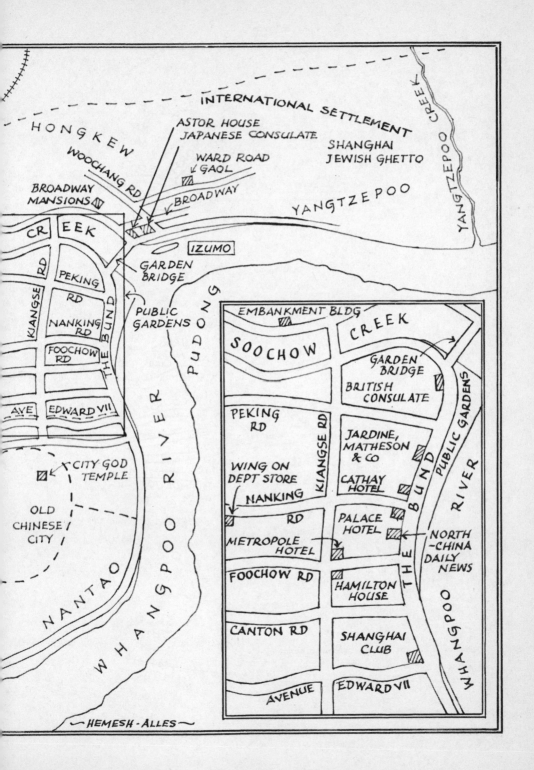

SHANGHAI GRAND

Prologue

The Shao family's directions were good.

Outside the Zhujiajiao bus station, a pedicab driver in a beige painter's cap had glanced at the black-and-white map I'd printed out at the business centre of my hotel and muttered, "*Hao, hao, hao.*" Flicking away his cigarette, he'd gestured for me to take a seat on the upholstered seat behind him, and I'd watched as he stood on the pedals in no-name sneakers, using his full weight to generate a little momentum. As we approached the first of half a dozen humpbacked bridges, he'd leaned down to flip the switch of a jerry-rigged electric motor. With the uphill work being done for him, he'd sat back in his saddle and we'd both been able to enjoy a venerable Chinese vista: a waterscape of flat-bottomed wooden sampans, their sun canopies hung with red paper lanterns, being poled up and down the canals of an ancient water town.

Now, as we stopped outside a walled complex surrounded by a moat and whimsical sculptures of flute-playing boys astride giant carps, I re-read the text of the last message Pearl had sent me.

"After you enter the cemetery, look at the left-hand side, the third block. My grandparents' location is in the middle of the first row." A shaven-headed Buddhist monk in ochre robes pointed the way through a gatehouse roofed with upcurving eaves, and I walked towards a subdivision of tightly serried rectangular gravestones, whose outermost row overlooked a tiny parcel of fenced-off lawn patched with brown.

I found what I was looking for in the twelfth plot. It was a formal wedding portrait of a young man and woman, set flush with the polished granite surface of the gravestone. Most of the other tombs were topped by ill-lit head-and-shoulders photos of men in Western business suits, or women with puffy perms and frilly blouses. This one's careful composition, and the couple's high-collared silk gowns, bespoke the elegance of a less austere era. The almost perfect oval of the woman's face, matched, like a diffusing smoke ring, by the elliptical frame surrounding her, was offset by a wispy black bang combed down in a curve that sat flush with her thin black eyebrows. At one corner of her mouth I detected the hint of a dimple. Her smile, like that of the man beside her, was calm and complacent, suggesting shared childhood secrets that have settled, in early adulthood, into a comfortable complicity.

It was the man in the portrait, though, who commanded my attention. His jet-black hair was slicked away from a high, amused brow over eyes that, as one admirer phrased it, called to mind "black grapes on a white jade platter." Although he was Chinese, the lower half of his face – full lips, a square chin and a long, aquiline nose with elegantly raked-back nostrils – looked more Middle than Far Eastern. Clean-shaven in this photo, he was more often seen with a thin moustache and a goatee that, when he put on the long robes of a Confucian scholar, evoked at once a Mediterranean romantic hero and the mysteries of the Orient. Part Rudolph Valentino's *Sheik*, part Fu-Manchu as played by long-forgotten Hollywood star Warner Oland, he was an irresistible combination of East and West.

The gravestone recorded the names of the couple, confirmed that they were husband and wife, and gave their dates of birth (hers 1905, his a year later). It also indicated the dates of their deaths: his at the height of the Cultural Revolution, hers in the same year government troops mowed down pro-democracy protesters in Tiananmen Square with machine guns and assault rifles. The neighbouring gravestones' reverse sides were blank, but theirs was inscribed: four columns of characters were carved into the granite, twenty-eight bright pink ideograms in all. Taking a photo, I promised myself that as soon as I got back to my hotel I would have the inscription translated. I hoped it would provide a clue to the mystery that had brought me back to China.

For now, though, the puzzle remained. The trail I had been following ended at this exiguous grave on the distant outskirts of Shanghai.

The man buried in Gui Yuan cemetery is known to Mandarin-speaking Chinese as Shao Xunmei. During his lifetime, speakers of the Hu dialect, still the primary language of communication for fourteen million people in the Shanghai area, called him Zau Sinmay. Before the Second World War, hundreds of thousands of readers in the West knew him as Mr. Pan, a charming and chimerical poet and publisher with a houseful of children, a good-for-nothing rake for a father, and a long-suffering wife. His misadventures in a series of *New Yorker* vignettes in the late thirties humanized the reputedly inscrutable Chinese for a well-educated Western audience. For his literary admirers, Zau Sinmay was one of the first writers to bring the sensibility of *fin-de-siècle* Europe to the Middle Kingdom. In the bestselling novel *Steps of the Sun* he was Sun Yuin-loong, who, after sweeping the heroine Dorothy Pilgrim off her feet by reciting poetry between puffs of opium smoke, proves a passionate if maddeningly inconstant lover. For Christopher Isherwood and W.H. Auden, who arrived in China just as the first wave of a Japanese invasion reached the mouth of the Yangtze River, he was Mr. Zinmay Zau, the only contemporary Chinese writer whose verse was translated for inclusion in their one-of-a-kind travelogue *Journey to a War*. A pioneering publisher of *manhua*, the proto-*manga* that were a popular sensation in pre-revolutionary Shanghai, Sinmay would see his distinctive features caricatured by cartoonists and the misadventures of his dissolute father parodied in *Mr. Wang*, a weekly strip about an impecunious nobleman's comical attempts to save face by avoiding his legions of creditors.

By the time he met Emily "Mickey" Hahn, the Missouri-born adventurer who would become his concubine (and eventually his second wife, in a convoluted marriage of convenience), he'd transformed himself into the director of a company that pumped out glossy colour weeklies on a German-made rotogravure printing press – then the most modern in China – even as he adopted the long brown gowns and whiskers of the Mandarin scholar.

His American lover's candid chronicling of their relationship in the *New Yorker* made him an international celebrity, and often the one Chinese person the foreign intelligentsia insisted on meeting when their ocean liners called at Shanghai. Sinmay was a French decadent poet's most garish Orientalist fantasy made flesh.

Among Shanghainese writers, the lifestyle of this Cambridge-educated cosmopolitan provoked awe. "The young master's residence is one of Shanghai's superior mansions," wrote a contemporary.

Built entirely in marble, surrounded by a large garden, and approached by eight pathways wide enough for automobiles, the estate looked like a manifestation of the eight hexagrams with a tall Western building in the middle. The center of the house formed a hall magnificently decorated like an emperor's throne room . . . and there was the host's private study, where he entertained guests. Here, too, the interior decoration was exceptionally opulent; there was an authentic bust of the poetess Sappho recently excavated in the volcanic city of Pompeii – this item alone was worth five thousand dollars. Furthermore, there was a manuscript of the English poet Swinburne that had been acquired for twenty-thousand pounds in London . . . In the center of the room stood a Steinway piano . . . and right next to it there was a pile of music scores bound in jade-tinted snakeskin.

Though much was exaggerated in this account of the Zaus' family home on Jiaozhou Road (the Sappho bust was a reproduction and the manuscript by Swinburne, one of Zau's favourite poets, was over-appraised), the writer had left out other things: the poet's collection of priceless Song-dynasty ivories, for example, and a Jean-Auguste-Dominique Ingres canvas he'd picked up in Paris. At a time when most Shanghainese were living tightly packed into complexes of brick rowhouses and the typical writer was forced to rent a pavilion room over another family's kitchen, Zau's extreme wealth provoked envy, and sometimes out-and-out enmity.

For readers in the United States, the swan song of Pan Heh-ven, as he was known in the vignettes, came in March 1940, when the *New Yorker*'s readers learned of a risky trip behind Japanese lines to recover what little was left on the shelves of the family pawn-shop in a little country town near Nanking. In the twentieth century, the last news that readers would have of Zau was an essay by Mickey Hahn in the late 1960s, describing how he'd introduced her to the rituals of the opium pipe. Zau Sinmay – a.k.a. Shao Xunmei, Sun Yuin-loong, the Chinese Verlaine, and the quirky Mr. Pan so beloved by readers of the *New Yorker* – became another skeleton in a drowned world, the pre-revolutionary Shanghai of gin slings and sing-song girls, rickshaw coolies and Bolshevik spies.

In the West, the story of what happened to Sinmay in 1949, when the Chinese Communist Party pulled a "bamboo curtain" from Manchuria to Canton, has never been told.

On this overcast March morning, the final resting place of Zau Sinmay and his wife Sheng Peiyu was a study in shades of grey. Zau's surviving children, with the help of his granddaughter Pearl, had recently relocated the couple's remains from their family tomb – among pine trees and fieldstone walls in the proverbially lovely city of Suzhou – to this crowded cemetery on the distant outskirts of Shanghai. Tallying up the graves and the niches for cremated remains in the surrounding columbaria, I calculated the population of these few acres of ground to be well over 100,000. It was a city of the dead, one where individual lives had been reduced to granite headstones placed less than a foot apart, arranged in row after identical row.

The cemetery reproduced the high human density of the *shikumen*, the maze-like complexes of rowhouses whose coal-dust-stained bricks provided the backdrop against which the vast majority of people in Shanghai, until quite recently, lived. At one time, Sinmay had derived much of his income from the rent paid by tenants in entire city blocks of *shikumen* owned by the Zau family.

Now, in death, he occupied the right half of Tomb No. 12 of the first row of subdivision A1 of the eastern division of Gui Yuan cemetery, on the farthest outskirts of Shanghai Municipality. Invasion, revolution, imprisonment, and finally death, had permanently placed one of China's most celebrated cosmopolitans among the ranks of the people known, in the reductionist terminology of Marxist sociology, as "petty urbanites."

Before returning to the pedicab, I pulled an object out of my daybag and placed it above the birthdate of the man I'd first come to know as Zau Sinmay.

It was a black ballpoint pen – an inexpensive lagniappe from my guest suite – inscribed with the name of a certain hotel on Shanghai's Bund.

And therein lies a story.

美

I fell for Shanghai – the city of legend, and the city as it is today – as the Year of the Pig gave way to the Year of the Rat in clouds of smoke and the stench of gunpowder. In its courtyards and laneways, the echoes from strings of firecrackers created an aural map of the contours of a city singularly slow to shed its past. On that first visit, the World Exposition of 2010 was still three years in the future, and the decanting of the population from the old city centre of wood, brick, and stone to exurban high-rises of concrete, steel, and glass had yet to hit full speed. The old China hands I met said I should have seen the place fifteen years ago. (Of course, that's what old hands say, no matter where you go.) I was too busy marvelling at all that had survived into the twenty-first century to bother gainsaying them.

While I was duly impressed by the glittering new skyline rising on the Pudong riverfront, to my surprise I found myself strolling past the onion-dome of a Russian Orthodox church on the plane-tree-shaded boulevard of the former French Concession, and taking high tea in the Tudor Revival mansion of a long-dead British newspaper magnate. A half-century of stagnation, combined with a new will to preserve heritage architecture – if as nothing more than a backdrop for movie shoots and wedding photos – had conspired to preserve much of old Shanghai. I roamed through

buildings that felt like sets from the film *Blade Runner*: the corridors of Gothamesque towers, whose glassed-in lobby directories
still listed the names of upper-crust tenants from the thirties, were
now lit by bare electric bulbs, crowded with bicycles and scooters,
and redolent of herbal concoctions being boiled behind triple-
locked metal doors. I didn't know it at the time, but as I wandered
the sidewalks of the district once known around the world as the
International Settlement, my imagination was already taking up
residence in a city I'd never known: the wicked old Paris of the
Orient, a city whose major landmarks had been preserved in aspic
for half a century.

The more I learned about pre-revolutionary Shanghai, the
more fascinated I became with the people who had washed up
there. There was Morris "Two-Gun" Cohen, a Jewish brawler
from London's East End, who, after saving the life of a Cantonese
cook on the Canadian prairies, was named a general in the
movement to liberate China from seven centuries of Manchu
domination. There was "Princess" Sumaire, the niece of the
wealthiest Maharajah in the Punjab, who, after working as a fashion model in Paris, scandalized Shanghai society with her open
bisexuality and high-profile affairs with Japanese aristocrats and
Gestapo agents. There was the triple agent Trebitsch Lincoln, a
professional shape-shifter, whose career – from rabbi's son in
Budapest, to Protestant missionary in Montreal, to shaven-headed
Buddhist abbot in Shanghai – read like the back cover of a
paperback thriller. It was as vivid a cast of chancers, schemers,
exhibitionists, double-dealers, and self-made villains as had ever
been assembled in one place – and they all crossed paths in the
hotel lobbies, exclusive clubs, and dockside dives of pre-war
Shanghai.

If I was mesmerized by the personalities who congregated in
this "paradise of adventurers," I fell in love with Mickey Hahn, the
St. Louis-born journalist and adventurer who put the whole crazy
scene down on paper. In an attempt to mend a broken heart, she'd
impulsively hopped an ocean liner out of San Francisco and ended
up living in China and Hong Kong for eight years. The *coup de*

foudre came when I saw a portrait of her, taken about the time she was sharing drunken confidences with Dorothy Parker in the ladies' room of the Algonquin Hotel. In the photo her hair is boyishly short, her skin pale against a black blouse, and her full lips are parted as she gazes up at a capuchin monkey (named Punk) perched on her left shoulder. In the heyday of the flapper, she looked like a proto-beatnik, one of nature's born individualists. I started to read her books: a travelogue about walking across the Congo with a three-year-old pygmy boy; her recollections of defying sexism to become the first female mining engineer to graduate from the University of Wisconsin; an essay about living on D.H. Lawrence's ranch in New Mexico, where she picked up a taste for corn liquor and dating cowboys while working as a trail guide. I liked her style (daring in fashion, breezy in prose), her utter lack of snobbery and prejudice, her fragile yet intrepid heart. In the long-out-of-print books about her Asian adventures, she took me exactly where I wanted to go: on an insider's rickshaw ride that criss-crossed a bygone Shanghai, down alleys reverberant with the rattle of mah-jong tiles and scented with sweet almond broth, opium smoke, and the chemical bite of Flit insecticide.

And I got to know her friends, who were legion. There were the *taipans*, the wealthy businessmen she liked to shock by puffing on a cigar at such nightspots as Ciro's and the Tower Club, and their wives, the *taitais*, among them Bernardine Szold-Fritz, whose salon brought together the Chinese and European intelligentsia. (Bernardine, deeply enamoured of Zau Sinmay, would later regret the night she introduced the poet to Mickey.) There were such roving reporters as Martha Gellhorn, also from St. Louis, who, on her honeymoon with Ernest Hemingway, made a point of tracking down Mickey for contacts in the Chinese military. There were the expat newsmen of China – the so-called "Missouri Mafia" – among them John B. Powell, the corncob-pipe smoking editor of the *China Weekly Review*, and Edgar Snow, who would follow a muleteer into the remote mountains of Shaanxi Province and return with the first articles by a Westerner to profile Mao Tse-tung and his rebel army.

Most intriguing of all was Sir Victor Sassoon, the third Baronet of Bombay, who, after photographing Mickey in the nude in a private studio in his penthouse suite, set tongues wagging when he gave her a powder-blue Chevrolet coupe in which to buzz around town. Sir Victor, who spoke the best Oxbridge English, could trace his ancestry from an ancient line of Sephardic Jews who served in the court of the Babylonian Pasha and claimed descent from the fifth son of King David. While the world slid into the Great Depression he unapologetically made the rounds of Shanghai's most fashionable nightspots in top hat and tails, usually wearing a fresh carnation from his own gardens in his lapel, looking for all the world like the caricature of a multimillionaire on a Monopoly "Chance" card.

Mickey's friendships weren't limited to the Shanghailanders,* the privileged expatriates who styled themselves the natural ruling class of the China coast. She learned to speak Shanghainese and, later, to read and write Mandarin; her various apartments became salons for Chinese writers, and hideouts for communist guerrillas on the run. It was Mickey's flirtation with Zau Sinmay that ultimately brought her the connections that would make her into a respected biographer of China's leading political dynasty. And it was their ongoing relationship – which saved Mickey's life during the Japanese occupation – that may well have put Zau into his early grave.

Now, seven years after my first visit to Shanghai, I found myself returning from a cemetery on the edge of the city, my questions about the fate of Zau Sinmay still unanswered. From my plastic bucket seat on a pastel-pink bus on the elevated Huyu Expressway, I had a privileged view of the new metropolis. Though we were hurtling along at fifty miles an hour, the glass-and-concrete towers continued to scroll by for almost half an hour – apartments

---

* While "Shanghainese" is used to describe both the dialect spoken in Shanghai and the city's Chinese residents, since the nineteenth century residents of European and North American descent have favoured the unfelicitous term "Shanghailander" – probably for its suggestion of islanders, surrounded by a vast sea of humanity.

stacked twenty, thirty, forty storeys high – growing more tightly spaced as we got closer to the Bund. Through a scrim of pollution I descried a highwayside sign for the State Grid Corporation, China's coal-dependent electrical utility, whose blue neon flashed "Clean Energy Towards a Harmonious Future."

After pausing at a multi-lane toll plaza my bus merged into the traffic on the upper deck of the Yan'an Elevated Road, a bold piece of civil engineering that is also a royal road into the urban past. We were following the route of an ancient creek, Yang Jin Bang, which by the thirties was called Avenue Édouard VII – the French name for one of the few British kings palatable to Shanghai's Gallic community – and marked the boundary between the International Settlement and the French Concession. During the Japanese occupation it was renamed Great Shanghai Road, and for a few years after the Second World War it became Zhongzheng Road (after the Chinese name for the nationalist leader Chiang Kai-shek). Since the fifties it has been Yan'an Road, in honour of the mountain hideaway where Mao Tse-tung holed up after the Long March. Now an elevated multi-lane expressway, intertwined with pedestrian overpasses, by night its neon-lit underbelly casts a frigid blue glow on the lanes of traffic at street level.

The building of the Yan'an Elevated in the nineties cut a swath through the historic centre of Shanghai, but some landmarks were spared. On my right, the upper tiers of a building shaped like a neo-baroque wedding cake loomed over the expressway. This was the Great World, a phantasmagoric entertainment centre, built by the Chinese inventor of a bestselling brain tonic. In its heyday it teemed with acrobats, magicians, acupuncturists, storytellers, and sing-song girls. It was here that two errant shrapnel bombs fell from a damaged plane one afternoon in 1937, killing over a thousand refugees who had gathered outside the building to receive rations of rice – an event that some historians argue marked the true beginning of the Second World War in Asia.

The Great World, once a flagrant symbol of decadence, is now a city-block-sized shell, its long facade empty except for a few souvenir and herbal-medicine shops. After reaching the bus's final stop at the Pu'An Road station, I crossed a pedestrian overpass that took me to what had once been one of the nerve centres of expatriate life in pre-war Shanghai: the Shanghai Race Course. Now renamed People's Square, it is the heart of the city, a teeming complex where three busy metro lines meet, topped by a vast plaza that includes museums, a symphony hall, and an urban planning exhibition centre. Skirting its eastern edge, I turned east onto Nanjing Road, Shanghai's main commercial conduit – an aorta or a cloaca, depending on your point of view – since the city's earliest days as a treaty port.

From that point on, every step took me back in time, through a Shanghai only lightly touched by the decades. I walked past the sprawling department stores, past Sun Sun, and Sincere, and Wing-On, and their green, orange, and red neon signs, which flickered on in the dusk. I walked past the crowd queued up for takeout outside Sun Ya, a Cantonese restaurant that, when Zau Sinmay and his circle used to frequent it in the thirties, was famous for its bird's nest soup and ice-cream sundaes. I walked past a group of elderly women who had gathered to waltz, erect and graceful, in the pedestrianized street, to music from a CD player perched on a bench. I walked quickly, because a solitary foreigner on Shanghai's main drag was still accosted by girls who offered "*massageee*" and touts in tight leather jackets hissing: "What you want? Rolex? Purse? Beautiful girl? Sex?" I weaved my way between the blue tourist trains that had taken the place of electric trolleys and man-powered rickshaws, until Nanjing Road started its gentle curve towards the riverfront, and a sharply pitched pyramid of weather-stained copper, topped with the billowing red and yellow flag of communist China, came into view.

At the east end of Nanjing Road, at the exact point where the city meets the Huangpu River – and where Chinese commerce has always met the waterfront that has led to the rest of the world – lay Sassoon House, and atop it, my destination: the hotel that was once known around the world as the grandest in the Far East.

This was my home in Shanghai: the house built by, and for, Sir Victor Sassoon, reckoned in the thirties to be one of the five or six richest men in the world, who erected Asia's first real sky-scrapers, and created the elegant apartment houses and nightclubs that made the world want to cross oceans to see Shanghai. I pushed through a revolving door, and my pace slowed as I crossed a lobby which, from floors of polished marble to soaring coffered ceilings, captured the streamlined beauty of Art Deco at the height of its elegance.

The Cathay Hotel was Sir Victor's pied-à-terre in Shanghai; he lived in a luxuriously appointed penthouse apartment on the eleventh floor. It was here that Noël Coward wrote the play *Private Lives*, that Charlie Chaplin and Paulette Goddard dined at the hotel's Dragon Phoenix Restaurant, and that Douglas Fairbanks danced on the sprung teak floor of its eighth-floor ballroom. At a time when the Chinese were barred from such Western bastions as the Shanghai Club and the Cercle Sportif Français, its rooftop nightclub provided the venue that allowed Zau Sinmay and China's brightest minds to mingle with the global elite. And it was in this hotel that Sir Victor, who had been waiting to meet a woman like Mickey Hahn all his life, became enraged as he watched her slip away from the bubble of Euro-American society into the rich life of Chinese Shanghai.

It was at the Cathay, too, that Zau Sinmay's American lover first stayed when she arrived in Shanghai – "in Room 536 or thereabouts," according to her fictionalized account of her love affair with the Chinese poet. The suite I had booked was also on the fifth floor, on the Nanjing Road side.

That night, I closed my eyes on one of the world's great views: the barges and twinkling tourist boats on the Huangpu River, turned Lilliputian by the mega-tall skyscrapers that twinkled exuberantly on the opposite bank.

Opening my laptop the following morning, I read an email from a Chinese friend, who overnight had translated the inscription I'd found on the back of Zau Sinmay's grave.

It was a poem first written in 1930, and it read:

Who do you think I am?
A loafer, a miser obsessed with money, a scholar,

Someone who wants to be a minister, or a die-hard hero?
You are wrong, you are totally wrong,
I am a natural-born poet.

I chuckled. It was typical of Zau Sinmay, I thought, that his epitaph took the form of a riddle in verse.

He was one of the twentieth century's most fabulously entitled aesthetes, yet unlike Sir Victor Sassoon and Mickey Hahn, his fate has remained unknown outside of China. Since my first visit to Shanghai, I had learned all there was to know about the life and career of Mickey Hahn. After visiting the Lilly Library in Bloomington, Indiana, where the 10,000-plus items in the "Hahn mss" are stored in dozens of bankers' boxes, I had spent months poring over the prose, published and unpublished, and correspondence that comprehensively documented her life – first in India ink, then in typescript on onionskin paper and Western Union telegrams, and finally, by the early nineties, in emails recorded by dot matrix printers. In Dallas, I had spent a week photographing the cramped handwriting and tiny snapshots that filled the pages of Sir Victor Sassoon's thirty-five journals, stored at the DeGolyer Library at the Southern Methodist University. There, too, I had been graciously welcomed by the niece of his late wife, who took me on a tour of the old Sassoon mansion while sharing stories that showed how Sir Victor had held on to his love of velocity and novelty well into the age of Sputnik and Elvis Presley. In contrast, the final act of Sinmay's life – the story of what became of him after China's communists pulled a "Bamboo Curtain" from Canton to Manchuria in 1949 – has never been recounted in the West.

What happened to Sinmay after politics and history had conspired to rob him first of his home, then of his printing press and family fortune, and finally of his reputation? The poem on the back of his tomb, though it brought me no closer to an answer, made me more determined to dig deeper.

For what happened to Zau Sinmay, I knew, also happened to Shanghai. For a brief, shining period, this was one of the most cosmopolitan places on the face of the earth – a city where Confucian scholars studied the philosophy of Bertrand Russell, where

Midwestern farm boys were tutored in the calligraphy of Tang-dynasty poets, and where Vietnamese detectives engaged in running gun battles with secret-society hitmen in the streets of the French Concession. In a time before email, cell phones, and social media, it was a place to which the ambitious, the wily, and the desperate could escape to discard old identities and recreate their lives from scratch. It was in Shanghai that chambermaids became White Russian princesses, and the sons of impoverished peasants made themselves into crime overlords. It was here, too, that the co-existence of breathtaking wealth and abysmal poverty created the crucible for the ideologies that have transformed Asia, and continue to shape global geopolitics in the twenty-first century.

The place where so many of these lives intersected was the famous building whose mailing address was 20 Nanking Road: the Cathay Hotel, the house built by Sir Victor Sassoon. Its opening in 1929 heralded the beginning of the city's golden age of glamour. An explosion outside its revolving doors eight years later would mark the beginning of the end of old Shanghai, and with it the West's long romance with the idea of "Cathay" – the mysterious, supine, unchanging Orient long cherished by the Western imagination.

The pen I'd laid atop Zau Sinmay's grave was inscribed with the words "Peace Hotel," the name the hotel was given after the Chinese Communist Party took power. By the time "Cathay" gave way to "Peace," China had undergone invasion, occupation, world war, and revolution, and three intensely lived lives had been sundered and dramatically transformed. Of the protagonists of this story, only one would remain behind to witness what history had in store for Shanghai.

Human history is written, for those who take the time to read it, into the physical fabric of the world. In Shanghai it is scrawled into the patterns of the streets and legible in the surface of the bricks and stones of buildings that, through the years and against the odds, have continued to stand. It was precisely because I know that history is not only written on paper that I'd decided to return to Shanghai, to discover what, if anything, its streets could tell me about the people who had once led such full and vivid lives there.

From my fifth-floor window, I watched the Bund coming to life. Seventy years ago, bells atop the British-run Custom House played the Westminster Quarters, providing a comforting echo of the chimes of Big Ben over the Thames half a world away. On this morning, as the clock faces marked seven o'clock, loudspeakers atop the same building made the riverfront resound with a recorded version of the Cultural Revolution anthem "The East is Red."

Even this early in the morning, the pavement below was alive with the exuberant life of a great Asian city. Joggers weaved among people flying dragon-shaped kites and vendors tending steaming pots of corn on the cob. An elderly man on a bicycle smiled serenely as he pedalled past a traffic cop in a white cap, who berated him, in a perfunctory way, for riding on the sidewalk. I pulled on my jacket and went out the door, ready for another day of walking the streets.

The resolution to Zau Sinmay's story, I knew, was out there somewhere, written into the bricks and alleyways of Shanghai. I had a lot of reading ahead of me.

PART ONE

"During the last thousand years, a Sassoon
has never been known to be wrong."

– Ernest O. Hauser,
"The Fabulous Sassoons,"
The American Mercury, 1940.

1: Shanghai, January 28, 1932

The room boy had just cleared Sir Victor Sassoon's desk for tiffin – the multi-course luncheon that, on Thursdays, included a Bombay-style vegetable curry accompanied by a bottle of ice-cold Bass ale – when the blast occurred. Suddenly and authoritatively, every molecule in the penthouse of the Cathay Hotel was displaced by a vastly percussive thud, almost tectonic in its intensity, followed half a beat later by a watery, all-encompassing *whoosh*. For a moment, the entire building seemed to lurch backwards, like a stout man rocked on his heels by a gust from a Pacific typhoon.

Sir Victor approached the windows that faced north towards the Public Gardens. A geyser of filthy water was already subsiding into a cloud of vapour on the river in front of the Japanese Consulate in Hongkew. Shock waves from the explosion had sent the bat-winged junks on the Whangpoo River bobbing like toys in a bathtub. From the looks of it, the Chinese had detonated a naval mine not fifty yards from the *Izumo*, the flagship of Japan's Imperial Navy in China.

So, this was how it was going to be. Tokyo and Nanking weren't content to confine their squabbling to Manchuria. They were going to bring the fight to his doorstep.

That the Asiatics were at each other's throats was one matter. That their chosen battleground was the greatest metropolis in the Far East, a city whose greatness derived from the sustained industry of the Western powers, was quite another. Ever since the Japanese had sunk the Russian fleet at Port Arthur in 1905 – the first time a Western power had been defeated by an Oriental one – they had been swaggering about Asia like they owned the place. In Shanghai, the number of their factories had been steadily growing, as had the number of resident Japanese, so that they now outnumbered the combined British and American population. In spite of their assurances that Tokyo's intentions in Shanghai were peaceful, belligerent elements in the Imperial Navy had taken advantage of a Chinese boycott of Japanese-made goods to launch their fleet, on the pretext of protecting Japanese citizens in Shanghai. Less than a week before, Rear-Admiral Shiozawa had solemnly assured Harry Arnhold – chairman of the Municipal Council, and one of Sir Victor's most trusted lieutenants – that Japan had no intention of trespassing on the neutrality of the International Settlement. Yet the following day, 500 Japanese marines had landed on the wharves of Yangtzepoo, half a mile from the front door of the Cathay Hotel. The copy of the *North-China Daily News* atop Sir Victor's desk reported that a dozen Japanese destroyers had sailed from Nagasaki the day before. Even now they were crossing the 500 miles of the East China Sea, destination: Shanghai.

Sir Victor picked up the telephone receiver and called down to the lobby. Carrard, the Swiss-born manager at the front desk, assured his employer that the staff had reported no deaths or injuries. So there was that: he wouldn't be walking out into a lobby strewn with bloodied bodies. Before he reached the door, an impulse made him pivot on his walking stick and reach for his motion-picture camera. Whatever drama was occurring outside, it was bound to be photogenic.

In the corridor, the Chinese lift operator was waiting for him, white-gloved hands holding back the gates. As the indicator needle counted down the floors, Sir Victor's anxiety mounted. Until now, he had had no reason to regret his decision to move the Sassoon family's base of operations from India to China. In Bombay the previous summer, he'd announced his decision to quit the subcontinent with some satisfaction.

"The political situation in India does not encourage one to launch out in a big way for the time being," he'd told the editor of the *Times of India*, who he'd summoned to his office. "India under Swaraj [self-rule] will have a great deal of internal trouble. On the other hand, China now is getting over her civil wars."

The interview had appeared on front pages in London and New York. The Indians, long restless under British rule, now seemed intent on self-sabotage. Two years earlier, a self-righteous lawyer had marched over 200 miles from his Gujarati ashram to the Arabian Sea. Kneeling on the beach, Mohandas Gandhi had bucked the tax laws of the Raj through the simple expedient of boiling a lump of mud in seawater to illegally manufacture his own salt. Now, as head of the Congress Party, Gandhi was calling for a complete rejection of British authority. The flag he proposed for an independent India was made of handspun cloth. Bang in the middle was a simple rendering of a foot-operated spinning wheel, said to symbolize Indian self-reliance. For Sir Victor, it was a personal affront: the thousands of mechanized spools of the twelve Sassoon mills in Bombay, which kept the British Empire supplied with well-priced cotton, had also spun the family fortune.

In truth, life in India had become tiresome for Sir Victor. Bombay meant sweating in formal whites at excruciatingly long banquets with the Viceroy; yet another burra peg of whisky at the club to ward off the withering humidity; the stultifying Colonial atmosphere of inertia, bureaucracy, and over-taxation. Since he had started visiting the Sassoon offices in Hong Kong and Shanghai, China had impressed him with its immense potential. Shanghai was gin slings at late-night cabarets, horse races with spirited Mongolian ponies, and pliant sing-song girls with outlandish nicknames. The city, inevitably, had its share of self-styled blue bloods who thought it clever to mumble anti-Semitic remarks behind his back. But they were outnumbered by an ever-growing population of cultured White Russians, straight-talking American entrepreneurs, preposterous European adventurers, and educated – and increasingly prosperous – Chinese. For a man who knew how to make the best of a complex situation, this most complex of cities felt like home.

On the eve of the stock market crash, Sir Victor had transferred sixty lakhs of silver taels – the equivalent of $29 million – from Bombay to Shanghai. Even now, new Sassoon hotels and apartment buildings were under construction in the Chinese city, the French Concession, and the International Settlement. While stockbrokers leaped from skyscrapers on New York's Wall Street, Sir Victor had been raising new towers on Shanghai's Bund; as the global depression bit deeper, the neon had continued to glow bright in only one city. All over the world people dreamt of coming to exotic, seductive Shanghai.

Sassoon had made sure of that with his grandest gesture: the construction of the Cathay Hotel. Its very name was a declaration of faith in the future of China. Since the day it opened in 1929, when the press had dubbed it the "Claridge's of the Far East," its reputation for up-to-date elegance had made Shanghai an essential port of call for luxury ocean liners. Already the hotel registry was filled with the signatures of celebrities. Noël Coward had been one of the first guests: he'd written an entire play while laid up with influenza in his suite. The arrival of every new ocean liner brought launches filled with well-heeled visitors. The most fashionable arrived with a booking for a room at the Cathay.

The presence among them of comely young women kept Sir Victor hopeful. He had known love once; they had met during his university years, while he was summering in London. Parental opposition cut the affair short; her family wouldn't hear of their daughter marrying a Jew. (To even his closest friends, he never spoke her name aloud; she was always "that woman.") Back at Cambridge he'd substituted defiance for despair, founding a "Club for Bachelors" with his fellow undergraduates. The initiation ceremony culminated in a blood oath, sealed one night over magnums of champagne, never to marry. Until now, he'd kept the faith, cultivating the role of cynical man of the world, flippant about affairs of the heart. When he had liaisons, he was careful to keep them brief. Fortunately, it was easy to ward off the gold-diggers who assailed him: their motivations tended to be as transparent as their charms were extravagant.

For Sir Victor, building the Cathay was a gesture of defiance: if he could not find happiness in London, Bombay, or Hong Kong, he would build a world of his own, beyond the confines of Empire. In Shanghai, he was in the process of turning a malarial swamp into a garden of delights. The Cathay was his prize orchid on the Bund, one that was already luring the world's most fabulous social butterflies. He was confident that, one day, he would go down to the lobby and she would be there – a woman who could fire his imagination and match his passion.

It wouldn't be today, though. If the news spread that the Cathay Hotel was at the heart of an active combat zone, nobody – apart from a few crazy reporters – would be coming to Shanghai at all. As the clatter of his steel-tipped walking stick echoed through the lobby rotunda, people turned to gaze at the rangy, middle-aged man with sleek black hair and a full moustache, a long Roman nose, and a monocle clamped into his left eye. Lately, American guests had taken to asking for his autograph. People told him he was a ringer for the Hollywood leading man Adolphe Menjou.

Today, though, no one dared impede his progress towards the revolving door. The castle on the Bund was under assault, and its lord had appeared to inspect the integrity of the fortifications.

Outside, he began to pace the building's perimeter, his gaze drawn upwards by the narrow granite ribs that separated the columns of slender windows on the building's facade. At street level, the colonnade of the hotel lobby and the ground-floor shopping arcade ran to the end of Nanking Road. The next three storeys were occupied by the corporate offices of Sassoon House, among them E.D. Sassoon & Co., headquarters of the private banking and trading company that was the cornerstone of the family's business in the Far East. Next came the Cathay Hotel itself: 215 rooms and suites on five floors, each with a private bathroom. Atop the guest floors, an entire level was devoted to dining and dancing. At the front of the building, nearest the riverfront, the first three tiers of the tower emerged from the roof: the Chinese-style Tower Grill, the Jacobean-style banquet hall, and the penthouse from which he had just descended. Atop it all was a pyramidal roof of verdigrised copper culminating in a look-out, 202 feet above street level, reserved for the spotters of the Shanghai Fire Brigade.

To some eyes the Cathay suggested a fanciful Art Deco rendition of a Chinese skyrocket. For Sir Victor, its granite streamlines recalled those aerodynamic sedans, their very silhouettes evoking velocity, that had lately been coming out of America. It was a fine contrast to its neighbours, the banks and head offices of the Bund, whose rusticated cornerstones and Corinthian columns suggested immobility, tradition, and the solidity of capital and Empire.

As a condition of building the Cathay, Sir Victor had convinced the Municipal Council to let him straighten out the dog-legged Nanking Road. The building's southern perimeter tapered towards its northern edge, which ran diagonally along Jinkee Road, so that the two sides met in a near-point at the hotel's riverfront facade. From the air, the Cathay formed a flat-bottomed but perfectly legible "V."

Not coincidentally, this was how Sir Victor signed his correspondence. Later that year, a vast apartment complex he was building to house his employees would complete the signature. When it was finished, its sinuous facade would form a stylized "S" on the far side of Soochow Creek. Reading from left to right, a passenger in a seaplane above the Bund would see the letters "V" and "S" stitched into the very fibres of Shanghai. Sir Victor Sassoon would be the first man in history to have monogrammed his initials into an entire city. It was a fitting emblem for a man who had derived so much of his fortune from the manufacture of cotton.

Only five years earlier, naysayers had told him no real skyscrapers would ever rise on the banks of the Whangpoo River. In Shanghai the mud of the ages went down, in places, a thousand feet. Sir Victor's engineers had solved the problem by sinking 1,600 piles, made of a composite of concrete and Douglas fir shipped from the Oregon coast, to a depth of sixty feet into the slime. On the piles sat a concrete pontoon, atop which was perched the ferroconcrete structure of Sassoon House. This made the Cathay the only hotel in the world where the guests slumbered atop a gargantuan raft, floating free in semi-liquid alluvial muck.

The explosion on the river had put the structure to its first real test. It appeared to have passed: as he continued his inspection of the colonnade, Sir Victor could detect no cracks in the granite. "Tug" Wilson, the architect, had done his job well.

As he walked farther along the east side of the building, Sir Victor was forced to keep his eyes on the street before him. At the best of times, the point where Nanking Road debouched onto the Whangpoo waterfront was chaotic. Here, outlandishly mutilated beggars keened for coppers and rickshaw coolies trawled for custom, as electric trams shouldered their way through the crowds. Now, stepping onto the Bund, the riverfront promenade that curved as elegantly as the blade of a Sikh policeman's kirpan, he saw pandemonium.

Over the water, the smoke from the exploded mine near the *Izumo* was dissipating into the ambient winter haze. From between the gossamer arches of the Garden Bridge, which spanned Soochow Creek, an uninterrupted torrent of humanity poured onto the Bund. The arrival of the Japanese was clearly causing panic across the creek in Hongkew. Sweating coolies pushed barrows with enormous wooden wheels, laden with the contents of entire households. Children in padded cotton jackets clutched rag dolls and toy trains to their chests; the topknots of the tiniest bobbed and swayed as they swung in baskets that dangled from poles over the shoulders of older brothers. One old man carried a birdcage; another a grandfather clock. That winter's flooding in the Yangtze had already made the city's Chinese districts swell with homeless peasants. Once again, the International Settlement was about to become a haven for China's most desperate refugees.

Sir Victor planted himself at a spot at the corner of the hotel, by the end of the Nanking Road colonnade, spread the legs of the tripod on the asphalt, and screwed the motion picture camera into place. Just as the motor started to whir, and he began to swivel the lens to take in the panorama, he heard the report of a rifle. A foot above his head, a windowpane shattered.

Damned if somebody wasn't shooting at him.

Hastily folding up the tripod, he made a beeline for the nearest entrance to the hotel. The doorman, trained to keep out sightseers and riff-raff, at first blocked the revolving door with a gloved hand. Flushing as he saw who it was, he bowed deeply as his boss made for the bank of elevators that would whisk him to his office on the third floor.

In the E.D. Sassoon offices, Sir Victor retrieved the service revolver he'd had since the Great War from his desk, tucked it into his belt, and told his secretary to call for a car and driver. No one was going to take pot shots at him in front of the house that he'd built. The Japanese might have decided to play rough, but Shanghai's International Settlement had a few resources of its own.

Sir Victor spent that afternoon in constant motion, inspecting the defenses on the perimeter of the Settlement, snapping photos and chatting with the soldiers of the Volunteer Corps. In the aftermath of the explosion that had shaken the Cathay, the Municipal Council declared a state of emergency and named Brigadier-General George Fleming the Commander-in-Chief. The Scots Fusiliers, he learned, were manning five miles of barricades on the borders of the Settlement.

Pausing at a checkpoint, Sir Victor chatted with a young officer. The mayor of Shanghai's Chinese municipality, he said, had agreed to most of the Japanese demands, including an end to the boycott of Japanese goods that had precipitated the crisis. The wild card in all this was the 19th Route Army, a mob of Chinese soldiers from the distant south – many armed with rifles left over from the 1870–1 Franco-Prussian war, and hand grenades made of cigarette tins – who had washed up outside Shanghai after the nationalists' Northern Expedition. It was anybody's guess whether this lot would melt into the countryside or stand and fight against the Japanese.

The defenses, Sir Victor had to admit, looked solid. There were gunboats on the Whangpoo, and the entire Settlement was surrounded by barbed wire. Yet privately Sir Victor, who had served in a real war, felt the Volunteer Corps were playing at being soldiers. Only that morning, most had been dressed in business suits. The Japanese, in contrast, had sent over men ready to die in their uniforms.

By nightfall, he felt reassured enough that he had his driver take him to the Carlton Theatre, near the Race Course, to watch a Hollywood talkie. In *The Dawn Patrol* Douglas Fairbanks plays a devil-may-care Royal Flying Corps ace driven to drink as he watches his callous commanders, desperate to maintain the appearance of air superiority, send new men to their death under the guns of the experienced pilots under the command of the "Baron," Germany's most vicious pilot. For Sir Victor, the desperate revelry of the pilots on-screen recalled his own days in the Mess of the Royal Naval Air Service in Dover – before the crash that had shattered his leg. As entertainment, though, it was hardly distracting. The storyline reminded him of the uncertain show of force his fellow Shanghailanders were putting on outside, in the face of an enemy that might prove more relentless than even the Huns.

In his offices the following morning, he learned that all hell had broken loose while he'd slept. Good as their word, the official nationalist troops had begun to withdraw, but the rag-tag 19th Route Army had stayed to fight. Even now they were in a pitched battle with the Japanese. Much of the fighting, apparently, was taking place in Chapei, the densely packed Chinese city north of the International Settlement. Sir Victor had his driver put chains on the tires of the Studebaker, his sturdiest car, the better to negotiate any rubble and glass in the battle zone.

On Nanking Road, every doorway was occupied by refugee families. After crossing a checkpoint at Soochow Creek, which marked the northern border of the International Settlement, the car progressed slowly through the deserted streets. Entire blocks of rowhouses had been destroyed by Japanese bombs. Leaning out the car's window, Sir Victor snapped a photograph of the North Station, the terminus of China's first railway line, its main building engulfed in flames. Near the station, the fighting was more intense; the Japanese marines, unmistakable in their soft-soled split-toed shoes, puttees, and white helmets, eyed the big American-made car with suspicion. After being sniped at one too many times, Sir Victor ordered his driver to turn around.

Back in the Settlement, he shared a glass of whisky with the soldiers in the Scots Fusiliers blockhouse. The marines, they told him, had been seen moving through the streets of the Settlement, directly violating official Japanese promises to the Municipal Council.

That night, he was joined by his uncle David – the black sheep of the Sassoon family, affectionately known as Nunky – atop the Cathay Hotel. The roof was a privileged viewpoint over the fighting in the city's Chinese districts. Through binoculars, they watched the Japanese bombers dropping payloads in the area around the North Station. The surrounding streets were home to some of the Sassoon companies' cheaper rental properties, where up to ten families lived under a single roof. The civilian casualties, Nunky muttered to Sir Victor, would be enormous.

As they spoke, a member of the Volunteer Corps arrived to ask about using the tower of the Cathay, with its panoramic view of the waterfront, as a signal machine. Sir Victor nodded his assent, though this was hardly the kind of role he had envisioned for the Cathay: he wanted the hotel to be renowned as a luxurious sanctuary from the world's cares, not an observation post for bloody urban warfare.

Back in the Cathay penthouse that night, Sir Victor struggled with a mounting sense of despair. He was beginning to suspect he was building a real-estate empire on quicksand. In so doing, he might have gambled away a fortune that went back a thousand years, to the Abbasid caliphate in medieval Baghdad. To occupy his mind he pulled a thick volume, bound in oxblood-hued leather, from his writing table. It was a daybook, bearing the name of a local office-supply company, embossed with his name and title. He began to write, in a spidery hand, the entry for the day: "FRIDAY – January 29th, 1932. Fires started by aeroplanes spreading fast. Japs have broken their word not to use Settlement as a base or send troops through . . ."

He paused before putting down what followed. Though what he was about to write was true, they were words he would prefer no one else read.

"It really is a war."

2: Where China Meets the World

Before Shanghai was Shanghai, the patch of swampy foreshore that was fated to become China's gateway to the world, and the future site of the Cathay Hotel, showed no particular marks of distinction. If anything, the muddy stretch of riverfront where marshbirds stilt-walked among bending reeds repelled settlement. Only its geographical position, in a calm backwater near the point where the earth's greatest ocean meets its largest continent's most lengthy river, might have marked it out for a special destiny.

For eons the river that humans would come to call the Yangtze has drawn its waters from the limits of the Indian subcontinent. Flowing down from the landside-prone plateaux of Tibet, carving away at the metamorphic rock of three spectacular gorges, widening in places to a mile, it finally spreads its fingers to cast soil first gathered from the heights of the Himalayas onto the floor of the East China Sea. Every year, this magnificent machine for turning mountains into pebbles deposits 300 million tons of alluvium onto the seabed, extending the mainland of China twenty-five yards closer to the shores of California. The notch on the coastline that marks the location of modern Shanghai, which on a map suggests the cross-section of a barnacle projecting from the hull of a freighter, was formed, over geologic ages, by the Yangtze's successive changes of course. The lower Yangtze, whose slow-flowing waters shift in hue from turbid yellow to coffee-coloured depending on the season, has been in its present channel, its fourth, for only the last 1,300 years.

For its first human inhabitants, life in the Yangtze delta came with challenges. Prone to catastrophic flooding and subject to temperature variations of 130 degrees Fahrenheit in a single year, it provided a rich habitat for boar and deer, but also for the *Anopheles* mosquito, that privileged vector for the malaria sporozoite. On its floodplain, where the alluvial soil goes down 1,000 feet in places, nothing built by humans remains completely stable: even coffins have to be ballasted with weights to prevent them from being buoyed up and split open by the mud of the ages.

Yet the river has always provided a good living. The mineral riches of constantly renewed soil, gathered from the 700 smaller rivers that flow into the Yangtze, allowed for the cultivation of rice and tea. The mulberry tree, adored by silkworms, occurs naturally on the banks of the lower Yangtze. (During the Han dynasty, silk products made in filatures in the Shanghai area travelled overland all the way to Imperial Rome.) In countless creeks and tidal inlets, freshwater and ocean fish provided a reliable source of nutrition. The earliest known name for what is now Shanghai was Hu Tu Lei, after the Hu, a fishing contraption consisting of a palisade of rope netting strung between bamboo poles, rigged to stand erect with the rising tide.

The site of this fishing village, which would later become the heart of Shanghai, was not on the Yangtze itself. It was located fifteen miles south of the great river, at the meeting of two of its tributaries, near the point where the Woosung meets the Whangpoo.* In prehistory, the Woosung was the greater river. Hydrological works undertaken by a general in the fourth century BC (the river is said to bear his family name, Whang; *poo* means "by the water") made the Whangpoo navigable, and eventually relegated the Woosung to the status of fetid urban canal.

As the Woosung silted up, cargo-laden rafts that had sailed down the Yangtze began to anchor near the fishing village on the Whangpoo. Tax collectors and other administrators followed the

---

* On modern maps, the names are transcribed "Wusong" and "Huangpu." For the purposes of this narrative, I have chosen, with a few exceptions, to use place and proper names that were common in China in the years before 1949.

boats, and the site at the confluence of the tributaries of the Yangtze came to be known by the two Chinese characters *Shang* and *Hai* – meaning, respectively, "above" and "sea."*

By the mid-sixteenth century Shanghai had become a small but prosperous city known for its poets and musicians, wealthy merchants, and erudite scholars. Its location put it within easy striking distance of the Japanese pirates who terrorized the coast. The *wokou*, or "dwarf bandits" – as diminutive, in the eyes of the Northern Chinese, as they were rapacious – sacked the Shanghai region five times in 1553, finally burning the city of wood and paper to the ground. It was rebuilt in more solid form a mile south of the fishing village, behind twenty-four-foot-high fortifications. Within these city walls, ovoid in outline, were compressed streets formed by sinuous paths between temples, government offices, teahouses, and guild buildings.

By the end of the eighteenth century, the Imperial bureaucracy in Peking ranked Shanghai a "third-class county seat." While it remained a speck on the map compared to nearby Hangchow and Soochow, it was clearly far more than a fishing village. The masts of the junks on the river, the bustling wharves, and the large warehouses for silk and cotton announced it as a prosperous, if not terribly important, settlement on the eastern edge of a venerable empire.

Only the location of the little walled city, which sat like a hundred-year-old egg on the Whangpoo River, portended a bright future. Located halfway up China's Pacific coast, it was a natural entry point into the rich heartland of the Middle Kingdom, providing a secure mooring at the embouchure of a largely navigable river in whose watershed lived one in five of the world's inhabitants during the early decades of the nineteenth century. It was fortuitously situated, in short, at the exact point where

---

* The city's name is often, and conveniently, interpreted as meaning "above the Pacific Ocean." A less glamorous but more convincing translation is "upper sea," after a local name for a minor tributary of the Woosung.

China met the world, making it a doorway to a civilization to which foreigners from a world away were already seeking entry.

In the case of Shanghai, they would physically knock that doorway down. One afternoon early in the summer of 1832, the *Lord Amherst*, a 350-ton vessel that had set sail from the port of Macao, elbowed its way past the multi-masted war junks on the Whangpoo River before dropping anchor among the sampans that floated near the little fishing village at the mouth of the Woosung. Inside its hull were some of the finest products of the British Empire: calico from Manchester, broadcloth from the Cotswolds, raw cotton from the mills of Bombay. Though commissioned by the British East India Company, the ship didn't fly the red ensign of the royally chartered company. Aboard was the Reverend Gutzlaff, a Protestant missionary from Pomerania travelling without his collar or soutane. For the purposes of the voyage, Gutzlaff, who was fluent in several Chinese dialects, had changed his first name from Charles to "Chia-li" and dubbed the ship's supercargo – Hamilton Lindsay, charged by the Company with overseeing the ship's cargo – "Hu-hsia-mi." Disguised as merchants bound for Japan, they were on a secret mission whose goal was to "ascertain how far the northern Ports of the Empire may gradually be opened to British commerce."

Proceeding to the walled city by rowboat, past wharves and large warehouses, Lindsay, Gutzlaff, and two of the ship's stoutest tars, Simpson and Stevens, strode through the city gates. When they approached the upturned gables of the Yamen, the offices of the Taotai – the highest representative of the Qing dynasty in Shanghai – the Chinese guards tried to shut and bolt the wooden doors against the intruders.

"We were only just in time to prevent it," Lindsay would later recount,

and pushing back the gate, entered the outer court of the Yamen. But the three doors leading to the inner court were shut and barred as we entered . . . Messrs. Simpson and Stevens settled the matter by two vigorous charges at the centre door with their shoulders, which shook them off their hinges and brought them down with a great clatter.

Inside the great hall of justice, they discovered the Taotai was absent that day. When Lindsay, intent on presenting a petition that would allow them to openly trade and distribute Bibles to the people of Shanghai, dared to take a seat at the table without first being given permission, the highest-ranking official glared at him, stood up, and left the room without a word. The remaining officials, after offering the barbarians cups of tea, entreated them to return at a later date.

In spite of the frosty official reception, Gutzlaff and Lindsay judged their visit a success. During the eighteen days the *Lord Amherst* remained at anchor in Shanghai, Gutzlaff and Lindsay managed to take note of the local topography, as well as the fact that up to 400 cargo ships – most of them big, four-masted junks from the north – were sailing past the mouth of the Woosung River every day. More importantly, all through their sojourn runners from ashore had rowed up to the ship, bearing messages from local merchants entreating them to sell their cargo. The merchants, they quickly realized, had no interest in Gutzlaff's Bibles, the pages of which would later be found stuffed into holes in the houses of the poor to keep out drafts. But if the honourable Hu-hsia-mi had any *yangtu* – "mud from the Western seas" – in his hold, they were eager to negotiate.

On this voyage, Lindsay had no *yangtu* to sell. To maintain his cover as an innocent trader, the product the Chinese merchants most desired had been deliberately omitted from the *Lord Amherst*'s cargo: the highest quality opium, harvested in Bengali poppy fields, processed in Calcutta, and shipped by fast, monsoon-beating opium clipper to Canton. For the East India Company, which had a monopoly on its import, opium was a cash cow. In China, its import and smoking had been banned by Imperial edict for over a century. To carry it into an untested market like Shanghai would have been an open provocation.

But Lindsay and Gutzlaff, seeing how eager local merchants

were to trade, knew that the nominal opposition from Manchu bureaucrats would be easily overcome. Shanghai, they reported to the Company on their return to Macao, would soon be open for business.

美

The splintering of the carved wood of the Taotai's door by the crew of the *Lord Amherst*, the event that marked the beginning of Shanghai's modern history, occurred at a low point in Chinese history.

For much of its existence, China's civilization has been the most advanced on the planet. The organized harvesting of rice and millet on her rivers goes back 12,000 years, predating Mesopotamian agriculture by four millennia. While Europe was slumbering through the Middle Ages, China was a unified, centralized state capable of such huge infrastructure projects as the construction of a network of bricked roads that put the capital, then the sacred city of Sian, within eight days' travel of most major cities. Almost a century before Columbus reached the mainland of South America, the explorer Zheng He was mapping the coast of Africa in five-masted ships that carried crews of 500, beside which Christopher Columbus's *Santa María* would have looked like a sampan.

When the first British trade delegation was permitted into the Forbidden City in 1793, bearing clocks, a spring-suspension coach, and airguns, the Qianlong Emperor responded with a message to King George III that read, in part: "We have never valued ingenious articles, nor do we have the slightest need of your country's manufactures." Though the first part of the proposition was disingenuous – the Chinese have *always* delighted in ingenuity – the Middle Kingdom had already invented, in one form or another, most of the devices sent from Europe. By 1800, China was already using spinning machines and steam engines, had long since invented multi-coloured printing, the handgun, and the smallpox inoculation, and was marketing a larger share of its harvest, over longer distances, than any nation in Europe. It was easily the largest economy in the world, and a society at least as urbanized as France or England.*

While the methods of the Europeans were clumsy, their timing was excellent. China, as one sinologist has noted, has only been weak, divided, and poor in rare periods in its history. The early decades of the nineteenth century happened to be one of them. The Han dynasty, roughly contemporaneous with Ancient Rome, had presided over a golden age that saw the building of the Grand Canal linking cities through a network of inland waterways, and the extension of the Silk Road trade route as far as the Mediterranean. The Ming dynasty, which succumbed to decadence and infighting among the palace eunuchs after three centuries of rule, was succeeded by the Qing dynasty in 1644. The Manchus, as the Qing rulers called themselves, were originally nomadic horsemen from the northern plains of Manchuria, known for their skill at archery, their penchant for frugal living, and distinctive hairdos: the women wore sculpted coifs lacquered with elephant dung, while the men sported braided ponytails, also known as queues, that hung down the backs of their silk robes. Two great Manchu leaders, Kangxi and his grandson Qianlong, presided over an expansion that saw the conquest of Formosa, the pacification of Tibet, and the stabilization of the Imperial borders. By 1750, Qing power was at its peak: emissaries from Vietnam, Korea, and Burma brought tribute to the Emperor (with only Japan demanding to be recognized as equal) and a wave of emigration created outposts with substantial Chinese populations all over South-east Asia. Near Peking the Qianlong Emperor built a vast summer palace, meant to display everything within, and without, the borders of the Celestial Kingdom. When, a century later, Queen Victoria's soldiers burned and looted these "Gardens of Perfect Brightness," they were astonished to find a palace, built in the best

---

* China's most populous cities were also bigger, by far, than any others in the world; as early as the thirteenth century, Hangchow – whose city limits are now found an hour by high-speed train south-west of Shanghai – had a population of seven million.

Italian Baroque style by a Milanese painter named Castiglione, at the heart of the Oriental pleasure park.

The British, it turned out, weren't the first *waiyi*, or "outer barbarians," to come to China. Not by a long shot.

Western contact with Zhongguo (the "Middle Kingdom," as China is known to the Chinese) went back to at least the second century, when a Roman ambassador carried presents of tortoise shells and rhino horns to Han-dynasty courts. Merchants such as Niccolò Polo travelled over the silk routes to meet Kublai Khan as early as 1269 (his son Marco's book about his voyage from Venice to Peking would be the first to introduce the Western world to China). In the seventeenth century, a Jesuit priest who had come to Peking was surprised to meet a man named Ai Tan from the Silk Road city of Kaifeng, who told him he was part of a Jewish community that had already been in China for 700 years. Relations with Russia, whose hunters and settlers had made incursions into the north-eastern wilds of the empire, were first normalized in 1689; the Czarist general Alexander Suvorov would ride into battle against Napoleon under banners of Chinese silk.

The *waiyi* who came by sea, rather than overland, would prove the most troublesome for the Chinese. Portuguese ships, carrying merchant-navigators from a seafaring nation with an appetite for silk and other trade goods, had started to appear in Asian waters early in the sixteenth century. In the 1550s, the Chinese allowed Portuguese middlemen, who had found a niche trading Japanese silver for Chinese silk, to occupy Macao – the eight-square-mile tip of a peninsula segregated from the Cantonese mainland by a barrier that stands to this day – at an annual rent of 500 silver taels.* Macao grew from a scattering of thatched huts into a bustling Iberian trading post in the Orient, full of white-walled warehouses, stuccoed fortresses, and baroque churches. From Macao, the first Chinese-speaking Jesuit priests were sent to the

---

* The tael, traditionally a little boot-shaped piece of precious metal weighing 34 grams, is still the unit used to measure silver in Shanghai.

court of the new Qing dynasty, where they functioned more as cultural interpreters than as active proselytizers for Christ.

By the early nineteenth century, the Middle Kingdom was a troubled empire. The Qianlong Emperor's grandson, who was in the twelfth year of his rule in Peking when the *Lord Amherst* sailed into Shanghai's harbour, was an indecisive man who wandered the Forbidden City in patched robes and fretted about the welfare of the palace's troupe of 650 musicians. He was hopelessly ill-equipped to rule a nation-civilization of 300 million, where contact with the outside world was already producing massive social cleavages.

The greatest challenge came from the importunate British, enriched and empowered by the opportune discovery of the resources of the New World. As China struggled against internal revolts and border skirmishes in its wild north-west, England had grown rich on lumber and pelts from Canada, sugar from the Caribbean, and taxes from the American colonies. And while China continued to burn wood, England discovered the easily accessible coal that helped to fuel the factories, trains, and steam-ships of its industrial revolution.

"The Empire of China," wrote Lord Macartney, the emissary who led the trade delegation that brought steam engines and tele-scopes to the Qing court, "is an old, crazy, first rate man-of-war, which a fortunate succession of able and vigilant officers has con-trived to keep afloat for these one hundred and fifty years past, and to overawe their neighbours merely by her bulk and appearance."

In 1832, the year Lindsay and Gutzlaff's sailors knocked down the gate of the Taotai's Yamen, the empire had been struck simul-taneously by floods, drought, and famine. In such troubled times, when Heaven seemed to have withdrawn its mandate from the Qings, the old wisdom for dealing with the cow-smelling *waiyi* – "leaving them outside, not inviting them in, not recognizing their countries" – no longer seemed to apply. On the day the *Lord Amherst* finally sailed out of Shanghai's harbour, war junks pur-sued it, though none too closely, shells from their stern guns popping in the air like harmless Lunar New Year fireworks. It was a face-saving gesture that allowed the Taotai to report to the Emperor in Peking that the barbarians had been successfully shooed out of the city.

When other foreign ships followed, however, their holds would be filled not with metaphysical opiates, but the real – and immensely profitable – thing. In just a few years, it was Indian opium, rather than the Holy Bible, that would bring about an almost magical transformation of the little patch of muddy fore-shore that was blessed (or cursed, depending on one's point of view) to be situated where the Yangtze meets the Pacific, and China meets the world.

3: The Sassoon Gamble

On a Monday afternoon late in November 1893 – three days after the celebrations marking the half-century anniversary of Shanghai's founding – a portly man in early middle age walked down the steps of the Shanghai Club. Silas Hardoon, the property manager of E.D. Sassoon & Co., had just passed an agreeable hour in a leather armchair, sipping whisky and flipping through the special Jubilee edition of the *North-China Daily News*. Now, as he returned to his employer's office on the Bund, he read the banners that hung from guy-wires strung between the telegraph poles, emblazoned with mottoes in a variety of languages. In bold letters, one of the English-language banners demanded: "In what region of the earth is Shanghai not known?" He was able to decipher the Chinese characters on another, which read: "Busy mart with ships from distant shores; Chinese and foreigners mark their happy delight."

The decorations were left over from the previous Friday's celebrations. The event, all in Shanghai's foreign community concurred, had been a great success. On Nanking Road, native merchants had planted themselves on high-backed chairs in front of their shops, whose facades announced their wares with painted characters the height of a tall man. As Chinese women climbed to the rooftops of three-storey buildings to get a better view of the festivities, the officers of HMS *Alacrity* paraded by, followed by a French naval brigade pulling two field guns. From streets named for China's greatest cities, and newly paved with cubes of granite, the crowd followed the marchers onto the waterfront. As a special favour, native spectators had been allowed into the Public Gardens – from which dogs and Chinese were normally excluded – to

glimpse the illumination of a wrought-iron fountain built specially
for the Jubilee, before being hurried off the grounds by Municipal
Police officers. On a bandstand erected on the broad lawn where
Nanking Road met the Bund, the Reverend William Muirhead,
the city's oldest foreign resident, had exhorted a crowd estimated
to number 200,000 to recognize how far Shanghai had come, and
in how little time.

"We have steamers, telegraphs and telephones in communication with all the world; there are cotton and paper mills and silk
filatures of foreign invention; dockyards and ship-building yards."
Gesturing in the direction of the nearest major building – gratify-
ingly for Hardoon, it was the offices of E.D. Sassoon & Co. – he
pursued: "We note also those splendid hongs and houses, banks
and offices in front, imparting an air of beauty and order to the
Settlement." He concluded, "Christ and Christianity are the one
great want of the country – and it is all-important that the want
should be supplied!" The remark was greeted by thunderous
applause from the foreign spectators, and silence from the Chinese.

Though a weekend – and with it the Sabbath – had since
supervened, the "huzzahs" elicited by the Reverend Muirhead's
remarks still echoed in Hardoon's ears. It was true that, even in
the twenty years he'd been there, Shanghai had been utterly transformed. The riverfront north of the walled Chinese city had
become the centre of a bustling and many-cultured city. The mile
of jetties that stretched towards the stone bridge that marked the
border of the French Concession was fronted by the facades of
private clubs, hotels, and the two- and three-storey hongs – complexes that resembled baronial mansions, mixing business office,
warehouse, and residence, with living quarters for junior employees on the ground floor – of the largest European and American
trading houses. From the square clock tower of the new Custom
House – where the collection of all tariffs from water-borne trade
was overseen not by Chinese bureaucrats but by Sir Robert Hart,
a Methodist martinet from Northern Ireland – the Westminster
chimes rang on the quarter hour, from bells cast in Croydon. The

first impression of the Orient that struck passengers alighting from steamers newly arrived from San Francisco, Vancouver, and Europe's great ports via the Suez Canal, was of the stately stone facades of a small Western capital. It was no Liverpool or New York – not yet – but its fame was growing.

On that afternoon, however, Hardoon found himself inclined to be cynical about the festival of self-congratulation to which Shanghailanders had treated themselves. During the quarter century he had spent in China, he had come to understand only too well the way they thought. Though he spoke English, acquired while in the employ of the Sassoons in Bombay, he did so with a thick Arabic accent. And if he now wore the waistcoat and pocket watch of the thoroughly Westernized gentleman, he would never forget that he had spent his early years in Baghdad wearing the straps of *tefillin* under his robes and a skullcap beneath his embroidered turban. Though he had attained a position of prominence with one of the city's most respected trading houses, he knew that to most Shanghailanders, he – like David Sassoon, the patriarch of the Sassoon dynasty – would always be a Jew, and thus an outsider.

Silas Hardoon continued his stroll to the north extreme of the Bund, only turning on his heels when he reached the hong of David Sassoon & Sons, where for years after his arrival he'd slept on a thin mattress in a tiny room on the building's upper floor. Even now, the memory of his association with his former employers was bittersweet.

If it weren't for the Sassoon dynasty, Hardoon knew, he would be nothing. In Baghdad, the family had been legendary. Sheikh Sason Ben Saleh – the Prince of the Captivity, and civil leader of the Jewish community in Mesopotamia – had claimed descent from King David, and rode to the palace of the Pasha in robes trimmed with gold. When a new governor began an anti-Semitic reign of terror, the Sheikh's son was forced to flee across the Persian Gulf with the family's pearls sewn into the lining of his robes. The young David Sassoon, after starting life anew as a trader in Bushire, a city on the Persian Gulf south of Tehran, heard of new opportunities arising in India. Bombay, whose seven islands had

originally been ceded by Charles II to the East India Company for
a rent of £10 a year, was fast emerging as a leading port. In 1832
– the same year Gutzlaff and Lindsay knocked down the Taotai's
door in Shanghai – David Sassoon sailed from Bushire to Bombay,
where he nailed his *mezuzahs* to the doors of his new home at 9
Tamarind Lane. He thrived in the booming port, trading first in
dates, horses, and pearls, and then in the more lucrative commodity of opium, all the while cannily buying up prime dockland
property.

Hardoon's parents, who had joined the diaspora of Baghdadi
Jews to Bombay, enrolled their son in one of the Sassoons' charit-
able schools. When it was discovered he had a talent for numbers,
the young Hardoon was singled out to travel to the Sassoon
offices in Hong Kong. He had only been seventeen at the time:
too young, he knew now, for such a dramatic change. He still
didn't like to think about the argument that led to his sudden
dismissal from David Sassoon & Sons, six years after his arrival.

Hardoon's stroll took him past the colonnaded balcony of one
of the grandest of the hongs, Jardine, Matheson & Co. Its facade
was still decorated with Jubilee lights in the shape of the profile of
St. Andrew, a tribute to the firm's Scottish roots. The sight of the
"Noble House," as the Chinese called the hong, always reminded
him of his first glimpse of the waterfront of Shanghai, from the
third-class deck of a steamer.

He'd left Hong Kong for Shanghai in 1874, without a coin in
his pocket. Taking pity on him, his old employers had given him a
job as a watchman in the David Sassoon & Sons godown, or warehouse, on the Bund. Already fluent in Cantonese, he had quickly
picked up the local Shanghainese dialect – a skill that allowed him
to close a series of lucrative real-estate transactions with the local
Chinese, redeeming him in the eyes of the Sassoon family. He came
to admire Elias, the second son of patriarch David, who had been
dispatched to Shanghai from Bombay just seven years after the
opening of the Treaty Port. Unlike his father – who on formal
occasions wore a turban and billowing white trousers bound at the
ankles – the bespectacled, slightly stooped Elias favoured the grey

suits of the British business class. When the Sassoon patriarch died in 1864 and his older brother Abdullah took over the family firm, Elias set up his own company. E.D. Sassoon & Co., while diversifying into Indian cotton and wool to supply markets in China's cold northern provinces, competed aggressively with David Sassoon & Sons in the opium trade. The Chinese, at first confounded by the unfilial spectacle of competing Sassoon offices on the Bund, soon resolved the issue by dubbing David Sassoon & Sons *kau*, or "old" Sassoon, and E.D. Sassoon *sin*, or "new" Sassoon.

The real money in Shanghai, Hardoon had realized even before he became a property manager at E.D. Sassoon, lay in real estate. While working as a watchman, every week he'd set aside one shilling from his meagre salary of twelve, until he had enough to buy a shack, which he rented to a Chinese family for a few silver dollars a month. With that money, he'd purchased another, and then another, until soon he was renting out dozens of flats in the foreign concessions. Thanks to Shanghai's unique status as a foreign enclave and the quirks of Chinese history, his real-estate holdings were already helping him acquire a fortune, one string of copper cash and silver dollar at a time.

As he reached the corner of Jinkee Road, Hardoon noticed that the bandstand, still festooned with the flags of the world and red Chinese lanterns from the Jubilee, had yet to be taken down. Had he been asked to take the stage alongside the very Reverend Muirhead, Hardoon's account of Shanghai's early years, given his insider's knowledge of the city, would have been quite different.

Clergymen and missionaries liked to say that the foreign presence in China was a noble endeavour, a way of bringing religion and the other benefits of civilization to the benighted. But from the start, the West had sent crucifixes and Bibles to China alongside chests packed with opium.

The first British traders in China had no trouble filling their cargo holds with silk, porcelain, and tea, paid for with the de facto currency of the Far East, beautiful but bulky dollar coins minted from silver from Mexican mines. These products were eagerly snapped up by consumers in European and American cities, caught up in the West's first wave of Orientalism. But the ships tended to return to the Far East with empty holds, for the Chinese had no interest in the products of the Occident, save one: opium. Qing troops were likely introduced to *madak*, Javanese opium mixed with tobacco, by Dutch traders in Taiwan. The habit spread to palace eunuchs in Peking, wealthy women, the provincial gentry, and finally to the poor, who found that it warded off hunger and allowed them – for a time at least – to bear hard physical labour. Demand was so great that the clippers (yacht-like ships with raking masts and sharp bows) that brought the opium from India never even had to make landfall. Anchoring offshore, first in Canton and then in new markets up the coast, they transferred their cargo to the floating warehouses called opium hulks. Multi-oared native vessels called "centipedes" or "scrambling dragons" would swarm the hulks, and the chests, each weighing up to 160 pounds, would be rushed to smugglers' dens inland. For the merchants, the profit on a single chest could be as much as £100. By the early 1830s, 24,000 chests of opium were being imported from India a year – enough to sustain the habits of two million addicts. With the balance of trade corrected in favour of the foreign powers, a torrent of silver started to flow out of China in the direction of England, France, and the United States.

In the same month that the *Lord Amherst* sailed into Shanghai's harbour, the Emperor in Peking declared *yangtu* to be the source of all China's woes. One of his most upright officials, the commissioner Lin Zexu, was charged with bringing an end to the trade. Lin wrote directly to England's new queen, Victoria, imploring her to stop the import of "foreign mud." When his letter went unanswered, he sent his troops to the south of China, where the habit was particularly widespread.

The British counterpart to Macao, the Portuguese merchant's enclave, was Shameen, a fifteen-acre cigar-shaped island crowded with warehouses and separated from Canton's thirty-foot city walls by a canal no wider than a mid-sized avenue. Lin, after ordering that two million pounds' worth of raw opium be seized from Shameen's godowns, had the drug mixed with lime and salt and washed into the Pearl River strait. This grand gesture had two consequences. The merchants were immediately able to charge famine prices to addicts, causing the price of a single chest of opium to sextuple. And the traffickers abandoned Shameen – called, by one historian, "perhaps the least pleasant residence for a European on the face of the earth" – for a rocky, near-deserted island known as Xianggang, eighty miles south of Canton, which would soon become the colony of Hong Kong.

One merchant in particular was outraged by the effrontery of the Chinese. William Jardine, who'd started life as one of seven children on a small Scottish farm, had realized what fantastic profits could be made in opium "tonnage" while serving as a surgeon on an East India Company clipper. In Canton, he became an independent trader, eventually teaming up with fellow Scotsman James Matheson. To the Chinese, he was the "Iron-Headed Old Rat," a name he'd earned after implacably receiving a series of blows at the gate of a Canton official's rooms where he had come to deliver a petition. When Jardine's opium was seized by Commissioner Lin, the stubborn Scotsman sailed to England, on funds raised by the other merchants to lobby for military support for British interests in the Far East. Parliament authorized 4,000 troops to sail to China, under the command of a cousin of the British trade superintendent who had led the exodus from Shameen to Hong Kong.

In the summer of 1840, the fleet laid siege to Canton and occupied key cities to the north. They sent their secret weapon, the iron-sided paddle-wheeler the *Nemesis*, whose shallow, five-foot draft allowed her to operate in coastal waters in virtually any tidal or wind conditions. With her two thirty-two-pounder guns, the *Nemesis* – the Chinese called her the "devil ship" – was able to blast China's best war junks to splinters. Within a year Britain had seized control of the Grand Canal linking Peking to Hangchow, and her troops had occupied the forts at the mouth of the Yangtze River. The Daoguang Emperor was forced to sue for peace.

The Opium War, as it became known, had been a funny kind of conflict: Britain, already experiencing imperial overreach in India, had no intention of colonizing China's vast territory. In Peking, the Qing, who had lost their first war in 200 years of rule, persisted in thinking of the British as pirates who would soon enough be on their way. The Treaty of Nanking, signed in a British ship moored on the Yangtze, ceded the new trading outpost of Hong Kong to the British Crown in perpetuity, and opened five Chinese coastal cities – from south to north, Canton, Amoy, Foochow, Ningpo, and Shanghai – to residence by British subjects. Subsequent treaties with France and the United States enshrined China's subjugation into international law. The establishment of the Treaty Ports, as Shanghai and the other cities became known, announced to the world that China was open for business. (In Bombay, the patriarch of the Sassoons heard of the Treaty Ports by accident: the elder David, in the habit of going to the post office to collect his mail himself, began to make enquiries after noticing his competitors were receiving bags of letters with Chinese postmarks.)

Article 21 of the treaty with the United States established the principle of "extraterritoriality," which meant that an American who committed a crime on Chinese soil would be tried "according to the laws of the United States." Because Britain had cleverly stipulated that its citizens would be granted all privileges that in the future were accorded to other foreign powers, immunity from Chinese law applied to almost all English-speakers, whether they were diplomats or vagrants. In practice, "extrality," as it was known in its abbreviated form, meant, in the words of one later Eurasian commentator, that Westerners "could enter China without a passport, stay as long as they liked, rob, steal, murder . . . and bring in narcotics and opium and guns without being punishable by law."

When the *Nemesis* steamed into Shanghai, ten years after the *Lord Amherst*, the paddle-wheeler took only two hours to pulverize the forts at the mouth of the Woosung River. Though the Qing soldiers offered stiff resistance – "no one," a British commander reported, "who witnessed the obstinacy and determination with which the Chinese defended themselves would refuse them full credit for personal bravery" – they were forced to retreat. The British, after scaling the Old City's walls, established their military headquarters in the City God temple. In the coming months, the soldiers plundered old Shanghai, hacking apart exquisite wooden carvings to use for fuel. They sold the finest pickings to the most mercenary of the local merchants, lowering jade sculptures and blackwood chairs over the walls on ropes at nightfall in exchange for a few pieces of Mexican silver.

When the looting had ended, Captain George Balfour, the first Consul to Shanghai, negotiated with the Qing's top official in Shanghai, the now tractable Taotai, the terms that would shape the city for the next hundred years. Twenty-three "Land Regulations" allowed foreigners to rent land outside the walled city on a permanent basis and forbade Chinese from holding title (though it was understood, naturally, that the Emperor was the *actual* owner of all land under Heaven). To the north, 470 acres of foreshore were set aside as the British Settlement. Captain Balfour, who recognized the strategic importance of controlling the mouth of the Yangtze, chose the site of the recently defeated Woosung forts – which not too long before had been the fishing village of Hu Tu Lei – for the British Consulate. Between the walled city and the British Zone, the 164-acre French Concession included a stretch of Whangpoo riverfront that would become known as the Quai de France. North of the British Zone, the United States was allotted 1,309 acres of land on the far shore of the Woosung River.

Under the Land Regulations Shanghai became, as one speechifier had exulted from the bandstand at the city's Jubilee, "the unique instance of a republic dropped down on an alien empire."

South of the land claimed for the British Consulate, a line of stakes was driven into the mud at the water's edge. The Taotai informed the foreigners that to preserve the rights of coolies,*

---

* "Coolie," an Indian term applied to unskilled labourers throughout Asia, was ennobled on the China coast into *kuli*, which in the Mandarin pronunciation meant "bitter strength."

who for centuries had used the towpath to haul rafts towards the Yangtze, no building would be allowed within thirty feet of the Whangpoo River (a distance soon doubled, laying the foundation for the promenade later known as the Bund). Moreover, the foreigners would have to negotiate title from local residents, plot by plot. At the time, the Whangpoo waterfront, then the northern suburbs of the walled city, had a population of just 500 Chinese farmers and fishermen.

"It consisted largely of burying grounds, vegetable gardens, with shops and shanties, small and miserable in appearance," the Reverend Muirhead recalled of the land adjacent to the riverfront. "Open and offensive ditches were in all directions, and one had to be careful, alike by day and night, in walking to and fro, lest he should be engulfed in these pitfalls. The roads, narrow and unpleasant, were in some instances laid with uneven stones or consisted of the original mud." What would later become the easternmost stretch of Nanking Road followed the course of a creek whose willow-shaded banks meandered towards the Whangpoo.

Though the merchants that followed the soldiers found the people of Shanghai more open to business than the notoriously xenophobic Cantonese in the south, some resisted all intercourse with the new arrivals. When the Taotai and the British council paid a courtesy visit to an old lady, she flatly refused to sell the riverfront land on which her ancestors were buried.

"She went so far in her opposition to all proposed bargains," recalled the editor of one of Shanghai's earliest newspapers, "that after pouring on the head of the party a torrent of colloquial Billingsgate, she actually, I blush to say it, *spat in the Taotai's face* and declared that she would *never* sell her patrimony to foreign devils!"

The newspaper's editor failed to record how the old lady was talked, or coerced, into selling. But by 1857, the colonnaded buildings of Augustine Heard & Co. had risen on that same patch of land. When the New England opium dealer was ruined by the Panic of 1873, a financial crisis that led to years of depression in the United States and England, the land was snapped up by the

Sassoon family, who chose the prime site at No. 20, the Bund, as the headquarters of E.D. Sassoon & Co.

美

At the corner of Peking Road, where coolies smoked and chattered, the poles of their idle rickshaws on the pavement, Hardoon passed a white obelisk. The monument to the grandly named "Ever Victorious Army" made him chuckle: it commemorated one of the stranger episodes in China's recent history, and went a long way to explaining why he was fast becoming the wealthiest foreigner in Shanghai.

Four years after the Treaty of Nanking, a village schoolteacher named Hong Xiuquan, having failed the Qing exams that would have allowed him to wear the robes of a scholar, decided he was the younger brother of Jesus Christ. Inspired by a superficial reading of Christian missionary tracts, he raised an army of 10,000 followers that he dubbed the Taiping – the "Heavenly Kingdom." The Taiping grew their hair long, lived communally, allowed women into high leadership roles, and vowed to wipe out corruption and opium addiction. By 1853 they had terrorized the country as far north as Nanking, a city that became their base for over a decade. In the same year, the Small Swords, a band of soldiers claiming to be inspired by the Taiping, broke through the old city walls of Shanghai.

Shanghailanders at first welcomed the self-proclaimed Christians – before deciding they were dangerous fanatics. Frederick Townsend Ward, a freebooter from Massachusetts, was paid to lead the hastily improvised "Ever Victorious Army," a mostly Chinese fighting force, against the Small Swords. Though the "Battle of the Muddy Flat" (which took place on what was later to become the Race Course) was a fiasco in military terms – Ward was killed by a stray bullet, and his troops were rendered impotent when confronted with a shallow ditch – the rebels were driven away; the battle led directly to the creation of the Volunteer Corps, sworn to the defense of the Treaty Port. The Taiping Rebellion, which caused twenty million deaths in thirteen years, was finally ended by infighting and put down by Qing forces in 1864.

The real significance of the Taiping madness, Hardoon knew, lay in the flood of new residents it brought to Shanghai's foreign settlements. Three hundred thousand desperate Chinese refugees poured in from Nanking alone. In the French Concession and the British Settlement (the British and American Settlements, the latter never recognized by Congress, merged to become the International Settlement in 1863), entrepreneurs threw up tightly-serried rowhouse tenements to house the newcomers. Rural land bought for a few hundred Mexican silver dollars soared to $12,000 an acre. Though many refugees returned to the countryside at the end of the fighting, the pattern for the future had been established. Every time famine, flood, or an extortionate warlord ravaged the countryside, more refugees poured in, so that by 1891 Shanghai was home to 1.7 million people (only 5,274 of whom were European or American).

And it was on this concentration of humanity that Hardoon was growing rich. Every month, he personally collected the rent at every one of his properties, surprising new tenants with his ability to converse in Chinese.

Hardoon had been sitting in the kitchen of one of his rowhouses, waiting for a delinquent tenant, when he first met Liza Roos. The product of an affair between a Chinese woman and a French sailor, she eked out a living as a seamstress and wet nurse; some whispered she'd been a "flower-seller," Shanghai slang for a prostitute. Hardoon was entranced by her exotic charm: despite her European appearance, she was a Buddhist who treated herself with traditional medicine, relied on fortune-tellers, and preferred to go by her Chinese name, Luo Jialing. When they married, they mixed Sephardic and Chinese tradition; at the ceremony, they simultaneously repeated "*hareath*" as joss sticks burned beside them.

Blue-blooded Shanghailanders, Hardoon knew, considered his marriage to a half-caste the height of eccentricity. But through Jialing he had come to love the concentrated energy of Shanghai.

As he walked past Foochow Road he heard the *"Hi-yi-ho-ah-yum!"* of labourers straining to lift a 500-pound hammer on a pulley, followed by a thud and a *"hoom-ah!"* as they dropped the wooden piling into the Whangpoo mud. A line of crouching gardeners chattered and laughed as they cut grass with tiny scythes, progressing along the lawn before the Custom House a few inches at a time. From a lane, the odour of fried beancurd, plucked lip-burning hot from a vat of oil with outsized chopsticks when it turned yellow and crisp, mingled with the stench of the "honey carts" carrying human manure bound for vegetable plots outside the city.

Shanghai would excuse Hardoon his foibles, for he had amassed the thing it respected the most: money. In a way, the Jubilee year had also been his coronation. Not only was he named a councillor on the French Concession's municipal government, in recognition of his property holdings, but he'd become a member of the most exclusive bastion of the British elite: the Shanghai Club, which was closed to all Chinese, no matter how wealthy or noble.

He couldn't help wondering what the future held. While at the club, he'd read an editorial in the *North-China Daily News* that had set him thinking about the destiny of the city to which he had committed his future.

"Is there anyone," asked the editor, "who is not proud of being a Shanghailander? Of the hundreds of children who will be entertained to-day and to-morrow, some will no doubt be present at Shanghai's next Jubilee in 1943. What the city will have become then it is not easy to foresee."

The future of Hardoon's employers in the Far East was even harder to predict. When Elias died suddenly in 1880 while inspecting the Sassoon tea plantations in Ceylon, his son Jacob, who had overseen the construction of up-to-date cotton mills in Bombay, was sent to the "new" Sassoon offices in Shanghai. Though Jacob had proved an excellent manager, his younger brother David had nothing in common with the commanding family patriarch after whom he'd been named. As diminutive as he was charming, David spent half the year in London chasing after actresses and dancers. In Shanghai, when he deigned to appear at the Sassoon offices, David kept his nose in the racing sheets. If the Sassoon name was to endure into the twentieth century, a sharper business mind than his would have to step into the breach. Elias, he knew, had a grandson in England who would have his bar mitzvah the following year. One day this Victor, or another of his generation, might be convinced to seek his fortune in Shanghai.

Hardoon's afternoon walk ended with his arrival at a tile-roofed building, fronted by rows of arched windows, on the corner of Nanking Road and the Bund. Approaching the building the Chinese referred to as "new" Sassoon afforded him a strong measure of satisfaction. Its central position on the riverfront lent it even more prominence than the great British institutions of the Shanghai Club and Jardine, Matheson & Co.

The fact that at the heart of Shanghai's foreign concessions – ostensibly built to bring Christianity to a heathen empire – sat a building owned by direct descendants of King David, harmonized neatly with Hardoon's innate appreciation for human complexity.

It was at the exact spot where Silas Hardoon's stroll ended, on that afternoon in 1893, that the fishermen of the village of Hu Tu Lei had once worked their tide-borne traps. And it was precisely on this patch of shoreline – where the *Lord Amherst* had dropped anchor, where a stubborn Chinese lady had spat in the Taotai's face rather than sell her ancestral land, and where a New England opium dealer's warehouse had been replaced by the hong of the "new" Sassoon – that the Cathay, the greatest hotel in the Far East, was destined to rise.

PART TWO

"When you come to think of it, there's an awful lot
to know about me, if you take the trouble."

– Emily Hahn,
China to Me, 1944.

4: St. Louis, May 27, 1916

It was one of those late spring days when the sun melted the asphalt on Fountain Avenue, staining her bare feet and calves with streaks of soft tar, and the St. Louis heat made Mickey long to be inside in the coolness of the family home. In the parlour, the walls were lined with bookshelves and a big *Webster's Dictionary* sat open on a lectern. (Its middle pages had come loose as a result of all the words she'd looked up. The good ones, she'd noticed, seemed to start with "l": licentious, libidinous, lascivious.) When the weather was fine, books were off limits; her mother seemed to think that too much time spent reading would somehow use up the limited stock of vision allotted to young eyes. In the Hahn household, reading for pleasure was restricted to thirty minutes a day.

In spite of her nickname – given to her by her mother because of a supposed resemblance to a chummy Irish saloonkeeper featured in the newspapers – Mickey was no tomboy; she found playing outside boring. At the age of eleven, her hair was cut into a Dutch bob whose drooping strands bracketed cheeks still puffed with baby fat. As a toddler she'd worn a brace to correct a twisted leg, which gave her an excuse to linger in the parlour and leaf through picture books while her brother and four sisters played outside. Now, if she tried to sneak a book unnoticed to the kitchen table, she would inevitably be scolded and reminded of all the children in China who would be grateful to have her dinner.

That afternoon, Mickey left her sisters playing in Fountain Park and slipped into the backyard. She'd discovered that the cleft of the peach tree there made an ideal hiding place for forbidden fruit. In the shadow of their high board fence, she could read undetected for hours.

She'd already made her way through all the approved children's classics on her parents' bookshelves. David Copperfield, who ran away to Dover with just three halfpence in his pocket, had satisfied her craving for adventure, as had Huck Finn, who rafted down the Mississippi, the same river that ran through her hometown. Lately, though, she'd developed a taste for more exotic locales. She'd revelled in the adventures of Kim, the Irish orphan who befriended snake charmers and Tibetan lamas as he ran barefoot through the backstreets of Lahore. Recently she'd read *The Wallet of Kai Lung*, which followed a wandering storyteller who got the best of bandits and barbarians alike as he roamed the camphor forests, willow banks, and temple gardens of China.

Standing on tiptoe, she reached into the tree and pulled out a hardcover book. Its dustcover showed a yellow-faced man with a drooping moustache, slits for eyes, and hands that gripped a scimitar – apparently in readiness to be plunged into the breast of the half-undressed woman beside him, whose bare arms were chained to a gilded Buddha. Decent young ladies were not supposed to read Sax Rohmer's books. Mickey couldn't get enough of them.

Propped up against a fencepost, her toes in the cool grass, she sensed her breathing become shallow as the virtuous Dr. Petrie described his first encounter with the insidious Fu-Manchu.

"In his long, yellow robe," recounts the hero,

his masklike, intellectual face bent forward amongst the riot of singular objects upon the table, his great, high brow gleaming in the light of the shaded lamp above him, and with the abnormal eyes, filmed and green, raised to us, he seemed a figure from the realms of delirium.

Fu-Manchu, discovers Petrie, is the leader of the Yellow Peril, a secret society of thugs and dacoits dedicated to placing "Europe and America beneath the scepter of Cathay." His weapons include scorpions and pythons, bacilli and fungi, poisonous black spiders with diamond eyes, and a leashed marmoset, trained to obey his commands, that he is fond of caressing with slender, claw-like fingers.

Following the criminal mastermind to London's East End, Dr. Petrie witnesses the curious rituals of the opium den:

Holding a needle in the flame, he dipped it, when red-hot, into an old cocoa tin, and withdrew it with a bead of opium adhering to the end. Slowly roasting this over the lamp, he dropped it into the bowl of the metal pipe which he held ready, where it burned with a spirituous blue flame.

The nefarious doctor, however, has merely feigned intoxication to get the better of Dr. Petrie.

He came forward with an indescribable gait, cat-like yet awkward, carrying his high shoulders almost hunched. He placed the lantern in a niche in the wall, never turning away the reptilian gaze of those eyes which must haunt my dreams forever. They possessed a viridescence which hitherto I had supposed possible only in the eye of the cat – and the film intermittently clouded their brightness – but I can speak of them no more . . .

Mickey tried hard to remember if she'd ever encountered eyes like that. The only Oriental person she knew was the old man who ran the laundry. Some of the children were afraid of him, and called him "chink," but she liked to go to his shop. He always seemed to be laughing and let her play with his kitten, until her mother, who believed cats transmitted typhoid to children, forbade her to go.

As the sun lowered in the sky, the first flares of low-hovering lightning bugs became visible in the hibiscus bushes. The downstairs maid called her name again – supper was on the table – but she read on, oblivious to all but the mysteries of Cathay.

It wouldn't be long before Mickey had the luxury to read whatever books she wanted, whenever she wanted to read them. And soon enough, she would be living her own adventures in distant lands and writing stories about experiences that, to her younger self, would have seemed – if not as lurid as Sax Rohmer's – at least as improbable.

Oddly enough, the most gripping of them would feature exotic primates, Oriental secret societies, opium pipes, and long-fingered intellectuals in silk robes.

5: The Flapper's Progress

By the spring of 1935, Sir Victor Sassoon's doubts about coming to China had vanished. After all the bother three years back – the naval mine that rocked the Cathay Hotel, the bombing of Chapei by the Japanese – peace had returned to Shanghai.

In the end, it had been a funny little war. For the Chinese, the invasion became known as the "January 28 Incident." Incredibly, the soldiers of China's 19th Route Army stood and fought, humiliating the Japanese and temporarily driving them back to their destroyers on the Whangpoo River. (Only the arrival of 8,000 Japanese reinforcements would force the ill-equipped, unpaid, and underfed Chinese soldiers to withdraw for good.) Scorned by the nationalist leadership in the capital of Nanking, the 19th Route Army became heroes to the ordinary people of China. Their resistance was the first modern evidence that Chinese soldiers had the heart, and the skill, to stand up to foreign invaders.

The cost, though, was enormous. The Japanese had boasted they could take Shanghai in four hours. The battle lasted for five weeks, and cost the lives of 3,000 of their best troops. The shelling, bombardment, and street fighting destroyed 85 per cent of the buildings in Chapei, and killed 10,000 Chinese civilians.*

Some Shanghailanders of Sir Victor's acquaintance had actually cheered for the invaders. The Japanese, who were allowed to vote in local elections and hold seats on the Municipal Council, were seen as "honorary Westerners." Many British and American busi-

---

* The "January 28 Incident" also marked – five years before the fascists bombed Guernica in Spain's Basque country – the first aerial terror bombings of a densely populated city in the history of modern warfare.

nessmen hoped they would chastise the Chinese masses for their nascent nationalism.

All through the incident, Sir Victor had kept up a public display of unflappability. In the evenings, he made appearances at the Horse and Hounds bar in the Cathay lobby, chatting with guests and offering tourists free rounds of pink champagne. When the sweating aide-de-camp of a Chinese general appeared with apologies for the sniper's near-miss – the bullet that had almost hit his movie camera turned out to have been Chinese, not Japanese – Sir Victor graciously accepted the bag of sweets proffered as a peace offering.

And then, one by one, the soldiers of the 19th Route Army had melted into the countryside. By the end of the first week of March, the "Circle of the Sun" of the Japanese flag was flying over the rubble that was all that was left of the North Railway Station. Satisfied they'd made their point, the Japanese withdrew, and an uneasy peace returned to Shanghai.

The League of Nations had chosen the Cathay Hotel as the site for negotiations to end the conflict. As the delegates checked in, Sir Victor took the opportunity to express his confidence in Shanghai's future to Sir Miles Lampson, Britain's Minister to China, and Lord Lytton, the head of the commission. (The agents of the Special Branch of the Municipal Police foiled an attempted assassination in the hotel, after discovering a Chinese man had smuggled three hand grenades into Room 511 in his luggage; the idea, apparently, was to show the world, while its eyes were on Shanghai, that China's nationalist government could not guarantee the security of its greatest city.) The markets had interpreted the relative lack of damage as a sign of the inviolability of the foreign settlements. The war, as Sir Victor was at pains to tell reporters, had for the most part "kept its place," and the Japanese and Chinese had treated the residents of the International Settlement with gentlemanly restraint.

In the years that had followed, the Japanese seemed to have suspended their aggressive posturing in Shanghai. After installing the last Emperor of China, Henry Pu Yi, as their puppet leader in north China, they professed satisfaction with their holdings in Manchuria – or Manchukuo, as they now called it. In Shanghai, Japanese nationals seldom strayed from Little Tokyo, on the north side of the Garden Bridge, and seemed content with their two seats on the Municipal Council. The local taipans believed that the "Sons of Heaven" could be persuaded to share, rather than seize, power in Shanghai. The pie was big enough, after all, for everybody to get a slice.

The tourists, too, had returned, and Shanghai was earning a reputation as the gayest city in the world. Every day the "world-girdlers," as they called themselves, poured off liners that had passed through the Panama or Suez canals, threaded through the Hawaiian Islands, or rounded the Cape of Good Hope. This month alone the *Sumatra* would be arriving from Trieste, the *Resolute* from Hamburg, the *Naldera* from London, the *Tancred* from Oslo, the *President Jackson* from Seattle, the *Empress of Russia* from Vancouver, and the *Glengarry* from Port Said. Shuttled by steam launch to the jetties in front of the Custom House on the Bund, most of the visitors proved to be "four-minute guests," wandering the lobby of the Cathay for a little window-shopping in the arcade. The more prosperous checked in, staying for a night or a week, making the ballroom and the Horse and Hounds ring with laughter and song late into the night.

Sir Victor himself had recently returned to the Far East, after a summer in London and Monte Carlo, on a Lloyd Triestino liner. As the *Conte Verde* sailed into the Adriatic, he'd organized a fancy-dress cocktail concert. "Ladies and gentlemen," an invitation sent to the first-class passengers read, "are Kindly requested to appear in Venetian Dress to make the feast more attractive." To ensure the proceedings were jolly he'd slipped the barman the recipe for one of his signature drinks, the lethal Green Hat, which he'd renamed the Conte Verde in honour of the ship. Guests were forewarned of its potency in a printed menu.

"Sir Victor Sassoon's Famous Cocktail," it read. "For the real he Men. 2 parts Gin, 2 parts Cointreau, 2 parts Vermout Française, 2 parts Crème de mente, 1 part lemon."

Glowing a sinister green, the Conte Verde produced instant levity in its consumers. The party had been a great, sloppy success.

As had Sir Victor's Circus Dance, in which the cream of Shanghai's high society had been invited to a Cathay Hotel ballroom transformed for the night into a big top. The city's leading taipans had come wearing the satin shirts of high-wire artists, and one taitai had come dressed as a convincingly slippery-looking seal. The Chinese acrobats of Long Tack Sam's troupe had elicited gasps as they cartwheeled through the crowds. All of this had suited Sir Victor, who appeared dressed as a ringmaster, complete with top hat, false moustache, and whip.

As things threatened to slip out of control, he'd needed the authority conferred by the latter. One young woman had had the effrontery to gatecrash in costume ("Pretty girl," he noted in his journal, "but cannot allow that.") Sylvia Chancellor, the wife of the head of the Reuters agency in the Far East, and John Keswick, a director at Jardine's, had smuggled a live donkey to the party in the freight lift. The beast had proceeded to defecate on the floor in the midst of the dancers.

"Get it out of here," Sir Victor had been forced to snap at Keswick, who was dressed as Don Quixote. Sylvia Chancellor had ended the night by falling asleep on the dance floor.

In spite of such displays of disrespect from the British Shanghailanders, Sir Victor was finding life both amusing and gratifying. His many enterprises were thriving, and, between lunches at the Royal Air Force Association, dinners at the Shanghai Club, and late nights at the Majestic Ballroom, his dance card was so full that he'd decided to hire a young woman to work full-time as his social secretary.

Lately, life itself had become an adventure. Shanghai's renown was attracting the most preposterous scoundrels, wayfarers, and quick-change artists. Returning from a business trip to Hong Kong aboard the *President Grant*, he'd been introduced to Sun Fo, the son of the late Sun Yat-sen. The nationalist politician, currently the mayor of Canton, was a morose nonentity, but his burly bodyguard turned out to be good company. Holding forth in a bastard Cockney–Canuck brogue, Morris "Two-Gun" Cohen recounted how, after being caught stealing a pocket watch in a tough part of London's East End, he'd been sent into exile on the Canadian prairies. There, he'd knocked the gun out of the hands of a thug trying to hold up a Chinese restaurant he frequented. One thing led to another, explained Cohen, and he'd been enrolled in a secret society sworn to the overthrow of the Manchus. In China, he became an aide-de-camp to Dr. Sun and then an arms dealer, before becoming the first foreigner to be made a general in the nationalist army. For Cohen, it made perfect sense that the Chinese got along with the Jews: they had a lot in common.

"We are good friends but damned bad enemies," he confided to Sir Victor. "We don't want trouble, but if someone picks on us, we like to be on top at the end and we don't mind how long it takes."

Sir Victor was spending weekends at Eve's, a Tudor-style hunting lodge built in Shanghai's western suburbs on land he'd purchased from one of the partners at Palmer & Turner, the firm that had built the Cathay. ("Eve," as Sir Victor had been known in university, was an acronym for his full name, Ellice Victor Elias.) Most nights, though, he slept in his eleventh-floor penthouse overlooking the Bund.

Crossing the lobby of the Cathay the previous day, he'd struck up a conversation with a stylish dark-eyed woman, who wore her deeply waved hair in the short bob they were favouring in America. Her name was Helen Asbury; she'd just arrived from Yokohama, and was travelling with her sister. He'd first noticed the striking pair of brunettes earlier in the day, when he'd paid a visit to Bernardine Szold-Fritz's salon.

Under the heading "FRIDAY – April 12th, 1935," he wrote:

"Met Mickey Hahn + Helen Asbury. Dined with Helen in K. Suite. Fetched Mickey from Pen Club + took them both to Eves."

Mickey was just the kind of woman he had been waiting for. She was quick-witted and up-to-date, with a voluptuous figure and a jaunty, disillusioned manner. It certainly didn't hurt that she was

Jewish – though, like Sir Victor, more by background than by any regular observance. In only a few minutes of conversation, she revealed they had something else in common: they were both nursing broken hearts.

From that day on, the name "Mickey Hahn" – quickly shortened to "Mickey" – would appear with increasing frequency in Sir Victor's journals.

美

Emily Hahn was born in the middle of a St. Louis cold snap on the morning of January 14, 1905. She was the seventh of eight children. Of the six who survived past infancy, all but Mannel, the eldest, were girls. Her father, Isaac, was the son of a German Jew who had died young after exhausting himself working as a peddler in the rural Midwest. Isaac would eventually become vice-president of a Missouri grocery and dry goods firm, earning a good enough living that the family could afford to hire an "upstairs girl" to nanny the children and a "downstairs girl" to cook. A good story-teller with an exhibitionistic streak, Isaac was also an outspoken atheist whose idea of a fun family evening was picking apart Bible passages for logical inconsistencies.

Emily's mother, Hannah Schoen, felt she'd been cheated out of an education because of her gender. Her parents were conservative Jews from Bavaria who, while insisting their eldest daughter stay at home, had been willing to send their sons to college. Hannah became an early advocate of equal rights for women. In her youth she scandalized the neighbourhood by putting on bloomers to ride a bicycle to the office where she worked as a stenographer. From an early age the Hahn girls – Rose, Dorothy ("Dot"), Helen, Emily, and the youngest, Josephine ("Dauphine") – knew that their mother would fight to help them realize their ambitions. Hannah was delighted when her two youngest daughters wore knickers to school and were photographed by the *St. Louis Post-Dispatch* to illustrate an article about "immodest attire."

The Hahn household was lively and cultured. In the parlour,

alongside the well-thumbed dictionary on the stand, the book-shelves were filled with volumes by Hugo, Dickens, and Kipling; guests were entertained by curly-haired Helen on the piano, red-headed Dot on violin, Mannel on clarinet, and Isaac's full-throated singing. Emily had to work hard to stake out a position for herself. Her mother, detecting a dab of Irish mischief in her face, nick-named her "Mickey," in honour of the alter ego of Finley Peter Dunne, a Chicago newspaperman who gained fame writing in the folksy cadences of the Old Country. (Mickey Dooley was famously of the opinion that a good newspaper "comforts th'afflicted" and "afflicts th'comfortable.") Mickey considered herself plump, awk-ward, and unfavoured. Since her father clearly doted on Dot and her mother had proclaimed Helen the family beauty, Mickey gave up vying for her parents' attention at an early age.

"It was the crushing mass of girls that got me down," she would write in a *New Yorker* article. "If the world wanted graceful, blue-eyed princesses with curls, it would have to make out with Helen. I had *Webster*."

She would always remember her childhood as idyllic, and look back at the St. Louis of her youth as a special place. Early in the twentieth century, when it was the fourth largest city in the United States, residents of the young metropolis had legitimate grounds for civic pride. Located at the mythical, if not geographic, centre of the country – on both the Mason-Dixon line, dividing north from south, and the Mississippi, which marked the passage from the civilized East to the Western frontierlands – St. Louis styled itself as a genteel Southern city with Northern aspirations. The World's Fair of 1904 bequeathed the city both an art gallery, modelled on the Roman Baths of Caracalla, and an aviary, a soar-ing confection of Gilded Age wrought-iron. On Saturday mornings Mickey rode her bike to Forest Park to attend art classes, where she drew pictures of Apollo and Hera in a picturesquely ruined pavilion, and strolled among the white ibises and hooded mergan-sers in the great outdoor birdcage.

The Hahn home still stands, in the centre of a rank of three-storey houses across from an oval patch of municipal green space known as Fountain Park, in the Grande Prairie neighbourhood. The old grade school on Euclid Avenue, which the Hahn sisters used to reach by walking across the park, has been closed; a "For Sale" sign has been attached to its iron fence. The fountain from which the park takes its name, a glorified Baroque birdbath whose basins are painted eggshell green, today shares the lawn with a statue of Martin Luther King, Jr., sculpted wearing a flowing cape. Today the local community is mostly African-American, but a century ago Grande Prairie was home to many German and Irish immigrants.

One short block from the park is the old Hodiamont Streetcar route, now a weed-patched urban trail, where Mickey used to catch a ride to Soldan High School a half-mile to the west. It was a school that drew children from well-to-do families who grew up on the *right* side of the tracks.

The Central West End, which remains one of St. Louis's wealthiest neighbourhoods, begins two long blocks south of Fountain Avenue. A century ago it was home to the Midwestern elite, and elaborate stone gateways decorated with iron horses' heads still restrict traffic, turning streets such as Kingsbury and Portland Place into exclusive urban enclaves. T.S. Eliot, whose bust stands outside Left Bank Books on Euclid Avenue, grew up in an exquisitely pointed Federal Revival townhouse on Westminster Place (his father owned a brick-making company). Tennessee Williams spent his boyhood in the apartment building on the corner of Walton Avenue. Mickey grew up in the vicinity of – if not actually in – a neighbourhood that fostered literary respectability.

Mickey was just starting to relish her role as the eldest in the Fountain Avenue house – Mannel had married a sculptor, and her three older sisters were at schools in the East – when her father announced he was moving the family to Chicago, 300 miles to the north, where his company had opened a new office.

At first Mickey hated Chicago, with its reeking stockyards and terrifyingly busy downtown streets; but the energy of the big-shouldered, bustling city of immigrants, home to the world's first skyscrapers, soon won her over. She rode the El to the Loop, where she found a copy of F. Scott Fitzgerald's first novel, *This Side of Paradise*, at Kroch's bookstore, and began to affect a red beret and spend her afternoons at the Art Institute.

In the tough hometown of Al Capone, friends were harder to come by than adventures. Her mother once wondered why she didn't bring any schoolmates home to their flat on Lawrence Avenue, on the North Side.

"It was my private opinion," Mickey would later write of her fellow students, "that they were out cracking safes somewhere, or rolling around on the floor of some opium den."

Slowly, though, the young men of Chicago, drawn by the charms of the sisters, started to make appearances in the Hahns' new home. Rose came home one day with a young mixed-race poet named Jean Toomer, something that would have been unthinkable in segregated St. Louis. Helen, the family beauty, flirted with a *Chicago Daily News* reporter who declared himself intent on marriage. (When Helen broke his heart, he fled to Europe, the launch of a globe-trotting career that would see John Gunther becoming the most celebrated American foreign correspondent of the thirties.) Mickey was delighted when Rose married a well-read lawyer named Mitchell Dawson. The newlyweds invited Mickey to a literary gathering, the first of many, where she was charmed by the banjo playing of the straight-talking, baseball-loving poet laureate of the Midwest, Carl Sandburg.

In her first week at college in Madison, Wisconsin, Mickey, who had decided to become a sculptor, saw her academic career take a sudden left turn. When she tried to enrol in a course with a popular engineering professor, the dean brusquely informed her that "the female mind is incapable of grasping mechanics or higher mathematics." She impulsively switched from general arts to the College of Engineering, then a male enclave. The seventeen-year-old co-ed, who had grown up in a house full of women, suddenly found herself surrounded by men. Mickey gradually made herself one of the boys. She began to wear baggy khaki trousers to class and cropped her hair boyishly short. On summer field-trips through the badlands, she kept pace with the fast-striding geologists, and developed a taste for stovepipe cigars. Four years after the dean told her it would never happen, Mickey became the first female mining engineer to graduate from the University of Wisconsin.

Since she'd been a child, lost in the pages of *Fu-Manchu* and *Huck Finn* or held rapt by her father's anecdotes about his road trips around the Midwest, Mickey had longed to travel. One summer day following her sophomore year in Madison, she and Dorothy Raper, her roommate, packed up a Model T Ford – they named it "O-O," after their cries of alarm every time the engine coughed – and set off for California. Before motels and interstates, the 2,400-mile trip was full of potential hazards. They packed a small-calibre handgun under the driver's seat, and wore peaked caps and combed their hair into sideburns in the hopes they might pass as men from a distance.

After adventures with mudholes and flat tires, and side trips to Albuquerque, the Grand Canyon, and the Petrified Forest, they reached Los Angeles after three weeks on the road.

"My parents complained that I was never the same after that summer in the Model T," Mickey wrote on her return to the family home, "and no doubt they were right. I was restless and discontented at home . . . anything served as an excuse to get away anywhere."

Mickey's first attempt at settling down didn't last long. At her first job, in the office of a St. Louis zinc and lead mining company, the boss asked her to file correspondence, while her male colleagues were sent into the field to do geological research. Numbed by the prospect of riding the streetcar every day to a job that bored her, Mickey made a deal with herself. She'd recently learned that Charles Lindbergh had graduated from the University of Wisconsin's engineering school just two years before her. One night, drinking near-beer with reporters from the *Post-Dispatch*, she vowed that if Lindy successfully made his flight from New York to Paris, she would take it as a sign that she should change her life. On May 21, 1927, she woke to banner headlines that read: "Lindbergh Does It!" The adventurer had made the first solo flight – thirty-three hours long – over the Atlantic Ocean.

The fact that Lindbergh had done it in a plane called the *Spirit of St. Louis* cinched the deal. Mickey quit her office job, and never looked back.

美

After hearing what fun Dorothy, her old Model T co-pilot, was having as a tour guide in New Mexico, Mickey lit out for the West to join the ranks of the "Harvey Girls."

Before cross-country trains introduced dining cars, the Fred Harvey chain was famous for the beauty and dexterity of the waitresses that staffed its wayside train-station restaurants. By the late 1920s, the Harvey Company had branched out into other areas of the tourism sector. In New Mexico, Mickey was enlisted to guide long-distance rail passengers on a side trip known as the "Indian Detour," meeting them at the station dressed in an alarmingly kitschy uniform that consisted of a khaki shirt, a bright velveteen overblouse, a poncho belt and silver girdle, and, "most dreadful of all, a stiff Stetson hat." Her job was to school the tourists (or "dudes," as she was instructed to call them) in local folklore as they were shuttled between Native American villages, ranches, museums, gift shops selling kachina dolls and Navajo silverwork, and, inevitably, a hotel owned by the Harvey company. She took moonlit horseback rides, attended parties where tequila and corn liquor flowed, and kept company with archeologists and tubercular millionaires who dressed in Levi's, boots and bandanas.

She stayed in New Mexico until Hannah, worried that her daughter had gone off the rails, paid a surprise visit and offered to pay for her postgraduate studies. In January 1928, at the age of twenty-three, Mickey moved to New York City to attend Columbia University.

Mickey's bohemian side resurfaced in Manhattan. She rented a room on Forty-fifth Street, where she hung satin curtains decorated with Chinese dragons. She drank bathtub gin and Bacardi cocktails in speakeasies, and rode the "A" Train to Harlem, where she became enough of a regular in the nightclubs that W.C. Handy, widely known as the Father of the Blues, gave her an autographed copy of a portrait of himself by the Mexican artist Miguel Covarrubias. An old friend from St. Louis, Davey Loth, encouraged her to substitute for him as a *New York World* reporter; one of her earliest assignments was a two-part exposé on opium trafficking in New York. When summer came, she spent a month in Taos with Covarrubias and his girlfriend, renting the house where D.H. Lawrence, in search of a wilderness utopia, had once sojourned.

Her ambition to become a geologist ended when she returned to New York. As Mickey rhapsodized over the texture of calcite in a lab at Columbia, a male colleague tried to shut her down with the comment: "Science isn't a series of paintings and poems, you know." Though she was offended, she had to admit he had a point. Reluctantly, she submitted to the evidence: her future would be about words, not rocks.

After getting Mickey her first break writing for newspapers, Davey Loth, who would eventually author fifty non-fiction books himself, invited her to sail to Europe to help him research a biography of Robert and Elizabeth Barrett Browning. In Venice, she rode in a gondola and glimpsed Benito Mussolini – at least she *thought* it was him – standing on some steps in a piazza. In Paris, where she made some quick money working as a tour guide, she met Rebecca West, who had just ended an affair with her sister Helen's Chicago suitor, John Gunther. It was the beginning of a lifelong correspondence with the English writer, who matched Mickey in the eclecticism of her interests and the intensity of her romantic life.

In London to continue research on the Brownings, Mickey began another long-term relationship: with the great circular reading room of the British Library, to which she'd return many times, always to a seat in Aisle K.

During her early adventures, Mickey never stopped writing. Her prose mostly took the form of correspondence with family and friends. Those who received her typed letters – almost all of them were single-spaced and filled the pages from margin to margin – counted themselves fortunate. Mickey was a natural storyteller, with a punchy wit and an eye for the telling detail. While she was attentive to the movements of her heart, she could also hold forth as entertainingly as a gruff monologist in a Midwestern speakeasy.

"Lisbon is built entirely on the sides of several mountains," she wrote to her mother on her first trip to Europe. "They pretend they don't know it for awhile and then all at once they capitulate and give you great staircases joining street to street." From London, she wrote to her father about a famous soprano: "Yesterday we had lunch with Rebecca and I mentioned Ursula Greville and she said 'Oh yes. She's mad you know, quite mad.' Just as if she herself wasn't."

Her gifts as a writer arose out of a habit she'd had since childhood. Whenever something happened to her – funny, prosaic, fantastic – she subconsciously turned it into the kind of anecdote that would have entertained her parents and siblings in the parlour in St. Louis. Her own family – educated, competitive, observant – was her ideal public. In her head, she was constantly composing a letter to Hannah or Helen.

Without Mickey's knowledge, her brother-in-law Mitchell Dawson – Rose's husband was another favoured correspondent – submitted some of her letters from New Mexico to the *New Yorker*. The magazine's literary editor, Katherine Angell, rejected them, saying her pieces were "too far west of the Hudson," but encouraged her to continue writing. Mickey persisted until one of her vignettes, a solidly Midtown record of a lunch conversation, was accepted. The opening line of "Lovely Lady" showed off Mickey's talent for recording telling bits of dialogue: "'You know,' I suddenly said, much to my own horror, 'you're a funny person to be married to him.'"

The "person" in question was Leslie Nast, a debutante Mickey knew from Chicago. Twenty-three years old – the same age as Mickey – Leslie had married Condé Montrose Nast, who was over thirty years her senior and the publisher of *Vanity Fair*, the major competitor of the up-and-coming *New Yorker*. The "funny" part was a reference to the fact that Leslie was a lesbian.* "Lovely Lady" was the first of almost 200 short stories, poems, "casuals," and features that Mickey would see published in the *New Yorker* over the next sixty years.

Mickey's nasty streak clearly appealed to Harold Ross. The *New Yorker*'s bristle-brush-haired editor invited Mickey to his office to congratulate her on her literary debut: "You can write bitchier than anyone I know, except maybe Rebecca West. Keep it up!"

Mickey liked to be noticed – another trait that probably emerged when she was competing for attention with her sisters in the parlour on Fountain Avenue. At Manhattan parties, she always made an impression when she appeared with Punk, a chattering, black-pated capuchin monkey, on her shoulder. She found common ground with other wits at the Round Table of the Algonquin Hotel, where she struck up a friendship, sealed in the ladies' room by alcohol and tears, with Dorothy Parker.

A book project that exploited her talents to the fullest was attracting interest from publishers. Her sister Helen, who'd come to New York to work as crossword editor at the *Herald Tribune*, had married Herbert Asbury, a reporter who went on to write the highly stylized true-crime bestsellers *The Barbary Coast* and *The Gangs of New York*. When Asbury overheard Mickey extemporizing about her boy troubles, he suggested that, rather than complain, she put the anecdotes down on paper. The result would be her first book, *Seductio Ad Absurdum: The Principles and Practices of Seduction – A Beginner's Handbook*.

Though she was only twenty-five when it was published, Mickey was an old hand at the seduction game. She would later tell her biographer that she'd lost her virginity at the age of nineteen, to a gentle, poetry-writing geology professor in Madison. By

---

* Or, as Gore Vidal, who was no slouch when it came to nastiness, would write: "Leslie was a daughter of Bilitis, then the most secretive cult in the United States." He also passed on the tidbit that her fingernails were known to be of a prodigious length and sharpness.

her mid-twenties, Mickey had shed all traces of baby fat and blossomed into a full-figured woman with an intriguingly androgynous style. Having come of age during the proto-sexual revolution of the short-skirted, cigarette-smoking, absinthe-drinking flapper, she was wised up about sex and not afraid to flirt. Men found her a fascinating challenge.

Seductio Ad Absurdum, presented as a series of mock-scientific case studies, was a slight volume – aimed at the kind of metropolitan audience that would later make *Sex and the Single Girl* and *The Rules* bestsellers – but its author clearly had wit and talent. Though dismissed as trivial by male critics (apart from her Chicago acquaintance Carl Sandburg), the book sold well. As it went into its third printing, Mickey relished playing *provocatrice* on the promotional tour. In a staged debate with the author and essayist Floyd Dell, she championed a spirited love life and more complex sexual identities. "I don't mean there should be no relationship between the sexes," she argued, in what could have been a motto for her later love life, "but let there be various relationships."

She had picked an unfortunate time to launch a literary career. *Seductio* went on sale on April 1, 1930, just as the first months of the Depression were snuffing out the last embers of Jazz Age frivolity. Mickey, who would later confess she hadn't really noticed the stock market crash, did notice that "long twisted streamers of men waited patiently" in front of the soup kitchen outside her tiny apartment in Greenwich Village. She also noticed that throngs of people were gathering under the ornamental bridges of Central Park at dusk, the better to reserve a dry spot to put down their blankets for the coming night. The *New Yorker*, which had saved up a huge stock of stories for a rainy day, had temporarily stopped buying her work. For the first time in her life, Mickey, the product of an upper-middle-class home where servants did all the cooking and housework, found that she was often going to bed hungry. She also found herself grappling with despair. After a near-death experience with a bottle of sleeping pills, she began to consider a friend's offer to pay for a course of therapy with an "alienist."

Instead of psychoanalysis, she opted for travel. With her college roommate Dorothy, she had once dreamt up a scheme to go swimming in Lake Kivu in East Africa. Later, she had met an anthropologist from Boston named Patrick Putnam who invited her to visit him in the Belgian Congo. Even a long shot in Africa looked better than poverty and gloom, which seemed a sure thing in Manhattan. Mickey returned to London, and on Christmas Day 1930 she sailed for the Congolese port of Boma by way of Bordeaux and Dakar, in the third-class cabin of a French cargo ship.

Mickey would stay in Africa for two years. In that time she would assist Putnam dressing wounds in a Red Cross outpost, temporarily adopt an orphaned Pygmy boy, learn to speak Swahili, care for a pet baboon named Angélique, serve as a judge in an adultery case in a Congolese village (where she shocked the crowd by inviting the wife to give her testimony), and watch Al Jolson amaze an audience in a Dar es Salaam cinema by singing on film in the first talkie, *The Jazz Singer*. Eventually, though, she came to the conclusion that Putnam was a miniature Kurtz, playing out his own sordid version of *Heart of Darkness* with his African mistresses. Disgusted, Mickey left the village and walked through the jungle for eighteen days with a party of porters, finally fulfilling her dream of reaching Lake Kivu (which, she cabled her college roommate, was as "dull as the ditchwater it did not resemble").

Her African adventures provided her with the subject matter for her next two books. *Congo Solo* was a lively travelogue, presented in journal form, in which she changed Putnam's name and omitted his most shocking offences. In a pattern she would repeat in years to come, she also wrote a version of what she had *actually* experienced, in lightly fictionalized form. *With Naked Foot* told the story of an arrogant anthropologist who believed the strong should rule the weak, and chained one of his three native wives to a tree by the neck for a week when he suspected her of cheating.

When Mickey returned to the family home in Chicago, she found her father close to death, his limbs turning gangrenous as his diabetes worsened. Using the nursing skills she'd learned in the Congo, she ended his agony with an injection of morphine. (Following his death, her mother Hannah would move to the affluent lakeside village of Winnetka, outside of Chicago, where Mickey's sister Rose and brother Mannel were raising families.)

Back in New York, the Depression, in spite of the hope held out by the new presidency of Franklin D. Roosevelt, had only dug deeper. One "college-bred" acquaintance had moved to New Jersey to work as a cook for six dollars a week. Sharing a tiny apartment with two friends, surviving on meals of coffee, bread, and bananas, Mickey distracted herself with a troubled affair with a New-York-born playwright.

Edwin "Eddie" Mayer, who had built a career in Los Angeles writing such successful – and instantly forgotten – movie hits as *Tonight is Ours* and *Thirty-Day Princess*, had begun his aggressive courtship after spotting Mickey in a restaurant in London. Their on-again, off-again relationship, which lasted for two years, mystified her friends. Eddie was a pudgy man with a frog-like face, a lazy eye, and a wife in Hollywood. Mean when drunk, he was always fanatically jealous. ("He knocked off the bottom half of my front teeth for smoking marijuana," Mickey told her biographer. "He was drunk at the time and I hadn't a weapon or things would have been different.") When sober, he treated Mickey to nice clothes and out-of-town trips. Their best days were spent together in England, where they shared a rented house for a few months while Mickey studied anthropology at Oxford as a visiting scholar.

The end of the affair came early in 1935. Mickey had flown to Los Angeles to meet Eddie. In the cab from the airport, he announced he was going back to his wife. Impulsively, she decided she would rescue herself, and her pride, by embarking on another adventure – this one in the Far East. (In a later novel, she would suggest it was a glimpse of a red silk curtain with bamboo woven into the pattern, from the back of a cab, that inspired her main character's voyage to the Far East.) From there, she planned to return to Africa. Her sister Helen, whose marriage with Herbert Asbury was on the rocks, suggested that a first-class ocean cruise would help them to shed their grief.

Since Mickey was already in California, suggested Helen, why not return to the Congo by way of China?

美

No matter what you thought of Mickey – and she would find many enemies over her long career – there was no one else quite like her.

St. Louis-born and Chicago-bred, she was the inheritor of an openness, pragmatism, and provincial awe at the achievements of Western culture that typified a certain kind of American early in the twentieth century. Out of St. Louis would come the "Missouri Mafia": graduates of the School of Journalism at the University of Missouri who would bring their clear-eyed brand of reporting to all corners of the world (but most passionately to China). Out of Chicago would come voices like that of Saul Bellow, whose characters blended the outlook of outside-the-mainstream Jewish immigrants with the brash self-confidence of a restless generation awakening to the possibilities of a youthful and prosperous culture.

Mickey could be a glib writer, and her delight in spoken language sometimes made her alight on easy formulations that were quick to date. At her best, though, she wrote like a combination of Bellow's wide-eyed, idealistic Augie March, one of Mark Twain's restless, observant boy heroes, and the wisecracking, seen-it-all flappers of Dorothy Parker's short stories.

By the time she was thirty she had become a fearless globetrotter, happily opting to rough it in situations where more genteel literary travellers would have checked into a grand hotel. She'd already packed a pistol across the American West, trekked across West Africa without an inflatable bath, and discovered what it was like to be down and out in Paris and London. In a time when too many Americans and Europeans refused to cross the colour bar, she looked at and talked to African-Americans, Congolese, and Native Americans as her equals. Born of an exhibitionistic, atheistic father and a proto-feminist mother, she was forced by her birth rank in a large family to establish herself as a shrewd observer and record-taker. Possessed of boldness, charm, and curiosity, secure in her large family's love and support, she had a talent for turning wherever she happened to be into home.

It is hard to imagine a more suitable witness than Emily "Mickey" Hahn to the maddeningly intense world that was Shanghai in the thirties. A product of – and already an old hand at negotiating – cultural collisions, she was set to arrive in a metropolis where the ideologies that would shape the twentieth century were about to send the world trembling.

On March 5, 1935, Mickey stood on the deck of the *Chichibu Maru*, a motor ship of the Nippon Yusen Kabushiki Orient Line, watching the skyline of San Francisco recede as vapour from the vessel's single funnel mingled with the fog beneath the Golden Gate Bridge. A week or two in the Far East, she thought, would be enough to cleanse her mind of Eddie, before she got into the real travel that awaited her in Africa.

She would spend the next eight years of her life in China.

6: Shanghai Grand

Guests signing the registry book at the front desk of the Cathay Hotel in the second week of April 1935 could congratulate themselves: they had truly arrived. Not only had they secured lodgings at one of the half dozen or so most luxurious hotels in the world; they also had the good fortune to be calling at Shanghai during one of its all-too-brief periods of peace and stability, and at the apex of the city's twentieth-century prosperity.

In the forty-two years since her half-century Jubilee, Shanghai had grown from an obscure outpost of Western trade in the Far East into a veritable metropolis. Half of all China's foreign trade now passed through its port, whose 35 miles of wharves could welcome 170 ships (and 500 sea-going junks) at one time. Since 1893, its population had almost doubled, making it continental Asia's largest city – in the Far East, only Tokyo was more populous – and the fifth-largest in the world.

A new arrival would have recognized Shanghai as a city as up-to-date as any of the great metropolises of Europe or the Americas. Buildings were kept toasty with centrally supplied coal gas; in 1865, Shanghai had become one of the world's first cities to have a municipal gasworks. The streetcars that criss-crossed the boulevards drew power from an American-owned diesel generating plant, the world's largest when it was completed. An automatic telephone call could be placed via an American-run exchange to book a flight to Soochow or Nanking on the Douglas DC-2s of the foreign-owned China National Aviation Corporation, whose pilots tended to hail from Indiana or Missouri. On Broadway, in the former American Settlement, Jimmy's Kitchen, started by an ex-navy cook who jumped ship after earning a modest pile playing poker, served hamburgers and corn-beef hash on plain wooden tables. The portions were so large, every client left with a doggy bag; owner Jimmy James insisted, however, that the bags be given not to the family dog, but to the beggars who waited outside. The bowling alley at the Country Club (where the pinboys were Chinese, but from which Chinese clients were excluded) was excellent, and the grounds of the Hungjao Golf Course were expertly maintained by attendants in ankle-length white gowns.

For all the familiar comforts of home, though, any tourist gazing from the window of a room at the Cathay would have been struck by the intimidating concentration of humanity, visible at all hours, where Nanking Road met the Bund.

"In no city, West or East, have I ever had such an impression of dense, rank, richly clotted life," wrote Aldous Huxley after a visit to the Old City. "Nothing more intensely living can be imagined . . . so much life, so carefully canalised, so rapidly and strongly flowing – the spectacle of it inspires something like terror."

More democratic-minded observers thrilled to the vitality on display. The Missouri-born journalist Edgar Snow, who came to Shanghai in 1928 to work for the *China Weekly Review*, described downtown streets filled with "crushing throngs spilling through every kind of traffic, precariously among old cars and new ones and between coolies racing wildly to compete for ricksha fares, gingerly past 'honey-carts' filled with excrement dragged down Bubbling Well Road, sardonically past perfumed, exquisitely gowned, mid-thigh-exposed Chinese ladies, jestingly past the Herculean bare-backed coolie trundling his taxi wheelbarrow load of six giggling servant girls en route to home or work, carefully before singing peddlers bearing portable kitchens ready with delicious noodles on the spot, lovingly under gold-lettered shops overflowing with fine silks and brocades, dead-panning past village women staring wide-eyed at frightening Indian policemen, gravely past gambling mah-jonng ivories clicking and jai alai and pari-mutuel betting, slyly through streets hung with the heavy-sweet acrid smell of opium."

Through a squinting first glance, foreign-run Shanghai appeared to be a model city for the internationalization of the world. The brass badges on the smart uniforms of the multinational Shanghai Volunteer Corps members featured the Union Jack, the Stars and Stripes, the German Eagle, the Portuguese shield, the French Tricolour, a Scandinavian cross, and the flags of seven other nations set in a circle amidst Chinese characters.* On Avenue Foch, one of the dividing lines between the International Settlement and the French Concession, stolid Vietnamese in pointed straw hats regulated traffic on the south side, while on the north the turbaned Sikh constables of the International Settlement cracked quarter-staffs made of ironwood, and confiscated the seats of any rickshaw driver who dared break the law.

Shopping was a preoccupation for visitors. The exchange rate was highly favourable to foreigners, particularly those with American dollars in their pockets. In the Russian-run boutiques on Avenue Joffre, they bought fur coats and wraps fashioned from kolinsky and sable trapped in Siberia. They patronized La Donna Silk Salon Modernique in the Cathay's shopping arcade, whose management required the male attendants to have their hands manicured several times a week so their fingernails would not tear the precious bolts of shantung silk and crêpe de chine. Picked up in the stretch of the Bund in front of the Cathay Hotel by motor buses operated by American Express or Thomas Cook, they were overcharged for jade Buddhas and other souvenirs in the Chinese city (the tourists' apparent inability to haggle was the despair of Shanghailanders, who blamed them for inflating local prices).

Whisked between the bird market, the Great World Amusement Centre, and the Lunghwa Pagoda, the more observant tourist might have noted signs of the poverty in the street. Hunger

---

* Even in this international corps, strict divisions were maintained. White Britons made up the "A" Company, mixed-race Eurasians manned the "B" Company, and Chinese the "C" Company. Members of the Jewish Company, led by a Methodist from Hampshire, wore a silver badge in the shape of the Star of David. The only professional company was a battalion of highly disciplined White Russians who had formerly served with the Czar's army.

drove Shanghai's poorest citizens to unimaginable extremes. As a boy, the son of the Slovak architect Ladislav Hudec (who built the Park Hotel, the Cathay's only serious rival) watched a wealthy Chinese man lean out of his limousine and vomit up a rich meal; beggars promptly appeared from side streets to eat what he'd thrown up. Newly arrived, the American disc jockey Carroll Alcott was taking his first stroll in the International Settlement when he saw an old Chinese woman crossing Peking Road drop a bowl of rice. When she stooped to scrape her evening meal off the pavement and back into the bowl, a limousine ran into her, breaking her back and killing her instantly. Stunned, Alcott continued on to the Bund, where he saw another elderly Chinese woman washing what looked like the head of a dirty mop in the Whangpoo River. On closer inspection it turned out to be noodles dropped by food hawkers, blackened by the tires of coal trucks, that she'd retrieved from the streets. An officer of the American River Police explained that, once she'd washed the noodles, she sold them to street urchins for a few coppers.

"We get about seven or eight dead bodies from this stream every day," he'd added. "Not a clean place to wash a meal."

Even the Cathay Hotel's most blinkered guests could not help noticing the cruel poverty, particularly the two infamous beggars who worked the pavement across the street from the Nanking Road entrance to the Cathay. One, nicknamed "Light in the Head," kept a single candle burning atop his shaven skull, which dripped wax on his forehead and cast a flickering light over his cadaverous face. The other was a woman known as the "Weeping Wonder," whose tears were so copious they formed in pools around her on the sidewalk. Even more heartbreaking were the street urchins who chased after rickshaws on Nanking Road crying: "No Mama, No Papa, No Whisky Soda."

The Municipal Police kept the numbers of the estimated 20,000 professional beggars who worked the International Settlement in check by periodically herding them into vans and driving them deep into the countryside, dropping a few in each village along the way, so as not to incur the wrath of local officials. Disease and hunger often took care of the rest. In 1935, a peaceful year, the Municipal Council collected 5,950 cadavers from the streets of the International Settlement.

These displays of poverty, constantly renewed by Shanghai's status as a haven from war, famine, and drought, were turned into spectacle by the sheer compactness of the city. The International Settlement, formed by the merger of the British and American Settlements, amounted to a mere 8.94 square miles. The French Concession, which measured half a square mile, functioned as a residential suburb of the International Settlement (to this day, its broad, plane-tree shaded boulevards are favoured by consular staff and expatriates with generous living allowances). Including the Chinese governed sections of the city, whose major streets were patrolled by the Shanghai Municipal Police, the entire city occupied just twenty-seven square miles – making it smaller than the island of Manhattan. A five-mile walk in any direction from the Cathay Hotel would have ended in cotton fields or rice paddies.

This made Shanghai one of the most crowded places on the planet. In the eight years leading up to 1935, over one million Chinese migrants poured into Shanghai from adjoining provinces, boosting the population to 3.5 million. In comparison, New York's Lower East Side was roomy. In 1935, Shanghai counted 129,583 people per square mile, and within five years it would attain the double of the maximum historic density of Manhattan's most crowded neighbourhood.

The situation was entirely man-made. In the nineteenth century, the leaders of the foreign settlements had resisted all attempts to expand Shanghai's perimeter, on the grounds that a compact city was easier to defend. The truth was that they had learned the same lesson that Silas Hardoon had decades before: namely, that a politically enshrined barrier to growth made their real-estate holdings multiply in value, often exponentially. At the height of their prestige and influence there were never more than 70,000 foreigners in Shanghai, accounting for just 3 per cent of the total population. In the French Concession, which was run by a Consul General who answered to the Quai d'Orsay in Paris and exercised the powers of a colonial governor, only 2,342 of the half-million residents were actually French citizens. (In fact, in "Frenchtown," as it came to be known, the French were outnumbered by the British.) Of the 1.12 million inhabitants of the International Settlement, only 38,015 were foreigners, the vast majority being either Japanese or stateless White Russians. Fewer than one in ten of these foreigners had the right to elect the fourteen leaders of the Shanghai Municipal Council, who styled themselves the enlightened overseers of an aristocratic republic (as opposed to the parasitic oligarchs of a semi-colony of the industrialized powers). Political control of the economic core of China's largest city lay in the hands of just 3,852 non-Chinese voters.

A special issue of *Fortune* dedicated to Shanghai, which would have been available on news-stands throughout the city in April 1935, summed up the situation:

Shanghai, the fifth city of the earth, the megalopolis of continental Asia, inheritor of ancient Bagdad, of pre-War Constantinople, of nineteenth-century London, of twentieth-century Manhattan – where the world's empires coinhabit twelve square miles [sic] of muddy land at the mouth of a yellow river – is unique among the cities. Shanghai's land is dedicated to safety.[*]

That safety, the *Fortune* writers pointed out, was guaranteed by the gunboats of the foreign powers anchored in the Whangpoo River, the truncheons of the Municipal Police, and the rifles of the Volunteer Corps.

Fortune also set out an extract, tantalizing at the height of the Depression, from the annual budget of a typical taipan. The manager of a foreign-owned firm could expect a $25,000 (US) tax-free salary that would buy him the services of ten to twenty

---

[*] *Fortune*, whose first issue appeared four months after the 1929 stock market crash, was the pet project of Henry Luce, who had been born in China to American missionary parents. The cover price of his "Ideal Super-Class Magazine" was one dollar – this in a year when *Time* magazine went for fifteen cents, and the average weekly wage for a factory worker in Shanghai was the equivalent of $1.70.

domestic servants, membership at several clubs, a houseboat, and a new Ford or a Buick with a driver.

"A bachelor," the magazine asserted, "will probably live in one of Sir Victor Sassoon's smart new apartments." Married men could expect to pay $250 a month to rent a house on the outskirts of Frenchtown with two or three acres of land. "Entertainment" was another significant expense ("biggest item: Liquor"). Near the bottom of the budget was the heading: "Charity: a small item."

Amidst colour prints of slender Chinese women in silk gowns, some of them topless, the lead article, entitled "The Shanghai Boom," singled out the Cathay Hotel as "one of the most luxurious hostelries in the world, rivalling the best in Manhattan and charging Manhattan prices." Pointing out that an acre of land on the Bund worth $68 in 1843 would be valued at $1.43 million in 1935, it further noted that anyone who'd had the foresight to transfer their money from American stocks to Shanghai real-estate would have trebled his fortune in seven years.

"One man in the world actually did this," the *Fortune* writers concluded. He was:

a Bagdad Jew by race, though technically an Englishman by birth. Now Shanghai's No. 1 realtor, he lives in the tower of his Cathay Hotel, gives wild, luxurious, and astonishing parties, possesses the only social secretary in the city, and strays away to England or India for no more than the few months the British income-tax laws permit him . . . He has left his imprint on Shanghai in the towering bulk of his buildings, he has found a sanctuary for his wealth, and he is great.

The first page of the report featured a black-and-white photo of Sir Victor, knuckles folded over an ivory-handled cane, wearing a soft felt hat, a double-breasted suit, and the broadest of smiles.

美

It hadn't been as easy as the *Fortune* scribes portrayed it; but then, as Sir Victor knew, nothing worth achieving was ever easy. Nor was the future quite as bright as they painted it. The salty streaks in his once pepper-black head of hair – the white had started to appear five years earlier, with the explosion of the mine outside the Cathay – bore testament to his worries.

He had first become aware of Shanghai's potential in 1903. Fresh out of Cambridge, he'd taken a leisurely tour of the Sassoon holdings in the Far East. In India he had stayed at his uncle Jacob's villa, where he'd made a show of tinkering with the spindles at the David Sassoon & Sons cotton mills in Bombay, all the while finding excuses to play polo with the local cavalry officers. Shanghai was more to his taste. His favourite uncle, David, while nominally a manager at E.D. Sassoon & Co., made it his true profession to profit from the pleasures of the China coast – the ne'er-do-well "Nunky," as Victor had called him since he was a boy, brought him to the sing-alongs at the Paper Hunt Club, introduced him to the Mongolian ponies at the Race Course, and showed him where to find jade-handled knives and ivory snuff-boxes, the collecting of which had become a passion.

On the third floor of Sassoon House, Silas Hardoon, the firm's long-term property manager, had earnestly warned him that the Japanese mills would drive down textile prices worldwide by drawing from the vast pool of cheap Chinese labour. But Victor was more attentive to Hardoon's tales of the fortunes to be made in the Shanghai real-estate market. His late grandfather Elias, Victor realized, had shown foresight in buying prime property on the Bund.

After his sojourn in the Far East, Victor returned to England. Though already singled out as the most promising member of the fourth generation of the David Sassoon dynasty, as a young man he was more interested in high speed than high finance. In London, he ran up long bills at Nunky's tailor and wine-merchant and developed a reputation for reckless driving; he cut a dashing figure at Brighton and Ascot, where he could be seen clambering out of a roadster in a top hat and morning coat, with a monocle jammed into his weak left eye. Most of all, he loved the new sport of aviation. Thrilled when Louis Blériot crossed the Channel in a monoplane, Victor became a founding member of the Royal Aero

Club; as a pioneering British aviator he was the proud holder of Pilot's Licence Number 52.

His love of velocity was almost his undoing. One windy morning in 1915, while serving as a sub-lieutenant in the newly formed Royal Naval Air Service, he went up in a biplane on a training mission over the cliffs of Dover. At 1,000 feet, a spring in the engine broke; glancing down at the disabled crankshaft, Victor saw flames shooting up between his shins. As the plane dove, none of the pilot's desperate tugs at the control stick could stop their downward spiral. The subsequent plunge into a farmer's field left the pilot tangled in the rigging, one ankle broken. Victor, whose role as observer put him in the front of the plane, felt the brunt of the impact: the crash broke both of his legs.

He spent eight months cocooned in a cast, and emerged with his right leg markedly shorter than his left. For the rest of his life, recurring pain in his hips would force him to rely on walking sticks. At Cambridge he'd been fond of tennis, boxing, swimming, and dancing. To be thus sidelined from an active life was a torment. If he developed a reputation for having a dark, sardonic wit, it came from too often being a wallflower at extravagant balls of his own devising.

After the First World War, Victor turned his energies to the family business. As chairman of E.D. Sassoon, his father Edward Elias, vexed by what he saw as overtaxation by the Inland Revenue, set up trusts to gradually funnel the firm's English assets to India and China. Victor was dispatched to Bombay to oversee the family's cotton mills and dye-works. Dividing his time between his suite at the palatial Taj Mahal Hotel and Eve's, his bungalow in Poona, he built United Mills into the largest cotton manufacturer in India, with 6,500 looms. Though the firm prided itself on its enlightened paternalism and paid the best industrial wages in the country, Victor, who served on the Legislative Assembly, knew that change was in the air. Militants who wanted the British to quit India were making bonfires of imported cloth. Victor was particularly frustrated by the leader of the Congress Party, Gandhi, who was leading peaceful protests against British rule and whom Victor suspected of being tied up with the communists.

After his father's death in 1924, Victor – now the third Baronet of Bombay, and entitled to refer to himself as Sir Victor – began visiting Shanghai with increasing frequency. The more he got to know the place, the more he found his heart was in China.

True, the Middle Kingdom had been a shambles since 1911, when the Celestial Court of the Manchus, gnawed from the interior by inbreeding, decadence, and opium addiction, had fallen to earth and shattered like a termite-ridden pagoda. After briefly becoming a republic, the nation had disintegrated into fiefdoms ruled by rival warlords. Its weakness proved a boon for foreigners: in China, unlike India, the British could enjoy the benefits of colonial power without any of the costly responsibilities of actually administering a colony. Shanghai in particular profited from China's pain.

The events of 1927 had proved a litmus test for the city. After the death of their founder, Sun Yat-sen, the nationalists – the Kuomintang, or the "Keep the Nation Together" party, as they were known in Chinese – marched north from their base in Canton under the command of a wasp-waisted general named Chiang Kai-shek. The goal of the Northern Expedition was to reclaim the divided northern provinces from the warlords. In the early twenties, the nationalists, seeing their efforts to garner financial and material support from the United States and other Western powers rebuffed, had turned to the Soviet Union for aid. A shaggy-haired Bolshevik named Mikhail Borodin – "a large, calm man, with the natural dignity of a lion or a panther," in the words of American journalist Vincent Sheean – had converted many of the nationalists to the cause of international communism. Meanwhile, a rival group, the Chinese Communist Party, whose name in Chinese, Kungch'antang, means "Share Production Party," had held its first meetings in the backstreets of Shanghai, home to China's largest urban proletariat.

In March, as the nationalist troops approached the city, Shanghailanders braced for revolution. A young communist named

Chou En-lai called for a general strike, and close to a million Chinese workers took to the streets. The Volunteer Corps were put on alert, gunships were called to action on the Whangpoo River, and barbed-wire barricades went up around the International Settlement. The fear was that Chiang Kai-shek's troops would join with the communist strikers, an alliance that would spell doom for foreign power in Shanghai.

Fortunately, at least for the Sassoon interests in Shanghai, Chiang Kai-shek proved more than willing to shut down the communists, whom he saw as rivals to his power. Sterling Fessenden, the American secretary general of the Municipal Council, and a notoriously feckless man with a soft spot for Russian taxi dancers, allowed a one-time breach of the International Settlement's sanctity. At the same time, a deal was struck with two of Shanghai's leading gangsters. "Big-Eared" Du Yuesheng, who had started his career with the Little 8-Legged Band smuggling opium into the International Settlement in coffins, was the undisputed kingpin of Shanghai's opium trade. "Pock-Marked" Huang Jinrong was at once the head of Chinese detectives of Frenchtown's Sûreté and the leader of the Green Gang, the city's underworld enforcers.

The picturesque pair made Chicago's Al Capone look like a penny-ante thug: while their sinister power was rooted in five-century-old secret societies, they also moved effortlessly in high society, where they passed as respectable financiers and philanthropists. Fessenden's Municipal Police turned a blind eye as the gang bosses' men were set loose in the Settlement, picking off communist strikers with their Mausers. Chiang's troops, armed with British guns and armoured cars, were permitted into the foreign zones. By some estimates, 10,000 young Chinese, almost all of them unarmed, were slaughtered in the violent purge that followed.

For ending a mob uprising, "Big-Eared" Du was revered by Shanghailanders as the city's saviour (he would later be entered in the official Shanghai *Who's Who* as "one of the leading financiers, bankers and industrial leaders of China" – an astounding tribute to a man who was said to keep a dried monkey's head in the back of his gown for luck). In the decade that followed, during which Du and "Pock-Marked" Huang exercised undisputed dominion over the underworld, organized labour in Shanghai didn't stand a chance: the wages paid by industrialists remained pitifully low, working conditions in their factories abysmal. Chiang's reward for ending the Red Menace in Shanghai was reportedly $3 million, paid out in Mexican silver by the grateful bankers of the Bund. The Northern Expedition had achieved the nationalists' twin goals of pacifying the urban communists and ousting the most important rural warlords. An unelected Kuomintang government took power in the new capital of Nanking, marking the beginning of ten years of Republican rule.[*]

A few months after the slaughter, on December 1, 1927, Chiang married a celebrated beauty in a lavish ceremony in the Majestic, the hotel that was Shanghai's premier venue for such events before the opening of the Cathay. The Generalissimo's alliance with Soong Mei-ling, who had been educated at Wellesley College in Massachussets and whose Harvard-educated brother, T.V. Soong, was the nationalist finance minister, sent a clear signal to the world: Shanghai was open for business.

Sir Victor was particularly receptive to the message. A pivotal sojourn in Shanghai in the spring of 1928 made him decide that his future lay in China rather than India. After checking into Suite 104 of the Majestic – a hotel he would soon add to his real-estate empire – a journal entry recorded a night spent enjoying the city's frenetic nightlife.

The early evening of May 3, 1928, found him seated next to the wife of an American naval officer. (He noted: "Big blonde. Understand divorcing husband. Bit of gold digger + should say tease.") After dinner, he went to see a boxing match in the Carlton Café and Theatre, whose ballroom could host a crowd of 2,000 under a ceiling of leaded glass. Then he went on for drinks at the

---

[*] Nanking means "southern capital." Between 1928 and 1949, the name of Peking – which means "northern capital" – was changed to Peiping, meaning "northern peace."

Del Monte club, run by Al Israel, the "Ziegfeld of Shanghai," who staffed his French Concession gambling den with beautiful White Russian hostesses and a 200-pound barman named Thurman "Demon" Hyde. He finished the night at a cabaret on Thibet Road that – after becoming famous for briefly forcing its dancers to dress in black and act like cats – had recently caused a stir in the foreign community for hiring Cantonese hostesses. Sir Victor noted, "At Black Cat there were Chinese dancing partners, an innovation since beginning year." He was agreeably surprised to see the better class of Chinese mingling with white Shanghailanders. It was a sign that times were changing, at a suitably gradual pace. He finished the entry with, "Bed 4 am."

A city that could keep a man approaching fifty amused until the wee hours of the morning was worth investing in. Soon afterwards, following a meeting with fifty business associates at Sassoon House, Sir Victor noted in his journal: "Definitely decided on Hotel. Wilson the architect is a good man."

The architect in question, "Tug" Wilson, would build most of Sir Victor's greatest buildings in Shanghai. The hotel was the Cathay, which in a few months would start rising on the Bund – on the exact spot where the stubborn old Chinese lady had once spat in the face of the Taotai, rather than sell her property to a foreigner.

The keystone of the Sassoon empire in Shanghai was laid in 1926, when Sir Victor began his long association with Palmer & Turner.* The architectural firm had already shown it was up to the challenge of building on Shanghai's treacherous soil by erecting the Hongkong and Shanghai Bank building at No. 12, the Bund. This domed building, which weighed 50,000 tons and occupied 300 feet of precious riverfront, instantly became a landmark: to this

---

* One of the oldest architectural firms in the world, Palmer & Turner moved to Hong Kong after the Second World War, and reopened its offices in Shanghai, under the name P&T Group, in 1990.

day, visitors push through the front doors to gawk at the octago-
nal entrance hall, which is decorated with mosaics representing the
world's great cities. (Shanghai is portrayed as a gowned damsel
looming over the Bund, her left hand over a ship's wheel, her right
shading her eyes as she gazes down the Whangpoo.) Ever since its
opening, Chinese passers-by, hoping some of the bankers' prosperity would rub off, have stroked the bronze paws of the two
lions out front – the crouching cat representing security, the rear-
ing one symbolizing protection.

The interior of the building's rooftop dome, whose curving
walls were decorated with flying trophies, flags, and the first propeller manufactured in China, was used as a meeting place for the
Royal Air Force Association Club. Sir Victor's First World War
flying experience qualified him for membership, and the ceremonial dinners he attended gave him ample opportunity to admire
the workmanship that had gone into the building. Its architect,
who had orchestrated the arrival of the pine pilings from Oregon
and the 16,000 blocks of white granite from Kowloon, was
George Leopold Wilson; his friends knew him as "Tug." Working
under orders from the head office in Hong Kong to "dominate
the Bund," he'd completed the job in just two years. Always
impeccably groomed and sporting his signature round spectacles,
Wilson was the kind of man Sir Victor could talk to: he enjoyed
polo and steeple-chasing, and had an asset in his wife Kathleen,
one of Shanghai's leading socialites. In the years to come, Wilson
would be the chief architect on every important building erected
by the Sassoon interests in Shanghai.

The cornerstone of the Sassoon empire would be the building at
No. 20, the Bund, which was to replace the E.D. Sassoon & Co.
headquarters that had risen on the site of the old American opium
hong. Laying the foundation of the new Sassoon House proved
to be the biggest challenge. Ever since the Han dynasty, Chinese
architects had coped with the problem of building on mud
through the use of friction piles: posts were driven into the ground

to a depth where the pressure exerted by the surrounding earth was greater than the load borne by the posts. Traditionally, wooden pilings – driven by massive hammers raised on pulleys by teams of grunting workers – were used to establish the perimeter of a building. As long as the wood remained below the water table, rot would not set in. The friction pile technique, however, had rarely been tried on buildings taller than four storeys. When a Palmer & Turner partner asked engineers at the Massachusetts Institute of Technology for advice on erecting modern skyscrapers on ancestral mud, they proposed the same solution arrived at by the ancient Chinese: why not cover masses of driven timber pilings with a giant concrete raft?

Wilson rose to the challenge. On the perimeter of the trapez-oidal wedge of land that faced the Bund, concrete-and-wood piles were driven to a depth of sixty-two feet. The piles supported a thick raft of concrete, poured in a grid pattern, atop which the new Sassoon House began to rise. Partway through construction, and after the first four storeys had already been completed, Sir Victor sorely tried Wilson's patience by announcing he wanted to add a luxury hotel to the building's upper floors. Construction was briefly halted as the plans were redrawn. On May 29, 1928, a new company, The Cathay Hotels, Ltd., was founded; its direc-tors included Wilson and H. E. Arnhold, who served for several terms as chairman of the Municipal Council. The merger between E.D. Sassoon & Co. and the venerable Arnhold Brothers & Com-pany, whose fortune had been made in the development of Hankow, was hailed as one of the biggest in the history of the Far East.

When the Cathay officially opened in the summer of 1929, Sir Victor was on the other side of the world, taking in shows at Paris's Folies-Bergères and enjoying the nightlife on Hamburg's Reeperbahn. (His was not the first name in the hotel's registry; the honour went to a now-forgotten playwright from Brooklyn, who signed her name "Mrs. 'Buddy' Hazel.") It was a fondly-awaited moment, then, when he was able to write in his journal, "Arrived S'hai 6:30. Staying Suite I Cathay Hotel."

The Cathay, after all, was more than just another hotel. As a man accustomed to the best accommodation in the world – the Taj Mahal in Bombay, the George V in Paris, Claridge's in London – Sir Victor knew that he'd built something glorious. And now he was staying at *his* hotel, built to *his* specifications.

When he dropped his bags at the Cathay Hotel, on Monday, March 31, 1930, Sir Victor had finally come home.

Other Sassoon buildings soon followed, each establishing a new standard of luxury in its class. A few hundred yards south of the Cathay, the stepped tower of the fourteen-storey Metropole, a hotel aimed at business travellers, rose at the corner of Foochow Road. The movement of its concave facade was continued across Kiangse Road by the mirror-image Hamilton House, a luxury apartment tower. The pair of Gothic Art Deco towers, on a curved intersection designed to suggest a miniature Piccadilly Circus, created an impressive, amphitheatre-like urban space. Completed in 1932, and decorated with Persian rugs and Jacobean furniture, the Metropole catered to busy executives (for years, the Rotary Club held raucous Saturday-night meetings there, lubricated by flagons of U.B. Beer produced at Sir Victor's Union Brewery). Across the street, Hamilton House combined office space and residences for doctors and dentists on its lower floors with the city's most up-to-date and extravagant apartments, some of them spread over three levels.

North of the Cathay, Embankment House rose like a ship's prow over Soochow Creek. Built as an apartment complex to house Sassoon company employees, it was the largest building in Asia on its completion in 1932. The challenge of erecting such a massive structure on soft soil had led Sir Victor to found the Aerocrete Company, which manufactured a lighter, "aerated" concrete that reduced the load of interior walls. It was the erection of the serpentine Embankment House that completed his plan to monogram his initials into Shanghai, following the "V" traced by the Cathay Hotel with a gargantuan "S."

In 1929, as the worldwide depression began, 22,000 new buildings rose in Shanghai. The eastern hemisphere's most celebrated tycoon was far from being the only real-estate developer in Shanghai; but his faith in the city's future fuelled the boom that saw the erection of the tallest buildings in the world outside North America.

Key to Sir Victor's long-term strategy was his slow acquisition of Silas Hardoon's property. By the time Sir Victor came to China, his grandfather's former real-estate manager had established himself as the richest foreigner in Shanghai. He had also developed a reputation for eccentricity. Liza Roos, his Eurasian wife, had encouraged Hardoon's headlong plunge into Oriental culture. While he continued to collect the rent in person from his tenants in the lowliest rowhouses, and lease his properties along Nanking Road to the city's most profitable department stores, Hardoon built himself an extravagant Oriental pleasure garden and had the Koran translated into Chinese. (The book's frontispiece featured a portrait of Hardoon in the robes of a Manchu merchant prince.) He lived in a sprawling pagoda-roofed home complete with a throne room, modelled on a building described in the famous Qing-dynasty novel *The Dream of the Red Chamber*. The couple legally adopted eleven Chinese and European children, who were ferried to Shanghai's best schools in an ancient maroon Rolls-Royce.[*] For all his great wealth, Hardoon worked in an unheated office with an unpainted floor, where on cold days he could be found bundled in an overcoat, doing his accounts at a clumsily planed pine desk.

When Hardoon died in the summer of 1931, his three-day funeral – held in Aili Gardens, a twenty-six-acre estate whose bamboo groves and arched bridges were hidden away behind high

---

* "Nothing in my rich store of Shanghai memories," Mickey Hahn would write in 1937, "is as delightful as the picture of a group of these children, blond and graceful in the Nordic fashion, striking attitudes and executing difficult steps in the best traditional manner." Though the Hardoon children wore Chinese clothes at home, they attended British public school, and the boys were circumcised and brought up as Jews.

iron gates painted vermilion – confounded the world's press. As huge sticks of Chinese incense burned at the grave, and after a rabbi had conducted traditional Jewish interment rites, 5,000 mourners passed before a wax effigy of the deceased holding a pair of chopsticks in his hands.

In the months before his death, Sir Victor recorded several meetings with Hardoon in his journals. The man had assembled a fabulous property empire, especially along Nanking Road, which was on its way to becoming Shanghai's Fifth Avenue. Sir Victor managed to snatch up some of the choicest lots. The rest of Hardoon's property, valued at $150 million, languished in probate or was sold off piecemeal to cover estate taxes and legal costs.

Sir Victor's fondest hope was that foreigners and wealthy Chinese alike would opt for apartment living. Sassoon's buildings offered a fully serviced, air-conditioned alternative to rising damp, malarial mosquitoes, mould, and other perils of living in low-rise brick rowhouses in what was essentially a swamp. Grosvenor House was his biggest gamble. Located within sight of his Cathay Mansions, a Frenchtown residential hotel that boasted a roof garden and its own bakery, its name was a tribute to the elegant hotel on Park Lane in London's Mayfair, which had opened in 1929 (not far from the Sassoon family townhouse on Grosvenor Place). From a seventeen-storey tower in the Streamline Moderne style, concrete ribs spread outwards like stylized, incurved bat wings. The management gave long-term residents a choice of Old English or American Colonial-style suites complete with claw-foot bathtubs, parquet floors, high ceilings, and servants' quarters. The building's automatic elevators were powered by electricity from the same diesel power plant that kept the streetcars of the French Tramway Company running.

Grosvenor House was meant to welcome its first tenants in 1932, but the January 28 Incident that year brought construction to a near halt. When it finally opened, three years behind schedule, Sir Victor sent a black-and-white snapshot to his mother with a typewritten note that revealed his worries about Shanghai's future.

Modestly describing Grosvenor House as "a very large block of flats," Sir Victor added: "I only hope there will be enough people left with enough money in Shanghai to keep the flats occupied!"

美

If Shanghai's long-term prospects sometimes worried him, Sir Victor never regretted building the Cathay. His evening stroll through its lobby and corridors, a near-nightly ritual, always reassured him about the elegance and solidity of the hostelry he'd built on the Bund.

On its opening, six years earlier, the Cathay's modern appointments had instantly announced it as the best address in the Far East. While guests at Astor House, the sprawling grand hotel located on the north bank of Soochow Creek since 1859, still had their toilet buckets emptied by "night soil" collectors, the Cathay's modern plumbing included a flush toilet in every room. Purified water was piped in from the Bubbling Well spring two miles away. In many of the grand hotels of the Orient, air circulation was ensured by rotating ceiling fans, or even punkah wallahs (servants who manually operated fans made with cheesecloth stretched over bamboo frames by pulling long cords). At the Cathay, incoming air was washed in a spray of atomized water, which kept the temperature agreeable on even the most humid summer days. Old Asia hands agreed Shanghai's Cathay made Singapore's Raffles Hotel look like an antiquated pile.

To staff his dream house, Sir Victor had sought the greatest talent from Shanghai and abroad. He had poached the Cathay's manager from the Taj Mahal Hotel, the best address in Bombay. The general manager of Cathay Hotels, Ltd. was Louis Suter, who he'd stolen away from Claridge's, London's most aristocratic hotel. The man responsible for the hotel's insignia – a pair of stylized bas-relief greyhounds that undergirded the leaded-glass ceiling of the lobby's rotunda, and ran along the exterior in a marble frieze – was Victor Stepanovich Podgoursky, the same hard-drinking White Russian, a graduate of the Moscow Art School, who'd created the stunning Venetian mosaics in the entrance hall of the Hongkong and Shanghai Bank. The light fixtures in the halls were decorated with moulded, opalescent glass produced by the master French craftsman René Lalique. (Even the shaving mirrors in guest bathrooms were surrounded by Lalique's illuminated glasswork.) Sconces in the form of robe-swaddled "Ladies of the Fountain" lined the corridor that led to the ballroom, on whose polished floor couples danced to the music of Henry Nathan, a New York jazzman whose band was the pick of Shanghai's best clubs.

Sir Victor continued his walk-through of the lobby. In the central shopping arcade, visitors were window-shopping for Rolexes through the plate glass at Alexander Clark's boutique, and inspecting the gowns on the mannequins at Madame Garnet's shop. He waved a hand at the two statuesque White Russians he'd recently hired to work at the tobacco counter, which offered the finest hand-rolled cigars from Havana and Manila.

The hotel's best rooms were the nine "apartements de-luxe," on the hotel's Bund side. The Indian suite was all filigreed plaster-work and peacock-hued cupolas. In the Chinese suite, whose dining and living rooms were separated by a semicircular moon gate, guests sat on lacquered blackwood chairs beneath an oxblood red ceiling. For the whimsically inclined, Jacobean, Modern French, and Futuristic suites were also available. A staff of 400, who could be summoned by buzzers in every room, meant service was near-instantaneous. The room-service menu included *capon Souvaroff* cooked with Madeira, foie gras, and truffles, and *crêpes Georgette* sprinkled with finely-chopped pineapples marinated in Kirsch. Every morning, copies of the *North-China Daily News* were delivered to the 205 guest rooms, their folds and wrinkles painstakingly ironed out by room boys.

As he stepped out of the elevator on the eighth floor, Sir Victor's arrival provoked whispers from the guests who were wait-ing for the maitre d' to seat them at the hotel's restaurants. All who had eaten at the Cathay agreed that the hotel's food was among the best in Shanghai. Overseeing seventy Chinese cooks, the French head chef Victor Boudard stocked his pantry with Per-sian figs, Caspian caviar, peaches from California, butter from Australia, and *foie gras* from the Périgord. (Sir Victor's extensive land holdings meant that he could guarantee his guests that traditional fertilizers, rather than human waste, were used to raise the vegetables served in his kitchens.) The former reading room, on the same floor as the ballroom, had been turned into the Peking Room, whose best tables overlooked the Bund. Its walls and ceilings – even its radiator grilles – were festooned with riotous chinoiserie: soaring gilded bats representing happiness, flaming pearls perfection, and a coiled dragon the old Manchu Emperor. Every square inch of the room's coffered ceilings was covered with intricate carvings and Chinese characters.

Later in the year, Sir Victor would oversee the opening of the Tower Club, a new nightspot on the ninth floor. The space would be tiny, no bigger than a basement jazz club in Harlem. The manager he'd chosen was Freddie Kaufmann, a flamboyant Jewish stage actor who had recently fled Berlin, where he'd run the Jockey, the club where Josef von Sternberg was said to have met Marlene Dietrich. Freddie had been given instructions to create a truly exclusive atmosphere.

The Cathay, all who knew it agreed, was the acme of comfort and good taste. One of the earliest celebrities to visit had been Noël Coward. Arriving from Tokyo just five months after the hotel's opening, the playwright had been forced by a bout of 'flu to hole up in the Cathay Suite. Propped up in his bed with a writing-block and an Eversharp pencil, he'd completed the first draft of the play that was to become *Private Lives* in just four days. Two years later, Douglas Fairbanks had charmed a crowd of 200 in the banquet hall, flashing a brilliant smile as he numbered Shanghai among the world's top five cities. (Hollywood, he'd said, was another, "because it supplies the emotional food for the universe.")

One night, Sir Victor had dined with Will Rogers, the cowboy vaudevillian and 1928 presidential candidate who had run on behalf of the "Anti-Bunk Party." Rogers had gratified his host by referring to him in his syndicated "telegrams" as the J.P. Morgan of China and India. "We have to get his OK," the straight-talking

Rogers wrote in his newspaper column, "to see if we can have sugar with our coffee."

Walking the long corridors of the guest floors, Sir Victor elicited bows from the page boys, who shuffled almost inaudibly on the buff-and-green carpets in their felt-soled shoes. Occasionally he heard laughter and shouts as the walnut doors to the guest rooms opened and shut. Riding the elevator to the rooftop, he nodded to the knots of women in gowns and *qipaos*, and men in evening suits who had left the ballroom to smoke and chat. As he approached the iron railing on the roof's edge, he detected in the cool spring air a hint of the unmistakable "eau de Chine" rising from the sewage-filled Soochow Creek.

Rising, too, was a new Chinese middle class. The sons and daughters of the *compradors*, the middlemen who had worked for the hongs in Silas Hardoon's time, now wore suits and polished wingtips rather than gowns and cotton shoes. They were increasingly confident, and gently ironic in their dealings with Shanghai's foreign elite. In the *North-China Daily News* that week, he had read about a speech in which the prominent writer Lin Yu-tang chided the foreigners for their materialism. Lin was quoted as saying that the man-made Cathay Hotel was as nothing compared to the grace of the branch of a dead tree.

Sir Victor looked at the vacant lot on the other side of Jinkee Road. It was the site the nationalists had reserved for their new bank. Sir Victor had been shown the architectural drawings: the thirty-three-storey Bank of China, as currently planned, would tower over the Cathay. He wasn't particularly worried. His man on the Municipal Council, Harry Arnhold, assured him that the Chinese plans would be rejected on technical grounds. The Cathay Hotel would remain the tallest building on the Bund.

The bet he had made seven years before had paid off. The skyscrapers he'd raised on the mud had transformed the city's skyline, and the Cathay had become the instantly recognizable symbol of a thriving Shanghai. The article in *Fortune* was Sir Victor's apotheosis, raising him to the rank of one of the gods of international finance.

The Chinese that Sir Victor knew were not particularly religious. They were, however, superstitious, and paid close attention to portents and the significance of numbers. There was a saying among them that war came to Shanghai in five-year cycles. In 1927, Shanghai's foreign community had stared down China's communists and warlords by aligning with Chiang Kai-shek and such gangsters as "Big-Eared" Du. In 1932 they'd kept the over-reaching Nipponese invaders out of the International Settlement. If you credited the Chinese calculations, destruction would visit Shanghai again in 1937.

Perhaps. The Japanese were still lurking about, and the communists were rumoured to be gaining strength in their mountain hideaways. If that were the case, Sir Victor reflected, as he turned away from the city and towards the laughter rising from the eighth-floor balconies, he'd better spend the next two years getting as much out of Shanghai as he possibly could.

7: Mickey Checks In

The rusty steamer operated by NYK, the Japan Mail Shipping Line, entered the mouth of the Yangtze, crossing the knife-edge boundary where the silt and filth of the mighty river stains the blue waters of the East China Sea a murky brown. Veering to port at the red canister buoy that marked the location of the Woosung Bar, where a tongue of mud and sand had created treacherous shallows, the ship began to navigate the calmer waters of the Whangpoo River. As she steamed upriver, vegetable farms quickly ceded to oil-tank farms – vast circular reservoirs, painted with Chinese characters, and their English equivalent, "The Standard Oil Co. of New York" – followed by solid lines of wharves, at which the ships of a half-dozen different nations were docked. Anchoring at a buoy off the NYK wharfs, the ship came to the end of her routine overnight run from Yokohama. In the hold were letters and parcels from the largest city in Japan, destined for the largest city in China. On its deck was one very disgruntled American woman.

Mickey Hahn's first impressions of Shanghai were coloured by the fact that she was, by her own admission, in a deep sulk. She did not particularly want to be in China. Nor did she particularly like what she saw. The sky was leaden, the water murky, the temperature on that early spring day far from clement. Apart from a few junks in the river, there was nothing especially Oriental about the scene. She'd been hoping to be greeted by pagodas and temple bells chiming in spice-laden breezes. Instead, she got low warehouses on a gritty workaday waterfront that could have been the docklands of Liverpool – or Brooklyn.

Her sister Helen continued to insist that, after crossing the

Pacific Ocean, they should at least spend a week or two in China. From the looks of things, Mickey thought a weekend might suffice.

The first leg of the journey had provided exactly what she'd needed. Every nautical mile separating her from the California coast lessened the sting of leaving Eddie Mayer. The ocean voyage was having the same restorative effect on Helen. Though it wasn't Mickey's habit to travel in first class – during her journey to the Congo, she'd bunked on the same steerage deck as the French soldiers – she'd appreciated the charms of the NYK liner, the *Chichibu Maru*. In their cabin, everything seemed one size too small: the bedsheets stopped at her ankles, the sink was too low, the mirror was the size of a postage stamp. It gave her the agreeable impression that, overnight, several inches had been added to her five-foot four-inch frame.

The crossing had been great fun. On shore in Honolulu, she and Helen had been told not to fraternize with the Japanese passengers – most of whom, they were informed, were spies – advice they'd proceeded to ignore. Fascinated by a white-haired American man in pince-nez they heard speaking fluent Japanese to a group of small men in kimonos, Mickey struck up a conversation. Eddychan, as his friends called him, though born in Japan, was the son of an American missionary. He spent the passage giving the sisters a crash course in Japanese culture. Every afternoon at three, they knelt with Eddychan on straw mats in the ship's tatami room, where he taught them how to say *konnichiwa* for "hello," and *dōmo arigatō* for "thank you." They took baths in the ship's pool with Eddychan's companion, Mr. Kuroda, the head of a leading textile works, and attracted stares from the ship's few British and American passengers as they memorized the verses of Japanese drinking songs. They weren't even angry when the ship's captain, after a fortnight at sea, admitted his ship wouldn't be calling at Shanghai, as originally advertised.

In Tokyo, they'd checked into the Imperial Hotel – a complex whose main building was designed by a fellow Midwesterner, Frank Lloyd Wright – and used it as a base for exploring Honshu, Japan's main island. Eddychan introduced them to his girlfriend, an unusually tall Japanese woman, who invited them to stay at their house in the oceanfront city of Kamakura. Walking on the beach, they'd seen a man in armour riding by on a great white horse – an eccentric neighbour, Eddychan explained, who liked to dress up in his father's samurai clothing. Impressed by the kindness of their hosts, Helen declared the warnings they'd been given in Hawaii not to trust the Japanese so much "applesauce." The only sign of anything sinister came from the officious customs officials, who'd made them fill out endless forms and examined the books in their luggage with exaggerated suspicion. If the representatives of NYK never really explained why the *Chichibu Maru* wouldn't be sailing on to China, at least they'd found room for the sisters aboard the Shanghai Mail. It was a dirty little tub, but they'd only have to spend one night on board.

Arriving in Shanghai, they were met by a steam launch that ferried them and their luggage the two miles from the NYK Wayside Wharf in the Yangtzepoo district to the Bund; the Whangpoo, a cabin boy had explained, was too silted up for big ships to anchor much closer to the heart of the International Settlement. On the way, Mickey found herself increasingly frustrated with Helen. She would rather have stayed in Tokyo – or be on her way to her ultimate destination, Africa, where she'd learned Matope, the Pygmy boy she'd "adopted" in the Congo, was awaiting her return.

The little launch docked in front of the open-sided sheds of the Customs Jetty. Ragged wharf coolies threw ropes over the bollards on the quay. As their trunks were unloaded, Mickey scanned the riverfront promenade. She saw brick walls, stodgy stone facades, crowded streetcars; to her right, an elegant skyscraper with a pyramidal roof rose above the others – the famous Cathay Hotel, she presumed. From a clock tower, chimes like the ones on Big Ben rang on the quarter hour. Except for the rickshaws, which were no different from the ones she'd already seen in Japan, there was nothing here that a Cook's tourist couldn't see in New York or London.

Years later, she would remember exactly what was going

through her mind the first time she saw Shanghai: "Just as I find a reasonably pleasant place" – by which she meant Japan –

in which to loaf about and read, I am dragged away again to stay for some uncomfortable days in a vulgar, loud city like this. I don't know and I don't care who these Chinese people may be, but everybody is aware that the Japanese are the only subtle Orientals. China is garish. China is red and gold and big, everything I don't like. Pooh.

An agreeably outlandish-looking woman was waiting for them on the pier. Immense jade earrings dangled from her ears; her head was wrapped in an elaborately folded silk turban. Bernardine Szold-Fritz, an old friend from Chicago, greeted the Hahn sisters effusively.

As Bernardine bundled them into the back of her limousine, giving her driver the address of Hung Fah Loh, a Cantonese restaurant on Foochow Road, she maintained a non-stop stream of chatter. She had arranged for some entertaining guests to join them for dinner: a French count and his Italian wife, a Pole naturalized as a Frenchman, one of China's best young essayists, and a Chinese customs official, who would take care of ordering from the menu. The restaurant, she added mysteriously, was known to have the best moon cakes in China.

Counts, writers, moon cakes. Perhaps, Mickey admitted to herself, Shanghai would be amusing after all.

美

Mickey Hahn landed in China at a good time, and she landed well. The only person she knew in Shanghai also happened to be the one person who seemed to know practically everybody in Shanghai.

Bernardine Szold-Fritz, the woman who greeted the Hahn sisters at Shanghai's Customs Jetty, was born to an upper-middle-class family of Hungarian Jews in Peoria, Illinois. She first met Mickey in Chicago, where she had landed a job working for the *Evening Post*. After her first marriage to a newspaperman ended, she had had adventures that rivalled (and often overlapped)

Mickey's: during her time as a reporter in New York she'd become friends with Dorothy Parker, and in Europe she'd gotten to know F. Scott and Zelda Fitzgerald, Gertrude Stein, and Isadora Duncan. While travelling in the Far East in 1929, she'd wed a taciturn Englishman named Chester Fritz. It was a providential alliance: Fritz, who had made a fortune trading in silver, was a friend of Sir Victor Sassoon's, and had a brokerage office just over the lobby of the Cathay Hotel.

Bankrolled by her husband, Bernardine became an expert matchmaker, on a mission to unite Shanghai's multicultural bohemia and the merchant elite of the International Settlement.

After seeing her at work in a social setting, Mickey would write – drawing an analogy from her university training in chemistry and geology – that Bernardine "had a soul of manganese dioxide or some such catalytic agent. Platinum, perhaps? It was a rare soul."

Bernardine's extravagance was legendary.* She liked to travel with three trunks of jewellery, and affected a bohemian Orientalist style that had no relation to what women in China – or anywhere else in the Far East – actually wore. In addition to her elaborate silk turbans, she was likely to appear with a pair of outsized tortoiseshell cherries dangling from her ears and a plaque of Balinese silver on her breast. Scorning bridge, tennis, and other pastimes of the taitais – the wives of the foreign business taipans – she spent her afternoons pacing her red-and-black-painted Frenchtown apartment, using a telephone with an absurdly long cord to arrange buffet suppers, teas, and meetings of her amateur dramatic company, the International Arts Theatre. In her salon, Bernardine brought together characters as diverse as Morris "Two-Gun"

---

* Her hospitality, however, was less well regarded. A 1940 book of recipes titled *Bon Appétit: Secrets from Shanghai Kitchens*, copies of which were sold to benefit the British war effort, features contributions from leading Shanghailanders, including a mouthwatering *filet de mandarin Bercy* from the kitchens of the Cathay Hotel. Bernardine's recipe for baked beans, in contrast, begins: "Take two tins Heinz pork and beans, put in a little Worcestershire sauce . . ."

Cohen, the scholarly dilettante Harold Acton, and the triple agent Trebitsch Lincoln.

The latter had particularly intrigued Sir Victor. Bernardine introduced him as a Buddhist abbot, but this was only the latest of the man's many identities. Born Trebitsch Ignácz, the son of a Hungarian rabbi, he had, at various times, been a Presbyterian missionary among the Jews of Montreal, a Member of Parliament in the British House of Commons, the organizer of a right-wing putsch in Weimar Germany, and an arms dealer to some of the most vicious warlords in northern China. In a nasal Mitteleuropean drone, Chao Kung, as Trebitsch now called himself, held forth about how the twelve stars tattooed on his forehead represented "spokes on the Wheel of Becoming." He was rumoured to be selling secrets to the Germans. In his diary, Sir Victor underlined the unusual name in red – his code for a new acquaintance, a blue underline indicating somebody he already knew – noting: "Trebitsch gives impression of being a charlatan."

During her first two weeks in China, Mickey's every move was chronicled by the English-language and Chinese press. The *China Press* had anticipated her arrival in a brief item: "Vicki Baum, author of 'Grand Hotel,' and Emily Hahn, author of 'With Naked Foot,' are coming to this city Friday." The "Teatime Chats" column of the same daily noted, "Miss Hahn, considered one of the cleverest of America's youngest writers, is here for the sole purpose of enjoyment, and to satisfy her love for travel."

Mickey gladly surrendered to what she called Shanghai's "social swirl." She attended a dinner for Pearl White, a fellow Missourian and "America's first movie star," famous for her starring role in *The Perils of Pauline*. At the International Arts Theatre, she dined with screenwriter and playwright J.P. McEvoy – who also created the popular comic strip *Dixie Dugan* – in whose Woodstock home Mickey had worked for a summer as a secretary after her return from the Congo.

"The IAT did concerts and lectures and debates and now and then a play," Mickey would later recall.

What made it good was that the concerts were Russian or

German or whatever, the debates took into account such extremely controversial subjects as 'Birth Control in China' (three Catholic priests attended, with skyrocket results), and the plays were damn good, especially Lady Precious Stream with an all-Chinese cast.

Helen, determined to see as much of China as possible, talked Mickey and the Fritzes into a trip to the country's new capital, Nanking. The sisters took the overnight train from the North Station. Greeted on the platform by the Kuomintang's Education Minister, Mickey was introduced as a Hollywood screenwriter and asked to lecture a lunch crowd on the secrets of movie-making in America. They rode horses to Sun Yat-sen's extravagant hilltop tomb, learned the correct way to raise a toast while drinking hot rice wine – turning down their small glasses after saying *"kanpei"* to prove they were drained – and were taken for a moonlit stroll on the shores of the Lotus Lake.

Back in Shanghai after their three-day trip, Helen and Mickey co-wrote a long letter to their mother in Illinois.

"We're very famous," wrote Mickey, "names and faces smeared all over every Chinese paper in the country." They were also, thanks to a certain millionaire bachelor, staying in the lap of luxury.

Now we're back at the Cathay Mansions, in a suite instead of a room, because Sir Victor made them give it to us at a terrific reduction. He owns almost all the important property in Shanghai. When we moved in yesterday we found a great basket of liqueurs – one of almost anything you can think of, including vodka, and on top a carton of delicious cream cheese. We'll just have to give them to Bernardine.

Helen added: "I'll be sailing about the middle of June, perhaps without Mickey because I think she wants to stay longer."

Bernardine had turned out to be a very useful acquaintance indeed. She'd helped Mickey land on her feet, and introduced the Hahn sisters to the "richest white man in the Far East" – and Sir Victor Sassoon was making them feel right at home.

美

There's no description of Mickey Hahn's first meeting with Sir Victor Sassoon in any of her writings. For a woman who exhaustively documented so many details of her life, it's a strange omission.

The moment may have been captured, however, in a photograph. In the May 1935 issue of *Town and Sportsman*, a glossy magazine that catered to Shanghai's smart set, Sir Victor Sassoon is shown "chatting with Mrs. Asbury and Miss Emily Hahn." A complacently smiling Helen, wearing a broad-brimmed white hat, has her eyes fixed on Sir Victor. The latter's attention is riveted on Mickey, who is captured in profile. She has a checkered scarf wrapped around her neck, and a dark curl falls over her cheek. Carrying a sheaf of papers in her right hand, she leans towards the tycoon with her mouth half open, as if caught driving home a point.

In his journal, under the date "April 12th, 1935," Sir Victor recorded meeting the Hahn sisters at a lecture on D.H. Lawrence at the International Arts Theatre. By that point he'd known Bernardine for over three years, and was on good enough terms with her to loan the International Arts Theatre studio space in a vacant office in a building a few blocks from the Cathay. After the lecture, Bernardine arranged a meeting of the PEN Club, the international authors' association, in Mickey's honour at the Mary Garden Restaurant. While Mickey was feted, Sir Victor spirited her sister away and dined with her in an empty suite in the Cathay. After the PEN dinner, Sir Victor fetched Mickey in his Rolls-Royce and they were all driven to Sir Victor's Tudor-style hunting lodge, Eve's, on Hungjao Road.

Clearly at ease in his presence, the sisters shared intimate details of their lives.

"Mickey v. sad," wrote Sir Victor in his journal. "Just broken off an affair. They are sisters + Helen is married to the author." In a later entry, he added: "M. seduced at 23. H. at 18." (Mickey, who'd actually lost her virginity at age 19, was being coy.)

"I was in Shanghai because my heart was broken," Mickey would tell her biographer many years later. Sir Victor, she thought, "was sorry for me. He liked girls with broken hearts."

Sir Victor's journals are full of artfully lit nudes, some in elaborate poses: one slender woman appears in several photographs naked and painted brown, striking athletic poses, or standing bare-breasted in front of a Buddha, the jewels from an elaborate headdress hanging over her nipples. After knowing the Hahn sisters for only four days, Sir Victor convinced them to pose for him.

"He invited Helen and me up to his studio," Mickey would remember. "She kept saying, 'I wish I had a good figure.' He said, 'But you have such a nice *nature*.' I think it amused him to think that he had pictures of practically all the women in Shanghai. None of them wanted people to know about it."

Identified by codes, or nicknames, the portraits in his journals include some of Shanghai's leading taitais – often scantily clad, though rarely completely naked. Being free of inhibitions was a point of pride for Mickey.* It was a trait she shared with Sir Victor, who would name one of his fastest racehorses Exhibitionist.

They also shared the status of outsider. Sir Victor was ostracized by some taipans because he failed to observe the colour bar still prevalent among older Shanghailanders: many of his friends, male and female, were Chinese. His Jewishness also permanently set him apart from the British upper class. One evening at the Cathay Mickey heard the son of the Earl of Glasgow, resentful that Sir Victor had horned in on his conversation with a young woman, bray loudly: "Back to Baghdad! Back to Baghdad!" She was amazed that he had the effrontery to insult Sir Victor in the lobby of his own hotel.

Though Sir Victor was inured to anti-Semitic impertinence, it had clearly affected his personality. Beneath his charm lay a vindictiveness that manifested itself in cutting sarcasm and practical jokes. He once poured an entire bottle of crème de menthe down the back of the suit of a titled employee of the British Embassy.

The cocktails he liked to mix for the Hahn sisters revealed

---

* If any nudes of Mickey have survived, they are not among Sir Victor's papers in Dallas: the only black-and-white photographs of the Hahns in his journals show the sisters seated, and fully clothed.

something of his personality. The taste of a decadent concoction like the Cobra's Kiss – an opaque mix of equal parts brandy, curaçao, and cream, given sting by three dashes of absinthe – captured, in liquid form, his complexity, suavity, and well-concealed asperity.

There was an appealing streak of melancholy in him, too. In spite of his carefree public persona, he seemed incapable of real intimacy and, perhaps, happiness. Convinced nobody would marry him except for money and position, he once confided to a relative that he didn't want to have children, for if they were happy and healthy he would be horribly jealous of them. His horror of physical contact with anyone maimed or disfigured made going out in public in a place like Shanghai difficult; running the gauntlet of beggars on Nanking Road made him visibly shudder.

Sir Victor, the Hahn sisters soon learned, also had a reputation for sexual voraciousness. Mickey was not the first to notice that the bathroom in his Cathay penthouse had two tubs. (He once confided to Baron Robert Rothschild that he liked sharing his bed, but never his bath.) In his journals, he records a meeting with "Dr. Voronoff of monkey gland fame." The Russian-born surgeon Serge Voronoff had gained international notoriety for transplanting thin slices of baboon testicles into human scrotums in the hope of rejuvenating old *roués*; the poet E.E. Cummings wrote of him as the "famous doctor who inserts monkeyglands into millionaires."*

Sir Victor treated Mickey and her sister – who clearly did not belong to the category of "gold-diggers" and "teases" – lavishly. Before their three-day trip to Nanking, Mickey had probably been lodging with the Fritzes, while Helen seems to have taken a room at the Cathay. Sir Victor records giving them the equivalent of $350 (US) so they could continue to stay at one of his properties in Shanghai. The money was enough to pay for a double suite at a luxury apartment in Frenchtown's Cathay Mansions, including all meals, for almost three months.

---

* During his 1930 visit, a *North-China Daily News* reporter asked Voronoff if the taipans of Shanghai would benefit from the operation: "The life led by many," the professor replied, "might necessitate rejuvenation."

If Mickey never recorded the exact details of their first meeting, she was clearly impressed by Sir Victor. As a recovering flapper and an acknowledged expert on masculine techniques of seduction, she recognized that he was a cut above any other man she'd met. He had style, refinement, and an irresistible, if melancholy, charm. It was obvious that life had left him wounded – both physically, in the plane crash that forced him to walk with canes, and sentimentally, after bigotry had prematurely ended his first love affair.

"I thought him unusually quick and witty, *especially* for a businessman," she would recall, many years later. "And he really liked me. He liked intelligence, I think, and I was intelligent."

It was the beginning of a sometimes stormy relationship that would last for decades.

美

"It is an unhappy truth that all the nicest and most interesting people seem to dash away from Shanghai and leave their friends lamenting." So began the unsigned item on the "Woman's Page" of the *North-China Daily News* for June 12, 1935. "Perhaps this is why Mrs. Herbert Asbury has also elected to depart on the *Chichibu Maru* to-day." The item further noted that the French-speaking wife of the author of *The Barbary Coast* had "an amazing capacity for making friends, and by now has half Shanghai, the French and Chinese community in particular, right at her feet."

Mickey, for her part, had left her suite at Sir Victor's Cathay Mansions and moved into a significantly less luxurious flat on Kiangse Road, just two blocks west of the Cathay Hotel. The green walls of her room, on the ground floor of a Chinese bank building, were festooned with silver grillwork meant to imitate a thicket of bamboo. The box couch she slept on was covered with dozens of brilliantly dyed satin cushions. (Helen, eyeing the décor, had commented, "It's cheap, did you say?" and decided to stay on at the Cathay Mansions until the end of her visit.) This was her new home, for, rather than continue travelling with her sister, she had decided to stay in Shanghai.

Now Mickey sat in her new home, typing a letter to her mother, and wondering if she'd made the right decision.

The Shanghai Summer has set in and I sit here with a couple of electric fans going and a terrible din coming through all the opened windows; China enjoying itself by stepping on horns, whistles, klaxons and sirens.

Helen left horribly early in the morning. I felt slightly dismayed as she disappeared in the distance, and more so when I discovered she'd left her white coat, which I'll try to send over with somebody else on the next boat.

It was an ideal time, she thought, for a writer to be in China. Though she was still fuzzy on the details, she already sensed that big things were at stake. The Japanese had just demanded the nationalist president resign, and the Chinese were threatening to join forces with the Soviet Union. "I can't be joyful at the prospect of war," she typed, "yet honestly I don't see what else can be done with Japan taking more and more . . . Even the aristocrats here, the ones I know, admit that Communism is the only way out."

Nobody seemed that worried about the future, though. The Shanghailanders, she wrote, were "more amused by Sir Victor's calling off his garden-party because the weatherman predicted rain and it's a fine bright day." Meanwhile, Shanghai's social life was, night by night, vanquishing her heartbreak.

The other day, she had shown one of Eddie Mayer's maundering letters to Sir Victor. "Although I believe that I am naturally a creative person," her former lover had written, "I have done almost nothing to date – certainly nothing to what I should have done in thirty-eight years . . ." Sir Victor had advised her against throwing away sentiment on unhappily married, self-pitying drunks.

Besides, there was so much to do in Shanghai. After typing just one page of the letter, she excused herself because she had to prepare for the night's entertainment: "Tonight is a Charity Ball and I am dancing in the American part of the entertainment; a barn dance in tennis-shoes and checked gingham and a hair-ribbon!"

It was definitely too soon, Mickey knew, to sail for Africa. A place like Shanghai bore investigating.

8: On the Shanghai Beat

On a warm Tuesday morning, Mickey Hahn walked towards the building known as "The Old Lady of the Bund." The six-storey structure, three doors south of the Cathay Hotel, presented the Whangpoo riverfront with an intimidating facade. Beneath a frieze depicting lithe ancients in various states of undress, the motto "JOURNALISM, ART, SCIENCE, LITERATURE, COMMERCE, TRUTH, PRINTING" was carved into Japanese granite between Doric columns. The turrets that rose from the corners of its flat roof, supported by bare-chested caryatids, suggested some Gilded Age robber baron's attempt to erect an impregnable citadel in singularly hostile terrain.

Mickey would have liked to find a job at the *Shanghai Evening Post and Mercury*, owned by the American insurance magnate Cornelius V. Starr, but a friend on the staff told her they weren't hiring. There was, however, a vacancy at another paper: a young reporter was marrying one of the "bank boys" (an Englishman with a plum job with one of the foreign banks) and would soon be leaving on her honeymoon. Bernardine Szold-Fritz, who seemed to know everyone, wrote a letter introducing Mickey to the newspaper's manager.

She rode the elevator to the fifth floor, turning the heads of reporters and Chinese copy-boys as she walked through a news-room thick with cigarette smoke. The *Daily News*'s long-time editor Ralph Thomas Peyton-Griffin, known to his friends as "Peyt," listened to Mickey as she listed her experience writing for the *New Yorker*, *Harper's*, and the *New York World*. Stubbing out a half-smoked Ruby Queen cigarette, he told her he'd have to stop her right there: in Shanghai, a person couldn't just walk in off the street and expect to get a job. According to the Land Regulations, all white women who worked in the International Settlement had to be signed on "at home," *before* they came to Shanghai.

But given your qualifications, he'd added with a smile, perhaps we can make an exception.

The interview had lasted all of five minutes. Less than two weeks after washing up in Shanghai, Mickey had landed work at Shanghai's leading daily, and the oldest newspaper – in any language – in China. Mickey was a reporter at the *North-China Daily News.*

美

Shanghai by the mid-thirties was unquestionably one of the world's great cities. In terms of its English-speaking foreign community, though, it was no more populous than Muskogee, Oklahoma.

Addicted to gossip, and thirsty for news that could have a direct impact on their day-to-day lives, the 30,000 or so British and American inhabitants of the International Settlement and the French Concession were served by a remarkable variety of media outlets. Shanghai was home to forty radio stations; some, like the powerful XCDN, which broadcast out of Sassoon House, blanketed the whole region. In restaurants, bars, casinos, hotel lobbies, and almost all foreign, working-class and middle-class Chinese homes, radio sets transmitted the latest news and gossip to an information-hungry population. Between ads for Maxwell House coffee and Bakerite Bread, XMHA played the hits of the day: Shirley Temple warbling "On the Good Ship Lollipop," Fred Astaire purring "Cheek to Cheek," and Nelson Eddy belting out "Ah! Sweet Mystery of Life."

Every national community had its own privileged sources of entertainment and information. The French listened to Maurice Chevalier crooning on radio station FFZ and read the *Journal de Shanghai*, a thin daily subsidized by the French Consul-General which featured photo spreads of the latest styles from Paris. The Japanese, and those sympathetic to their ambitions in Asia, listened to Shirley Yamaguchi singing on XQHA and read the *Shanghai Times*, a daily owned by an Englishman but, since 1924, bankrolled by the Yokohama Specie Bank. Exiles nostalgic for Mother Russia listened to Tchaikovsky on XRVN and read the *Shanghai Zaria*. Germans picked up the *Deutsche Shanghai Zeitung* (which in 1936 would become an organ of the Nazi Party), and listened to Adolf Hitler's speeches on XGRS, which by the end of the decade would become the most powerful station in the Far East.

Shanghai's media scene drew the newshounds of the world. Some were young American vagabonds who worked for a few months before drifting off to Bangkok or Batavia. Others established reputations working the China beat. A surprising number of the best reporters came to China, like Mickey Hahn, by way of the American Midwest – a situation that led to muttering about the predominance of a "Missouri Mafia" in the Far Eastern press corps.

First to come was Thomas Millard, an eccentric *New York Herald* drama critic, and University of Missouri alumnus, sent to cover China's anti-imperialist riots at the turn of the century. He fell in love with the East and stayed on to edit the *China Press*, the nation's first American-run newspaper. Millard cabled the dean of his alma mater's School of Journalism – founded in 1908 and the first "J-School" in the English-speaking world – in search of a graduate to help him set up a new venture. Answering the call, a thirty-year-old Missourian named John Benjamin Powell arrived in Shanghai in 1917. Millard met Powell in the lobby of the Astor House Hotel, and made his pitch: he wanted someone to help him run a journal of politics and opinion, which would soon be renamed the *China Weekly Review*. As Millard downed the first of many whisky sodas, he introduced Powell to the hotel's manager, Captain Harry Morton, who said he could give Powell a room in "steerage" for $60 a month [US]. The hotel, located on the north end of the Garden Bridge in Hongkew and considered, before the opening of the Cathay, the grandest in Shanghai, turned out to be especially good lodgings for a journalist.

"If you sit in the lobby of the Astor House and keep your eyes open," an old Shanghailander told Powell, "you will see all the crooks who hang out on the China coast."

Early on, Powell made a crucial discovery. Members of Shanghai's relatively small English-speaking foreign community weren't the only ones buying newspapers. "The largest English-reading group was the younger generation of Chinese, the intellectuals, graduates and undergraduates of mission and municipal schools, who were just beginning to take an interest in outside world affairs." It was a potentially vast market, and one Powell cannily tapped by selling space to Chinese advertisers. Powell became a staunch defender of Chinese independence, and one of the first to publish eyewitness accounts of Japanese war crimes.

Another University of Missouri Journalism School graduate – originally from Kansas City —was Edgar Snow, who in 1928 came to Shanghai by way of New York to work at Powell's *China Weekly Review*. He soon incurred the wrath of his fellow expatriates, including his employer, by writing a bitingly sarcastic essay entitled "Americans in Shanghai." Published in the *American Mercury*, it portrayed a parochial outpost filled with "such peculiarly American institutions as navy wives, shot-gun weddings, Girl Scouts, Spanish–American War veterans, a board of censors, daylight holdups, immaculate barbershops, a Short Story Club, wheat cakes, and a Chamber of Commerce."

Shanghai's foreign community had been the target of other such attacks. In 1926, Arthur Ransome – later the author of the beloved *Swallows and Amazons* series of children's books – wrote a panegyric for the *Manchester Guardian* entitled "The Shanghai Mind." Ransome, fresh from meeting Trotsky and Lenin as a reporter in the Soviet Union, wrote that Shanghailanders were "those who look round on their magnificent buildings and are surprised that China is not grateful to them for these gifts," and seemed to have lived in a "comfortable but hermetically sealed and isolated glass case since 1901."

Snow one-upped Ransome in betrayal – infuriating even Jon B. Powell – by portraying his compatriots as materialist philistines. (He also printed the address of a popular brothel frequented by

Americans: 52 Kiangse Road, two blocks away from Mickey Hahn's new apartment.) Snow's subsequent travels in famine-ridden rural China, where he saw human flesh being sold openly in outdoor markets, sharpened the sense of outrage at injustice that would soon make him the best-known foreign chronicler of the rise of the Chinese Communist Party.

When Carl Crow of Hannibal, Missouri, gave up his job on the crime beat of the *Fort-Worth Star Telegram* to come and work for Millard in 1911, he wasn't exactly sure whether one sailed across the Pacific or the Atlantic Ocean to reach China. Over the next quarter century, though, he made himself into the most famous of the old China hands. After founding Shanghai's first Western-style advertising agency, the genial, rotund curmudgeon wrote such bestsellers as *Foreign Devils in the Flowery Kingdom* and *400 Million Customers*, highly readable how-to guides for businesspeople hoping to exploit the world's most populous market. With Cornelius V. Starr's money, Crow founded the *Shanghai Evening Post and Mercury*, China's leading American-run newspaper, in 1929. He selected the UPI's correspondent in Peiping as its editor. The Minnesota-born Randall Gould put out a broadsheet that could have been sold on the streets of Minneapolis or Chicago: it featured a crossword puzzle, the daily "Ripley's Believe it Or Not" cartoon, and ads for the latest talkies from Hollywood at the Grand Theatre. Initially sympathetic to the nationalists, Gould would follow an increasingly anti-Japanese editorial line.

Unlike the *North-China Daily News*, the American newspapers gave voice to Chinese writers, among them L.Z. Yuan, whose *Evening Post and Mercury* column "Through A Moon Gate" was a wry take on day-to-day life in Chinese Shanghai.

Also in Shanghai were some of the world's busiest foreign correspondents. Hallett Abend, a gossip columnist in Hollywood's silent era, covered northern China for the *New York Times*, using his sixteenth-floor apartment in the Broadway Mansions – part of the Sassoon property empire – as his base. (Ralph Shaw, a *North-China Daily News* reporter who would publish a salacious memoir called *Sin City*, wrote that Abend "made no secret of the fact that he preferred male company always. He had many boyfriends to whom he was said to be most generous.") For years Abend, who had excellent contacts in the Japanese military, was hated by the nationalists – he claimed that he once punched one of Chiang Kai-shek's sons in the nose – though he became one of the early voices warning of Tokyo's expansionist plans in Asia.

The press corps Mickey was joining might have been a hard-drinking boys' club, but allowances were made for female talent. Helen Foster, born into a family of Utah Mormons, became a convert to communism after meeting her future husband Edgar Snow in Shanghai's Chocolate Shop; she would write under the pseudonym Nym Wales. Edna Lee Booker, war correspondent for the *China Press* and the *Atlantic*, was famous for scooping her male rivals, landing exclusive interviews with China's most feared warlords.

Mickey's new job was at the old stalwart of Shanghai's newspaper scene. The *North-China Daily News* – founded in 1850 as the weekly *North China Herald* – was the purest expression of the reactionary voice of the "Shanghai Mind." Anything that seemed to further the prosperity of Shanghai's foreign community, especially its British establishment, received the paper's support. For many years, this included Japanese military expansion in China, deemed a stabilizing influence for business and preferable to rule by the nationalists, who many feared had come under Bolshevik influence.

The paper's owner, Harry Morriss, a British Catholic of Jewish descent, was a millionaire who rivalled Sir Victor Sassoon in business and leisure. Like the Sassoons, the Morriss family owed their fortune to early success in the opium trade. Every week, horses from the Morriss and Sassoon stables competed at the Race Course. The grounds of the Morrisses' French-Provincial-style manor (today a guest house favoured by Communist Party officials) covered one hundred acres of expensive land in the heart of the French Concession.

For all its stodginess, Mickey found the *North-China* newsroom a lively place to work. Limping through the office most days was a tall, bespectacled former lieutenant of the Russian Imperial Army, whose leg had been smashed in the First World War. With his fluid pen, Georgii Sapojnikoff drew cartoons that captured the essence of life in foreign Shanghai – and earned him the respect that made him the only Russian member of the British-dominated Shanghai Club. Jim, the office's "number-one boy," was actually an elderly, silk-trousered Chinese man who oversaw the vast Chinese printing staff, and owned entire city blocks in Hongkew, north of the Garden Bridge. Though its coverage of Shanghai was hampered by an utter lack of Chinese-speaking reporters, the paper was kept up to date on events in the underworld by "leaked" reports from the Chinese detectives of the Shanghai Municipal Police.

"I liked the whole atmosphere of the paper very much indeed," Mickey would later recall. "It made me feel that I was near the more colourful parts of the British Empire: Hong Kong and Singapore and Ceylon and all that."

Working the city beat for the *North-China Daily News*, the unique world that was Shanghai – at the peak of its prosperity and infamy – began to unfold for Mickey Hahn.

What she would make of it all, of course, was up to her.

美

"My days were crowded," Mickey said of her work at the *Daily News*.

I would wake up reluctantly in that hideous little flat, eat breakfast in the darkness of the dining room, served by a lacklustre boy I had inherited along with the green and silver, and hasten to the office. Usually my day's assignment could be polished off in the morning. It might be an interview with some retiring magnate . . . or perhaps a swimming pool was being opened by an advertising club. Or I might dream up a piece myself, about a Chinese drugstore that hung cages of real Indo-Chinese sloths around to attract trade. As long as I had a column that wasn't news, so that our readers would not be distressed by having to think, I was all right.

A typical assignment was a profile of the prolific British romance writer Dorothy Black, who stepped off the SS *Naldera* on April 21, 1935. "Shanghai is debauched!" Black complained to Mickey. "Nothing China might do to us can be half as bad as what we've done to China! Everywhere I go I see little yellow Garbos and dusky Clark Gables. I have tried and tried to buy a Chinese lantern and all I can find are the things we pay ten cents for in the Woolworth store – but here they cost a dollar. We've taught them to want shoddy things instead of their own beautiful inventions." (A letter to the newspaper's editor, signed "Noblesse Oblige," pointedly asked: "If this good lady wants a Chinese lantern, why does she not go into the Chinese city where they are sold?")

As a visiting literary celebrity, Mickey continued to make the news, as well as report it. Her novel *Affair*, a grim story of a doomed love affair based on her experiences in the winter of 1929, when she'd shared a Manhattan apartment with impoverished roommates, had appeared to mixed reviews and poor sales in the United States.

"The Disillusioned," a squib on the editorial page of the *Shanghai Evening Post and Mercury* read, "are literary folk who possibly know too much for their good – except that it helps them make a living. Eugene O'Neill, who saw Shanghai chiefly from the inside of a hotel sickroom, was one of them. Noël Coward was another. George Bernard Shaw was a charter member. Certainly Miss Emily Hahn, currently with us, 'belongs.'"*

Her new job left ample time for leisure. After writing an article in the morning, "I might meet a girl for lunch at the Cathay, with drinks first in the lounge; that meant we would pick up men and make a party of it."

The Cathay's location on the Bund made it a natural center for Mickey's social life. In a lightly fictionalized account of her first weeks in Shanghai, she describes her heroine, after registering in "Room 536 or thereabouts, the Cathay," taking in the scene in the hotel's lobby:

---

* The provocative tone of the item suggests it was written by editor Randall Gould, whose baiting of Mickey, which would later erupt into a literary feud, may have sprung from an unavowed crush.

She was evidently not one of the sleek, bright-plumed birds of passage who made the Cathay lobby such a pleasant place at the noon hour, which is called 'tiffin-time' in Shanghai . . . among the little tables there was a fresh stir for every new woman, and the Shanghai girls, neglected for the time, said disdainfully to one another, sipping tomato-juice, "The Empress must be in." They were not referring to any splendid lady, but to the Canadian-Pacific liners which brought them such effective competition.

It helped that she knew the owner of the hotel. She would meet Sir Victor for lunch on the eighth floor, and they would head off for drinks at the swank club of the Canidrome in Frenchtown, or for dinner with friends at Eve's. Mickey frequently appeared on his arm in public, attending parties for his beloved sister-in-law Guilia, the widow of his younger brother Hector, who had become Princess Ottoboni after marrying an Italian count. It was a tribute to Mickey's charm, for Sir Victor, whose journals are full of curt and often brutal judgments of other women, was easily bored.

On weekends, they'd drive across the Garden Bridge to the grandly named Ming Hong Yacht Club, which was in reality a little wharf in Hongkew from which local taipans launched houseboats crewed by Chinese sailors. Sir Victor liked to race a yacht he'd had built in Norway, or take friends duck-shooting. Mostly, he used a refurbished houseboat he'd christened *Vera* to putter around the canals. Sometimes they had great adventures extricating themselves from mudbanks; more often, he used it as a kind of stationary drinking club. One of Sir Victor's snapshots from late in the spring of 1935 shows Mickey lounging on board, atop a canvas-covered lifeboat, in deck shoes and chinos, chatting with Bernardine against a backdrop of a half-dozen junks in full sail.

Meanwhile, Mickey continued to discover Shanghai. "I visited Chinese schools and gave courtesy lectures, I inspected new little factories so that I could write them up, I looked at Russian painters' pictures, which were mostly pretty bad in my opinion."

She was also becoming aware of the prevailing attitude towards the natives. Shanghailanders seemed to look upon the Chinese as quaint – or infuriating – servants, dwellers in picturesque villages, or, at best, descendants of the emperors of a once-great civilization. "If I had left it to the newspaper," Mickey wrote, "I would scarcely have known that Chinese existed save for faraway-sounding names in news stories of battles and engagements upriver with bandits. The American *Shanghai Evening Post and Mercury* gave a better actual picture of conditions as they were, simply because the Americans were aware of the Chinese as people and most of the British weren't."

Bernardine, to her credit, was not only aware of the Chinese, but devoted to including them in her salon. Mocked by many British and American elites as a pretentious bluestocking, she was in fact presiding over a significant moment in the history of the Treaty Port. Mickey's arrival coincided with the first time that native Shanghainese were meeting socially with Shanghailanders of European and North American background.

Since Shanghai's earliest days as a Treaty Port, foreigners and Chinese had carried out business together and shared the same streets, all the while living drastically separate lives. The key figure in bridging the worlds was the comprador, a word that originated in Macao, where early Portuguese traders relied on Cantonese middlemen to trade with native merchants. In the nineteenth century, Shanghai's compradors, who tended to come from Ningpo and the nearby water-town of Soochow, were treated like chief stewards on a baronial estate: indispensable aides, but hardly social equals.

A symbol of the relationship between foreigners and their Chinese compradors was the trade language known as pidgin. Taking its name from the purported Chinese pronunciation of "business," pidgin was a classic example of what anthropologists call a "contact vernacular." Like Chinook, the jargon shared by European traders and the aboriginals of North America's northwest coast, pidgin was used as a *lingua franca* to facilitate business. Putting English, Chinese, Indian, and Portuguese words into Chinese sentence formations, pidgin was infantile-sounding, but effective. *Kumshaw* meant "tip"; *much more betta* meant "the best"; *chota hazra* (from the Hindustani) indicated tea with toast and jam, a typical Shanghai breakfast; and *no-joss!* meant "no dice!"

A 1935 newsletter provided to guests at the Cathay Hotel offered a handy guide for translating English phrases into pidgin, among them: "I want some tea at once, understand?" (*Catchee tea chop chop, savvy?*); "Do you mean it?" (*Talkee true?*); "I want a bath, get me some hot water" (*My wanchee bath, pay my hot water*); and, for shoppers: "Can you send this to the Cathay?" (*Cathay side can sendee?*).

Pidgin encapsulated the relationship that prevailed between cultures in Shanghai for the first years of the Treaty Port. In theory, white taipans – some of whom had spent decades in China, or had even been born there, without ever bothering to learn the language – gave orders. Their proxies, the Chinese compradors, carried them out. In practice, the compradors controlled all communication with suppliers and often vast Chinese staffs, which afforded them enormous power. Compradors acquired fortunes through "squeeze," the practice, engaged in by houseboys and national politicians alike, of keeping an undeclared commission for all services rendered.

By the end of the First World War, the figure of the pidgin-speaking comprador in long gown and silk trousers had given way to a young man who boasted an impeccably tailored Western business suit, a name Americanized with Rotarian-style initials, and an accent that bespoke the finest Oxbridge or Ivy League education. One of the consequences of the turn-of-the-century Boxer Rebellion – in which foreigners in Peking's legation quarters had been attacked with the tacit support of the Qing empress dowager – was that China was forced to pay a crippling indemnity to the foreign powers whose property had been damaged in the uprising. The United States, by agreeing to use its part of the Boxer Indemnity to fund the education of Chinese students in American universities, was instrumental in creating an administrative and business class that looked to the West for inspiration.

The foreign-educated sons and daughters of compradors formed the upper echelons of the new nationalist government in

Nanking. In the Shanghai of 1935, they could be found dancing the jitterbug at the Paramount Ballroom or listening to Filipino jazz bands at the Black Cat. The more culturally-minded attended literary gatherings hosted by leading Shanghailanders.

Harold Acton, the flamboyant British dilettante, painted a vivid portrait of the cosmopolitan scene on display at Bernardine's salon.

We were all much too physical: Emily Hahn, like a voluptuous figure from a Moroccan mellah; . . . some giggly Chinese flappers with permanent waved short hair, who had blown in late from a mah-jong party . . . there were Chinese painters in the Western-style – one had exhibited at the Royal Academy; representatives of Western firms who welcomed an escape from business; the first German Jews aware of the trend at home; journalists and professors.

Even the jaded Acton, whom Evelyn Waugh would acknowledge as partial inspiration for the wicked dandy Anthony Blanche in *Brideshead Revisited*, was impressed. "No crowd could have been more jumbled, and one had to thank Bernardine for shaking up the old bran-pie."

It was no surprise that, within hours of her arrival in Shanghai, a woman as democratically-minded as Mickey Hahn had begun doing what many lifelong Shanghailanders prided themselves on *never* doing: mixing socially with the Chinese. Her next move, though, would surprise even Bernardine. Mickey was about to fall in love with one of Shanghai's most famous poets – a dashing young man who was fabulously wealthy, beguilingly beautiful, and Chinese.

PART THREE

"Without beauty, what sort of world is possible?"

– Zau Sinmay,
"Her," 1926.

9: Shanghai, April 12, 1935

Sinmay was pondering how to slip out of the crowded room unnoticed, when she walked in.

He had almost turned down the invitation to yet another of Bernardine Szold-Fritz's "cultural" evenings at the International Arts Theatre. As honourable as this taitai's intentions were, her attentions were becoming tiresome. She seemed to regard him as her latest Oriental curio, an exquisite porcelain doll she could bring out to enliven a gathering when conversation flagged. On one of his recent visits to her salon, she'd asked Sinmay for a demonstration of Chinese martial arts. Suddenly finding himself surrounded by reverential pink-and-ivory faces, he'd solemnly and silently sketched out a few ludicrously elaborate gestures in the air. Of course, he'd made up the improbable display on the spot: he was a scholar, after all, not a common boxer. It was what he called "*chi yang ren,*" or "kidding the ocean people." As he'd pointed out to a friend later, in spite of what "Mrs. Manners" (as he called Bernardine behind her back) thought, each Chinese person could not do *all* the things the Chinese were known for.

Then he saw her, on the other side of the room. She looked nothing like the women who usually came to Bernardine's affairs – big-boned Englishwomen with long teeth, or wide-eyed Americans with braying laughs. With her lustrous hair cut boyishly short, and ample curves shown off by a mannishly tailored suit jacket, she was as stylish as the bohemian women whose androgynous looks had bewitched him on Paris's Left Bank. It was her eyes, though, large and unusually round even by Western standards, that arrested him. When Bernardine introduced them – before possessively ushering him away to meet another guest – and his dark gaze met hers, he thought he heard a sudden intake of air between her full red lips: a tiny gasp. For his part, the meeting had been a moment not of surprise, but of recognition.

But then the lecture started. He found a seat in the same row as her, a few chairs down. Though he tried to direct his attention to the man on stage, who was lost in an over-earnest discussion of the novels of D.H. Lawrence, he found himself shooting her sidelong glances, and arching his eyebrows in amusement when he saw the start of a blush pinkening her neck and pale cheeks.

Now, as the lecturer droned on about "phallic consciousness," Sinmay tried to remember where he had seen eyes like those. Suddenly, he was transported back to Naples. On his first trip to Europe, he had been stopped in his tracks by a fresco that had been rescued from a volcano-wrecked villa in Pompeii. It represented a young woman with dark, wide-set eyes, an aquiline nose, and full lips, to which she lifted a stylus. Her androgynous beauty had seemed to beckon, as with a lover's gaze: "Come to me, my Sinmay!" Later, in England, he would learn that it was meant to represent Sappho. Her poetry, along with the modern decadents she inspired, would come to obsess him. He had always dated the real beginning of his life as a poet from the day he had glimpsed the lyricist of Lesbos.

The woman he had just met, he suddenly realized, had the *same eyes*. And something else came back to him. In that room in Naples, there had been another portrait of the same woman; but in this one, she was depicted standing beside a man wearing white robes, who held a scroll beneath his darkly goateed chin. They stood together, dark eyes staring boldly across the ages. At the time, he had been struck by how, with his high cheekbones and wispy moustache, the man looked dark-skinned and non-European – could, in fact, have passed for Sinmay himself. The image had created a longing in him. Ever since then, he wondered if he would ever find a woman who would be his equal, in life as in art.

Now, he was sure, he had seen her. Just as quickly, though, she had disappeared; before the lecture was over, she'd ducked out the same side door Sinmay himself had been eyeing.

10: Cathay and the Muse

Later, when she'd come to know him intimately, she was able to precisely anatomize his charms.

"His body was slight, in loose white pyjama-like underclothing," wrote Mickey.

His hair was lank, silky, glossy black, unlike the stiff wiry heads of the others. When he was not laughing or talking his ivory-coloured face was perfectly oval, but one did not think of perfection, one looked at his eyes. In their oblique and startling beauty they were full of light and life. Blood flushed his cheeks only faintly, long smooth cheeks under the wing-like eyes.

The eye sockets that swept from a high-bridged nose called to mind a portrait on an Egyptian tomb, and the soft carved mouth was "decorated like those of his ancestors, marking sharply the corners of his lips. His tiny beard, no more than a brush of whiskers at the end of his chin, was a sly joke at his youth. In repose his face was impossibly pure, but it was rarely in repose."

She was writing of Sun Yuin-loong, the love interest in *Steps of the Sun*, a lightly fictionalized account of their affair; but it was a letter-perfect description of Zau Sinmay. (As a child, Sinmay's "milk name" – the affectionate but temporary first name Chinese parents give their children – was Yuin-loong, which means "Dragon in the Sky.")

With his long fingers, clouded gaze, and thin moustache, he matched the descriptions of the evil Dr. Fu-Manchu Mickey had thrilled to as a child. But in Sinmay's case, the overall effect was one not of corruption and malevolence, but of exotic beauty and wistful charm.

It wasn't long, after their first glimpse of each other at the

International Arts Theatre lecture in April, 1935, until Sinmay saw Mickey again. At a dinner Bernardine had arranged in a Chinese restaurant in Yangtzepoo, north of Soochow Creek, Sinmay found an excuse to sit next to her. As the other guests drank tea, spat sunflower seeds onto the ground, and sucked on oranges, their initially awkward conversation turned into easy, familiar chatter. A lively discussion of modern literature carried over to the pavement. As Mickey waited outside, hoping somebody would hail a taxi for her, the conversation around her shifted to Chinese. Suddenly Sinmay said: "Oh, excuse us for forgetting our foreign guest. We are all going now to my house. Would you like to come?"

Mickey replied, "Yes, of course I would."

Leaving Bernardine and her friends on the curb, she walked off with Sinmay and his entourage into the hot night of the Chinese city.

For an American as well read and worldly as Mickey, the notion of China and the Orient was, by the thirties, freighted with a rich cultural baggage.

China, for those who grew up in the American West, was the ultimate Other. North Americans' first sustained exposure to the Chinese came with the wave of emigration that followed the discovery of gold in Sutter's Mill, California, in 1848. Many Chinese workers arrived by way of San Francisco – whose Cantonese name was *Jinshan*, or "Gold Mountain" – before drifting off to lay the tracks of the British Columbia section of the Canadian Pacific Railway, or to open the restaurants, laundries, and grocery stores in Chinatowns that sprouted from San Diego to Victoria. Others arrived as victims of the "pig trade," through which Treaty Port merchants "Shanghaied" peasants through trickery or force and transported them in horrifically crowded ships to Peru, the American South, and the Caribbean, to work as indentured labourers on plantations. More than three quarters of the emigrants came from the hinterland of Canton, a region plagued by floods, earthquakes, typhoons, and, later, the social dislocation brought on by

the quasi-Christian excesses of the anti-Qing-dynasty Taiping
Rebellion. To the people of the American and Canadian West,
these southern Chinese, who dressed in robes, plaited their hair
into Manchu queues, and ate strange food with long sticks, were
"Celestials" – an allusion to the "Celestial Kingdom" of the Qing
dynasty that also suggested beings so alien-looking they could
only have fallen from the sky. In the United States, the Chinese
Exclusion Act – the only law in its history to single out a single
nationality or ethnicity from immigrating – was passed in stages
until 1902 (and not repealed until 1943). In Canada, where
poorly-paid Chinese workers had died in their hundreds digging
tunnels and laying tracks across the Rocky Mountains, a "Head
Tax" of up to $500 was levied on new arrivals from China until a
new law, enacted in 1923, stopped Chinese immigration outright
until after the Second World War.

For many Westerners, China was synonymous with Cathay, a
term that recalled the mysterious kingdom sought by the first
European explorers who came to the Asian mainland by sea.
Before them, overland travellers from Persia had spread legends
of a Mongol-controlled northern land called "Khitan" after the
pastoral nomads who lived there; and Marco Polo's *Travels in
the Land of Kublai Khan* contained a story called "The Road to
Cathay." It was the Jesuits based in Peking who resolved the mystery through historical scholarship: Cathay was just another name
– if a particularly euphonious one – for China.

China also meant products, foods, and ideas already familiar
thanks to centuries of commerce. During the Enlightenment, a
wave of Orientalism saw Voltaire writing a poem in praise of the
Qianlong Emperor, while the European gentry ate quail and
sweetmeats off exquisite blue-and-white dragon-patterned "china"
manufactured in the porcelain works of Jiangxi Province. The tea
the Sons of Liberty, dressed up as American "Indians," dumped
into Boston Harbor was a variety of oolong from the mountains
of Fukien Province. Since the beginning of the twentieth century,
the inner reaches of China had been penetrated by the salesmen
of Standard Oil of New York, who sold their famous *mei foo* lamps

for a few cents in the hopes of then provisioning 400 million consumers with a lifetime supply of kerosene (they brought back with them a strange game called mah-jong, dating to the early Ming dynasty, that would see tiles covered with Chinese ideograms becoming a feature in parlours from Beverly Hills to Miami Beach). Americans learned to love chop suey, sesame chicken, and fortune cookies – delicacies unknown in the Middle Kingdom, but elaborated for New World palates by Chinese-American cooks.

China suggested poverty and starvation, but also refinement, aesthetic beauty, and a countryside locked in a timeless idyll. News of recurring famines in the Yangtze Valley meant generations of North Americans grew up being told to finish their vegetables, as there were "children starving in China." Starting with *The Wallet of Kai Lung* in 1900, the British fantasy writer Ernest Bramah introduced English-language readers to a mysterious Orient, where long-whiskered scholars composed pastoral lyrics in bamboo groves and concubines with bound feet were borne to seven-walled pagodas in sedan chairs. *The Good Earth* (published in 1931, and later made into a movie with *Scarface* star Paul Muni as the hard-working protagonist Wang Lung) presented a more nuanced view of rural China. Written by Pearl S. Buck, a "mish-kid," or child of missionaries, born to a Southern Presbyterian couple who proselytized in Kiangsu Province, the bestselling novel created an image of the Chinese people as honest, long-suffering peasants, sorely tried by natural and man-made disasters.*

China, by the thirties, was a byword for injustice, but also a rallying point for revolutionaries. *Man's Fate*, by the French adventurer André Malraux, drew attention to the 1927 deal

---

* Buck's second husband edited the lavishly illustrated *Asia*, one of the great magazines of the twenties and thirties. A typical issue of "The American Magazine of the Orient" might feature John Dos Passos's account of a boxcar ride to Mount Ararat, Somerset Maugham anatomizing the life of a Shanghai taipan, or Edgar Snow describing anti-opium campaigns in nationalist China. Mixing scholarship with gripping reportage, while analyzing and frequently decrying Western imperialism, *Asia* had a large readership of armchair Orientalists.

between Chiang Kai-shek, Shanghai's gangsters, and the foreign bankers of the International Settlement that had ushered in the city's real-estate boom. Published in English in 1934, the novel told a story of intrigue involving Soviet and Japanese spies and Chinese revolutionaries entangled in a botched attempt to assassinate Chiang Kai-shek in Shanghai's foreign concessions. Though Malraux had never set foot in China, his riveting storytelling brought worldwide sympathy for the plight of China's masses.

China, and Shanghai in particular, meant glamour and international intrigue. In *Footlight Parade*, Busby Berkeley choreographed a drunken, tuxedoed James Cagney stumbling through opium dens in search of his Shanghai Lil. The cross-dressing Peking Opera star Mei Lan-fang, a friend of Sir Victor's and a frequent guest at the Cathay, performed in New York and befriended Charlie Chaplin in Hollywood. In *Shanghai Express*, director Josef von Sternberg told the true story of the hijacking of a Peking-bound express train in which twenty-five Westerners were held hostage. (The cast included a dimple-cheeked Anna May Wong, a native of Los Angeles's Chinatown, and a boa-wrapped Marlene Dietrich, who drawled: "It took more zan *vun* man to change my name to Shanghai Lily.")

China, thanks largely to a Birmingham-born vaudeville sketchwriter turned popular novelist, was also popularly associated with sinister dealings. Sax Rohmer published the first Dr. Fu-Manchu short story in 1912, and in thirteen novels published over the next half-century the moustachioed super-villain's plan for domination of the white race was repeatedly foiled by his unintentionally comical propensity towards chattiness.

The prototype for Ming the Merciless in the *Flash Gordon* comic strips, Fu-Manchu was despised in China as the ultimate negative stereotype. (In 1932, the Chinese embassy in Washington lodged a formal complaint when, in MGM's *The Mask of Fu-Manchu*, an assembly of "Asians" was told they must "kill the white men and take their women.") His congenial fictional antithesis was Charlie Chan, a Chinese-Hawaiian detective played on-screen by the Swedish-American actor Warner Oland. As he solved crimes around the world, the portly Charlie, assisted by his zoot-suited "Number-One Son," mouthed such mock-Confucianisms as "Cold omelette, like fish out of sea, does not improve with age."

Mickey Hahn, by the time she arrived in Shanghai, had been exposed to all these portrayals of China and the Chinese, and more. She considered *The Good Earth* a splendid, but not perfect, book, and mocked the stilted dialogue of the Chinese characters in *Oil for the Lamps of China*, a bestseller about the struggles of Standard Oil salesmen and their families in Manchuria and the Yangtze Valley. At a movie theatre in Shanghai's French Concession, she was able to watch *Charlie Chan in Shanghai*, about a plot to smuggle drugs into the International Settlement. (The mostly Chinese audience, she observed, deemed Oland's accent acceptable, but were disappointed that his dialogue was written in Cantonese rather than Mandarin.)

For Mickey Hahn, the essence of China – its otherness, timelessness, danger, beauty, glamour, and intrigue – coalesced in a single word: opium. Enjoyed by Sherlock Holmes in the backstreets of London's East End, the ruin of white youth in the dens of the white slavers of the Barbary Coast, and the indulgence of decadents from Samuel Coleridge to Jean Cocteau, the languor-inducing drug of legend encapsulated all the mystery of the Orient.

"Though I had always wanted to be an opium addict," she would write, many years later, "I can't claim that as the reason I went to China."

Opium was what would keep her in Shanghai, though, and for much longer than she'd planned.

After leaving Bernardine's party at the restaurant in Yangtzepoo, Mickey found herself in a party of half a dozen Chinese writers, entering the large front yard of Sinmay's house, a gabled Victorian home of roughcast brick. The ground floor, while barren of carpets and all but the most rudimentary furnishings, seemed to be full of people. An old man sprawled on a couch. Four or five children gawked and giggled as she entered. Sinmay introduced her to a young woman in a plain black dress – this was his wife, Peiyu – before inviting his guests upstairs. In a dark bedroom, Mickey took a seat on a spindly chair as Sinmay and a friend reclined on flat couches, between which a tray covered with unfamiliar implements had been placed on a white sheet.

Mickey watched as Sinmay used two long steel rods to manipulate what looked like a ball of taffy over the glowing wick of a lamp fuelled by peanut oil. As his hands flashed in knitting-like gestures, the substance thickened, changing colour from dark brown to tan. Chattering away in the Shanghainese dialect all the while, Sinmay wrapped the solidifying wad around the end of one needle and tamped it into a crater-like aperture in a pottery bowl. After fixing the teacup-shaped bowl into a long tube of polished bamboo, he held the projecting cone of hardened taffy over, but not actually in, the flame. As it bubbled and evaporated, Sinmay lifted the bamboo pipe to his lips and sucked, in little, regularly-repeated puffs. The complex herbal, caramel scent of the cloud of blue smoke he exhaled was one she'd already detected while wandering the back alleys of Shanghai.

Suddenly, she flashed back to the Fu-Manchu books she'd read in her backyard in St. Louis, and something clicked. "You're smoking opium!" Mickey cried, startling the other guests, who seemed to have forgotten her presence.

"Of course I am," Sinmay replied. "Would you like to try it?"

"Oh, yes," Mickey replied.

Beckoning for her to lie down, Sinmay showed her how to use one hand to keep the pipe steady. Sucking on the bamboo pipe, she almost felt sick, but her throat didn't close, and she managed to keep the smoke down. As she exhaled, Sinmay cautioned her to remain seated, or she'd feel dizzy.

At first, she didn't feel much of anything. Yet, as the talk turned to books and Chinese politics, she lapsed into a contemplative mood. "I listened with keen interest to everything the others had to say in English, and when they branched off into Chinese,

I didn't mind. It left me to my thoughts. I wouldn't have minded anything. The world was fascinating and benevolent as I lay there against the cushions." She watched, rapt, as Sinmay and his friends smoked four more pipes each.

After a while, one of Sinmay's friends asked Mickey how she was. "I don't feel a thing," she replied. "Perhaps opium has no effect on me." Sinmay told her to look at her watch. It was three o'clock in the morning.

"You have stayed in one position for several hours, you know – you haven't moved your arms or head," said Sinmay. "That's opium. We call it *Ta Yen*, the Big Smoke."

And so Mickey's relationship with Zau Sinmay began, in an aromatic puff of body-lulling poppy smoke, like an addiction.

美

Zau Sinmay, born in 1906, was the product of a strategic alliance between two of Shanghai's wealthiest and most prominent families.

His grandfather, Zau Youlian, gained fame for his brilliant missions as a Qing court envoy to Czarist Russia, and was one of the last Chinese governors of Formosa (before the 1895 Japanese occupation of the island that was to become Taiwan). After relocating to Shanghai from the family seat in neighbouring Zhejiang Province, he ensured that his youngest son, Zau Heng, was married to one of the daughters of Sheng Xuanhuai, a wealthy industrialist responsible for founding China's first Western-style bank and university. The union of these two families should have produced a powerhouse dynasty – but unfortunately Zau Heng, who briefly served as the mayor of Shanghai, was a hedonist with a ruinous taste for all the pleasures of the city.

Sinmay, as the eldest of Zau Heng's seven children, grew up among Shanghai's foreign and Chinese elite in a house on Bubbling Well Road (as the western stretch of Nanking Road was then known) in fabulous privilege, catered to by domestics and taught English in a mission school. The young Sinmay was intensely conscious of his family's illustrious past. "My ancestry is one of the most, if not *the* most colourful in China," he wrote in an unpublished essay Mickey would help him translate into English. One of his forefathers, he claimed, was

the first fortune-teller in China . . . among our foremothers we have another queen, or rather the favourite concubine to the emperor, the son that was born by her did actually succeed to the throne; this is why we had two life-sized eunuchs painted on the gates of our family temple.

The ceremonial party to celebrate his first haircut as a child, he wrote, "was attended by practically everyone who was famous, or rich, or influential in Shanghai." Even the features he had inherited from his ancestors, he believed, were illustrious:

that dragon-like face, that brush-straight nose, and eyes that are homes of sympathy and understanding: they are characteristic of Shao [Zau]; but a type so rare nowadays, that to find its like, one must go right back to the scrolls and paintings of the Tang dynasty.

Sinmay further claimed that his maternal grandfather Sheng, a man who could "turn clay into gold," was, on his death, "the richest man in China, leaving twenty millions worth of bonds and title-deeds to be fought for by his sons and daughters."

The overthrow of the Qing dynasty, when Sinmay was just five years old, brought an end to the family's generations-long idyll. He could still remember, he told Mickey, a shellburst that shook the family home, a harbinger of the Revolution of 1911. The men were forced to cut their Manchu queues, and the sedan chairs in which family members were carried through the streets by coolies – a symbol of imperial privilege – were quietly moved to a summer house in the garden, later to be replaced by horse-drawn fiacres and carriages.

Zau Heng's reckless spending precipitated the family's decline. When Sinmay was four, his father tried to acquire a "small white elephant" from a visiting circus for his son as a pet. After his brief term as mayor, Zau Heng kept concubines throughout the city, gambled incessantly, and developed a heavy opium habit. His antics made him the model for the hero of a popular comic strip called *Mr. Wang* – it was even turned into a film by Shanghai's hyperactive movie industry – about an elderly rake constantly on the run from his creditors. Capable of signing IOUs across the city in his children's names, Zau Heng gradually sold the family's once vast real-estate holdings to pay off debt collectors.

For a time, his eldest son was able to enjoy the family riches. As a young man, Sinmay dressed in a purple tweed suit and an imitation snakeskin belt of horsehair, and tore around Shanghai in a bright red Berliet. The hacks of the voracious "mosquito press" – so called because, after drawing blood, they could be counted on to buzz away to new offices to avoid being shut down by the police – delighted in chronicling his affair with a notorious *femme fatale* named Prudence. In a case of mistaken identity, Sinmay was arrested for the murder of one of the actress's admirers; he would later boast to Mickey that during his three months in jail he had learned four ways to commit murder.

Sinmay was merely sowing wild oats. Since he'd been a teen-ager, he'd known the woman he was going to marry. At the funeral of his wealthy grandfather Sheng Xuanhuai he'd been introduced to Sheng Peiyu, a pretty young cousin from Soochow. A month later, when the families were staying together at an inn in Hangchow, she caught him trying to take a surreptitious snapshot of her as she stood on the shore of West Lake.

Peiyu was less impressed by Sinmay: for her taste, her cousin was too short in stature, too long in the face. Her sisters and aunts, however, found him charming, and he courted his cousin ener-getically, even telling Peiyu he had changed his milk name of Yuin-loong to Sinmay in homage to her.*

They were engaged to be married when they were still teen-agers. First, though, Sinmay would have to complete his education. He had promised his father he would go to Cambridge to study political economy. Before he left, Peiyu knitted him a white sweater, and Sinmay wrote her a poem, which was printed in a

---

* "Peiyu" means camellia. It is also the beginning of a well-known line from a classical Chinese poem that includes the phrase "sinmay," which, in its Mandarin rendering, means "truly beautiful."

local newspaper. She would carry the yellowed clipping with her until the day she died.

Sinmay sailed from Shanghai on a German cargo ship in 1925. Stopping to tour Italy with an American friend of the family, he bought a bright green waistcoat embroidered with flowers, and a black bowler hat, and was followed in the street by people who thought he was a circus performer. It was in Naples's archeological museum that he was transfixed by the Pompeiian portrait of Sappho.

Upon his arrival in Cambridge he asked the Reverend Arthur Christopher Moule, the professor with whom he was lodging, about the identity of this beautiful woman.

Immediately recognizable in the cobbled lanes of Cambridge for his fringe of silky white hair, the eccentric sinologist was the son of a clergyman posted in the Chinese city of Hangchow. Reverend Moule introduced Sinmay to a professor of Greek literature at Jesus College, who suggested he read Sappho's leading modern interpreter. Sinmay swooned over the poems of Algernon Swinburne, whose response to European decadence often took the form of Sapphic verses invoking sadomasochism and cannibalism. Encouraged by Moule, Sinmay abandoned political economy at Emmanuel College, and plunged into literature.

Though his time in Europe was an intellectual awakening, Sinmay found the day-to-day life in his attic room in Cambridge dull. Moule's wife was a harsh disciplinarian, and even a sentimental relationship with a flaxen-haired farmer's daughter named Lucy, inspired by his reading of *Tess of the d'Urbervilles*, seemed tepid fare compared to the wild nights he had known in Shanghai. For real pleasure he crossed the English Channel, where he spent two summers studying at the École des Beaux-Arts.

"His two best friends introduced him to the Latin Quarter," Mickey Hahn would write of the Sinmay character in *Steps of the Sun*, "and he was enchanted with it. They lived in a small cheap hotel on the Left Bank and pretended to be poor students. They wore slouch hats and old clothes, and only rarely did they dress up and venture into the American part of the city."

A grainy photo from the summer of 1925 shows Sinmay in a tight suit, white slacks, and a broad-brimmed hat, with four other Chinese members of the "Celestial Hound Society." One was Xu Beihong, a painter whose combination of Western perspective and firmly delineated forms applied to traditional themes would make him one of the masters of modern Chinese art. They became "sworn brothers," taking a formal oath to always treat each other like close family. In Paris, too, he came face-to-face with his döppelganger, a literature student for whom he was often mistaken at Cambridge. Xu Zhimo would become a great friend, as well as one of China's most influential modernist poets.

"I spent all my money in Paris," Sinmay once told Mickey, with a faraway look in his eyes. "The women liked me *so* much."

After returning from Paris to Cambridge, a cablegram arrived from Shanghai. Two of the family's rental properties had burned down and his father, deeper than ever in opium addiction, could no longer manage the family's affairs. One year short of taking his diploma, Sinmay sailed for home. There, he learned that the death of a childless uncle had made him a multimillionaire at the age of nineteen.

Peiyu was waiting for him. Their wedding took place at the Majestic Hotel, in the same ballroom where, eleven months later, Generalissimo Chiang Kai-shek would seal his alliance with Soong Mei-ling. It was 1927, the pivotal year when the nationalist government, after having triumphed over the warlords – and pulling off its bloody purge of the communists in Shanghai – established its power base in Nanking.

"I had just been married," Sinmay wrote in a short memoir,

when a telegram arrived from a former school-mate of mine asking me to be his secretary, as he himself had been appointed the Mayor of the New Capital the day before. Since it is every young man's ambition to be the builder of a new country, I accepted the opportunity immediately.

Sinmay was given the task of riding around Nanking on a horse, instructing workmen to raze the houses of the poor to build the broad boulevards. "We thought it was splendid, to tear down all of old China." Six months later, another telegram, this one announcing the death of his grandmother, summoned him back to Shanghai. Though he remained in touch with his nationalist friends, his brief career in nation-building in Nanking marked the end of his life in politics.

His voyage home from Cambridge had taken him through Singapore, where he'd picked up a copy of a Shanghai-produced literary journal called *Sphinx*. Excited to find other Chinese poets writing in the modern style he'd discovered in Europe, he decided to embrace the life of the gentleman-poet. Now, with his inherited money, he set up the Maison d'Or, a small bookstore and publishing house in midtown Shanghai, and began publishing a monthly review with a yellow cover (an allusion to the *Yellow Book*, the *fin-de-siècle* English quarterly that had published the work of William Butler Yeats, Arnold Bennett, and the artist Aubrey Beardsley). Sinmay's self-published *Flower-like Evil*, its title a nod to Charles Baudelaire's *Les Fleurs du mal*, marked his literary debut in 1926.

The poem "To Sappho" is typical, combining the rhyming structure of classical Chinese four-line poems with sexual imagery:

> *From a flower bed, amidst fragrances you are awake,*
> *A virgin's naked body, a bright moon it does make –*
> *I see again your fire-red flesh and skin,*
> *Like a rose, opening for my heart's sake.*

Another poem, "Peony," linked the standard Chinese trope of the flower with crimson-tinged imagery suggestive of brothels and opium dens:

> *A peony also dies*
> *But her virgin-like redness,*
> *Shaking like a harlot*
> *Is enough to make you and me go crazy in the day*
> *And have wild dreams at night.*

Readers in Shanghai had never been exposed to such voluptuous blasphemy – at least not in the Chinese language. The impact of Sinmay's poems relied on his skill in playing with assonance and sibilance in the original Shanghainese. As was the case with the French poet Arthur Rimbaud's strongly phonetic verse, much of its essence was lost in translation into English.

"China has a new poet, its very own Verlaine," rhapsodized his friend Xu Zhimo, who, now returned from Cambridge, was himself becoming known for his passionate verse. Sinmay also began to write short stories; in his elegant prose style, critics detected echoes of another of his literary idols, George Moore.

Sinmay was indeed a new phenomenon. Equally capable of composing an impeccable *duilian* poem – the intricate haiku of China, in which every character is counterweighted in the metrically identical line that follows – or writing a Dostoevskean exploration of the inner life of a gambler, he adeptly occupied the literary terrain where East met West. If his early work lacked the nuance of Charles Baudelaire's ambivalent response to modernity, he compensated with a native son's deep-rooted understanding of Chinese culture.

What's more, Sinmay's wealth permitted him to cultivate the figure of the urbane boulevardier, with a Chinese twist. In Republican-era Shanghai, kidnappings made being a *flâneur* risky, so he usually opted to be chauffeured in his brown Nash sedan. Scorning the suits and ties of the Westernized children of the compradors, he opted for the mustachios and long brown robes of a Qing-dynasty scholar. It was as if the aristocratic Jean des Esseintes, the protagonist of Joris-Karl Huysmans's decadent novel *Against Nature*, had come to life in Jazz Age Cathay – with genuine ivory filigree in the place of French wallpaper, and reliable access to the best Indian opium.

In an effort to save the family fortune, Sinmay imported a rotogravure press from Germany. With the launch of his Modern Press, followed by the Epoch Book Company, a publishing empire was born. In 1932 Sinmay launched a satirical newspaper, the *Analects*, hiring as editor Lin Yu-tang, who would become a well-known interpreter of Chinese politics and culture in the American popular magazines of the forties. The Modern Press also published the photograph-filled *Modern Miscellany* – a Chinese answer to

Life – and *Shanghai Sketch*, a leading venue for the creators of *manhua*, the cartoons (a Chinese counterpart to Japanese manga) that first blossomed in pre-war Shanghai.

Sinmay's sociability, energy, and love of culture were legendary. Though he lacked the aptitude for business of the stereotypical *Shanghairen* (Shanghai person), he made up for it in worldly charm. Paying a surprise visit to the literary salon that convened in the Sun Ya Restaurant, he befriended a father–son team of Francophiles and used their Truth-Beauty-Goodness bookstore in the French Concession as the model for his own Golden Chamber bookstore. He welcomed the caricaturist Miguel Covarrubias, with whom Mickey Hahn had vacationed in New Mexico, and wrote a lengthy tribute to him in a local magazine. As a founding member of the Chinese branch of PEN, the international writers' association, he welcomed Rabindranath Tagore, an early advocate of Indian independence whose novel *The Home and the World* had helped him to become, in 1913, the first non-European to win the Nobel Prize in Literature.

One of Sinmay's biggest coups was organizing a feast for the Irish playwright – and vegetarian pacifist – George Bernard Shaw. In China, communists and nationalists alike were excited by Shaw's stopover in Shanghai on his 1933 round-the-world cruise, keenly anticipating – and dreading – the oracle's pronouncements about China's future. Shaw, then seventy-seven and treated like a living literary landmark, was less enthusiastic about the trip: he claimed he had only embarked on the *Empress of Britain* because his wife Charlotte wanted to see the world before she died. In Shanghai, Shaw could only be convinced to come ashore when Soong Qing-ling – the widow of Sun Yat-sen and a fellow member of the World Anti-Imperialist League – invited him to her French-town mansion. At an afternoon PEN Club meeting, Shaw was served a tiffin catered by the Gongdelin Restaurant, a famous Buddhist restaurant on Nanking Road. The guests included the Chinese opera singer Mei Lan-fang and the acerbic and ascetic leftist writer Lu Xun.

The white-bearded Shaw was encircled by Chinese writers, all hoping to shine in conversation. Lu Xun, who kept a dignified distance, reported them "bombarding him with questions as if consulting the *Encyclopedia Britannica*." Shaw, tiring of the third degree, announced he would have to leave.

"At that instant," reported the *North-China Daily News*, "Mr. Zau Sinmay carried in two large parcels and placed them on the table. Mr. Shaw leaped to his feet. 'Hooray,' he chortled, 'I knew I'd get a present; that's the only reason I came.'"

While Lu Xun looked on in disgust, Sinmay stole the show by presenting Shaw with an embroidered robe and a collection of miniature clay opera masks. While the scrum continued, Sinmay quietly paid the bill for everybody in the restaurant – including Lu Xun.

The banquet for Shaw would prove to be a turning point for Sinmay. By annoying Lu Xun, he had made a powerful literary enemy. At the same time, he had consolidated his friendship with Bernardine Szold-Fritz, who was also present that day. Sinmay's earliest letters to Bernardine – cordial at first, before becoming jocular and even confessional – date from around the time of Shaw's visit in 1933, and he would soon became a fixture at Bernardine's salons. The increasingly passionate tone of her letters suggests her growing infatuation with him.

A 1935 letter, typewritten on crumpled onionskin paper, captures the tone of their relationship. Bernardine has clearly been badgering the poet to attend to literary-club business. Sinmay chides her, light-heartedly:

Why do you ask me over and over about whether you may or may not bring the two authors to the P.E.N. dinner? . . . What could be [of] more interest than to dine with lady authors who are, at the same time, pretty girls? But you may as well warn the two ladies not to be surprised when they find that there could be so many stunned Romeos in this far east.

In the margin alongside "two authors" is written, in what is clearly Bernardine's looping hand, the words "Mickey Hahn + Helen."

It was the first hint of the radical change that was about to overtake Sinmay's happy, privileged life.

11: The Fantastic Mr. Pan

In the autumn of 1935, Mickey Hahn began to write the first of a series of *New Yorker* vignettes that would chronicle a friendship with a maddeningly mercurial poet and publisher named Pan Heh-ven. The sketches proved so popular that they were compiled into a book entitled *Mr. Pan*. Its dust cover was illustrated with a cartoon of a long-whiskered, narrow-eyed man, caught in mid-stride with a cane and a cigarette in his right hand and manuscripts under his left arm. Though he is dressed in a high-collared Chinese robe, the shoes on his feet are wingtips.

Pan Heh-ven, of course, was Zau Sinmay, whose every utterance had become fodder for Mickey's creative non-fiction.

In one of the early vignettes, Mr. Pan is a guest at a dinner arranged by a Bernardine surrogate with a comical enthusiasm for all things Oriental. He is "pale and wraithlike, bearded with a few wisps of real Chinese hair, gowned in sober brown . . . calculated to make the most hardened tourist gape and gasp." Mr. Pan is already, it is clear, growing weary of taking his hostess's friends sightseeing, and facetiously proposes a scheme to the narrator in which he will grow a pigtail and she will learn the sayings of Confucius ("just memorize the easy ones") so they can charge for their services as tour guides.

As the narrator's friendship with Mr. Pan grows, she is invited to his tall, thin house, with windowless walls, in Yangtzepoo. The Pan home, barren of rugs and all but a few furnishings, overflows with servants and relatives. The chauffeur, he tells her, is a distant cousin. The odd-looking man who sleeps on the downstairs sofa is employed running errands; it is only with some difficulty that Mr. Pan remembers that this Mr. Chow, a leftover from the time

he planned on having a stable, was once his jockey. (He asks
Mickey if she will try to get Mr. Chow a job as personal secretary
to "Shanghai's local British millionaire"; Sir Victor Sassoon, alas,
preferred young women in that role.) There is no mention of
opium pipes; Mickey would have to wait thirty years before the
New Yorker was ready to publish her account of trying "The Big
Smoke."

Mr. Pan's family tree is complex. He has five brothers, among
them the Fat Brother (who is helping the communist guerrillas),
the Half-Witted Addict Brother, and the Traitor Brother, who
finds work with the Japanese as a tax collector. (Mickey would soon
enough see the Traitor Brother dressed in silk and diamonds and
surrounded by bodyguards, in the Cathay Hotel ballroom.) His
father, the former mayor of Shanghai, is a tall, distinguished old
rake. At one point, Mickey shares a ride with him in the family's
Nash; the patriarch claims to be going to see a Charlie Chaplin film
but in fact disappears down a back alley in search of a gambling
den, or worse.

Most fascinating to Mickey is Mr. Pan's wife.* Her mother,
Mickey learns, was a sing-song girl – a Chinese geisha – and grew
up with bound feet. Peiyu herself speaks in the susurrating accents
of Soochow, the nearby water town renowned for its beautiful and
cultured women. Peiyu is temperamental (she flies into door-
slamming rages that make the entire household tremble) and
traditional in style (she favours a high Manchu collar and a straight
tunic). In their jewel-box of a home, she also lives a shockingly
sheltered life. Mickey has to encourage Mr. Pan to take his wife
dancing, and finds herself close to tears when he tells her how
happy he is that, for the first time in her life, Peiyu – then in her
thirties – has crossed a street in Shanghai by herself.

The twenty-eight Mr. Pan stories that would appear in the
New Yorker present a portrait of a complex, contradictory, and
charming man. At ease in English, French, Mandarin, and Shang-

---

* In her *New Yorker* pieces, Mickey made no attempt to disguise the name
of Sinmay's wife, whose name she romanizes as "Pei-yü."

hainese, Mr. Pan is a true cosmopolitan. Yet he is also old-fashioned, superstitious, and unapologetically Chinese. While he breakfasts on bacon and eggs and bread from a French bakery, his staple is "coolie food," plain dishes of bean sprouts and salt fish, and nothing delights him more than expounding at length about the origins of the sweet stuffed glutinous rice dumplings of Ningpo, or "lion heads," the spicy fried meatballs of northern Kiangse Province. When Mickey considers renting a house facing a long street, he advises her the "wind-and-water," or *feng shui*, is bad. "Any devil can come straight down that street and into your house, through this window – and this one – and the door downstairs. Oh, terrible! You must refuse to take this house."

After complaining of the stifling heat in Mr. Pan's house, Mickey asks him why he doesn't open the back window. Blaming his wife, he replies, "Something to do with wind and water. Of course it would be much cooler, but we dare not. It is Peiyu's superstition, you see. I humour her. You say 'humour'?"

Mr. Pan, who uses the narrator's apartment as his downtown pied-à-terre, introduces her to his quirky intellectual friends. In the vignette "Cathay and the Muse," Mickey describes meeting a snobbish disciple of T.S. Eliot addicted to epigrams, and a translator of *Magnificent Ambersons* author Booth Tarkington who prides himself on his rough, idiomatic American English. "China is simply stuffed with Henry Jameses," she notes. "I think James must have been a Mongolian throwback." One night at eleven o'clock, a poet she calls Mr. Shakespeare arrives with a friend and a bag of peanuts, demands vodka, and tells her that they had heard she was a second Sappho "and a true decadent." It is only with difficulty that she gets the amorous scribe out the door.

For readers in the West, Mr. Pan was something completely new. This was no Fu-Manchu, plotting the overthrow of the white race, nor a Charlie Chan, mouthing comical Confucian platitudes. Though proudly rooted in traditional culture, he was also an urbane man of unique, and even intimidating, sophistication – and about as far from the nobly suffering, illiterate peasants limned by

Pearl S. Buck as one could get.* Mickey's pen portraits of Mr. Pan, if they occasionally lapsed into caricature for comic effect, also provided a modern and nuanced alternative to the prevailing Western image of the inscrutable – or scheming, or impoverished – Oriental. At the height of its pre-war popularity, the *New Yorker* sold more than 171,000 copies per issue to a readership that included some of America's most affluent and politically influential households.

What old China hands had failed to do with a hundred well-intentioned editorials, Mickey achieved by portraying a modern Chinese family – and the travails of the Pans in a Shanghai facing siege – as fully-fledged humans.

To *New Yorker* readers, Mickey presented herself as an amused observer of the peccadillos of Mr. Pan. Behind the scenes, though, she was the lover of his real-life model, Zau Sinmay – and her ambiguous position in the Zau household, and status as the concubine of a Chinese poet, was about to make her already picturesque life in Shanghai into something far more scandalous.

As an inveterate self-chronicler, Mickey had a talent for making the raw material of her life into saleable words. She'd already spun her adventures in the Congo into both a gripping non-fiction travelogue – sanitized for legal reasons – and a novel which, with the relevant names duly changed, hewed closer to what she'd actually experienced. While her Mr. Pan stories set forth a version of her relationship with Zau Sinmay for official consumption, her lightly fictionalized version, *Steps of the Sun*, gets closer to the emotional truth of their affair.

Early in the novel, Dorothy Pilgrim, waking from a nap in Room 536 of the Cathay Hotel, decides to go to a party at a salon in the French Concession. She is battling heartbreak – a man in

---

* Sinmay, for his part, was ironic about the author of *The Good Earth*. Noting to Mickey the fact that Western-style cemeteries were favoured by the Chinese for nocturnal love-making, he proposed the epitaph: "Villagers, please don't fuck. Here lies Mrs. Buck."

Hollywood has spurned her – and looking for distraction. At the party she has her second meeting with Yuin-loong, a handsome Chinese poet with an impish smile. (Yuin-loong, or "Dragon in the Clouds," was, of course, the milk name Sinmay was given as a child.) They shock their host, the fussy bohemian Marcia Peters, by running out the door together arm in arm. In the back seat of his limousine their bodies slide together and they grip each other close, lips crushed, arms straining.

Breaking the clinch, Yuin-loong laughs, breathless, "I *knew* this would happen. I knew when I first saw you." He takes her to a Chinese hotel near the Race Course, the kind of place where you could bring a prostitute or order opium on room service.

The following day, Marcia pumps Dorothy for information about what happened next. "He's so attractive, I've often wondered – wasn't he different at all?"

"He's very gentle," Dorothy replies. "I'm sure he's had dozens of women, all colours; he was completely self-confident."

Their affair continues, in seedy hotel rooms, and then in a tackily furnished love nest a couple of blocks from the Cathay Hotel. Dorothy is fascinated by Yuin-loong's beauty, but also by his mind. Lounging in a silk robe spotted with burns from his favourite brand of Turkish cigarettes, Abdullah Imperials, he recites lines of Tang-dynasty poetry or expounds on T.S. Eliot's *The Waste Land* while exhaling opium smoke. She finds his love-making "intensely conscious," deeply and wisely sensual. As the affair progresses they even talk about having a child: Eurasian girls, he says to her dreamily one day, are *so* pretty.

Yuin-loong has a wife at home, "a lovely woman, small and slender, her straight little body blurred to the slightest degree by pregnancy." With her sleek black hair drawn back from her white face, "she might have been a statuette of glazed porcelain."*

The presence of children in the house – a boy with long black

---

* Peiyu's appraisal of Mickey was less lyrical. "She was tall, with short black curly hair," Sinmay's widow wrote in a memoir published in China in 2012. "She was neither thin nor fat, but had a big bottom. Though she didn't have blue eyes, she was good looking . . . I liked her, though I envied the fact that

hair who looks like a miniature version of his father, four girls, another on the way – gives Dorothy's conscience a pang. But soon the two women become friends, and go out shopping and to the movies together. With typically convoluted logic, her lover explains that while in nationalist China it is now illegal for a man to have a concubine, he is in fact *two* men. Since he is heir to both his uncle and his father, he has the right to two wives.

In real life, Mickey was also welcomed into Sinmay's home. Peiyu seemed to be willing to view Mickey as nothing more than another of her husband's many friends and business associates.

"Slowly I am collecting the Chinese language," Mickey wrote to her sister Helen. She was spending long evenings in the Zau home, chatting with Peiyu and playing with the children. "I know just what will happen, though; in the end she will be speaking excellent American and I will know nothing." She asked Helen to send clothes and toys for the children she was coming to think of as hers: the oldest was Little May, a seven-year-old boy, who drew and painted beautifully, the youngest Siao Pau, or Little Treasure, who would only play with rattles that were red.

Mickey found herself becoming part of the Zau family. "Personally I think we will all die here – of starvation, not of old age. I don't really mind. They will give me a good coffin in Chekiang on the family estate." Peiyu, she added, had already given her a jade ring.

Sinmay paid her the ultimate compliment by bestowing a Chinese name upon her. He taught her to write the characters, which she traced out awkwardly in a letter to Helen:

項 *Sha*

美 *Mei*

麗 *Lee*

"Sinmay," the name the poet chose to replace his milk name, means "truly beautiful." The name he gave Mickey, Sha Mei-lee,

---

she was independent and could come to China and earn a living with her writing."

is a typically charming play on words. "Sha" is a family name whose pronunciation approximates Hahn. The first character in "Mei-lee" – which, spoken aloud, sounds like Emily – is also the same as the second character in Sinmay's name. In Chinese, the character "Mei" has several meanings, among them "beautiful," "America," and – fittingly enough – "pleased with oneself." By making sure his and her name shared a character, Sinmay was permanently yoking his name to Mickey's.

While her day job on the *North-China Daily News* opened up the privileged world of the foreign Shanghai, her relationship with Sinmay was allowing Mickey to see the life the Chinese population led. Foreigners and Shanghainese, she realized, shared the same streets, but experienced the city in a completely different way.

"It was not so much that I found a new world with Sinmay and his family," Mickey wrote, "but I went with them around to the back of the scenes and peered out at the same old world through a glow of strange-colored footlights. It was fresh and wonderful that way."

Not everybody was happy, she was discovering, that she'd gone over to the other side.

美

Mickey had never stopped seeing Sir Victor Sassoon. Between the time she arrived in April 1935, and the time he sailed for India late in November of the same year, her name appears in his journals over two dozen times.

Sometimes he invited her for dinner at Eve's, his villa on Hungjao Road. Sometimes they went to one of the thirty-six movie theatres in Shanghai, taking his car to see James Cagney "snap-shooting his way to fame and romance" in *Picture Snatcher* at the Grand Theatre on Nanking Road, or reserving balcony seats at the Art-Deco Cathay Theatre, one of Sir Victor's French Concession properties. He was happy to have her in his box at the Shanghai Race Course. Though she knew nothing about horse racing, she was amused by the little Mongolian ponies – in China, she wrote, "the largest jockeys in the world ride the smallest horses" – and loved going on opening day, when all the banks and shops in the city closed and taipans in top hats and tails showed themselves off before the grandstand. Most often, they just talked, over long tiffins and lunches at the Cathay Hotel.

Bernardine Szold-Fritz, meanwhile, was stirring up trouble: she'd taken it upon herself to alert Sir Victor to the fact Mickey was ruining her own reputation.

"Once at a dinner here we were talking about games," Bernardine wrote to Sir Victor,

and Mickey told about playing a game called Truth in New York and in her turn she asked the others who was the last person they'd slept with. It was a chap on the New Yorker *whose name escapes me now and he refused to answer and she insisted and finally he said well, YOU!*

She asked Sir Victor, since he had influence with Mickey, to "try to keep her from telling her sex life to the town."

Replying on Cathay Hotel letterhead, Sir Victor scolded Bernardine: "It seems a little strange, after taking all the trouble you have done in warning one of your friends to be careful what she says in public, that you should somewhat lightheartedly repeat the very things which you deprecate being mentioned in the first case."

He was, however, concerned about Mickey's increasing immersion in the Chinese city. When she'd spent the night on his houseboat recently, she had seemed unable to stop sniffling. He noticed that her teeth were turning brown and that, in her bathing suit, her skin looked jaundiced – sure signs of the opium habit.

Over lunch at the Cathay one day, Mickey pronounced the name of one of his German Jewish friends, the owner of a dress shop, with Mandarin emphasis – as "May-ling." Slamming his hand on the table, Sir Victor shouted: "His name is Herr *Gamaling*! You're getting too damned Chinese."

Sir Victor blamed Sinmay. Bernardine, who resented losing her pet Chinese poet, had told him about Mickey's affair. He didn't particularly like the man, and thought he was a bad influence.

In spite of her differences with Sir Victor, when he sailed for

Bombay on the SS *Corfu* late in November 1935 to make his annual inspection of the Sassoon interests in India, Mickey confessed to Helen that she felt bereft.

"Victor left yesterday," she wrote.

He saved his last evening for Betty Moffett, her sister Connie, and me to make merry with our childish prattle, innocent adoration and baby kisses, and boy, did he eat it up. But really Helen I do love him; everything we know about him and all. I'll miss him awfully, since I have become a Resident and a cat like all the others. I saved up all my scratching to do with him, once a week in the Tower.

Everybody agreed that, with Sir Victor out of town, Shanghai wasn't quite as gay.

In the autumn of 1935, Mickey patched things up with Bernardine long enough to begin rehearsing for a role in a new International Arts Theatre production. The director, following a suggestion from Sir Victor, was Aline Sholes, Bernardine's sister; the play was Aristophanes's famous comedy *Lysistrata*, in which the eponymous heroine persuades the women of Greece to withhold sex from their husbands in order to end the Peloponnesian War. Mickey Hahn, naturally, would play the female lead.

In a city where rumours of war abounded, *Lysistrata* was a controversial choice. China's parlous political situation was making even Mickey nervous. "We expect war every minute," she wrote to Helen, "and last night when a car backfired in the middle of the 'Lysistrata' rehearsal and the other girls squeaked for joy and dashed to the window I turned sick and almost wet my pants."

The performance, at the Capitol Theatre on Soochow Road, provoked mixed reactions. "As we suffered from perpetual war in Shanghai, we thought it frightfully unsuitable," one British Shanghailander, the daughter of a tea merchant, recalled many years later. "I walked out in the middle."

"It seems I was very good," Mickey wrote to Helen. "I never knew I could act, but this part didn't call for much moving about. Mostly I stood in one place looking noble and intoning, 'Women of Athens!'" Mickey's own paper, the *North-China Daily News*, panned the play. Accompanied by a Sapajou cartoon portraying a bare-armed Mickey in a tunic, the notice acknowledged that "Emily Hahn as Lysistrata was excellent throughout," but criticized it as untrue to the original, declaring it a "very weak attempt to stage the fruity old comedy."

The review was signed "R.T. P-G.": Ralph Thomas Peyton-Griffin, the editor who had hired Mickey. "The editor of the paper is now very much in love with me," Mickey informed Helen, "and keeps sending me notes. I intend to get even somehow as soon as I have the time." She did, in a letter to the editor signed "Lysistrata": "I thought the audience liked us. In fact, I'm sure they did. They laughed at all the right times." She concluded on a serious note, "We are in China. Somewhat to the north a large tract of country is undergoing drastic political changes . . . don't you think we're wasting a lot of time over the dead body of an ancient Greek dramatist?"

If Mickey Hahn, the proudly non-political bohemian, was starting to pay attention to the news, it was thanks largely to her relationship with Zau Sinmay. "There seems to be something going on in North China," she'd written to Helen late in November. "The Japanese army captured a lot of railway stations, looked into a lot of baggage trains, and then suddenly went away again."

For now, though, it was the holidays, and there were parties to go to. She spent Christmas Eve at one of Shanghai's hottest dancing nightspots, the Paramount Ballroom. With a friend from the *Evening Post and Mercury*, she "accidentally" ignited a string of firecrackers under a neighbouring table, which turned out to be occupied by some of the city's most notorious Chinese gangsters.

"It is as if I had set off a small bomb under Al Capone," she wrote. "We were scared stiff, because somebody's pants had been burned off." Borrowing a diplomat from another table, she managed to make the offended gangster accept an apology – and then danced the rest of the night away with the diplomat.

Nineteen thirty-five was coming to an end. Mickey sensed the menace in Yangtzepoo every time she went to visit Sinmay's family.

Recalling her state of mind, a few years later, she would write: "There were Japanese across the creek, waiting. I began to know it, but I was happy."

12: Cosmopolis-on-the-Whangpoo

The building at 374 Kiangse Road, where Mickey Hahn rented her first flat in Shanghai, still stands. It is a five-storey commercial complex mixing offices and residences, next door to Lu Ya, a restaurant much loved for serving up flash-fried freshwater shrimp, spongy gluten, and other sweet and sour standards of Shanghainese cuisine.

The street itself is typical of the former International Settlement: a narrow, workaday corridor, tightly packed with low-rise apartment buildings, massage parlours, and noodle shops. At its north end, just before Suzhou Road – which in the thirties was called Soochow Road – an English- and Chinese-language plaque attached to a painted brick wall identifies the old Shanghai Waterworks Building, completed in 1888. To its south, the street runs up, after eight short blocks, against what was once Avenue Édouard VII – formerly the southern limit of the International Settlement, and now the easternmost stretch of the Yan'an Elevated Road. The only point where the street really attains elegance is at the corner of Fuzhou Road, where Sir Victor Sassoon's twin Art Deco towers, the Metropole Hotel and Hamilton House, still square off across a circus-like intersection.

Though the street's name has changed – it is now Jiangxi Middle Road – it retains its indomitable vitality. Vendors with deeply tanned faces stand at the street corners, baskets of cherries and lychees dangling from the bamboo poles balanced on their shoulders. Between the stop lights, pastel-hued Volkswagen taxis race with near-silent electric bikes. The drivers of cargo tricycles piled with stained mattresses, empty plastic water bottles, and other improbable loads grunt and puff as they race to beat the traffic light at Beijing Road. South of Nanjing (formerly Nanking) Road East, a venerable transvestite in a scarlet coat and lustrous black wig picks his way down the sidewalk in high heels, long nails clicking against the window ledge he uses to support himself. With his ruined face painted into a theatrical mask, and curling grey hairs protruding from moles, he is a daylight apparition from a long-vanished nightlife.

In 1936, according to the Shanghai city directory, a "Miss Emily Hahn" shared the third floor of the Shanghai Bank building with seven other tenants. When Mickey stepped out of the building on her way to the *North-China Daily News* office, she would have been plunged into the teeming street life of Republican-era Shanghai. Almost immediately, she would have been surrounded by rickshaw pullers, who, spotting a well-dressed foreign woman, would have trotted alongside her, asking, "*Where go, missie?*"

Mickey's first decision of the day – whether to brave the crowded sidewalks and get to work on foot, or pay a few coppers to be conveyed in comfort above the mob – was not an inconsequential one. The human-powered rickshaw, for many, was an all-too-obvious symbol of cruelty, inequity, and exploitation. As soon as you climbed into one, you were implicated in the economy of the Treaty Port. Shanghai allowed no one to remain aloof.

Mickey, naturally, would resolve the matter in her own unique way.

美

More than anything else in Shanghai – whose streets were lined with Western-style skyscrapers, and crowded with streetcars and the latest sedans from Detroit – rickshaws, which darted through traffic like water striders gliding over the surface of a pond, announced to newcomers that they were a long way from home.

Rickshaws were picturesque: on Nanking Road, high-class prostitutes cooed and puckered at potential customers from the back seat of lacquered "pheasant" rickshaws, whose pullers used them to moonlight from their regular employ with wealthy families. They were comfortable: the latest models had pneumatic rubber tires, backrests, spring cushions, and acetylene lights; in cold weather, pullers provided blankets for their clients' knees (during typhoon season, some would even piggyback passengers to their door across muddy streets). They were fast and manoeuvrable: they could deliver passengers to Old City alleys too narrow for cars to enter, and their pullers delighted in racing cars between lights – a race that, thanks to the congestion of the streets, they usually won. They were ubiquitous: in the early thirties, there were 23,000 rickshaws registered in the International Settlement, one for every 150 residents. They were easy for non-Chinese speakers to use: one stamped with one's right or left foot to indicate a turn, or in the middle to signal "stop." Finally, compared to taxis, which were usually driven by surly White Russians, they were cheap: a trip of a mile – and few trips in Shanghai were over a mile – cost about 20 cents in Chinese currency,* equivalent to the tip one left a taxi driver.

At the same time, a ride in a rickshaw was a sudden and vivid schooling in the inequities that had built Shanghai. At first glance, the pullers looked cheerful and tough: sporting recycled fedoras, they maintained a stream of chatter as their muscled legs, pants pulled above the knees, danced between the shafts. In the summer heat, though, when their ribs showed through ripped shirts, the suffering was apparent on their faces. Most pullers, crippled by chronic pain, were addicted to opium, often taken in the form of cheap and noxious "red pills," mixed with heroin and arsenic. Sikh policemen lashed them with *lathis*, ironwood quarterstaffs, for the smallest infractions, and drunk or belligerent clients often kicked them (the pullers called this "eating foreign ham"). Most Shanghai rickshaw drivers were former peasants – disproportionately from the northern part of Kiangsu Province – ruined by rural bankruptcy brought on by natural disasters or civil war. For them,

---

* In 1935, following a collapse in the price of silver, the nationalist government took China off the silver standard and limited currency issuance to four major government-controlled banks. In the mid-thirties, $1 US bought three new Chinese dollars.

"plowing the pavement" was a hard living: the average monthly income was nine Chinese dollars ($3 US), half of what a factory worker earned.

Much energy was expended by the foreign community in justifying their reliance on rickshaws. On the Woman's Page of the August 18, 1937 edition of the *North-China Daily News*, a cartoon of a skinny man pulling a rickshaw laden with three Chinese women was topped by a poem titled "Not As Hard As It Looks":

> *The rickshaw-wheels spin round and round,*
> *The coolie's feet just skim the ground.*
> *When the rickshaw cart is full,*
> *Then he really doesn't pull,*
> *No, he really doesn't pull –*
> *He's pushed!*

The rickshaw pullers themselves were fond of a Chinese proverb that got at a deeper truth: "There is no light load if one has carried it for a hundred paces."

Pulling a rickshaw could be cruel, extenuating work. A survey by the Shanghai Social Bureau found that the average lifespan of a puller was forty-three years. At the same time, they provided much-needed employment: on average, each puller supported a family of 4.23 people, and the public rickshaw business, which by the late thirties was entirely Chinese owned, was estimated to feed 340,000 mouths in Shanghai.[*]

Not everybody used rickshaws. Many missionaries in Asia made a virtue of turning down rides. Edgar Snow, the biographer of Mao Tse-tung, was surprised to learn that although Gandhi was over sixty when he met him, he walked everywhere, refusing on principle to be pulled in a rickshaw.

For her part, Mickey Hahn didn't hesitate to ride in rickshaws. The very fact of being in China, she believed, meant you were

---

[*] No new rickshaw licences were issued in Shanghai after 1949; the last rickshaw was sent to the Shanghai Museum in 1956.

implicated in a system based on exploitation. "Why balk at a rick-sha," she wrote in her memoirs,

> *when you are doing just as much harm in every other way, merely by living like a foreigner in the overcrowded country of China? The shoes I walk in have been made by sweated labor; the shoemaker, beaten down by my bargaining, takes it out of his workers, and so they are being exploited (by me) just as much as the ricksha coolie is. And so, because I want to go wearing shoes . . . I use rickshas too, without wasting time in insincere pity and oratory.*

As a writer, Mickey decided she couldn't afford to remain aloof. So, when she wanted to get somewhere in a hurry, she did what just about every foreigner in Shanghai did: she beat the traf-fic and climbed into a rickshaw.

美

Mickey didn't have far to go to discover the real life of Chinese Shanghai. A block north of her flat on Kiangse Road, a non-descript brick archway in the middle of a row of two-storey storefronts offered a portal into a world far removed from the cool corridors of the Cathay Hotel.

The *shikumen*, or alleyway complex, at 434 Jiangxi Middle Road, still stands. Leaving the sidewalk and walking beneath the arch, whose keystone bears the characters for "Alley of Three Har-monies," means entering the hidden inner life of a Shanghai city block. After a few steps, the sounds of traffic and the smell of exhaust are replaced by the hum of outdoor air-conditioning units, and the air becomes redolent with frying garlic, stewing meat, and the liquorice notes of simmering medicinal herbs. Off the main lane, narrower alleyways, separating the rows of attached two-storey homes, branch off at right angles. Telephone lines, electrical wires and bamboo poles tangle in cat's cradles over doorways; bicycles lean against exterior walls. Brick facades, some overgrown with creeping vines, are painted charcoal grey, the wooden window frames a faded oxblood red. Everywhere are signs of small com-merce: a sink for rinsing dishes outside the back door of a noodle shop, a cobbler's last next to the rows of neatly paired sneakers of an informal shoe-repair shop. Overhead, water drips from quilted jackets, whose arms are threaded through bamboo poles that protrude like ship's spars from second-floor balconies. Bedroom windows look into kitchens; rooftop patios are separated by mere inches. With its abrupt angles and beguiling acoustics, the *shikumen* is a theatrical space, ideal for the nurturing of intense feuds, passionate love affairs, and all varieties of urban drama.

The Shanghai that Mickey Hahn lived in was a vast patchwork of such *shikumen*. Visionary entrepreneurs like Silas Hardoon had made fortunes by compressing migrants, who clambered for safe haven from rebellion and civil war, into identical rowhouses in the secure confines of the foreign concessions. They were built quickly and cheaply – though solidly – with the object of squeezing the maximum living space, and profit, out of relatively small urban lots. The main alleys that separated the rowhouses were thirteen feet wide – wide enough for rickshaws, but not cars – with tributary lanes only eight feet wide. The name *shikumen*, which means "stone gate," was meant to suggest a genteel rural past: in ancient China, the entrance to a palace consisted of five layers of gates, the outermost of which was known as a *kumen*.

Shanghai's *shikumen*, however, were far from palatial. Population pressures led them to be relentlessly subdivided. By the thirties, an alleyway home originally built for one family typically housed twenty-four people, and Municipal Council surveyors found as many as fifteen families sharing a single home. Tiny pavilion rooms – the *tingzijian* – over kitchens were rented to college students, writers, and unmarried tenants. The largest *shikumen* complexes consisted of as many as 700 separate homes. *Shikumen*, whose layout fostered sociability, were the secret to Shanghai's astonishing population density, and the stage for the historical dramas that would transform China in the twentieth century.

It is estimated that, for most of the twentieth century, three out of every four people in Shanghai – all but the very rich and the very poor – lived in a *shikumen*. Wealthy Chinese were more likely to live in townhouses with their own yards, like the three-storey Victorian home in Yangtzepoo where Mickey Hahn first smoked opium with Zau Sinmay. (It was the destruction by fire of a large *shikumen* complex the Zau family owned near the Race Course that forced Sinmay to return to Shanghai before completing his studies at Cambridge.)

Continuing a block past the Alley of Three Harmonies, and just 300 yards north of her apartment in the Shanghai Bank building, Mickey would have come upon a waterway that was home to some of Shanghai's direst urban poverty. Today it is a tranquil urban canal, where a few municipal barges are moored against concrete banks; but in the mid-thirties, Soochow Creek was Shanghai's most notorious aquatic slum.

It was on Soochow Creek that many destitute peasants completed their long voyage from the disaster-stricken countryside to Shanghai. Thousands of families slept on flat-bottomed sampans, which were linked by duckboards laid from deck to deck; they were so tightly packed that it was said you could walk from one bank to the other, a distance of seventy-five yards, without getting your feet wet. When the boats started to disintegrate, some families dragged them ashore, turning them into shacks known as *gundilong*, or "rolling earth dragons."

The banks of Soochow Creek were lined with single-roomed straw huts whose windowless bamboo walls were plastered with mud. Some slum dwellers were unemployed, or eked out a precarious living as beggars. Most, though, worked full-time; Shanghai's *shikumen* and shanty towns provided the vast workforce that kept the British-owned factories of the International Settlement, and the Japanese-run mills in Yangtzepoo and Chapei, thrumming day and night. Some of Shanghai's biggest paper, flour, and cotton mills were located right on Soochow Creek, whose waters received the mills' untreated effluent.

Rewi Alley, a New Zealander who worked for the Municipal Council as a factory inspector during the thirties, discovered that in the Japanese districts barefoot children of ten were locked into the factories at night and forced to sleep on rags laid atop the same machines they operated by day. When the writers Christopher Isherwood and W.H. Auden visited in 1938, Alley regaled them with horror stories. "In the accumulator factories," they reported in *Journey to a War*, "half the children have already the blue line in their gums which is a symptom of lead-poisoning. Few of them will survive longer than a year or eighteen months. In scissors factories you can see arms and legs developing chromium-holes."

A communist-led movement to improve working conditions in Shanghai's factories was brought to a sudden halt by the purge in which Chiang Kai-shek – funded by the bankers of the Bund and in collaboration with the city's worst gangsters – hunted down and killed labour leaders. Since 1927, Asia's largest urban proletariat had been under the thumb of industrialists, warlords, and mobsters – with the tacit approval of the nationalist government in Nanking. Foreign factory owners were the beneficiaries: in Shanghai, they reaped outlandish profits by paying the world's lowest industrial wages.

Sir Victor, to his credit, kept his companies aloof from this seamier side of the economy. In Shanghai, his fortune rested on smart real-estate investments. In India, where the family money came from textiles, he took pride in the Sassoon reputation for generous paternalism. While he strenuously opposed the unions, he made sure his workers in Bombay's cotton mills were paid some of India's highest wages.

A common refrain in Republican Shanghai, one Isherwood and Auden reported hearing from well-meaning tourists and intellectuals, was: "Oh dear, things are so awful here – so complicated. One doesn't know where to start." When they reported this lament to Rewi Alley he replied, with a ferocious snort: "I know where *I* should start. They were starting quite nicely in nineteen twenty-seven."

美

Unbeknownst to Mickey Hahn as she enjoyed her new life in Shanghai in the mid-thirties, the seeds for the revolution that would completely transform China had already been planted in the city's *shikumen*.

In June 1920, a moon-faced peasant's son from Hunan named

Mao Tse-tung rented a house, with three students from the same province, near the tramway car sheds off Hardoon Road, on the edge of the International Settlement. Then in his mid-twenties, Mao had just completed a leisurely sight-seeing trip from the capital, where he had been working as an assistant librarian.

Washing up in Shanghai – after his shoes had been stolen, and without a copper in his pocket – Mao slept in an attic room in the shared house located in the Alley of Benevolence and Kindness.* Rent was paid to Silas Hardoon, who had by then become Shanghai's wealthiest landowner; to cover his share, Mao took in laundry and delivered newspapers. Doing laundry for a living wouldn't have been so bad, he told his biographer Edgar Snow years later, if he hadn't had to spend most of the money he earned on streetcar fare delivering clothes to customers.

Mao had grown disgusted by the corruption of Chinese politics. Working at Peking University, a hotbed of revolutionary politics, had sharpened his appetite for change. After the First World War, the League of Nations had ceded Germany's former territory in China to Japan, rather than returning it to China. Outraged at this betrayal by the Western powers, in 1919 students led mass protests in the streets of Peking. For Mao, and many other young intellectuals, it was a signal that China must look within, rather than to the West, for political salvation.

At that point in his life, Mao did not consider himself a Marxist; the first Chinese translation of the *Communist Manifesto*, after all, had appeared only that spring. He supported the "New Village" movement, led by Japanese anarchists who sought to create a classless society through shared resources and forced labour. In Shanghai, though, he had a fortuitous encounter with a charismatic professor named Chen Duxiu. Chen was singled out as one of China's leading Marxists by the Comintern, the global arm of the Soviet Communist Party dedicated to fostering international

---

* The *shikumen* complex has since been replaced by a luxury mall. Mao's former residence, preserved as a museum, is located next to the five-star Shangri-la Hotel's steakhouse.

revolution. In August 1920 – shortly after Mao had left Shanghai for Hunan – Professor Chen and seven other Marxist intellectuals, with the guidance of a Bolshevik emissary, founded the Chinese Communist Party.

Mao was present at the party's First Congress, held in Shanghai in July 1921. Fifteen delegates, posing as university professors on a summer excursion, met in a two-storey *shikumen* house on Joyful Undertaking Street, in the French Concession. In attendance was a Dutch Comintern agent who went by the name of "Maring." After a stranger unexpectedly wandered into the meeting – a prelude to a police raid – Mao and the other delegates fled to Hangchow, where they concluded the meeting on a canopied boat of West Lake, pretending to be tourists writing poetry.

In its early years, the party was a left-wing appendage of Sun Yat-sen's Kuomintang. Mikhail Borodin, the larger-than-life delegate from Moscow's Politburo, encouraged the communists and nationalists to maintain a united front against the warlords. After Sun's death in 1925, the Soviets encouraged the Chinese communists to gradually infiltrate the Kuomintang. In Stalin's words, China's communists would use the nationalists "like a lemon," squeezing them dry before discarding them.

Events, however, followed their own logic. That spring, the killing of a Chinese communist worker by a Japanese foreman in a Shanghai mill led to mass demonstrations against the presence of foreigners in China. When the protesters stormed a police station in the International Settlement, the panicked officers – whose commander was enjoying a long lunch at the Shanghai Club on the Bund – fired on the crowd. Eleven Chinese protesters were killed. The "May Thirtieth Movement," which eventually spread to twenty-eight other cities, would come to be seen as the first nail in the coffin of foreign domination in China. It was also a boon for the communists, causing membership in the party to increase tenfold in a matter of months.

In the decades that followed, Mao would return to Shanghai many times. With his second wife, Yang Kai-hui, he raised two children in a *shikumen* house in the French Concession. Later, he would speak fondly of the intellectual ferment of the Treaty Port's backstreets, referring to urban-based intellectuals as "men from a Shanghai *tingzijian*," an allusion to the tiny pavilion rooms rented out to poor scholars in *shikumen* houses.

Mao – who by 1927 was convinced that revolution in China would be led by the rural poor rather than factory workers in Shanghai, and that "political power is obtained from the barrel of a gun" – holed up with a small army in a mountain lair in Hunan Province. The Kuomintang, meanwhile, captured Mao's second wife in the capital of Hunan and had her shot. (Around the same time, Chiang Ching, the woman who would become Mao's fourth wife – and the ringleader of the Gang of Four during the Cultural Revolution – was making her name in Shanghai as the slender, dark-eyed movie star Lan Ping, or "Blue Apple.")

The communists that remained in Shanghai, following the Soviet-sanctioned "urban path," came to a sticky end. In 1931, the Special Branch of the Shanghai Municipal Police, which also functioned as the intelligence-gathering arm of the British Secret Service, discovered a mailbox maintained by a Soviet agent that helped them to identify every communist still operating in Shanghai. For the next five years, Patrick Givens, chief of the Special Branch, and a ruthless "Red"-hunter, made a ritual of regularly handing over alleged "subversives" to the Kuomintang authorities for imprisonment or summary execution.

By the end of 1935, by which time Mickey Hahn had been in Shanghai for eight months, there were estimated to be no more than one hundred active members of the Chinese Communist Party left in the city. The previous autumn, Mao, hounded from a new hideaway in south-east China by Chiang Kai-shek's forces, had joined 86,000 fleeing communist troops taking the first steps of what would become known as "the Long March."

At the same time Mickey was enjoying gin slings on Sir Victor's houseboat, Mao's troops were slogging through a black, viscous swamp; half of them would die along the way, in skirmishes with tribespeople, or of malnutrition and suppurating sores. After just over a year, the 6,000-mile march, which circled northwards towards Shensi Province, ended on the desolate plateau of the Yellow River. Mao and his lieutenant, the French-educated intellectual Chou En-lai – along with the 5,000 or so other communists who had survived famine, exhaustion, and the marauding of the nationalist forces – found shelter in the area's *yao-dong*, dank cave dwellings carved out of the yellow earth.

After years of "eating bitterness," Mao had transformed himself from a Shanghai laundryman and tenant of Silas Hardoon into the great hope of the Chinese Communist Party. Tall, long-haired, hardened by the ordeal of the Long March, and now thoroughly schooled in Marxist dialectics, he was an impressive figure. Even Moscow had declared him the "tried and tested" political leader of the party.

On Christmas Eve, 1935 – which Mickey Hahn had celebrated by setting off firecrackers under a gangster's table in the Paramount Ballroom – Mao sealed his ideological leadership of the party at a meeting of the Politburo in the walled county town of Wayaobu, 800 miles from Shanghai. Desperate to rebuild the party, he proposed a new policy to the assembled faithful. The Red Army would stop confiscating the land of rich peasants. Local warlords – and even the Kuomintang – would become allies, not enemies.

"We are Chinese," he argued. "We eat the same Chinese grain. We live in the same land . . . Why should we kill each other?"

From then on, declared Mao, the ultimate goal would be to defeat the real enemy: the Japanese.

At the time, Mickey Hahn, like most people in Shanghai, had no idea who Mao Tse-tung was.

She had, of course, heard talk of the "Reds." But for Shanghailanders in 1935, names like Kiangse and Yenan meant very little; some taipans even denied the existence of Soviets, while the *North-China Daily News* dismissed the Red Army as bandits and rural brigands. Most foreigners were still trying to make up their minds about Chiang Kai-shek, who, in spite of clear evidence to the contrary, was considered by many to be a dangerous left-wing radical.

As Mickey got to know Shanghai better, she started to understand its inequities. For an ambitious writer, the city offered an infinite array of subject matter. Life in China also offered some distinct material advantages.

For most Westerners, moving to Shanghai meant a huge leap in social and economic status. The cost of living was fantastically low. A bespoke suit, made by some of the world's best tailors with excellent Australian wool, cost only $6 – a sixth of what it would have cost in the United States. Even the notoriously underpaid British Army soldiers stationed in Shanghai could afford to pay room boys to make their beds and polish their buttons.

For Mickey, who had lived in New York in the months after the stock market crash, fretting as her clothes grew ragged while lines formed around soup kitchens in the Village, Shanghai was a dream.

"I'm spending only a third of what I would in New York," she wrote to her mother, who implored her to join her in Winnetka, Illinois. "And I have much more to write about . . . I'm in the middle of a book; I'm in the middle of a magazine; I'm in the middle of China!"

In Shanghai, Mickey hobnobbed with multimillionaires, had new skirts and suits tailor-made every week, and spent weekends at the races and the yacht club. She even had a servant – a temperamental cook who was known for an obscure delicacy made of spun sugar – just as her family had in St. Louis when she was a girl. His pay amounted to the equivalent of $5 a month, at a time when American factory workers were paid $5 and $15 a day.

"What I didn't know at the time," Mickey would write of her first year in Shanghai,

was that the whole giddy structure rested on rice. Rice, in 1935, was so cheap that as far as we Caucasians were concerned it didn't cost anything. The Chinese had a different idea of it, but I'm talking about us ignorants. Cheap rice means cheap labor. Cheap labor in a vast city like Shanghai means cheap production: furniture and house-

work and clothing and green stuff. In placid ignorance I sat on top of a heap of underfed coolies. I didn't run into debt; on the contrary, I was living easily, just within my means.

It wouldn't take long for Mickey to wise up about the real source of Shanghai's prosperity. And soon enough, she would be providing haven and material support to guerrillas, and finding herself on the wrong side of the war of civilizations that was about to overwhelm the Far East.

For the time being, though, Mickey certainly saw no pressing reason to leave Shanghai. She was having a grand time, and living like a queen.

PART FOUR

"It was a fascinating old Sodom & Gomorrah
while it lasted!"

– Edgar Snow,
Journey to the Beginning, 1958.

13: Shanghai, November 3, 1936

Sir Victor picked up the speaking tube in the back of the limousine and instructed the chauffeur to drive west on Nanking Road. After a morning of work at the E.D. Sassoon offices on the third floor of Sassoon House, and a long luncheon with Nunky, he was in the mood for fun. That afternoon's duties would be more pleasure than business.

After almost a decade of building, all the elements of the Shanghai he had dreamt of – a city at once a haven for himself, and a beacon for the world's best and brightest – were falling into place. Sassoon House had risen again from the mud of the Bund, this time topped with a private penthouse nest where he could rest his head. With his luxury residential skyscrapers, he had brought lofty elegance to a city of brick rowhouses. His real-estate holdings, which ran the gamut from brothels in Hongkew, the U.B. brewery on Gordon Road, and the Jewish School on Seymour Road to his own Tudor-style retreat near the aerodrome, were so extensive he had lost track of what he owned. In just two more days, one of his most cherished projects would be complete.

The chauffeur, proceeding with the emphatic haste befitting his employer's status, was waved through intersections by Sikh policemen who spotted the licence plate "EVE 1." The car slid past the wedding-cake spires of the secular temples of Shanghai commerce, the Chinese-owned department stores Wing On, Sincere, Sun Sun and – grandest of them all – the new Sun, still under construction at the corner of Nanking and Thibet Roads. They sprawled over entire city blocks formerly occupied by pawn shops and opium dens – land that had once been in the hands of Silas Hardoon. Sir Victor was glad he had snatched up some of the most valuable of these properties, but Wing On was beyond his grasp: the Cantonese-Australian family who had founded the store still leased it, at an exorbitant rent, from one of Hardoon's adopted sons.

Sir Victor had once paid a discreet visit to its rooftop, which played host to a pleasure garden well loved by the Chinese. It was quite a spectacle. Pretty Shanghainese girls with marcelled hair sucked on watermelon seeds and nibbled dried duck gizzards, while parents herded their children between pony rides, displays of the juggler's art, and the caterwauling of painted opera singers. The Wing On rooftop was like Brighton Pier on a midsummer weekend: a jolly time for the common people, but hardly his cup of tea. The atmosphere in his own pleasure garden, a little farther down the road, would be altogether more rarefied.

His one regret was that he hadn't been able to open its doors earlier. Nineteen thirty-six had turned out to be the year many of the world's luminaries chose to visit Shanghai. Though it pleased him that the best of them had signed the Cathay's registry book, he was also frustrated that the hotel's nightspots couldn't accommodate bigger crowds; the Tower Night Club was tiny, and the ballroom was starting to look out of date. When celebrities passed through town, he would prefer to entertain them in a more up-to-date club – ideally, one that he himself owned.

Sir Victor had spent the previous winter away from Shanghai. His semi-annual sojourn in India had been dull, except for the morning the portly Aga Khan, celebrating his Golden Jubilee, had himself weighed on a giant scale in a public square and donated the equivalent in gold to charity. ("You have never seen such a crowd of people in your life," he'd written to Princess Ottoboni, the widow of his brother Hector. "He weighed only £16,000, which rather surprised me.") In Bombay, he'd noticed that the Taj Mahal, the subcontinent's most palatial hotel, had spruced up its public areas and added cabarets; its owner, Sir Nowroji Saklatwala, had clearly been impressed by his recent sojourn at the Cathay. The saddest moment had come over Christmas in Calcutta, when he'd been forced to put down his beloved thoroughbred Star of Italy, the winner of three Viceroy's Cups.

On his return to Shanghai in March 1936, Mickey Hahn had met him on the wharf. Over dinner, in addition to complaining about Bernardine Szold-Fritz's latest outrages and pumping him for advice on dodging the tax authorities, she'd regaled him with stories about Charlie Chaplin and Paulette Goddard. The couple had made Shanghai a port of call on their Far Eastern tour. At a press conference in the Cathay Suite, Chaplin had denied there was anything Bolshevik about his latest talkie, *Modern Times*, which some viewed as a critique of the inhumane pace of modern life. Mickey, who knew all the Hollywood gossip, said Chaplin had met his fiancée when she was a chorus girl in a Busby Berkeley movie. ("Mickey says Chaplin likes young girls," Sir Victor noted in his journal, "and has been living with Paulette Goddard because though not young is childish.") Playing to his Chinese fans, who knew him as "Cho Pieh-lin," Chaplin had praised the beauty of local women, and was courtly with Butterfly Wu, the star of Shanghai talkies, to whom he was introduced at a tea reception organized by Bernardine.

Sir Victor had finally met Chaplin and Goddard on their second visit to Shanghai, after they'd completed a tour of Indochina, Bali, Java, and Canton aboard a chartered yacht. In the Tower Night Club, Chaplin told him he was keen to make a film set in China, about a White Russian countess reduced to making a living as a taxi dancer; he'd already written 8,000 words of the script. He and Goddard, rumour had it, had been married in a quiet ceremony in Canton.

Later that spring, Sir Victor had had an opportunity to become better acquainted with the Chaplins when they were seated at the same table aboard the SS *President Coolidge*, en route to San Francisco. The fancy-dress party held to mark Meridian Day, when the ship crossed into the western hemisphere, had been especially jolly. Everybody got a little tight: there were a couple of Guggenheims in the ballroom, and the movie director Walter Lang joined them at a table that was soon awash with champagne.

Chaplin had introduced Sir Victor to an acquaintance of Bernardine, an extravagant Frenchman named Jean Cocteau. He was travelling with a suave Moroccan man who introduced himself as Marcel Khill. In broken English, Cocteau had explained that he and his companion had bet a French newspaper that they could follow in the footsteps of Jules Verne's Phileas Fogg by circumnavigating the face of the globe – without resort to airplanes, balloons, or zeppelins – in eighty days.

Privately, Chaplin had confided to Sir Victor that Cocteau had spotted his name on the passenger list of a ship he'd taken from Hong Kong, and had been making a pest of himself ever since. While they were in a queue to present their passports, Sir Victor had made a point of saying to the chatty poet, a minatory growl in his voice: "It seems you're writing some very amusing things about us." The warning, he'd hoped, was implicit in his tone. A man who wrote trifles about his betters, after all, could expect to be excluded from their company.

After landing in San Francisco, Sir Victor had made the eighteen-hour United Airlines flight to New York – with stops in Reno, Salt Lake City, Cheyenne, Omaha, Des Moines, Chicago, and Cleveland – before sailing on the *Empress of Britain*. After spending a few weeks in England, he'd summered on the French Riviera, where, on one memorable day, he'd lunched with Victor Rothschild and the novelist Somerset Maugham in Monte Carlo, before moving on for a quiet sojourn at Princess Ottoboni's villa in Roquebrune. (While an ardent fascist, she maintained a residence in France to avoid the Italian income tax.) Though the Mediterranean air had been a tonic for the neuritis in his right leg, his thoughts were back in China.

No place could match Shanghai. Since his return, the pace of life had been frenetic. *Eve*, the thirty-foot yacht he'd had built in Norway, was winning races on the Whangpoo River. At the Cathay, Freddie Kaufmann had done a fine job of making the Tower Night Club the most exclusive address in town: one night, the *Evening Post and Mercury*'s gossip columnist had caught Sir Victor snapping his fingers to a throaty version of "Frankie and

Johnny" by the Australian songstress Gladys Verney. Shanghai had it all: afternoons at the races, evenings on the river, and nightlife that continued well into the next morning.

As they drove past the Race Course, Sir Victor grimaced at the sight of the new skyscraper that towered over Nanking Road. To his chagrin, a year earlier it had beaten out the Cathay as Shanghai's tallest building by fully seventy-two feet. The Park Hotel was a streamlined Gothic monolith, faced with dark, burned-brick tile. Owned by Chinese bankers, it had been designed by the Hungarian architect Laszlo Hudec. Its thirteenth-floor Sky Terrace, especially popular with the Chinese crowd, was providing real competition to the Cathay Ballroom. Not surprisingly, given its forboding appearance, it was also becoming a favoured resort of visitors from Nazi Germany.

It still annoyed him that Anna May Wong, whose gracile figure and stylish black bangs had made her the first Chinese-American movie star, had chosen to stay at the Park. Her February 1936 visit, Sir Victor knew, had not been easy. In China, where strict on-screen morals prevailed, she was infamous for the immodest display of her shapely legs in such Hollywood films as *Shanghai Express*. Wong, who had been born to Cantonese parents in Los Angeles's Chinatown, had told reporters that her first trip to the country of her ancestors was meant to be a cultural pilgrimage. When she stepped onto the dock in Shanghai wearing a sharp-angled black "tiger hat" of her own design, Chinese newsmen had been disappointed to discover that she spoke not a word of Cantonese nor Mandarin. (Later, she would even be taunted by peasants when she visited her parents' village.) Because she was Chinese, though, she was barred from many of Shanghai's foreign-run enclaves, including the American-run bowling alley in the Columbia Country Club. Happily, a reunion with a long-lost brother – a staged event filmed by the Hearst newspaper chain's H.S. "Newsreel" Wong – had taken place in the lobby of the Cathay.

After his car passed Mohawk Road, Sir Victor told the driver to turn right into a U-shaped driveway. On the lawn, gardeners in blue smocks were cutting the grass around a fountain with hand scythes. Sir Victor admired the elegant lines of the windowless, one-storey Art Deco building. Palmer & Turner, the architects of the Cathay, had built another masterpiece. In the early afternoon sun its white-washed walls looked austere, but at night, as the vertical marquee of glass and metal flickered to life with the word "Ciro's," those same walls, shimmering with brilliant lighting effects, would be an irresistible beacon to Shanghai's night owls.

Inside, it took a moment for Sir Victor's eyes to adjust to the low lights in the vestibule. The walls of black Chinese lacquer, set off by narrow silver streamlines, gave one the sensation of being inside a plush womb. The foyer, decorated with white rexine leather and wainscots in figured walnut from Australia, was equally luxurious. But the *pièce de résistance* was the main ballroom: half a dozen elevated dining areas were surrounded by a gleaming metal railing which the press of a button caused to sink, providing access to the dance floor. The room would seat over 200 – at a cover charge of five Chinese dollars – and every table gave unobstructed views of the stage, where Henry Nathan's orchestra, borrowed for the opening from the Cathay Ballroom, would play against a backdrop of mulberry-hued velvet curtains.

On its opening, Ciro's would become the most elegant, up-to-date nightspot in the city – if not the world.

Sir Victor's decision to open a nightclub of his own came after an incident at the Paramount Ballroom two years earlier. Arriving with guests from out of town, his party had been seated at a table far from the dance floor. Asked for an explanation, the waiter told him that, when he saw the gentleman used walking sticks, he assumed he wouldn't want to dance. When Sir Victor protested, the manager had had the effrontery to suggest he open a club of his own.

Ciro's, a nocturnal refuge in midtown, was his response to the insult. His return from the United States and Europe had been timed to coincide with its opening.

Slipping backstage, Sir Victor rapped on the door marked "Premiere Danseuse" and said hello to a voluptuous – and rather flirtatious, if he wasn't mistaken – brunette with enormous brown eyes. That afternoon's pleasant duty would involve watching Dorothy Wardell, a professional ballroom dancer newly arrived from the States, pose for publicity photos for the club's opening, two nights hence. Her moustachioed partner, Don Dade, bore a passing resemblance to a younger version of himself. ("Think Dorothy Wardell wants to throw Don away," he would write in his journal that night.) After the rehearsal, he would try to entice Don and Dorothy back to the Cathay with the offer of iced cocktails and hot dogs. Americans loved that sort of thing.

As he took a seat by the railing and listened to Henry Nathan's orchestra play while the pair went through the steps of a tango, he was imagining the gay Shanghai nights that were sure to come. The opening of his pleasure palace on Bubbling Well Road on November 5 would represent his immunization against impudence.

Nobody would dare insult Sir Victor Sassoon in the club that he had built.

美

Mickey Hahn was finding it hard to get any work done.

In 1936, Shanghai felt closer to the centre of the world than New York or London ever had. One day, Sir Victor's sister-in-law would ask Mickey to take an Italian nobleman out on the town, and she would find herself chaperoning some vague and elderly *marchese* to shop for Sung-dynasty vases and smoke opium. The next, she would be guiding a newsreel crew from New York to the willow-patterned teahouse and other Shanghai landmarks.

Almost every day, people arrived at the Customs Jetty from the four corners of the world – most of them, it seemed, carrying letters of introduction, and eager to meet the picturesque "Mr. Pan" they'd read so much about in the pages of the *New Yorker*.

In September, she'd been happy to meet Josef von Sternberg, the director of *Shanghai Express*, who came to town on the *Chichibu Maru*, the same ship on which Mickey had crossed the Pacific. Von Sternberg, wrote Mickey, "sent me an enormous pot of flowers and came to lunch, where he met Sinmay and talked about himself for 2 solid hours." Von Sternberg told them that his ship had run into a Chinese junk as it approached Shanghai; instead of circling back, the Japanese captain had steamed on, ignoring the screams of the drowning passengers.

After checking into the Cathay Hotel as "Mr. Sternberg," the Viennese director set out to discover Chinese Shanghai on his own. His most memorable excursion was to the Great World, the amusement centre that rose like a ziggurat on the northern border of Frenchtown. Owned by the gangster "Pock-Marked" Huang – who was also head of the French Concession's force of Chinese detectives – the city-block-sized complex, which included ten multi-function theatres, an open-air central stage for acrobats, and even a skating rink, attracted up to 25,000 customers a day. In the evening, thieves, gamblers, and prostitutes moved through crowds drawn by the most exotic of attractions. (One French visitor recalled seeing "a manager complacently pointing to his premier sideshow attraction – a pregnant girl of six!")

Even von Sternberg, inured to the decadent cabarets of Weimar Berlin, was impressed. "On the first floor," he wrote of his visit to the Great World,

were gambling tables, singsong girls, magicians, pickpockets, slot machines, fireworks, bird cages, fans, stick incense, acrobats, and ginger. One flight up were the restaurants, a dozen different groups of actors, crickets in cages, pimps, midwives, barbers and earwax extractors. The third floor had jugglers, herb medicines, ice-cream parlors, photographers, a new bevy of girls, their high-collared gowns slit to reveal their hips, in case one had passed up the more modest ones below who merely flashed their thighs.

Up and up von Sternberg went, passing fan-fan tables, massage benches, vendors selling dried intestines – even a full-size stuffed whale – until he reached the fifth floor, where tightrope walkers slithered back and forth, and the girls' dresses were slit to the armpits. On the top floor, "an open space was pointed out to me where hundreds of Chinese, after spending their coppers, had speeded the return to the street below by jumping from the roof."

Asked why there was no protective railing, von Sternberg's guide retorted, "How can you stop a man from killing himself?"

Sinmay was grateful for an introduction to another out-of-towner, the Welsh-born novelist Eric Linklater. Raised in the Orkney Islands, Linklater, who was wounded while serving with the Black Watch in the First World War, went on to become an editor at the *Times of India* in Bombay before moving to the United States as a Commonwealth fellow at Cornell and Berkeley. His experiences in Prohibition-era America became the basis for the character Juan Motley, who claims lineal descent from Lord Byron's Don Juan. Possessed by an afflatus that sends him into flights of poetic fancy – usually at the most inopportune of moments – the modern-day Don Juan has adventures in nudist colonies and speakeasies. *Juan in America* became an international bestseller. It was exactly the kind of middle-brow comic novel that appealed to the well-heeled, well-travelled readers who stayed at the Cathay Hotel.

Linklater came to China in the spring of 1936 in hopes of finding subject matter for a sequel. That he and Sinmay hit it off wasn't surprising: both were cosmopolitans familiar with the East and the West, and they shared a puckish sense of humour.

"Sinmay is somewhat steamed up about his literary career," Mickey reported to her family, "because Eric Linklater fell hard for him, I mean in a nice way, and while I was away they saw each other all the time and talked about publishing in England, and Linklater gave Sinmay a watch so he would be on time, but it broke."

Looking for respite from Shanghai's social swirl, Mickey made a few tentative excursions beyond the International Settlement. In February, she'd taken a four-day trip down the coast to Hong Kong, where she met David Sassoon, the uncle Sir Victor called Nunky. The seventy-three-year-old rake, who had been a jockey as a young man, took Mickey to the racetrack, where she was introduced as "the Girl Friend" of Sir Victor. Thanks to the "sweet old man," the trip "was a merry one, full of champagne, and gaiety." (It helped that the Sassoon horses won the Derby that year.)

In June, Mickey talked Sinmay into going north with her to Peiping. It would turn out to be her only trip to the ancient northern capital. Sinmay spent much of his time with students at Tsing Hua University, where professors, wrote Mickey, "simply called off classes when word got round that Sinmay had come." They stayed with Bernardine's friend Harold Acton, who had already met Mickey in Shanghai. Mickey was surprised to learn that Acton, lost in his translations of Tang-dynasty poetry, shrugged off reports of Japanese advances in none-too-distant Manchuria.

Mickey, who found Peiping pretty but dull, wrote to Helen that she had an "idea for an article, about how the aesthetes always take over the pretty towns of the world and act proprietory [sic] about them ever after."

Acton, for his part, wrote to Bernardine: "Mickey is very good company: I wonder if she will come to live in Peking? She rather belongs here." He was even more taken with her poet companion. "I so enjoyed meeting Sinmay at last. What a *charmeur!* and a fine poet in everything."

By that time, Bernardine was gritting her teeth every time somebody praised Mickey. Updating her family on what she'd taken to calling "The Great Bernardine War," Mickey wrote: "Sinmay found some of the letters she used to write him before I arrived, and they're love-letters, so I understand better what was ailing her."

The novelist Vicki Baum was next to fall for Sinmay's charms. Though born into a cultured, status-conscious family in *fin-de-siècle* Vienna, she'd made a name for herself as one of Germany's "New Women." Curious, physically vigorous, and emotionally independent, she worked as a journalist in Berlin, and was taught how to box – in the same gym where Marlene Dietrich trained – by a Turkish prize-fighter. After the English translation of her tenth novel, based on her work as a chambermaid at the Hotel Bristol, became an international bestseller, she sailed for New York in 1931 to attend the Broadway premiere of *Grand Hotel*.

It turned out to be a propitious time to leave Germany: Vicki was Jewish. The novel became the basis for the Hollywood film in which a negligee-wrapped Greta Garbo, playing an overworked Russian ballerina on the verge of suicide, delivers the lines: "I want to be alone. I just want to be alone." It also launched an enduring literary subgenre, later mined by Arthur Hailey and Neil Simon, in which a grand metropolitan hotel – with its anonymous comings and goings, glamorous public areas and workaday backstage – becomes a setting for romance and intrigue. As one of the long-term residents in *Grand Hotel* ironically laments, "People come and go; nothing ever happens."

In Vicki's book, of course, much happened: behind closed doors, ruined barons pilfered jewels, dying accountants fought a lifetime of regret with a final fling in luxury, ambitious stenographers seduced lonely industrialists. The author of *Grand Hotel* was no literary innovator – Vicki, in her own words, was "a first-rate second-rate writer" – but her books were highly entertaining, and marked by narrative sophistication, dramatic flair, and real flashes of cultural insight.

Vicki had come to Shanghai for the first time in 1935, on a round-the-world cruise. Introduced at one of Bernardine's literary dinners, she and Mickey forged a friendship that would last decades. When, on her return a year later, she checked into a suite at the Cathay Hotel, she insisted on meeting the famous "Mr. Pan."

"Vicki Baum came back (they all come back)," Mickey wrote in a letter home.

I gave her a Szechuen tiffin that burned her guts out. She thanked me heartily and will probably write a book about Sinmay . . . I liked her much better, naturally, as the minute she got here she phoned me wildly and broke two (2) dates with Bernardine to see me.

Vicki, who was also an expert at turning life into art, paid close attention to Sinmay's mannerisms and speech patterns.

"Why don't you do a *Grand Hotel* of Shanghai?" Vicki was asked by a *China Press* reporter who cornered her in the Cathay. Too many books, she replied, had already been written about

Shanghai. "I'm not going to write the great Chinese novel. I'll leave China to Pearl Buck. Why, I'd have to live here twenty years before I'd tackle a book about China." She was being disingenuous. As her trip continued – she would move on to Bali, an experience that would result in another bestseller – an idea for an ambitious novel, set in Shanghai, was already germinating in her head.

When *Hotel Shanghai* was published, two years later, the action would centre on a grand hotel – located on Nanking Road and overlooking the Whangpoo River – that matched the Cathay in all but a few details. It would also prominently feature a Chinese poet who, like Zau Sinmay, was educated in Britain, lived in Yangtzepoo, spoke in charming epigrams, and dressed in shabby robes despite his wealth.

As 1936 wore on, Mickey had begun to dodge visitors, even those who arrived with letters of introduction. "I just can't do what I did last year – parties all the time, and dancing every night. It gets incredibly dull after a year. I'm studying hard, writing hard." In August, she confided to her sister Helen:

Sinmay (and myself for that matter) are on the wagon. I mean opium. You know me; I never get habits, but he has been so worried about money and me that he was slipping and I kept step deliberately, so really this is much better for all of us, and the general outlook is brighter too.

Their abstinence from the opium pipe that summer would be short-lived. As with most things involving Sinmay, the situation was more complicated than she made it sound.

美

"You have made me out to be something like an idiot," Sinmay complained to Mickey after reading yet another of her stories about his alter ego, Pan Heh-ven, in the *New Yorker*.

"I'm sorry, darling," replied Mickey, and changed the subject.

It was true, Mickey knew, that she was engaged in appropriation of the most blatant kind. Through her pen portraits of Mr. Pan, not only was she trafficking in cultural stereotyping for the amusement of the magazine's sophisticated readership; she was also turning a real person – a friend and lover, to boot – into a caricature.

Turning life into narrative was a habit she'd developed in childhood, when she'd competed for her parents' attention with four talented, articulate sisters in the family parlour in St. Louis. What distinguished Mickey from her sisters – and many other writers – was that her exhibitionism was tempered by her skills as an observer. She knew when to stop holding forth, bite her tongue, and start taking mental notes. If the material was good, as it so often was with Sinmay, any remark she'd refrained from making at the time could be amply developed on the written page. Mickey had learned the rewards of delayed gratification. In print, she could say what she'd really been thinking at the time – far more effectively, and to a much bigger audience.

Mickey made no apologies. As a teenager, she might have agonized in writing about how her desire to amuse those around her ended up isolating her; but since then she'd accepted it as a genuine talent, one that had brought her a lucrative career. "I use people," she would write later:

I use myself, which means that I use everything I find in my brain – experiences, impressions, memories, reading matter by other writers – everything, including the people who surround me and impinge on my awareness. Sometimes I am asked, "Do you think it's nice of you?" and I reply honestly, "I don't know. It isn't a question in my mind of being nice or not nice. I can't help it any more than I can help breathing."

If you had any kind of relationship with Mickey – or any writer, for that matter – you naturally ran the risk of being written about. "People who mind should stay away from writers. I think they do, on the whole."

Sinmay, for his part, had a right to be prickly. When Mickey turned him into a caricature, he felt she was denying a love that was still very much alive. By the summer of 1936, though, their relationship was on rocky ground. Not content with being the on-again, off-again concubine of a Chinese poet, Mickey had started going out with other men. Shanghai offered many exotic specimens to sample.

At the Cathay Ballroom she was seen on the arm of Prince Spada Potenziani, an austerely handsome statesman who objected to his nation's invasion of Abyssinia and seemed to hate the fascist turn his Italy had taken.

"He worried so much," she wrote to Helen, "that he had a nervous breakdown and came out here to get well. He never speaks of Mussolini." Though he was then in his fifties, the Prince could be charmingly naive. Noticing her mood had suddenly changed, and that she looked tired, he implored her to tell him what was wrong. As she wrote to Helen, she merely had menstrual cramps. "I could have said, 'My dear sir, you may have been Governor of Rome, but you don't know so much about Life and Nature.'"

Next she became enamoured with an earnest British naval officer named Robert, who sent her long letters describing the mechanics of river navigation as his gunboat patrolled the Yangtze River. Things were going well until, at a dinner for Robert's fellow Royal Navy officers in Nanking, Mickey saucily raised a toast to Wallis Simpson, the American divorcée for whom King Edward VIII had abdicated the throne. The shocked silence that ensued was the death knell of another affair.

As for her relationship with Sir Victor, mutual fascination had subsided into a friendship that, though punctuated with occasional exasperation, was based on respect and affection. The fact that she fraternized with Sinmay, though, continued to annoy him. (When the subject of her private life came up, she wrote to Helen, "He makes remarks about Esquimeaux and Negroes, etc.") After knowing him for over a year, she had concluded, "there is no dreadful secret about Victor," apart, of course, from the fact, widely known, that he still held a torch for his first love. "The Girl," she wrote, "lives in London, somebody he has always thought of marrying some day but probably never will."

As for Sinmay, he was, Mickey had long since realized, volatile, maddeningly so, by nature; it was a quality she emphasized, to humorous effect, in her *New Yorker* stories. Though he was flattered to be transformed into an exemplar of the modern Shanghai cosmopolitan by the likes of Mickey and Vicki Baum, Sinmay was right to protest against his reduction to quirk-ridden caricature.

The life that he lived was far more complex than could be conveyed in a 500-word vignette – or even a book-length collection of them. He was responsible not only for himself, but for an extended family; a household full of servants and hangers-on depended on him. Moreover, he had enemies, both literary and ideological, and they were gathering strength.

By the time Mickey Hahn met him, Zau Sinmay was no longer a poster boy for the gilded youth of Shanghai. While the Shanghainese bourgeoisie, then reaching its apex of wealth and influence, continued to look to the West, the literary world had turned away from the vogue for European decadence that coincided with Sinmay's poetic debut. In 1936, Sinmay self-published a slender volume titled *Twenty-five Poems.* Though critics – and subsequently, scholars – would acknowledge it contained his most sophisticated verse, they also dismissed his aestheticism and obsession with images of beauty and evil as outdated. The anti-foreign student uprisings that followed the League of Nations' handover of Chinese territory to Japan in 1919 launched a literary renaissance that established *pai-hua,* based on popular speech (as opposed to the complex classical Chinese of the Qing dynasty), as the new written vernacular. Sinmay's elevated prose seemed ill-suited to a time when artists were grappling with the existential crisis that confronted China. *Twenty-five Poems* was reviewed as a self-indulgent anachronism. It was as if Edgar Allen Poe had brought out another volume of verse in the age of William Carlos Williams, Hart Crane, and Langston Hughes.

Sinmay's most influential adversary, and a living symbol of how the times were changing, was the prolific novelist, literary critic, and essayist Lu Xun. Though almost twenty years his senior, Lu Xun had much in common with Sinmay. Both men were the issue of wealthy landowning families whose fortunes had started to decline with the fall of the Qing dynasty in 1911. Lu Xun's father, like Sinmay's, unsuccessfully grappled with opium addiction. Both were educated abroad (in Lu Xun's case, in Japan). Both, because they rejected the Western attire of the Shanghainese comprador class, experienced discrimination at the hands of foreigners in their own country.

"Once and only once Sinmay called for me in the *North-China* office," wrote Mickey about her time working for the daily newspaper. "His pale face and long gown caused such excitement among the mild British reporters that he became self-conscious and after that made me meet him out on the Bund."

Lu Xun had a similar experience a few doors north, when he visited a British friend at the Cathay Hotel. When Lu Xun entered the lobby elevator, dressed in a blue cotton gown and rubber-soled shoes, the operator ignored him. After waiting a few minutes, he decided to walk up seven storeys. When his foreign friend walked with him from his room to the elevator two hours later, the operator sheepishly brought him back to the lobby.

Unlike Sinmay, Lu Xun used such incidents to diagnose the ills besetting contemporary China. In the fevered mind of the subject of *Diary of a Madman*, the Confucian injunction towards filial piety becomes an exhortation to cannibalism; in *The True Story of Ah Q,* a deluded peasant bullies those weaker than him, and rationalizes his most abysmal failures as glowing successes.

While Lu Xun professed to be amused by the incident in the Cathay elevator, he would later write,

To live in Shanghai, it is better to be fashionably attired than to wear rude clothing. If you dress in old clothes, the trolleybus driver will not stop where you ask him to . . . the doorman of a large mansion or apartment will not allow you to enter the building through the front door. That is why some people can tolerate living in a small room and literally feeding their bodies to bedbugs.

Lu Xun had spent many nights in just such small, insect-ridden rooms. The *tingzijian* of Shanghai's alleyway houses – those little pavilion rooms, above the kitchen, rented out to students and scholars – had provided shelter not only for him, but also for such masters of modernist prose as Ba Jin, Yu Dafu, and Mao Dun, whose 1933 novel *Midnight* was an excoriating critique of Shanghai's consumerism. Sinmay's family, meanwhile, belonged to the landlord class that had until recently owned entire *shikumen* complexes.

Lu Xun never considered himself a communist. In 1930, he had dabbled with politics, and gave the opening address to Shanghai's League of Left-Wing Writers. Dedicated to social realism, the League's nemesis was the Crescent Moon Society, which had been founded by the well-respected Xu Zhimo, the Cambridge-educated poet Sinmay had befriended in Paris. When Xu, whose emotional verse tracked his own well-publicized affair with a wealthy socialite, died in a plane crash in 1931, Sinmay lost an influential champion. But just as Sinmay never formally became a member of the Crescent Moon Society, Lu Xun left the League of Left-Wing Writers when it became apparent he wouldn't have a voice in shaping their policies. His exit was fortuitous: in an anti-communist purge, the nationalists rounded up and executed Shanghai's leading leftist authors, five of whom belonged to the League.

Lu Xun considered Sinmay the ultimate playboy. Though the sociable Sinmay had once given him a ride in the back of his limousine, Lu Xun refused to contribute to any of Sinmay's publications and accused him of using his wife's dowry as literary capital, portraying him in one essay as "the pampered son-in-law who, belittled by the family, enters the literary world with a great reputation . . . studying portraits of Oscar Wilde, with his buttonhole, his ivory-topped cane." He also suggested that Sinmay paid ghostwriters to compose his essays. At the time, Sinmay shrugged off the attacks. When Lu Xun died of tuberculosis in 1936, his funeral was attended by 10,000 mourners, and after his death, his renown grew – particularly within the Chinese Communist Party, whose members increasingly used his life and work as an austere rebuke to the art-for-art's-sake school of Zau Sinmay and his peers.

To Mickey, Sinmay confessed that he was about to give up on

his ambition to make a career as a poet. Piles of the self-published books that had launched his career gathered dust on the shelves of his bookshop on Soochow Road. In her fictionalized account of their affair, she interrogates him in a dirty bedroom in a Chinese hotel near the Race Course.

"Who are you, anyway?" Mickey's character asks. "Are you the Chinese Cocteau, for instance?"

"No, I will not say that. I am not a poet any more, and even when I was a poet, I was something like Swinburne, but not Cocteau."

"Well, who are you now?" she wonders.

"The Chinese Northcliffe," he replies, a reference to the British founder of the *Daily Mirror*. "I publish magazines and papers. Popular ones. You are disappointed?"

It was an accurate assessment of his new status. Sinmay's Modern Press and Epoch Book Company continued to publish an astonishing variety of magazines and journals. The skill – and cheap labour – of Shanghai's typographers and printers made such an enterprise possible, though rarely profitable. Sinmay was known as one of the first Chinese publishers to pay close attention to the design of magazines and books. He laboured over not only the quality of paper and the bindings, but also the layout of text on each printed page. Unfortunately, his volatile nature and lack of focus doomed most of his enterprises from the start. Only the *Analects*, the satirical newspaper edited by his friend Lin Yu-tang, would prove to be an enduring success.

Inspired by the realization that – as English magazines read from front to back, and Chinese from back to front – a dual-language issue would meet, poetically, in the middle, late in 1935 Sinmay launched *Vox*, with Mickey as co-editor. It lasted for just three issues. ("There was something in the idea that was fallacious to begin with," Mickey later acknowledged. "Just because Shanghai was a bilingual city, that didn't mean that people wanted to read their magazines in two languages, did it?") Their subsequent collaboration proved more successful, and durable. They would publish two separate magazines, drawing on the same artwork and some of the same articles, duly translated. The Chinese edition was to be called *Ziyou tan*, or Free Speech. The English, edited by Mickey, would go by the name *Candid Comment*. Editing – and largely writing – the twin magazines would further politicize these avowed aesthetes, bringing them into contact with Japanese spies, Kuomintang assassins, and communist guerrillas.

For, having been in China for nearly two years, Mickey Hahn found it impossible to remain aloof from local politics. Shanghai had a knack for drawing people in. Her letters home were no longer filled with accounts of parties, but reports of troubling events in the provinces.

"Everything seems wrong today," she wrote to her mother a few days before Christmas, 1936. A dockers' strike was holding up the mail, which, thanks to a new service by the China Clippers – Pan Am's flying boats, which hopscotched across the Pacific with splashdowns in Guam and Wake – had started to take days, rather than weeks, to cross the ocean. "We are all worried, not about war which could not be down here anyway, but about the whole apple cart."

At issue was the sudden disappearance of the leader of China, the Generalissimo Chiang Kai-shek. Rumours abounded in Shanghai; his brother-in-law, the Harvard-trained Minister of Finance T.V. Soong, had flown across the country and returned with news of his kidnapping by a warlord. "We are almost certain that Chiang is still alive," Mickey wrote,

but the delay is ugly, especially since T.V. Soong flew up to Sian yesterday, while everyone held his breath, and then flew back again with a lot of promises sent by that half-witted imbecile bandit. It is like watching a man in a cage with a gorilla who happens to be in a good temper for the moment, but at any time . . .

It was the first time that Mickey had really grasped a reality familiar to long-term residents of Shanghai: the ease of life, the beguiling cosmopolitanism of that city dedicated to security, was in fact the most fragile of constructs. The security was symbolized by the British and American gunboats in the Whangpoo River, whose presence was approved by the nationalists, as well as the gangster elite of Shanghai. If it all came tumbling down, Mickey suddenly saw, the residents of the International Settlement and Frenchtown would wake up to discover they were a long way from home, and living on a very hostile shore.

14: The Rise of the Dwarf Bandits

As 1936 drew to a close, Mickey Hahn was starting to suspect the people she'd met in Japan had pulled the wool over her eyes.

When she thought of Japan, images from her three-week stopover in Tokyo leaped to mind: snow-topped Mount Fuji, dainty figures in kimonos, and tea sipped from the finest porcelain. At the tourist agencies, earnest young men had been eager to share with them the best of Japanese music, drama, and art. None of this seemed to jibe with the reports of Japanese belligerence that filled the newspapers. From their base in the puppet kingdom of Manchukuo, the Imperial Army was seizing railway stations in the north. There were rumours they would soon march on Peiping.

Now she couldn't ignore the facts. The Japan they'd been exposed to had been a shimmering mirage; there was a "stricter pattern behind the delicate landscape." Real power in Tokyo was held by a militarist clique that had imperial designs on China.

"The Japs put one over on us," she would later write, "and we scarcely noticed."

Shanghailanders, a tough-talking lot, denied there was a real threat. Sir Victor and the other taipans who'd lived through the Japanese invasion in 1932 seemed to have an unshakable belief in the Settlement's inviolability. Sinmay and his Shanghainese friends, in contrast, seemed genuinely worried.

Mickey wrote home: "A lot of the Chinese think it's bad form to go out dancing or dining with things so delicate in Japan." That was understandable, but Sir Victor's new nightclub had just opened, and the town was jumping. She wasn't the kind to let nervous chatter stop her from living her life; if she were, she never would have left St. Louis. "I think the more scared you are, the better it is to go out dancing."

While Shanghai drank gin slings and danced through the night at Ciro's, though, covetous eyes were trained on the shining jewel of the China coast.

美

Japan and China had dramatically different responses to contact with the outside world. While Qing-dynasty China reacted to the prodding of the West by retracting like a sea cucumber, Japan swelled up like a distressed pufferfish.

When European traders and missionaries started arriving off the coast of Japan in the 1540s, however, the initial impulse of the shoguns – the military government that ruled the country – was similar to that of China's Celestial Court. The newcomers, who the Chinese called "foreign barbarians" and the Japanese *gaijin* or "outside people," had to be contained and closely observed.

While China's pre-modern history spanned three dozen separate dynasties, since AD 660, Japan had been ruled by the same family – the Yamato clan, considered direct descendants of the sun-goddess Amaterasu – with sovereign authority vested in the Mikado, or Emperor. By the seventeenth century, actual power was in the hands of the lords and samurai of the Tokugawa family, whose reaction to the growing influence of Spanish and Portuguese Jesuits and British traders had been the official policy of *sakoku*. Japan became a "locked country": for over two centuries, no foreigner was allowed to enter and no Japanese person was allowed to leave, under penalty of death. (To drive home their point, Japanese officials actually crucified Franciscan and Jesuit missionaries in Nagasaki.) The only zone excluded was the fan-shaped artificial island of Dejima in the bay of Nagasaki, where a tiny Dutch community was allowed to trade. As on Canton's Shameen island, and the peninsula of Macao, the foreign traders were segregated from the local population by closely guarded walls. Cannily, the Japanese used controlled exchanges with Dejima as a way to gradually absorb the fundamentals of Western technology, science, philosophy, and medicine – which they called "Dutch learning" – while keeping the foreign contagion at bay.

All this changed in 1853, when four men-of-war, led by the paddle frigate *Mississippi*, steamed into Tokyo's harbour. In China, it had been the British that came pounding on the door; in the case of Japan, it was the Americans, whose recent triumph in the Mexican–American war had emboldened them to seek out new business opportunities. Commodore Matthew Perry, a hard-nosed Yankee in search of coal for his ships and new sources of provisions for New England's whaling vessels, bore a presidential letter that began, ominously, "You know that the United States of America now extend from sea to sea . . ." The arrival of the Black Ships – so-called because of the coal-smoke they spewed from their funnels – caused panic among the coastal population. Japan was forced to sign its own version of China's Unequal Treaties which had allowed the British, Americans, and French highly favourable conditions for trade and extraterritorial rights for their citizens in her major ports.

The quick capitulation to the newly insistent *gaijin* provoked a rebellion against the hapless Tokugawa shogunate. In 1868, two clans united to overthrow the Tokugawa family, bringing the teen-age Emperor Meiji to the throne. It was an about-face in Japan's approach to the outside world – one that would rapidly transform it into a leading global power.

In the course of a decade, power shifted from a small class of landowning feudal lords to the samurai, formerly the salaried employees of the lords, who, by the late nineteenth century, con-stituted a landless military nobility nearly two million strong. Japan sent envoys to Europe and North America in search of new ideas and technologies. Over 300 European experts were brought in to perform a total overhaul of society's institutions. The educa-tion system was patterned on the French network of school districts; the navy was based on the British model; universities were organized on American lines; and the army followed the hierarchy of the *Deutsches Heer* of the newly unified Germany. The gov-ernment sold off newly built factories to the former samurai, launching a capitalist class steeped in *bushido* – "the way of the warrior," a neo-Confucian ethos that encompassed everything from frugality to mastery of martial arts to the proper way to commit *seppuku*, or ritual suicide.

At the same time, breakneck industrialization, spearheaded by such conglomerates as Mitsui and Mitsubishi, transformed Japan from a backwater into a major player on the world stage in just a generation. In a test of its newfound power, Japan in 1894 invaded Korea, formerly one of China's most faithful vassal states. After installing a regent in the Korean palace, Japan landed troops on the Chinese mainland; they proceeded to seize forts north of Shanghai and use the Qing military's own guns to blast the battle-ships and cruisers of China's northern fleet out of the waters of the Yalu River. The humiliating terms of a treaty signed the following year ceded the island of Formosa (later Taiwan) to Japan "in per-petuity" and gave the Japanese the right to trade on mainland China. Japan joined the club of industrialized nations that enjoyed extraterritorial rights in Shanghai. The new samurai-executive class, who had profited by paying puny wages to workers in their own country, now competed with the Sassoons and other British mill owners by flooding the world market with textiles and con-sumer goods manufactured by cheap Chinese labour in the factories of Shanghai.

Japan's next move shocked the world. When Russia completed a railway that allowed goods and soldiers to be transported from Moscow to Manchuria, Japan – with the financial support of Britain, who saw Russia as an emerging rival in Asia – challenged Nicholas II's aspirations in the Far East. The Czar's mighty Baltic fleet was ignominiously sunk in the narrow waters of Tsushima Strait, and the Chinese Eastern Railway, which linked Moscow to the Sea of Japan, fell into Tokyo's hands. In Russia, discontent over the defeat eventually boiled over into the Revolution that toppled the Czar and brought the Bolsheviks to power. After becoming the first non-Western nation to industrialize in the nine-teenth century, Japan had become the first Asian power to trounce a modern European nation.

The Japanese victory over Russia was the twentieth century's first intimation of a new world order. The 1905 battle of Tsushima Strait signalled that white men, until then the *de facto* rulers of the globe, were no longer invincible.

"When everyone in Japan, rich or poor, came to believe in self-respect," wrote a young Mohandas Gandhi, who was then living in South Africa, "the country became free. She could give Russia a slap in the face."

China's elite began to look to Japan as a non-Western model of modernization. Writers such as Lu Xun, Zau Sinmay's nemesis, and politicians such as Sun Yat-sen and Chiang Kai-shek opted to pursue their education in Tokyo. For the Chinese, it was an abrupt turning of the tables. The Japanese had long been considered an inferior race, both physically and culturally. Until its first contact with China in the fifth century AD, Japan lacked a writing system of its own, and its main belief systems – Taoism, Buddhism, and Confucianism – were imports by way of the Korean peninsula from the Middle Kingdom.

If Japan rose to power on its own terms while China underwent decline and subjugation, it was largely thanks to the way each country negotiated contact with the outside world. Japan, as a military Confucian nation that valued martial skill, was willing to subsidize a new class of industrialists who hastened modernization. China, a civilian Confucian state where access to power was achieved by writing poetry and passing exams, chose to squelch enterprise in its emerging middle class.

While Japan perceived Russia, Britain, and the United States as her long-term opponents, she was happy to use China as a convenient punching bag. During the First World War, as European powers were bogged down in trenches, Japan took possession of the German concession areas around the port of Tsingtao. In 1915 Tokyo issued its notoriously punitive "Twenty-one Demands," which, if agreed to, would have made China into another Japanese colony. The document, printed on paper watermarked with battleships and machine guns, provoked international outrage and massive protests in China. The Japanese, realizing they had moved too far, too fast, temporarily scaled back their ambitions.

By 1931, the year Sir Victor Sassoon made Shanghai his base, Japan had gained enough military strength to attempt an actual invasion. An explosion on the tracks of the South Manchuria Railway – the same tracks Japan seized from Imperial Russia – was blamed on Chinese dissidents. Though the blast had actually been set by a Japanese army lieutenant, and was reportedly so weak a train was able to pass over the same tracks minutes later, Japan used the "Manchurian Incident" as a pretext for the occupation of north-east China. Within six months, the homeland of the erstwhile rulers of Qing China had become the Japanese colony of Manchukuo, providing soy, corn, and sorghum for an expanding, resource-hungry empire.

By the time Mickey Hahn arrived in Shanghai in 1935, China had lost over half a million square miles of territory and thirty-two million of its own citizens to Japan. By the summer of 1936, wrote the Shanghai-based American correspondent Hallett Abend, all the "forces had already gathered that would propel Japan into attacking this country, and into attempting her push southward with the domination of Asia as her ultimate goal." But the United States was in an isolationist mood, and Abend found his articles about the atrocities in north China relegated to the back pages of the *New York Times*.

For a world struggling with the consequences of global depression and the rise of fascism in Europe, the machinations of the Japanese in China could be of but minor concern. Even Shanghailanders, confident of protection by the nationalists and Western gunboats, tended to minimize what was going on just 600 miles to the north.

"I don't think at that time I had given any thought to the Manchurian Incident," wrote Mickey Hahn, recalling her attitude after arriving in Shanghai, "because I'm pretty sure I had never heard of it."

Since then, Sir Victor Sassoon had told her plenty about the Japanese navy's abortive incursion in Shanghai in the first months of 1932, when the Cathay Hotel had been shaken on its concrete raft by the force of explosions on the Whangpoo. And she couldn't help but notice the ever-increasing number of Japanese civilians in the city. By the time she arrived, there were 30,000 – twice the combined British, American, and French population of Shanghai. As Japanese numbers grew, so did their demands. They were agitating for additional seats on the Municipal Council and insisting that the streets of Hongkew be patrolled by a Tokyo-trained police force.

When Mickey first arrived in China, she looked upon the Japanese presence as a sign of an appealing cosmopolitanism, and part of what made Shanghai an interesting place to live. It was becoming clear, though, that Japan's imperial ambitions included turning China into a colony. Some believed that they wanted to rule all of Asia. For the time being, the International Settlement's security depended on the existence of a functioning, if notoriously corrupt, military government in Nanking.

Which explains why Mickey was so shocked on the morning of December 12, 1936, when she learned that Chiang Kai-shek, the nationalist leader of China – and the only man with the authority to keep the Japanese in Shanghai in check – had gone missing.

Mickey Hahn, and anybody else who arrived in Shanghai in the mid-thirties, could be forgiven for believing that China was a country like any other on the planet.

After all, it had a national government, run by the Kuomintang Party, and a new capital, Nanking, criss-crossed by broad boulevards and filled with such impressive monuments as Sun Yat-sen's mountaintop mausoleum. It had an army – in terms of sheer numbers, one of the largest in the world – and a navy, whose gunboats proudly flew the flag of the Republic of China, a white sun on a background of blue sky. It even had a national philosophy, the New Life Movement, which promoted cleanliness, chastity, and honesty while discouraging such vices as gambling, opium smoking, and bribe taking.

It also had a leader. A framed portrait of Chiang Kai-shek, depicted with his hands in white gloves resting on a sword hilt, hung in every government office and railway station in China. The Generalissimo, as he was known, was officially the chairman of the National Military Council of the Republic of China.

Like so much else in modern China, the nationalists were a product of the shock of an ancient civilization's contact with the outside world. The party's founder, Sun Yat-sen, was born in a mountain village in rural Canton. His father was a participant in the Taiping Rebellion, the mutant Christian uprising against the Qing dynasty that rampaged through south China in the mid-nineteenth century. After graduating from medical school in Honolulu, Sun, disgusted by the ease with which Japan had trounced the Manchu military, founded the Revive China Society. When an uprising against Qing rule in Canton failed in 1895, Sun was declared an outlaw and went into a long period of exile. He roamed Europe, western Canada, and the United States – often with knife-wielding Manchu assassins in pursuit – trying to raise the funds, and forces, for a republican revolution.

Sun was passing through St. Louis – Mickey Hahn was six years old at the time – when, to his surprise, he read a headline announcing he'd been named the first president of the new Republic of China. The fall of the Qing dynasty was precipitated by the accidental explosion of a homemade bomb in the basement of a revolutionary group's meeting hall in Hankow, a city 500 miles upstream from Shanghai. District troops threw in with the rebels and successfully fought off Qing troops dispatched from Peking. The army, increasingly sympathetic to Sun's cause, mutinied and fifteen provinces in south and central China declared their independence. In Shanghai, half a million discarded pigtails, the "slave braids" that symbolized submission to the Manchus, littered the asphalt. On Christmas Eve 1911 Sun steamed triumphantly into Shanghai, the first time he'd been back to China in sixteen years of wandering.

Hopes for the new republic were quickly squashed. Sun's presidency lasted for only the first six and a half weeks of 1912.

Power passed to the hands of a portly, Peking-based general named Yuan Shi-kai, who caused chaos by announcing the foundation of a new Empire of China – with himself as Emperor. In the dozen years that followed, which came be known as the Warlord Era, the country fragmented into competing fiefdoms controlled by military strongmen. China had become an early prototype for the failed state.

The nationalists' shaky claim to power forced them to seek unlikely allies. In 1917, Sun was back in his native Canton. A traditional centre of resistance to the power of distant Peking, Canton was a breeding ground for such secret societies as the Triads. Originally founded by sailors on ocean-going junks and ships on inland waterways, the Triads found common cause with the nationalists for their opposition to the Manchus, who were seen as being too pliant to foreign occupation. Triad lodges sympathetic to the Kuomintang sprung up throughout the Cantonese diaspora – including the Canadian prairies, which was how Morris Abraham Cohen, one of the most colourful characters ever to warm a Shanghai barstool, ended up a general in Sun Yat-sen's employ.

Known up and down the Chinese coast as Ma Kun – Cantonese for "clenched fist," and as close as many Chinese could get to pronouncing his name – Morris Cohen definitely got around. Sir Victor Sassoon first met him on board a ship from Hong Kong, where he was working as a bodyguard for Sun Yat-sen's son, Sun Fo, who was then the mayor of Canton. Mickey Hahn met him at the Astor House Hotel, where he was a long-time resident.

"If General Two-Gun Cohen had never lived," a reporter for the *New York Times* marvelled after getting the full version of his life story, "Bernard Shaw might very easily have invented him."

Cohen, born to a Jewish wheelwright in a *shtetl* in Poland, escaped anti-Semitic pogroms when the family emigrated to the heart of London. Raised in the East End in the 1890s, "Fat Moisha," as he became known to the local bobbies, had a childhood out of a Charles Dickens story. Running free in the same streets where Jack the Ripper stalked his first victims – and Sir Arthur Conan Doyle had Sherlock Holmes slumming in dockside opium dens – he put his significant heft to use earning a few shillings boxing under the name "Cockney Cohen." He became a Yiddish-speaking Artful Dodger, working as a shill for a Petticoat Lane character known as "Harry the Gonof" and extracting wallets and watches from waistcoats in Whitechapel. Hauled before a magistrate, he was thrown into a reform school for Jewish boys, where he used the time to memorize long speeches from Shakespeare's *Richard III*. Upon his release, his father, intent on keeping Cohen out of trouble, shipped him across the Atlantic to tiny Wapella, Saskatchewan, where a cousin owned a small ranch.

Stopping for chop suey one night in a Saskatoon diner, Cohen noticed the elderly Chinese owner was trying to hide a diamond ring from a thug with a suspicious bulge in his coat pocket.

"I closed in till I was too near for him to use his rod," Cohen would later recall, "and socked him on the jaw. I let him get on his feet, gave him a kick in the pants – maybe two kicks – and told him to beat it."

The grateful owner, who turned out to be a supporter of the Kuomintang, initiated Cohen into his Secret Society in a clandestine meeting room above a Calgary grocery store. Convinced of the justice of Sun Yat-sen's cause, Cohen became a defender of the Chinese in Canada, and lobbied to abolish the racist "Head Tax" levied on new immigrants from China. Using the underworld connections he'd developed as a grifter on the prairies, he also arranged for the purchase of 500 Ross rifles from an associate in Chicago – thus launching his career as a "sewing-machine trader," as arms dealers in China were known.

Cohen arrived in Shanghai in 1922, where he was introduced to Sun Yat-sen at his modest home at 29 Rue Molière, in the French Concession. Sun asked him to command his large corps of bodyguards, and Cohen quickly rose through the nationalist ranks, becoming first a colonel, then a brigadier-general, and finally a major-general. (Such ranks, cynics muttered, were handed out like Lunar New Year's presents.) He soon became a legend throughout the Far East. Barrel-chested, his beetle brows accented by the bold-faced caron of an impressive widow's peak, he was a living symbol of the heroic early days of the nationalists. He was notoriously prickly about his dubious military credentials, bristling when people called him a bodyguard rather than "aide-de-camp." He qualified, however, as a genuine *shtarker*, the Yiddish word for strongman, earning the nickname "Two-Gun" through his skill with a pair of Smith & Wessons, which he liked to demonstrate by shooting tossed lightbulbs out of the sky. (His detractors claimed his Smith & Wessons were pre-loaded with No. 2 shot rather than bullets.) Taking up residency in hotels up and down the China coast – the Hongkong Hotel in Kowloon, the Victoria in Canton, the Astor House in Shanghai – he was known for throwing lavish parties and spinning elaborate yarns, delivered in an unlikely Cockney-Canuck brogue.

"My conviction," wrote the *Shanghai Evening Post and Mercury's* Randall Gould, "is that at an early age General Cohen must have kissed some Jewish equivalent of the Blarney Stone."

The newsman John B. Powell of the *China Weekly Review* recalled seeing him at Dr. Sun's French Concession house:

Cohen always sat on a bench in the front hall and carried a large revolver in his hip pocket, which caused the seat of his trousers to sag grotesquely. His title of 'General,' which was later conferred on him by a grateful Canton Government, was the subject of frequent puns in the local English newspapers, but Cohen was a faithful watchdog.

During the long interview with Sun Yat-sen that followed, Powell was surprised to discover the extent of the nationalist leader's bitterness towards Americans, whom he resented for not kicking the Japanese out of Korea when they had the chance.

In spite of his energetic campaigning on American soil, Sun continued, he'd failed to drum up any concrete support from politicians in Washington.

"Worst of all," Powell would later write, "America continued to grant diplomatic recognition to the most reactionary elements in China [the northern warlords] while ignoring Dr. Sun Yat-sen and his Kuomintang associates who were developing a more modern nationalist form of government."

To the distress of Cohen, and many in Shanghai's foreign concessions, the nationalists turned to the Soviet Union for material and political support. From their stronghold in Canton, they used Russian money to set up the Whampoa Military Academy, dedicated to building a military based on the Soviet Red Army. When Sun died of cancer in 1925, leaving Cohen to take on a less exacting job as a bodyguard for his son and his widow Soong Qing-ling (widely known as Madame Sun), the struggle for leadership of the Kuomintang came down to two men.

Sun's natural successor was the dashing Wang Jing-wei – dubbed "Baby-Faced Wang" for his youthful dimples – who had been schooled in Tokyo, Paris, and Moscow. The challenger on the right was the commander of the Whampoa Military Academy, the iron-willed Chiang Kai-shek. During the Northern Expedition, in which nationalist troops – carrying iron kettles, oiled-paper umbrellas, and ancient rifles, and expected to forage for their own food – marched from Canton against the northern warlords, Wang declared the city of Wuhan, 500 miles upriver from Shanghai, the capital of a new left-wing republic. Meanwhile, though, Chiang, collaborating with Shanghai's gangsters, had launched the 1927 purge of the city's communist-led labour movement. Wang's supporters in Wuhan were routed by a warlord suspected of being allied with Chiang, and his Soviet advisers were sent back to Moscow. With Wang's defeat, Chiang became leader of the Republic of China, a role he would play for forty-seven years to come.

Chiang Kai-shek was a strange mix of foreign and Chinese influences, which made him entirely a product of his time. Though born in a tea-producing hamlet one hundred miles south of Shanghai, he was educated at a military academy in Tokyo, where he absorbed the essentials of the samurai ethos. In Shanghai, where he would work as a broker on the Chartered Stock and Produce Exchange, he was introduced – via a millionaire anarchist art dealer known as "Curio Chang" – not only to Sun Yat-sen, but also to the boss of the Green Gang, "Pock-Marked" Huang. Though he traded in neo-Confucian platitudes and professed a nationalism motivated by the West's humiliation of China, Chiang became a devout Christian after his marriage to his Methodist, American-educated wife, Soong Mei-ling, who also happened to be the younger sister of Madame Sun.

Chiang was also a singularly charmless and famously quick-tempered man, with a knack for making enemies and a tendency to hold grudges. With his false teeth, thick Ningpo accent, trademark cloak, and the Sam Browne ammunition belt with which he wrapped his tiny frame, he struck some as a ridiculous figure. The American General Joseph Stilwell, who worked with the nationalist leader in the Second World War, was especially contemptuous of Chiang, whom he called "Peanut."

While he was a determined leader with a notorious cruel streak, Chiang was not an idea man of the calibre of Mao Tse-tung or Sun Yat-sen. Under his rule, reform of old Manchu institutions was modest and superficial. The nationalists were mocked for planting maple trees imported from the United States along roads that led nowhere out of Shanghai. While they established a new calendar with the founding of the Republic in 1912 as Year 1, the people continued to set off firecrackers to mark the Lunar New Year, as they had for centuries. For many, Chiang's Blueshirts – a paramilitary group made up of graduates of the Whampoa Military Academy, and zealous in their repression of communists – bore a troubling resemblance to the German Gestapo.

Journalist Edgar Snow, the biographer of Mao Tse-tung, dismissed the idea that Chiang was an Eastern Hitler or Mussolini. "Chiang Kai-shek wanted absolute power, but he did not really want to change anything," wrote Snow. "In a time of utmost chaos, he was often concerned with form, convention and propriety and inwardly concerned with prevention of change."

A symbol, and symptom, of this innate conservatism was the New Life Movement. Promulgated as an alternative to communist philosophy, it set forth hundreds of rules for daily living. Its tenets, listed in an article by Randall Gould, the American editor of the *Shanghai Evening Post and Mercury*, included:

— *Sit straight, don't throw food on or under the table, don't smoke or drink intoxicants.*

— *Walk to the left, not too slow or too fast for the inconvenience of others, apologize if you collide.*

— *Know at least 1,000 characters, read the newspapers daily, attend instructive meetings frequently.*

— *Control your emotions, eradicate prostitution and don't gamble, don't gossip on idle subjects for more than 15 minutes.*

In Shanghai the New Life Movement had been announced, by means of immense banners in the streets, in the summer of 1934. From the start, the mix of neo-Confucian morality and Boy-Scout-like earnestness was met with derision by the Chinese public.

"I was stopped on the street by a nice policeman because I wore a sleeveless dress," recalled the author Han Suyin. "Rickshaw coolies in the heat of summer, with a temperature of 101 degrees, were enjoined to run fully clothed, or to tie a towel round their shoulders in the pretence that they had a jacket on."

By the end of 1936, after being in China for nearly two years, Mickey Hahn understood that the nationalists – once the democratic hope of the nation – were deeply flawed. Sinmay's brief experience of serving on the national government in Nanking had left him with plenty to say about the true motivations of Kuomintang officials, who he saw as voracious in their quest for personal enrichment. Chiang, in spite of a justified reputation for personal honesty, was known to turn a blind eye to the worst excesses of his subordinates.

Even Morris "Two-Gun" Cohen told Mickey that the nationalists weren't what they used to be. As a bodyguard for Madame Sun, Cohen's duties were light. In Shanghai, he spent much of his time in the lobby of the Cathay Hotel, playing cards, which was where he had been introduced to Eric Linklater. When the British author's novel *Juan in China* was published, a Cohen-like character played a central role. Juan is introduced to Colonel Rocco, a former boxer and gangster now working as an arms dealer in China, in the New Celestial Hotel, an "almost Americanly tall hotel" on the Bund. It answers to the description of the Cathay, where Linklater stayed when he was in Shanghai.

"He came into the lounge," Linklater writes of Rocco, "quick and heavy-shouldered, like a boxer conscious of spectators, and stopped for a moment to look this way and that with the searching gaze of a ham actor in melodrama."

Juan learns that Rocco is mixed up in a deal to sell tanks to a General Wu Tu-fu, in Nanking. Informed that he may be walking into a trap, Rocco lifts his coat to show the butt of a revolver holstered under his arm.

"And nobody ever saw the big blow on my hip?" he adds, scornfully. "I've been in plenty traps, and come out again with the cheese in my pocket."

Linklater's nod to Morris Cohen captured his mannerisms, but also his current state of bibulous inactivity: by 1936, "Two-Gun" was living in the past. Nonetheless, he remained a fixture on the China coast, and Mickey would continue to run into him in the most surprising places.

In a similar way, the Nationalist Party's heroic days were behind it. China needed real hope for the future, not scolding from a party whose idea of societal change amounted to a ban on gossip and bad table manners.

美

The kidnapping of Chiang Kai-shek, which so upset Mickey Hahn and set Shanghai's International Settlement buzzing with rumours, was actually an event that had been a long time coming.

Among the Chinese population, frustration had been growing for years over Chiang's reluctance to fight the Japanese. Mickey noticed that even Zau Sinmay was writing in his Chinese-language newspapers that the time had come to stand and fight. ("Chiang Kai-shek," she wrote home, "made a speech about 'passive resistance up to the limit of peace,' and Sinmay is running an editorial asking Chiang politely what he considers the limit.")

Internationally, the tide was turning against old ideological splits. The rise of Hitler and Mussolini had led the Soviet Union's communists to renounce the militant, ultra-left line of the Comintern's "Third Period," in favour of a Popular Front against fascism.

By 1935, the stakes had been considered high enough that communists were enjoined to seek an alliance with socialists, liberals, and New Dealers – as well as such potentially useful "fellow travellers" as Ernest Hemingway, John Steinbeck, and Richard Wright. In Asia, Japan was singled out as the opponent against which Mao Tse-tung's communists and Chiang Kai-shek's nationalists needed to unite.

Chiang, however, remained obsessed with routing the Reds. While the Japanese pierced the Great Wall to occupy the hinterland of Peiping, Chiang focused on hounding the Red Army on their Long March. In the countryside, the communists were winning the battle for the hearts and minds of the over-taxed peasantry – the class that really mattered in China – by destroying the power of the landlord-pawnbrokers; the nationalists, at the same time, were actually introducing onerous new taxes. By 1936, the communists had scaled back early hardline tactics in favour of winning over rich peasants and shopkeepers with moral suasion. Mao had even signalled that he was willing to abandon the name "Red Army" and place its forces under the supreme command of the government in Nanking in order to defeat the invaders. But Chiang was intractable: before engaging with the Japanese, the communists had to go.

Chiang said as much to Chang Hsueh-liang, a thirty-five-year-old warlord who had dared write him a letter making a case for a united front. The "Young Marshal," as he was known, came by his hatred of the Japanese honestly: they had blown his father, the governor of Manchuria, to pieces, in the belief that Chang, a notorious womanizer and opium addict, would be turned into an easily manipulated puppet. Instead, the Young Marshal sought the help of Chiang Kai-shek's Australian-born adviser, W.H. Donald, who sent him to Europe to be cured of the opium habit. Upon his return, the now clear-headed Chang was shocked when Chiang ordered him to withdraw his troops from Manchuria. The Young Marshal, after Chiang gave him a tongue-lashing for daring to advocate détente with the communists, decided to force the Generalissimo to see reason.

The Young Marshal invited Chiang to the ancient capital of Sian to address his officers, who were in a mutinous mood. On the morning of December 12, 1936, Chiang, awakened by gunshots, fled out the back door of the cabin he'd been lodged in. The Young Marshal's soldiers discovered him shivering in a cave in his nightshirt, without his false teeth. Once he'd realized he'd been kidnapped and mastered his anger, Chiang started to listen to his captors. Many of them wanted him killed. It was the communist intellectual Chou En-lai – many of whose comrades had been slaughtered in Chiang's "White Terror" – who argued most forcefully that it was better for the nation if he was allowed to live. On Christmas Day, Chiang was released; the Young Marshal personally escorted him back to Nanking.

Though Chiang never formally agreed to the kidnappers' demands, from then on the Kuomintang quietly dropped their policy of "internal pacification" – code for the destruction of the Reds – in favour of "recovery of the lost territories." Soon after, the Red Army was put under nationalist command. It had taken extraordinary efforts, but the United Front against the Japanese had been achieved.

Though the significance of the alliance between the communists and the nationalists wasn't immediately appreciated in Shanghai, there was genuine relief about Chiang's release. Many had feared he would be executed – which, in addition to throwing the country into chaos, would most certainly have been bad for business.

"We acted like ostriches most of the time in the treaty ports," wrote Mickey Hahn of the kidnapping of the Generalissimo, "but this development was of such magnitude that even we, the half-wits of the world, paused and looked at each other, and stopped chattering for a little. Then he came back again, safe, and we laughed shrilly, and poured out more cocktails."

The "Shanghai Mind" had always been a tough thing to penetrate. The residents of the foreign settlements should have continued to pay attention, though, because 1937 was the year that everything would come crashing down.

15: Sweetie Pie Goes to Nanking

Nobody said not to go, so one weekend in August 1937 Mickey Hahn and her new roommate Mary Garrison made up their minds to take the train to Nanking. There would be dinner parties, dancing, and young men, and they could go horseback riding in the hills to escape the sweltering summer heat. They would be back in Shanghai by Sunday.

In truth, Mickey needed a break from the city – and particularly from Sinmay. For months now, their relationship had been foundering. She was grateful to him for helping her discover the Chinese side of Shanghai. But she was carving out a new life, and his attentions were becoming troublesome.

Nineteen thirty-seven had, so far, been an eventful year. She had quit her job at the *North-China Daily News* to take a teaching job. Though she loved being a reporter, she hated keeping regular office hours. At the Customs College on Connaught Road, established to train Chinese officials for the foreign-run customs service, she only had eight hours a week of classroom time. She liked teaching, and she liked her Chinese students, who were eager to learn English. (She was especially popular with the young men in her Shakespeare class, who slipped her love notes.) If she occasionally dozed off in class – a symptom of her continuing recourse to the opium pipe – the students seemed to consider it just another of her foreign eccentricities. She wasn't teaching for the sake of money: her salary was paid in steadily depreciating Chinese dollars. For regular income she relied on cheques from the *New Yorker*, for whom she was still writing "Pan Heh-ven" stories, sometimes at the rate of one a week.

In May, she'd finally left behind her gaudily-decorated flat in the bank building near the Bund. When Mary, an old family friend from St. Louis, had arrived in Shanghai, she'd talked her into renting a shared house off Yuyuen Road, one of the "Western Roads" that the Municipal Council had extended beyond the border of the International Settlement without Chinese permission. For less than she had been paying for her mouse-hole on Kiangse Road, they now had a spacious, two-bathroom home.

Since the spring she'd also had a car – another token of Sir Victor's appreciation. To her mother Hannah, she explained:

Once in a while Sir Victor, who is the nicest man in the world, finds some way to make me a present, and I take it without blushing, everybody does, because he is also the richest man in the world and unlike Mr. Rockefeller he seems to like to waste his money like that. So long as I never let myself slip into the habit of expecting him to help me, I think it's safe, don't you?

It helped that Mickey kept introducing the bachelor millionaire to young woman like Mary, a pretty and petite brunette. She had contemplated buying a small Morris, but settled on a shiny blue Chevrolet coupe with running boards and sporty streamlines. Mickey mostly took it out to Eve's, or the houseboat dock in Ming Hong. On one of her first trips, to her horror, she almost ran down a rickshaw driver on the Garden Bridge.

With one American dollar by then buying four Chinese dollars, cheques from home went a long way. Employing three Chinese servants – a chauffeur, a cook, and an amah – cost Mickey and Mary only $24 (US) a month. Russian hairdressers and manicurists made housecalls, they changed their lingerie twice a day, and kept the house filled with freshly-cut flowers.

Sinmay resented Sir Victor's attentions, and especially the fact that he had bought Mickey a car. His solution, typically, was to provide her with a driver, recruited from his vast household of underemployed servants.

Sinmay was also starting to resent her new boyfriends. For a while, she'd been seeing a titled Polish diplomat named Jan – she dubbed him "Count Petroff" in one of her *New Yorker* stories – who blamed his lack of appetite on a stomach ulcer. ("A nice big hunk, but an opium addict," she would tell her biographer, many years later. "Avoid addicts.") The relationship lasted until he was transferred to deadly dull Peiping; she later found out that he had pilfered a valuable jade pipe and hundreds of dollars from her and her friends.

Stung by Mickey's flings, the normally cool Sinmay lost his head. After she'd left town for a rendezvous with a British boy-friend who captained a gunboat on the Yangtze, he sent her an impassioned letter reproaching her for her new love interests, her friendship with Harold Acton, and everything else that stopped her from paying attention to him.

What a hell you have put me in! I could see you tearing yourself into pieces and offering them to princes, sailors and fairies of different nationalities . . . I want to come back . . . I have been hysterical since I left, and have been quarrelling with everybody.

The letter was handwritten, in Sinmay's exquisite calligraphy, in red ink – a colour traditionally used in Chinese obituaries. He was signalling, in his melodramatic way, that she had put him near death.

He even confessed his distress to Bernardine in a typewritten letter. "My public life is over, the life of my self-importance. I rose from my death and found M." – interpolated, in Bernardine's handwriting, are the words "Mickey Hahn" – "I wanted the world to belong to me, but now I want her. Of course it sounds selfish; but I have acquainted her with my situation and she is not afraid to face the fact. The worst may come but we are hoping for the best."

She made up with Sinmay, of course. When Peiyu became pregnant with her sixth child in 1937, Sinmay told Mickey she was free to take lovers – so long as she continued to love him best. In truth, though, she was done with being his concubine. She spent the spring and summer working through the ebb and flow of their relationship by writing. By July she had produced a 150,000-word novel, which ended with the main character leaving her lover, a Chinese poet, for a British navy man named Kenneth. When Sir

Victor read it, he suggested she call it *Whirlpool*.* "I suppose," she wrote to Helen after she'd completed the first draft, "I have built up a lot of self-reliance, unbeknownst to myself, while I waited for Sinmay all that time, and am my own independent self once more, and an avowed bachelor . . . I do love that little bastard, but it's like playing marbles with quicksilver, honestly."

A weekend getaway to Nanking with Mary Garrison would be a welcome escape from all the drama, as well as the summer heat in Shanghai. They left on a Wednesday, carrying hatboxes and a basket containing Sweetie Pie, a duckling Mickey had bought from a peddler on the Bund for ten cents. Frequent delays meant the train ride from North Station, which normally took five hours, turned into a sixteen-hour slog. Over lunch on a gunboat moored on the Yangtze River, with Robert – the British naval officer Mickey had been seeing for several months – they learned that the situation in Shanghai had deteriorated while they'd been travelling. The Chinese had scuttled junks across the mouth of the Whangpoo to hold up the Japanese navy, and there was fighting in the streets of Hongkew.

It was no time, Robert scolded them, to be taking pleasure trips. Hadn't Mickey heard about the latest incident, in which two Japanese soldiers had been shot at the Hungjao Aerodrome? (She had, of course, but by then there had been so many incidents, she didn't pay this one much mind.) Well, Robert said, if she expected to teach on Monday morning, they would have to get right back on a train.

The return trip was an odyssey. The station was filled with Chinese soldiers, cheerful and ready for a fight, carrying their kit on bamboo poles. They shared a compartment with a German named Wally, an Indian man in a grey flannel suit, and plump Mr. Lee, who spoke English with a Nanking accent. They sat on their hatboxes and fed Sweetie Pie toast until they were kicked off the train at Soochow. After spending the morning in a foul-smelling

---

* It would be published in 1940, to disappointing reviews, as *Steps of the Sun*.

farmer's field, they ran across the tracks to board a Shanghai-bound train. The last leg of the trip was uneventful, except near Kashing, where they held their breath as a Japanese bomber flew overhead.

They returned to a Shanghai in chaos. As they disembarked at South Station, the train was mobbed. Mary screamed as she was buffeted on the platform by refugees; her basket was crushed flat but Sweetie Pie, though compressed, survived. They emerged from the crowds, and Wally managed to find them a single rickshaw to carry their luggage. To get home, they had to walk four miles through streets resonant with the *whizz-bang* of artillery shells.

Back at Yuyuen Road, they invited their travel companions for dinner and congratulated themselves on their adventure. "We had coffee and brandy, and cigarettes," Mickey wrote in a dispatch published in the *New Yorker* four weeks later, "and Sweetie Pie had a long swim in the bathtub."

It was only after talking to Chin Lien, their cook, that she realized how bad things were. If they'd put off their return by even an hour, they might never have gotten out of Nanking: the trains were now filled with refugees trying to escape the Japanese, and Chinese soldiers pouring in to fight the invaders. "Twelve hundred Chinese," she wrote, "had been killed in Shanghai that day – by Chinese bombs."

Her estimate of the death toll was off, but not the essential facts of the matter. They had come home just two hours after the events of what would come to be known as Black Saturday. The greater truth – that, in less than three days, the Shanghai she loved had become a thing of the past – would take longer to sink in.

PART FIVE

"The hands of the clock outside Sir Victor Sassoon's fabulous hotel were to tick to 4:27 and then stop dead: and so for a few frantic seconds were the hearts of the 3,000,000 Chinese, Russians, Japanese, Britons, French, Americans, Germans, Filipinos, Koreans, Italians and representatives of about thirty-two other nationalities who starved or feasted in Shanghai, the modern Babylon."

– Rhodes Farmer,
Shanghai Harvest, 1945.

16: Shanghai, August 14, 1937

The forecasts had been dead wrong. Though it was shaping up to be a typical midsummer day in Shanghai – temperature in the low nineties, overcast, humidity near unbearable – the newspapers had forgotten to mention the little matter of the wind. The weather that morning, the front page of the *China Press* had indicated, would be "cloudy, fine, breezy." In all likelihood, that big typhoon blowing in from Guam would completely sidestep Shanghai.

But as Rhodes Farmer, an Australian-born reporter for the *North-China Daily News*, rushed towards the Bund that morning, he had to hold on to his fedora to keep it from being snatched from his head and blown all the way back to the Race Course. On his walk from his flat, he'd watched the human scarecrows emerging from the dives and flophouses of Hongkew being tossed around like leaves. Now, the gale-force winds that reached eighty miles an hour snatched the glasses from his face and lofted them fifty yards down Nanking Road, where they landed on the streetcar tracks. A group of Chinese refugees huddled together in a doorway, blue smocks drawn around their heads to protect them from the flogging rain, laughed and pointed as the white man in the billowing mackintosh narrowly missed being crushed by an oncoming streetcar. As he reached the point where the Cathay Hotel faced the Bund, Farmer looked over a Whangpoo swollen with rain, towards the Rising Sun flag on the bow of the four-stack *Izumo* as it flapped wildly in the gale.

This bad weather might be good news for the Chinese, Farmer realized, as he shook the rain off his coat in the lobby of the *North-China Daily News* building. A typhoon would make the ongoing arrival of the Japanese fleet, and with it close to 10,000 troops, a disordered affair. Meanwhile, every few minutes trains from Nanking, filled to standing room with nationalist soldiers, were arriving at North Station. If Chiang Kai-shek could mobilize his air force, the storm might provide just the cover needed for the kind of air attacks that would stymie the long-awaited Japanese landing.

Any way you looked at it, Farmer reflected, as he strode through a newsroom abuzz with the chatter of typewriters and the stutter of the news wire, this Saturday was not going to be one of Shanghai's slow news days.

美

Sir Victor had a knack for absenting himself from Shanghai at the most inconvenient moments.

As he paced his office on the third floor of Sassoon House on the afternoon of August 14, Lucien Ovadia, Sir Victor's right-hand man when it came to all affairs relating to the Sassoon holdings in the Far East, realized it was an observation he had been making with increasing frequency, and no small measure of bitterness. Naturally, Sir Victor had been in Shanghai that spring for the festivities around the coronation of King George VI, when the Cathay and every British-owned building on the Bund had been brilliantly outlined with incandescent lights. Now that war was knocking on Shanghai's door, however, he was 3,000 miles away.

Since coming to China to work for E.D. Sassoon & Co. in 1935, Ovadia had become inured to playing the role of wise consul to the free-spending playboy. The year before, Sir Victor had impulsively decided to invest in a molybdenum deposit outside of Hangchow. When Ovadia discovered the ore would have to reach port by being hauled overland in bamboo relays, the only way he could talk Sir Victor out of throwing away half a million pounds was by threatening to resign.

In spite of such set-tos, the pair had much in common. They were cousins – their mothers were sisters – and both shared complex, cosmopolitan backgrounds: Ovadia, though of Spanish nationality and born in Egypt, had begun his career in finance in

Manchester. Unlike Sir Victor, though, who was constantly travelling the world on ocean liners – and increasingly, airplanes – Ovadia liked to think of himself as a responsible steward of the Sassoon interests in the Far East. Bald and heavily built, he was more likely to spend an evening poring over balance sheets than making the rounds of the tables at Ciro's.

The Japanese, during Sir Victor's absence, had found another spurious pretext for war. On July 7, 1937, an Imperial Army company garrisoned near the Marco Polo Bridge – the famous eleven-arched granite bridge mentioned in the Venetian explorer's memoirs – claimed Chinese soldiers had fired on them in the night and killed one of their number. Though the missing soldier turned up in a brothel the following day, a genuine battle ensued, and the Japanese military decided to "teach China a lesson" by subduing Chinese forces in the north. A full-scale invasion of the area around Peiping had followed.

Sir Victor had been informed of the Marco Polo Incident via the ticker-tape machine in his office in Bombay. He had yet to learn about the latest outrage. Four days ago on a dark road not far from Eve's, Sir Victor's country resort, two men in the uniform of the Japanese navy's elite Special Landing Force had been found dead next to a bullet-ridden sedan at the entrance of the Hungjao Aerodrome. Not far from the car a third body had been found, dressed in a Chinese uniform. Shanghai's new mayor maintained that the Japanese soldiers were spies killed in a shoot-out by Chinese paramilitary sentries. There were rumours, though, that the whole thing was a set-up, and the nationalists actually wanted the war, if it was to come, to be fought in Shanghai – thereby stretching Japan's resources by opening a second front.

If so, they'd succeeded. As they'd done five years earlier, the Japanese had sent a fleet steaming across the East China Sea. The previous day, Chinese snipers had begun firing on the troops as they landed in Hongkew, provoking the predictable flood of panicked residents across the Garden Bridge into the International Settlement. From his windows overlooking the Bund, Ovadia could see refugees, buffeted by the typhoon's gusts, huddled against every tree, bench, and immovable object on the riverfront.

Ovadia considered placing a trunk call to the Sassoon offices in India. Things were clearly heating up, and he was the one left behind to hold down the Sassoon fort in Shanghai. There was plenty at stake. Even now, President Quezon of the Philippines was a guest – he'd hosted a huge luncheon for the Filipino community in the ballroom – and Mrs. Theodore Roosevelt, the daughter-in-law of the late American president, had checked in with her son Quentin. The presence of such prestigious guests made him nervous. Already that morning he'd seen the silver-sided bombers used by the Chinese air force drop from beneath the clouds and make runs on the Japanese flagship. Their bombs had splashed harmlessly on the surface of the Whangpoo, but he wagered they'd be back.

If Ovadia made the call, he knew he'd get a reassuring lecture from Sir Victor about how the Cathay Hotel had withstood explosions before. Besides, it was a race weekend in Bombay, and Sir Victor would almost certainly be in his box, watching the ponies.

Shortly after teatime, he heard the propellers again, clear and keening through the typhoon's gusts.

美

Something, it was immediately obvious to Claire Lee Chennault, had gone terribly wrong.

Early that Saturday morning the retired United States Army Air Corps captain had left the nationalist base at Nanking, at the controls of an unarmed Hawk 75 monoplane. Chennault had come to China that June on a three-month contract to do a survey of the nationalist air force – such as it was. It hadn't taken him long to realize that Chinese air power was a mirage. Before his arrival, its expansion had been overseen by advisers and pilots from fascist Italy, who initiated a practice of adding airplanes to the official roster even when they happened to be total wrecks. Of the 500 planes officially available to engage the Japanese, Chennault discovered that only ninety-one were fit for combat. (The general who broke the news to Generalissimo Chiang Kai-shek narrowly avoided being shot.) Nor, in Chennault's opinion, were most of the pilots fit to fly. The Italian flight-training school, he would later write, "graduated every Chinese cadet who survived the training course as a full-fledged pilot regardless of his ability."

As his plane approached Shanghai, swooping and banking to evade the rainstorms over the Yangtze, his anxiety grew. The night before in Nanking, Soong Mei-ling – or Madame Chiang, as foreigners knew Chiang Kai-shek's wife – had burst into tears as she implored him to protect China from Japanese invasion. The Generalissimo had put his wife in charge of overseeing the air force; she was responsible, she explained, for acquiring those faulty planes. There was no one in China who had the experience to organize an aerial combat mission against the Japanese.

"They are killing our people," she had sobbed to Chennault. When he'd asked her what the nationalists would do, Madame Chiang had thrown back her head and proclaimed, voice twanging with the Southern accent she'd picked up at college in Georgia: "We will fight." (Chennault, impressed, wrote in his diary: "She will always be a princess to me.")

Chennault stayed up all night making plans. It made sense, he decided, to attack the ships on the Whangpoo, which were likely to be used to provide artillery support to ground forces. He'd decided the nationalists' Curtiss Hawk dive bombers could be deployed against the Japanese navy's light cruisers, and a half dozen Northrop 2E light bombers should be enough to finish off the *Izumo*, their flagship.

But he hadn't counted on the severity of the typhoon, or the alarming incompetence of the pilots. That morning, he'd decided to participate in the capacity of unarmed observer. Now, as he flew over Shanghai, he watched as a Chinese plane's bombs fell far short of a ship on the Whangpoo, which responded with blazing guns. To his shock, he saw the ship had a Union Jack prominently painted on its afterdeck. The Chinese bombers had picked for their target the *Cumberland* – a British cruiser. Then, taking Chennault for one of the attackers, the ship's gunners turned their turrets on his plane; bullets pierced his wings. He put the monoplane into a vertical climb, and headed back to the base. The last thing Chennault saw as he headed back to Nanking was that the *Izumo* was untouched, while a column of thick smoke rose from the Bund.

It was only when he returned to the base that he learned what had happened. The Chinese pilots he'd sent to sink the Japanese ships had been trained to bomb at a fixed speed from a height of 7,500 feet. Forced to dive below the clouds because of the typhoon, they'd failed to adjust their sights to the new altitude, and dropped their bombs as soon as they'd seen the bulk of the *Izumo* fill their crosshairs.

To his horror, Chennault was informed that two 1,100-pound bombs had been dropped in the heart of the world's most crowded city. "Unknowingly," he would later write in his memoirs, he'd set "the stage for Shanghai's famous Black Saturday – a spectacle that shocked a world that was not yet calloused to mass murder from the sky by thousand-plane raids or atomic bombs."

As an experienced Shanghai newsman, Rhodes Farmer knew just where to go when the action on the riverfront heated up. The rooftop of the Cathay Hotel, three doors north of the *North-China Daily News* building, offered a privileged vantage point. As he pushed through the revolving doors and waited for the elevator to take him to the ninth floor, he noted by the clock in the lobby that it was twenty minutes past four.

A few dozen people had gathered on the tennis-court-sized roof terrace. The winds had momentarily died down, which allowed Farmer to approach the railing at the edge of the roof closest to the Bund. Below him, thousands of spectators had joined the refugees at the corner of Nanking Road to observe the fighting. He watched as a sortie of medium Chinese bombers dropped through the low clouds, and the *Izumo*'s anti-aircraft guns pivoted and started barking. Suddenly, one of the planes broke formation and veered towards the Bund; four bombs fell from its belly. Two would fall into the Whangpoo, sending dirty water and bits of broken sampans raining down on the Bund. The other two were lofted towards the hotel by a gust from the typhoon. The twin blasts that followed rocked the Cathay on its foundations.

Farmer staggered back into the hotel and, finding the elevator operators had abandoned their posts, ran down the stairs back to the lobby. He emerged to a scene of devastation on Nanking Road. Yellow fumes and white plaster dust filled the air. The refugees who had been huddled in the doorways had been reduced to heaps of mangled flesh, their blue smocks reddening with blood. On the corner was a decapitated Sikh policeman, his arms outstretched as though trying to hold back oncoming traffic. A Lincoln Zephyr parked outside the Cathay's entrance was ablaze, its whitewall tires smouldering; the chauffeur's body was calcinated inside. Pieces of gore were mingled with the Rolexes in the shattered display windows of the Cathay arcade.

"Beneath the dead hands of Sir Victor Sassoon's clock outside the Cathay," Farmer would write later, "I saw a Japanese girl in very high heels and Western clothes. She was stepping over the dead, directing the rescue parties to those whose lives might still be saved."

Inside the hotel, an eerie calm prevailed. Farmer made his way to the Horse and Hounds Bar, which had been spared the main effects of the blasts. Two Chinese stewards behind the bar produced a bottle of brandy. A White Russian picked up a severed thumb from the floor, and asked, "Any of you lose this?"

Farmer, gulping down his drink, made a mental note: the hands of Sir Victor's clock had stopped at 4:27 p.m. In years to come, he would remember it as the exact moment that the party had stopped in Shanghai.

After helping load some of the injured into hospital vans, Farmer stumbled back to the offices of the *North-China Daily News*. He joined his fellow professionals, who were at their desks struggling to report on what they'd witnessed. They'd write a few paragraphs on their typewriters, head to the restroom to throw up, and then return to work.

美

When the blasts came, Lucien Ovadia was at his desk in the third-floor offices of Sassoon House. The shock hurled him to the floor. He must have lost consciousness for a moment, because the next thing he remembered was the ringing of a telephone. Crawling to the desk, he picked up the receiver. It was Louis Suter, the general manager of Cathay Hotels Ltd., reporting the obvious: a bomb had exploded outside the hotel's entrance.

Ovadia emerged from the elevator into a wasteland of shattered Lalique glass. The mezzanine, where the orchestra played, was hung with body parts. The canopy over the entrance had been vaporized. The Cathay's lobby now opened directly onto Nanking Road.

At the front desk, Suter, though ashen-faced, was able to report what had happened. After the explosion he'd run out into Nanking Road and bent to help the first victim he saw; when he tried to pull him out of the rubble, though, he saw the man's legs had been blown clean off. He had mechanically moved on to the next victim, until the first of the ambulances arrived. It was as though a giant mower had been pushed through a field of humanity.

It could, Suter added, have been worse. A party of two dozen American schoolteachers who were having tea in the lobby lounge had left the arcade a few minutes before the explosion.

With some anxiety, Ovadia asked the manager if he knew of the whereabouts of Mrs. Roosevelt.

Suter told Ovadia that she had been having tiffin with her son in the Peking Room, on the eighth floor. She'd been upset because, while they were dining, they'd witnessed a Chinese mob chase a Japanese man down the Bund and beat him to death with bricks and their fists and feet. When the *Izumo*'s anti-aircraft guns had started firing on the attacking Chinese planes, Suter had advised them to leave the hotel. The Roosevelts had been bundled into a waiting car outside the entrance just eight minutes before the bomb fell, and rushed to the safety of a friend's house. The Chinese telephone boy who had taken a message for Mrs. Roosevelt moments before the bombing, Suter was sorry to report, had been killed.

The damage, in the manager's opinion, was significant but not structural. The Palace Hotel across the street had suffered a direct hit on its roof; its first three storeys had been completely gutted. Suter recommended they board up the front of Sassoon House and have the Volunteer Corps guard the arcade against looters.

The newspapers would later confirm Suter's reports. Of the many hundreds killed in that terrible day's bombings, only four were foreigners.

Ovadia, though still stunned, was also relieved. At least he would be able to report to Sir Victor, that, as horrible as the devastation had been, none of the Cathay Hotel's guests were among the human wreckage.

In times of peace, the Great World was crowded even by Shanghai standards. Now that war had returned, the amusement centre on the corner of Thibet Road and Avenue Édouard VII was a thrumming hive of human activity. On the stages where acrobats and jugglers had until recently performed, rice was being distributed to refugees fleeing the violence in Chapei and Hongkew. Since the previous day, the temple of vice that had so astounded Josef von Sternberg had been given over to virtue, doing duty as a makeshift shelter.

On the sidewalk, refugees had formed a line to enter the building. When explosions were heard from the Bund, a wave of panic had briefly washed through the crowd. Eighteen minutes later, two planes approached from the Whangpoo River; a cheer went up as people noticed the white-sun insignia of the nationalists on the bombers' tailfins.

Then, one of the planes started losing altitude, as though it had been damaged. As it neared the Great World, two dark dots dropped from its underbelly. The first struck the traffic control tower in the middle of the road, vaporizing an Ammanite policeman in a peaked hat who had been directing traffic. The second exploded a few feet above the ground, spraying the six-storey ziggurat with shrapnel. Gas pressure from the detonation stripped bodies of their clothes, which, as the shock subsided, were seen piled up five feet high against the entrance to the Great World.

The aftermath was even more horrific than the scenes of devastation created by the bombs that had struck outside the Cathay Hotel. Falling in the thick human heart of Shanghai at a time when refugees clotted the sidewalks, the Great World bombs killed 570 people. All told, the death toll for "Black Saturday" would reach 825.

The West had been shocked by the fascist bombing of Guernica – the first such aerial bombing of a defenseless civilian population – four months earlier. Now the heart of a crowded metropolis was the target, and in a few minutes the number of dead and injured from just four bombs was double the toll achieved by three hours of carpet bombing in Spain.

For many, the fact that the Chinese bombed their own people was both galling and confusing. Some speculated the nationalists had targeted the International Settlement deliberately, to bring world attention to their cause. The real explanation was a combination of incompetence, human error, and chance. Interviewed in his hospital bed by a *Shanghai Evening Post and Mercury* reporter, the Chinese captain of the bomber responsible for the Great World carnage explained that the bomb racks had been damaged by a Japanese fighter, causing the accidental dropping of the plane's payload.

The concentration of newsmen near the site of the atrocities meant news of the tragedy travelled around the world quickly. When the bombs dropped, the famous Hearst reporter "Newsreel" Wong was only two blocks away. A cameraman for the "March of Time" newsreel service was sitting in the lobby of the Cathay when the bombs went off, and filmed the blazing Lincoln Zephyr on Nanking Road. Outwitting the nationalist censors, he threw his film cans to a friend as his tender pulled away from the Bund, and the footage – flown across the Pacific on a Pan Am China Clipper – was playing on movie screens around the world within days.

Only three days after Black Saturday, Barbara Miller, a staff writer for the *Los Angeles Times*, wrote a eulogy for the city she'd known in the early thirties:

With nice irony, the bomb gouged a mammoth hole in Nanking Road between two crowded hotels, the swanky Cathay of tourist fame and the old-time Palace. Shanghai, the Paris of the Orient, with more cabarets, country clubs, lavish living and degrading misery than any port from Honolulu to Suez, belongs to the past.

For most of the world it was obvious that, in the once-charmed city of Shanghai, everything had changed.

For the battle-calloused inhabitants of Shanghai – among them Zau Sinmay, Sir Victor Sassoon, and Mickey Hahn – the new reality would take longer to sink in.

17: After Saturday

No city with as much vitality as Shanghai could be shut down overnight. But in the days that followed August 14, 1937, the International Settlement came as close as it ever had to becoming a ghost town.

Since the previous Friday, when the Yangtze River had been closed to navigation, activity on the docks of the Bund and the Quai de France had come to a standstill. The only trains still running were filled with nationalist troops. The facade of Sassoon House was boarded up, and on Nanking Road the only restaurant open was Sun Ya – formerly the rendezvous of Zau Sinmay and his literary friends, but now filled with Cantonese refugees who paid for a few hours' shelter with the price of a meal. After the events of Black Saturday, such motion-picture palaces as the Metropol and the Nanking Theatre – both close enough to the Great World to be hit by debris – were locked and boarded up until further notice. A curfew was announced: lights had to be out by 11:30 p.m. in the International Settlement, 10 p.m. in Frenchtown. The Vienna Gardens and the Lido, once hopping nightspots, were turned into vast sickbays filled with soldiers. Taxi dancers and hostesses were allowed to comfort the wounded – until the prudish Chiang Kai-shek banned the practice. As thousands of refugees tried to crowd into Shanghai, the iron gates between the old Chinese city and the Settlement were closed.

On Black Saturday, Hallett Abend, the *New York Times*'s man in China, had been in Tsingtao, 350 miles north of Shanghai. Desperate to cover the fighting, he had shipped down the coast on the pitching deck of the private yacht of Harry Yarnell, commander-in-chief of the United States's Asiatic Fleet, in the tail end of the typhoon. Four days after the bombings he found the block between the Cathay and Palace roped off; in spite of the sand and disinfectant sprinkled on the sidewalks, the street still smelled like "a foul charnel house." Near the Great World, "the combination of the stench of unburied bodies and simmering August heat was unbearable."

Nor, Abend discovered, had the war finished with the International Settlement. The following Monday, he went on a shopping trip to Nanking Road. While his assistant was inside the Wing On department store ordering field glasses, Abend, who had stayed in their car to smoke a cigarette, noticed a silvery airplane passing overhead. Then the ground gave a sickening lurch, and he felt debris and rubble from the surrounding buildings showering down on the car's roof.

A bomb, he realized, had scored a direct hit on the department store. Abend, struck by the eerie silence, was aware only of the tinkling of falling glass and the rumble of crumbling masonry. Then his bloodied assistant crawled back to the car on hands and knees. He had been in the elevator with eleven other people when the blast hit; only he and the operator had survived. After making sure his assistant got to the hospital, Abend, still covered with plaster and blood, limped into the Country Club. As he gulped down a double brandy, he discovered a piece of glass the size of his little finger lodged above his right ankle.

The death toll of 600 was almost as high as that recorded on Black Saturday. Abend would later learn that a Chinese pilot, pursued by Japanese fighters, had panicked and dropped his bombs to lighten his load. One 750-pound shatter bomb lodged in the roof of an American naval warehouse where tons of mines and heavy shells were stockpiled; fortunately, it failed to detonate. Had it exploded, Abend believed, much of downtown Shanghai would have been erased from the map.

As horrible as such incidents were, Shanghai's foreign concessions were spared from actual armed conflict. Unknown to most Shanghailanders, a life-and-death struggle was under way for control of the city's Chinese districts. In the early days of the fighting, two of Chiang Kai-shek's elite German-trained divisions had successfully driven the Japanese in Hongkew back to their landing places on the wharves of the Whangpoo River. As new troops poured in from Japan – 40,000 in the first three weeks of the war – and the Imperial Navy took key forts downriver, Chinese divisions began to retreat into the countryside north of the city, burning shops and houses in Chapei as they fled.

When the Cathay's Tower Night Club reopened, it became the favoured gathering spot of foreign journalists.

One night, when Mickey had decided to put on an evening dress and join the reporters at the Cathay, she had a glimpse of the new order coming to Shanghai.

In front of the hotel where I stepped from car to kerb, three Japanese gentlemen walked by the glow through the front door. They were hatless and small and plump, business-men making their first fearless appearance after hiding for two months from rare mobs. They walked saunteringly, they glanced about appraisingly at this city, making plans . . . then the one-legged beggar who never misses anybody crawled along the pavement and held out his cap as he always does, as he did, I am convinced, the day the bomb killed six hundred people in this street. He never misses anybody, the cap was held out to me, but he seemed not to perceive those Japanese gentlemen.

Mickey found the Cathay filled with correspondents watching the dogfights and the shelling of the Chinese city. "There they are, crowded up against the bar in the Cathay Tower, showing off to each other all round the world, each trying to be more bored and international than the next." She found a strange beauty in night combat: "Over all, incessantly, appeared streaks of light, as though some great cat were scratching at the dark-blue velvet; stars shot across from one side of the window to the other, and explosions sent up brief fountains of liquid gold."

Japanese flags were raised over the city's Chinese districts, with one exception: the Joint Savings godown on the north side of Soochow Creek. Five hundred or so members of the 1st Battalion of the nationalist army's 524th Regiment had found refuge inside the warehouse's ten-foot walls, where they managed to hold off the combined might of the Japanese forces for four days. The siege of Shanghai's "Alamo" would inspire all of China. During a lull in the fighting, a Girl Guide who had wrapped herself in the nationalist banner snuck into the warehouse, allowing the Chinese to raise the white-sun flag. When the press of the world turned its attention on the "Lone Battalion," the Generalissimo realized their propaganda value. Madame Chiang, who had a talent for lapidary proclamations, declared: "They must die so China may live!" The soldiers themselves had other ideas: as Japanese machine-gunners reloaded, they scurried across a bridge, handing over their rifles to Municipal Police as they entered the safety of the International Settlement, to be rushed away in twenty British trucks. Against incredible odds, only one hundred of their number were killed in the siege.

As Chinese resistance broke down, a correspondent from the Hearst newspaper chain phoned Mickey to tell her that the fighting was moving north towards Nanking, and he'd be moving with it. By then, she was disgusted enough with what she saw as the voyeurism of the world press to yell into the phone: "You're all vultures. This means you'll all be leaving town; that's one good thing." She hung up so viciously, the receiver almost cracked.

At a time like this, Mickey, for one, had no intention of abandoning Shanghai.

If the outset of hostilities was marked in the hands of the shattered clock outside the Cathay Hotel – frozen at 4:27 p.m. on August 14 – the end came three months later, when the Rising Sun flag was raised to shouts of "Banzai!" over the last Chinese stronghold south of the old walled city. One of the last victims of the battle was Pembroke Stevens, correspondent for Britain's *Daily Telegraph*, who was shot through the head as he watched the fighting from a water tower in Frenchtown. Edgar Snow saw Stevens being carried down the stairs, wearing a red poppy in his buttonhole.

The Battle of Shanghai, which had lasted just under thirteen weeks and claimed the lives of over a quarter-million combatants

– 200,000 of them Chinese – ended at 3:34 p.m. on November 11, 1937.

美

When the fighting that signalled the outbreak of the Second Sino-Japanese War began, Sinmay discovered he was living in the worst possible location. The family home where Mickey Hahn had smoked her first opium pipe in Yangtzepoo, north of Soochow Creek, was also where the bulk of Shanghai's Japanese population made their homes. Now diminutive marines wearing puttees and split-toe shoes marched through those same streets, while looters ransacked vacant homes. After Black Saturday, Sinmay packed up his five children and his most prized possessions in a van and drove with his family to his sister's apartment in Frenchtown, where a dozen members of his household would share a single room.

After returning from Nanking, Mickey realized why her house in Yuyuen Road was such a bargain: it was located beyond the Settlement's borders, in what could easily become a lawless combat zone. (The Western Roads district soon became a notorious haven for Japanese-run opium dens, brothels, and roulette houses.) When a plane swept so low it almost hit the chimney, she and Mary moved to an empty house off Avenue Joffre, a busy boulevard running through Frenchtown.

By 1937 the historic French Concession, which began southeast of the Race Course, was French in name only. Only 1,200 of its million citizens actually had French passports. They were vastly outnumbered by Shanghai's 25,000 White Russians, who had made the mile-long Avenue Joffre into an unofficial "Moscow Boulevard" where bakeries posted Cyrillic signs advertising black bread, and tiny restaurants offered shots of vodka and bowls of borscht (a soup that features on many Shanghai menus to this day). In Frenchtown, brothels were licensed, and even such notorious prostitutes as the "Voluptuous Vampires from Vladivostok" (who shocked old Shanghailanders with their willingness to accept Chinese clients) were regularly inspected by doctors.

Unlike the cramped, commerce-driven International Settlement, Frenchtown was embellished by the panache of Gallic urbanism, which made it a favoured residential district for American and European diplomats. With the Old World charm of Tudor-style houses and faux Spanish villas on generous lots, and broad sidewalks shaded by plane trees, it was – and remains to this day – the only place in central Shanghai for an urban stroller to enjoy the pleasure of genuine Baudelairean *flânerie*. Such vestigial continental chic also made Frenchtown an ideal home for Sinmay. By December, Mickey had found the Zau family a home, nearly identical to her own, two doors to the west of her Avenue Joffre cottage. Soon the house was crowded with beds, wardrobes, spittoons, and newspapers stacked in corners. Sinmay would call Avenue Joffre home for the rest of his life.

After seeing the Zaus resettled, Mickey agreed to undertake a rescue mission. In the haste of their flight, the family had been forced to abandon their bulkiest possessions in the old home and office in Yangtzepoo. Now, Japanese sentries posted on the bridges over Soochow Creek turned back anybody without the proper papers – subjecting Europeans to slaps, and Chinese to prodding (or much worse) with their bayonets. In the company of an officer lent by a friend, the deputy commissioner of the Shanghai Municipal Police, Mickey was able to cross into Japanese territory. The house, Mickey discovered, had been ransacked, but they were able to save some furniture and family photos, as well as Sinmay's invaluable library of Ming-dynasty books and prints.

Rescuing the printing press would prove trickier. To show that she was the press's rightful owner, Mickey had signed an agreement that indicated Sinmay had sold it to her the year before. Sinmay worried, though, that the Japanese would see through the ruse.

"You must marry me," Sinmay proposed one day, "and then it will be really all right."

His wife, Sinmay explained, had come up with the idea. Since he and Peiyu had never actually signed marriage papers – "it is often that way in careless old families like mine" – Mickey could be his wife, which would give her a legitimate claim to ownership of the printing press. One morning in October 1937, Mickey signed a paper in Sinmay's lawyer's office, declaring she considered herself his wife "according to Chinese law." To celebrate the alliance, Peiyu gave her a pair of exquisite "mutton fat" jade bracelets, larded with white spots. Mickey organized a gang of twenty White Russian movers and, with four trucks, unbolted Sinmay's press from the floor of his Yangtzepoo office and moved it into a garage in the safety of the French Concession.

Though all parties considered the marriage a joke, Mickey was delighted that Sinmay promised she could be buried in the family grave.

"For some absurd reason," she wrote, "I ceased to worry about my old age."

She was also delighted with her spacious new Frenchtown cottage. It was surprisingly cheap – the previous tenants had been evacuated to Hong Kong. She decorated it with Soochow rugs for curtains and a parakeet in a cage. It also had a front garden that made a convenient playground for her latest companion.

After the death of Mary Garrison's duckling ("shell shock" was the probable cause) Mickey had renewed her passion for non-human primates, something she hadn't been able to indulge since being forced to leave her pet baboon, Angélique, in the Congo. Strolling down Bubbling Well Road one day she spotted a tiny ape, with enormous round eyes set in a pansy-shaped black face, being kept on a short leash in the window of the Shanghai Pet Store. "Mr. Mills," as he was dubbed (after the man from Malaya who told her she'd bought a *wau-wau*, or silvery gibbon) became Mickey's constant companion. Though he slept in a movable cage and swung from trees in the front yard (provoking complaints to the police from the Englishwoman who lived next door), Mr. Mills was no homebody. The vociferous ape, Mickey discovered, enjoyed being taken out for a night on the town. After pinning a diaper around his waist she would dress him in a tight-fitting Sunday coat lined with otter fur – tailor-made by a seamstress at the Peter Pan Toy Store on Avenue Joffre – strap a red fez to his head, and pay a visit to the Cathay Hotel. ("My Chinese pupils soon got used to him," wrote Mickey in an academic article entitled "Gibbons in Interactions with Man in Domestic Settings" – but "not so the patrons of such places as the Cathay Hotel bar.") As an observant exhibitionist, she was fascinated by people's reactions. Some clearly saw Mr. Mills as an affront to their humanity, demonstrating the kind of irritation "aroused by modern painting or sculpture . . . 'Is the artist, or the monkey, making fun of me?'"

For the rest of her life, Mickey resisted the idea that the passion of some independent women – among them Dian Fossey and Jane Goodall, who she would profile in her last book, *Eve and the Apes* – for non-human primates could be reduced to displaced maternal instinct. The fact was, though, that before acquiring Mr. Mills, she expressed her anguish in letters home about the way Sinmay's wife continued to have children; because she had stopped menstruating, probably due to her opium addiction, she feared she was infertile. Whatever her motivation, given the morbid turn life in Shanghai had taken, the irrepressible Mr. Mills – who, in adulthood, weighed thirty pounds and was as tall as a six-year-old boy – was a great comfort to Mickey. To keep him company she bought two macaques, which she kept in a cage in the front yard, antagonizing her neighbour even more.

Building a surrogate family was Mickey's way of signalling she had no intention of running out on Shanghai. In the days following Black Saturday, over 1,000 foreigners, mostly women and children, were evacuated from the city. The Americans – Mrs. Theodore Roosevelt and her son among them – were sent to Manila on the SS *President Jefferson*; the British to the colony of Hong Kong on the SS *Rajputana*. (Bernardine returned to the United States, where she set about building a salon in Hollywood. Her husband, Chester, who Mickey learned was having an affair with their White Russian maid, remained in Shanghai until 1943.)

Mickey's willingness to pooh-pooh fear and conformity had served her well: defying the nervous chatter that kept other people at home brought her the adventures on which she'd built a career. Shanghai, likewise, was a city built on a haughty disdain for all-too-real dangers; living there only intensified her devil-may-care attitude. (The anaesthetic qualities of opium almost certainly contributed to her nervelessness.) With Black Saturday, though, what Shanghailanders had long feared had finally happened: warfare – in its most brutal, mechanized form – had come to the Treaty Port. Mickey, who had made derring-do into a virtue, was loath to accept the new status quo.

When she wrote home, she tried to maintain a facade of domestic normalcy. In her first letter after Black Saturday, she wrote: "I think the first awful accidental bombing in the Foreign Concession will not be repeated. WE ARE VERY SAFE." But cracks were starting to show. On the afternoon of October 24, some friends decided to go horseback riding on Keswick Road, west of the Settlement; a Japanese pilot swooped down and machine-gunned them, killing a sentry and several horses. It called to mind the similar attack, two months earlier, on the British ambassador, Sir Hughe Knatchbull-Hugessen, who was strafed and severely injured in his car on the way from Nanking to Shanghai. The incidents reinforced the idea that, under the new regime, no one who strayed from the foreign concessions would be immune from attack.

When the Japanese scheduled a victory parade down Nanking Road for December 3, Mickey bet her roommate Mary five dollars there would be no violence. In fact, the procession – the Japanese had agreed to hand over their arms in respect for the International Settlement's neutrality – was marked by a series of dramatic incidents. A Chinese man jumped to his death from the top floor of the Great World amusement centre, with a yell of "Long Live China!" On Kiangse Road – the street where Mickey had lived until recently – another Chinese man threw a bomb that wounded three Japanese soldiers. For half an hour, the parade was brought to a standstill at the spot where the bomb had exploded outside the Cathay Hotel on Black Saturday.

Mickey was also taken aback by the sinking of the USS *Panay*, an American gunboat anchored in the Yangtze River near Nanking, which was attacked by Japanese planes on December 12. When she discovered the Japanese had flown back to machine-gun the survivors, she feared the incident would lead to immediate war between the United States and Japan. Neither country, though, was ready for such a confrontation. As sympathetic as President Roosevelt was to the plight of China – the Delanos had been partners in a Chinese tea-shipping firm, and his mother had spent her childhood in Hong Kong – he was aware the country was in an isolationist mood. Ninety per cent of the American public supported neutrality in Japan's war with China, and when the Japanese apologized – and organized a campaign of letter-writing in which schoolgirls sent handwritten condolences to the American embassy in Tokyo – everyone decided it had all been a regrettable mistake.

When the fighting swept northwards, the news that came from Nanking was shocking. The arrival of Japanese troops in the nationalist capital on December 13 was marked by an orgy of violence. It was a hideous tradition in the Imperial Army, Mickey knew from her Japanese friends, that commanders allowed soldiers three days of looting after they'd taken a city. The "Rape of Nanking," in which Japanese officers threw decapitated bodies into the "Ten Thousand Corpse Ditch," set a new standard of brutality. At least 40,000, and perhaps as many as 300,000, Chinese civilians died.

"Everything you read about Nanking is true," Mickey wrote home. "I know it. It is the older element in the army, the ones used to such actions from years of campaigning in North China. As soon as the gendarmerie got there, they were under control again, but it was three days too late." (Mickey was misinformed: the slaughter in Nanking went on for two months.) She was sickened by the thought of the broad boulevards and tranquil hillsides of Nanking, a city she'd come to know with Sinmay, running with blood.

"It is the most horrible war ever." As horrible as things seemed, though, she had no intention of leaving.

美

On September 17, 1937, a short article appeared in the *China Press* quoting the management of the Cathay Hotel: "Since August

14, we were obliged to close down temporarily. Now circumstances having become normal, or 'nearly' normal, we are able to reopen once more for the convenience of friends and patrons." No acknowledgement was made of the events of Black Saturday. Just a month and three days after the bombings, an orchestra led by cellist Joseph Ullstein played two sets in the Cathay's completely restored lounge, a few yards from where bombs had torn open the lobby.

In phone calls from Bombay, Sir Victor Sassoon had impressed on the staff the importance of reopening the hotel as soon as possible. The Cathay, after all, was a symbol of Shanghai's prosperity and security: as long as it welcomed guests, China would be considered open for business. After returning to Shanghai on November 3 – by way of an agonizingly slow ocean liner from Calcutta, and by air from Hong Kong – he was beginning to have doubts. When his plane had landed at the Lunghwa Airport in the midst of the nationalists' retreat, he'd seen the flames rising from a hundred fires in the old Chinese city. Things looked even worse than when he'd left the city on the *Empress of Japan* after the January 28 Incident in 1932.

It was a shame. Before the bombs, 1937 had been the gayest year he'd yet spent in Shanghai. In February he'd held a "Toy Shop" ball in the Cathay Ballroom, in which he'd expressed his gratitude to his friends and employees by inviting their children to come dressed as Raggedy Ann dolls and teapots. Ciro's had become the undisputed hotspot for nightlife, and lately he'd been feeling fit enough to go for a turn on the dance floor. An Italian doctor named Valvasone had been giving him massages for his bad leg, and told him he felt confident he would soon be able to walk – and even dance – without his canes. En route to India that summer, he'd been able to record in his journal: "Did dance steps without stick in cabin then walked upstairs without stick."

The damage to the Cathay, he knew, could be repaired; but if the Japanese invasion caused a mass exodus, he stood to lose everything. The nationalists, Ovadia told him, were already trying to put the squeeze on British banks to get more money for their war chests.

Strangely, though, since he'd returned, business had actually been improving. While imports and exports had suffered because of the war, the real-estate office on the third floor of Sassoon House was being flooded with enquiries for flats, offices, and warehouse space at almost any price. Conflict, as it had been since the days of the Taiping Rebellion, was a boon for owners of real estate in the International Zone.

Such gains, though, might only be temporary. As the weeks went on, he was finding it harder to project confidence about Shanghai's future. In December he had met with Mickey and re-assured her about her decision to remain in Shanghai. He gave her and her roommate Mary $500 each.* Privately, though, he was worried about the ever-increasing swagger of the Japanese. After their victory parade through the International Settlement, they seemed to think they were the masters of Shanghai.

"Two Japs noisy and insulting to England in Tower," he had noted in his journal early in December. In a later entry, he noted: "Japs getting truculent. Want control of municipal services. Things don't look good to me."

On the first day of 1938, Sir Victor sat down to write a letter to Derek FitzGerald, the manager of E.D. Sassoon's European interests, in London.

My dear Derek,

Things are looking really serious now, and I cannot see what is to be done.

The Japanese look like going the whole hog. They will take over the Customs and express their inability to meet the service of the loans. They will take over the currency and link it with their Yen, thus allowing no export of Capital by refusing remittances . . . only Japanese goods will enter China. In other words China becomes part

---

* Mickey wrote to her mother: "Victor is here, and everything immediately looks brighter, of course. And he is feeling so well and happy that he doesn't care about losing all that money which has gone up in smoke."

of Japan from a trade point of view . . . if we due [sic] anything like throttling their trade they will declare war on us, anticipating that they will be able to live on China by wholesale expropriation.

The solution, Sir Victor wrote, was something he was afraid his government would never do:

That is start withdrawing every Britisher from China including civilians from Hong Kong . . . and then stop all trade with Japan . . . this will be cheaper than starting an offensive before we are ready.

The final lines of the single-paged letter offered a glimpse of his real state of mind – and of just how bad things were in Shanghai:

Not showing this letter to the Staff as I do not want them to know how depressed I am.

Yours, V.

18: The Solitary Island

Shanghai in 1938 was a city in limbo. Since Black Saturday, the flood of refugees into the foreign concessions had swollen the population to over four million, so that it rivalled Berlin for the title of the world's fourth largest city. Many of the European and American women and children who had fled south had started trickling back. For them, life in war-harassed Shanghai, with its servants and luxurious estates, seemed preferable to the relative security of crowded refugee camps in Hong Kong.

They returned to find the International Settlement and Frenchtown hemmed in by hostile forces. When the Japanese forced the nationalist troops to retreat, they immediately replaced the mayor appointed by Nanking with their own Chinese straw man. The new authorities erected a semicircle of barricades and blockhouses on three sides of Shanghai's foreign concessions, with the Whangpoo River forming the fourth side. Half a million Imperial Army troops held the Yangtze Valley. Japan's navy was in undisputed command of the China coast, and her air force, operating from bases in Korea and Taiwan, had mastery of the Asian skies. The fact that the Chinese post office, Chinese radio and telegraph offices, and Chinese customs services continued to operate in Shanghai's international settlements was a constant irritant to the Japanese.

For the next four years, Shanghai would be what its residents called a *gudao*: a Solitary Island, isolated in a vast sea patrolled by a vigilant and heavily armed foreign power.

If Shanghai was in limbo, so was Mickey Hahn. The fact that the war had, by 1938, moved on to northern and southern China – Canton would fall in November, completely cutting the nationalists off from the coast – contributed to the illusion that life in Shanghai might continue unchanged. Her teaching duties had resumed with the reopening of the Customs College, and, as the value of the American dollar doubled against the Chinese yuan, her fat *New Yorker* cheques were going farther than ever. Not that they always arrived – the mail was often intercepted, and many of her outgoing letters were held by the Chinese censors.

By February, Mickey had made her new Avenue Joffre house into a reasonable imitation of home. In addition to Mr. Mills, she had a large cross-bred chow dog and two Siamese kittens; her cook, Chin Lien, kept a rhesus monkey with a bobbed tail who always seemed to escape from the kitchen when she had company over.

"I think I deliberately collect all these noise-makers," she wrote to her family, "because my early training makes it imperative that I be surrounded by noise before I can concentrate."

In fact, the house on Avenue Joffre often bustled like her childhood home in St. Louis. When Mary Garrison, after one too many run-ins with their temperamental cook, moved on to Sir Victor Sassoon's Cathay Mansions, another beautiful young woman took her place. Blonde, tragic, and mysterious, Lorraine Murray would bring a succession of entranced gentlemen callers to their door.

Mickey would end up writing a novel about Lorraine, an opium addict who, in addition to speaking exquisite Japanese, was a first-rate fabulist. They had been introduced by one of Lorraine's Chinese lovers, who was under the impression she was from South Africa. She told Mickey – who called her "Jean" in her memoirs – that she was from Australia, but when Mickey brought her for tiffin to Eve's, she told Sir Victor she was from Canada.

"At 15 companion to Japanese amb. to Canada's daughter," Sir Victor wrote of Lorraine in the telegraphic style he favoured in his journal:

He seduced her took her to Japan where kept her a year. Scandal through his wife. She sent away with little money. Reached S'hai Dec. '32. Stayed Metropole . . . Met Italian Pimp. He put her in brothels. Became tart kept for Chinese has slept with most Chinese including

TV Soong . . . Everyone tries to put her in business college. Is pregnant now to Luigi Barzini – going to H'kong to meet him – he is adopting child after as she tried commit suicide fortnight ago.

Gradually, Mickey learned what sounded like a plausible version of her life story. When the Canadian-born Lorraine was fifteen years old, she was noticed by a forty-year-old Japanese minister who also happened to be a prince and a member of the powerful Tokugawa family. He made Lorraine his mistress and took her around the world with him, deflecting suspicion by telling people she was his daughter's companion. Back in Japan, he hid her away in a geisha house until the gendarmerie got wind of the affair and put her on a ship (along with a substantial cash pay-off). In Shanghai she'd worked in a high-priced brothel run by a chatty, overweight former nurse from Canada; there, she'd become a favourite of wealthy Chinese clients – among them Chiang Kai-shek's brother-in-law, T.V. Soong. It was the nationalist finance minister who'd introduced her to Mickey, in the hopes she could find her work – or at least some female friends.

The year the romantically indiscriminate Lorraine spent with Mickey on Avenue Joffre was full of drama. After her affair with the dashing Italian journalist Luigi Barzini, she fell in love with a catty White Russian woman, who popped in one day to boast that she'd been invited to Sir Victor's box at the races.

"I did suggest to Sir Victor that he invite you," the Russian woman added, "but the fact is he didn't think it would be fair to his other guests. I mean to introduce the ladies to a girl who – well, who used to be a prostitute."

In despair, Lorraine took an overdose of the barbiturate Veronal – the first of many suicide attempts. In spite of such high drama, Mickey would count her as one of her best – and most endearing – roommates.*

---

* Mickey's novel *Miss Jill from Shanghai: A Beautiful Girl's Story of Salvation and Sin in the Orient* – published as an Avon paperback with a garish yellow cover in 1950 – documented the strangely happy ending to Lorraine Murray's adventures in China. During her wartime imprisonment in a civilian camp in Hong Kong, she was accepted by her fellow internees, and

Much of Mickey's time during 1938 was taken up with her latest publishing venture. The rescue of Sinmay's printing press, now secure in the garage on Avenue Joffre, allowed her to launch a sequel to their ill-fated bilingual magazine. *Candid Comment* was her attempt to bring the sophistication of the *New Yorker* to Shanghai. A front-of-the-book department, entitled "Of Possible Worlds" and written in the royal "we," consisted of short pieces in the style of the *New Yorker*'s "Talk of the Town." Sir Victor Sassoon helped out by purchasing full-page ads for the Tower Night Club, and a Eurasian cartoonist who went by the names "Chow" and Paddy O'Shea – he would die of tuberculosis at the age of sixteen – contributed vividly observed cartoons, in the style of Al Hirschfeld, of rick-shaw coolies, lute players, and other denizens of Shanghai's backstreets.

Mickey was not above using *Candid Comment* as a forum to air grievances and champion pet causes. The opening issue included a lengthy attack on the "Lady Next Door" who had dared to object to Mr. Mills's antics. The second had a poem in the gibbon's honour, with the verse: "He loves the girls with crinkly curls / And ladies with pompadours; / He likes bananas and gymkhanas / And peeks in cuspidors."

The magazine's pro-Chinese editorial slant attracted the attention of the Japanese. One visitor – whom she ignored – promised "increased circulation and plenty of advertising" if she would only convince her colleague Sinmay to tone down the anti-Japanese rhetoric in the Chinese version of the magazine.

The varied contents of *Candid Comment* reflected the bewilderingly varied company Mickey Hahn kept in real life. A frequent caller at the house was an extravagant Russo-Czech dancer with a Swedish name, Regina Peterson, who performed under the stage name Indra Devi. "Peter," as Mickey called her, had become fascinated with India in Moscow after reading a book by Rabindranath

---

experienced a rare sense of belonging. Over the years, Mickey would stay in touch with Lorraine, who after the war spent some time in Australia before marrying and settling permanently in England.

Tagore – the Bengali author idolized by Sinmay – and spent her days doing strange stretching exercises.

"Peter was in and out of the house all day, playing with the gibbons, trying in vain to make me take Yogi [sic] seriously," Mickey wrote. "Sinmay adored her in his own way; she appealed to his love of the bizarre."

Another regular visitor was Don Chisholm, the son of a dean at Johns Hopkins University, who edited *Shopping News*, a scandal sheet that made its money by charging a steep fee to "spike" stories that detailed the extramarital affairs and other peccadilloes of prominent Shanghailanders.*

The presence of "Peter" and Chisholm in her house, Mickey knew, was symptomatic of her scattered state of mind.

"Why was I such a patient slut?" Mickey would wonder, much later. "My foolish, insincere kindliness had let me in for all of this waste. It was certainly time to call a halt."

Yet she continued to let life happen to her. When one of Sinmay's younger brothers, who had become a general in a guerrilla army fighting against the Japanese, told her he was looking for a safe house, she obliged by letting a trio of revolutionaries move a radio transmitter – which they used to stay in contact with their headquarters in unoccupied China – into an unused back room. It was only after Malcolm Smythe – the deputy police commissioner who had helped save Sinmay's printing press – came over for tea, and wondered whether she too heard a strange *"gaak, gak, gakgakgak"* sound coming through the walls, that she politely asked them to move on.

The same room was then rented by a studious young Chinese woman who rarely left the house. Mickey soon discovered that Yang Gang, a friend of the American radical Agnes Smedley, was hard at work translating a series of Mao Tse-tung's speeches into

---

* Chisholm later read anti-British commentaries for the Japanese twice a week on radio station XMHA, becoming Shanghai's version of Lord Haw-Haw, the name given to a number of British- and American-born traitors who broadcast pro-Nazi propaganda from the Third Reich.

English. Mickey, hoping to bring news of the nationalists and communists' United Front against Japan to an international audience, agreed to publish the speeches. Ideologically, the publication of Mao's "Prolonged War," the first instalment of which appeared in the November, 1938 issue of *Candid Comment*, was the closest Mickey ever got to endorsing China's communists.

Mickey later told her biographer that she remembered Mao Tse-tung paying a visit to her Avenue Joffre house. That is unlikely: at the time, Mao, preoccupied with evading Japanese bombers, was 2,000 miles away, hiding in a cave outside the city walls of Yenan.

Given all the comings and goings, it wasn't surprising Mickey lost track of who exactly had crossed the threshold of her Frenchtown home. Most troubling of all was the sheer number of strangers who had begun to ring her bell. Towards the end of 1938, a succession of dignified and desperate Europeans came to her door – sometimes dozens a day – hoping to sell everything from handbags and rugs to porcelain and shoelaces. In Europe, they had been watchmakers and tailors and doctors, but were now reduced to pedalling family heirlooms. She talked to all of them, and did what she could to help.

They were all, she learned, Jews who had fled from Nazism in Germany and Austria. Every day, their numbers seemed to grow. She checked the lists of new arrivals for the name "Hahn," or her mother's maiden name "Schoen." Any one of them, she realized, could be a cousin.

Mickey's house on Avenue Joffre, which her reflexive sociability had made into a refuge for lost souls – as well as a menagerie for dogs, cats, and non-human primates – had turned into a microcosm of the Solitary Island. Just as a Shanghai hard-pressed by the influx of Chinese and European refugees had no time for long-term planning, the oddly comforting hustle and bustle in her Frenchtown home prevented Mickey from thinking about her own future. The still plentiful supply of opium kept the worst of her worries at bay.

Something, she was confident, would come along and shake

her out of the torpor that kept her rooted to the spot. She had no idea, though, what that something would look like.

美

In the months that followed Black Saturday, Shanghai had faced a humanitarian crisis. In late November, the Buddhist benevolent society responsible for burying the dead reported picking up 18,000 cadavers from the streets. Street fighting, aerial bombing, and shelling focused on the densely populated Chinese districts of Hongkew, Chapei, and Nantao. With the gates and bridges of the foreign concessions closed to the Chinese, 100,000 refugees flooded into the former walled city, Shanghai's historic heart. Thanks to the efforts of a one-armed Catholic priest, however, they were spared the worst effects of the fighting.

The Nantao Safety Zone, which was formally established on November 9, 1937, was the brainchild of a famously unorthodox Catholic priest named Jacquinot de Basange. The gaunt Jesuit kept a pistol in his cassock, and was known to use his wooden hand (he'd lost his right arm in a failed chemistry experiment) to whack uncooperative Japanese officials on the head.

"The Japanese have not gained entry here," Father Jacquinot proudly told reporters. "The only flags that fly over this place are the French flag and the standard of the Red Cross."

Makeshift barracks were set up in the Temple of the City God, rations were distributed, and Chinese officers – commanded by a 200-pound, bewhiskered Russian "Chief of Police" – patrolled the streets. Jointly administered by the British, French, and Americans, the Safety Zone was credited with saving half a million lives over the next three years. Enshrined in the Geneva Convention of 1949, it became the model for urban demilitarized zones in the twentieth century.

A year later, when refugees from European fascism began to arrive in Shanghai en masse, Sir Victor Sassoon was able to draw on Father Jacquinot's model. Late in 1938, when the orgy of anti-Semitic violence known as *Kristallnacht* made it clear there was no hope for a peaceful life under the Nazis, German and Austrian

Jews began to seek refuge around the world. In the United States, they would be turned back under the Johnson–Reed Immigration Act, which prioritized refugees from Nordic countries. Canada was only willing to accommodate farmers, thus excluding the great mass of city-born Jews. The 1939 "voyage of the damned" of the MS *St. Louis*, whose thousand German Jewish passengers were turned away from Halifax and Havana – and actually driven from the shores of Florida with warning shots – before being carried back to Europe and death in concentration camps, was an all-too-vivid illustration of how tightly the world's doors were closing to the victims of Nazism.

Shanghai became known around the world as the "port of last resort." All told, 18,000 Jews from Central and Eastern Europe would find refuge in the city (equal to the combined total admitted to Canada and Australia during the entire Second World War).

In the early days, Shanghai's Sephardic elites welcomed their Ashkenazi co-religionists. The first to arrive had embarked on Italian ocean liners at Trieste or Genoa, and travelled first- or second-class via the Suez Canal and Bombay, a three-week journey. Though many carried with them valuable family belongings, a ruinous Nazi "exit tax" allowed them to leave Germany with only ten marks (about $4 US, or $24 in Chinese currency) in their pockets. While Shanghai was unique among the world's great cities in that it required no passports, visas, financial guarantees or certificates of character from new arrivals, the customs authorities did demand a one-time entry fee of $400. Wealthy Sephardim like Ellis Hayim, Elly Kadoorie, and Sir Victor Sassoon – drawing from a trust fund operated under the pseudonym "Val Seymour" – paid the cautions that allowed many of the Jews to get past customs.

Sir Victor took the measure of the problem one morning when the Lloyd Triestino liner *Conte Verde* – aboard which he had cruised the seas in luxury many times – pulled into dock with 550 refugees aboard; he used his movie camera to record the throngs leaving the Customs Jetty on the Bund. In October 1938, a Committee for the Assistance of European Jewish Refugees, whose board included Hayim, Kadoorie, and the elderly Dutch financier Michele Speelman, was set up to coordinate donations from Europe and the United States. Sir Victor was by far the biggest contributor, making a one-time gift of $150,000 in Chinese currency. (The *China Press* estimated $90,000 would be needed to meet the material needs of the "émigrés" every *month*.) The Beth Aharon Synagogue, built by the late Silas Hardoon, was turned into a kitchen that fed 600 refugees a day.

Sylvia Chancellor – whose husband was the head of Reuters in the Far East, and who three years earlier had smuggled a donkey into Sir Victor's circus party – was one of Shanghai's most energetic philanthropists. To an interviewer, she described buttonholing Sir Victor:

I said to him at one of his parties, "Look here, I am sure I can rely on you to find us a building. These are middle-aged, professional men and their families and they need somewhere to live and something to eat and you're the man to do it."

In fact, Sir Victor was already hard at work. He established a fund to supply free milk on a daily basis to every refugee in Shanghai, and set up a variety of accounts to support the refugees, under the pseudonym "Val Seymour." He donated an expensive iron lung to one of the three hospitals set up to serve the community, and turned one of his buildings on Nanking Road into the Immigrants' Thrift Shop, where refugees could raise funds by selling their belongings. Thanks to Chancellor's prodding, he allowed the ground floor of his S-shaped Embankment Building to be used as a receiving station for new arrivals. Its kitchens, run by a Chinese caterer, fed 1,000 refugees a day. Later, Sir Victor arranged for more long-term housing for 2,500 refugees in Hongkew.

While the orthodox Sephardim paid special attention to the religious needs of the refugees, Sir Victor's aspirations for his fellow Jews in Shanghai were wholly secular.* He set up a voca-

---

* By 1938, Sir Victor's relationship with the faith of his ancestors was purely abstract. He conducted business, and even went to the races, on high holidays. He expressed no desire to be buried in a Jewish cemetery, and was a well-known sceptic on the subject of Zionism.

tional camp that trained young immigrants as mechanics, joiners, and carpenters, and arranged for 250 men to be trained by a Jewish commander for duty in the Shanghai Volunteer Corps. Mozelle Abraham, the wife of one of the leading Sephardic philanthropists, said of Sir Victor: "God will forgive him all his sins because of the charity he gives."

Thanks to Sir Victor and other wealthy Sephardim, Shanghai was able to absorb much of the first wave of immigrants. A section of Japanese-dominated Hongkew nicknamed "Little Vienna" became known as the place to go for Sachertorte and strudel.

Nobody could deny the extent of Sir Victor's contributions, said to be the most generous in the Far East, to Jewish causes. When controversy arose, as it did in the months leading to the Second World War, it would be about the justice of the Sephardic community's claims that Shanghai no longer had the resources to absorb any more immigrants.

Some refugees recorded their delight at arriving in a place that seemed to embody the promise of a truly international settlement. "Welcome to Shanghai," one placard held by a welcoming committee on the Bund read in 1938. "Now you are no longer Germans, Austrians, Czechs or Rumanians, now you are Jews, only Jews. The Jews of the world have prepared a home for you."

美

The sudden coming of German and Austrian Jews had a strong effect on Mickey Hahn. They were, after all, her people. "We are busy in lots of ways," she wrote to her family in the spring of 1939,

particularly with the thousands of Jewish refugees who have arrived lately, and are still arriving . . . Whenever Victor gets a job for somebody he is as cheerful as if he had settled the whole problem. I have never seen him so hard at work . . . We have lots of good doctors now, at prices we can afford; we have the best tailor in the world – I wish you could see my new suit, and a grey evening dress – and some of the artists are wonderful. Also photography, psychoanalysis – well, everything. Shanghai looks like Germany, with the Nazis left out.

There was a strange mix of sympathy and condescension in Mickey's reaction to the refugees. Her relationship to her Judaism, like Sir Victor's, was intellectual and cultural. Since her youth, she'd gotten used to thinking of herself as an up-to-date, scientific-minded cosmopolitan. In Shanghai, she was at the top of the social heap. At the Race Course, she sat in a multimillionaire's box; she was driven around town in a chauffeured Chevrolet; she had a gardener and a cook. They might share common ancestors, but the pedlars who knocked on her door asking for charity came from a different world. Her unease is evident in her writing from the time, which can come across as flippant, ill-informed, and lacking in *gravitas*. "Way off across the world, in Germany and the adjoining territories," she would write in her memoir *China to Me*, "Hitler was shouting and jumping up and down and bothering people generally."

Against the background of genocide and blitzkrieg, the voice of the wised-up flapper, reflexively blasé about other people's fears, rang hollow. An unpublished essay entitled "Shanghai, Land of Plenty" is a particularly cruel portrait of the refugees arriving in Shanghai. It opens with an anecdote told by an English friend, who has met two German Jewish girls named Sapiro on the boat from Hong Kong. Reading from an out-of-date guidebook, the girls had spoken unrealistically of the life they expected to lead in Shanghai.

"They were talking about putting up at the Cathay. It had been recommended to them, they said. The Cathay! I said, 'My dears, do you know what the Cathay charges by the day?' and they said 'Oh, that's all right; we'll put our money together.'"

Mickey and her English friend are then driven, by limousine, to a camp in Japanese-occupied Hongkew, where they plan to distribute biscuits to the refugees. She experiences a "spasm of pity" when she sees a woman wearing an out-of-fashion hat. "It was a silly shabby black straw, sitting on top of the oily brown hair of a middle-aged woman."

Then her friend spots the Sapiro sisters. Instead of feather beds at the Cathay, of course, they are sleeping in makeshift bunk beds of bamboo. To avoid embarrassment, the girls push violently through the crowd and escape into a nearby dormitory. "I had only a glimpse of them, of long noses and black eyes and frizzy hair," writes Mickey.

It is a bleak piece, which probably explains why it was never published in the *New Yorker*. One line is particularly cruel in its condescension: "It is only the left-overs, the poor, the spiritless or the stupid stubborn ones who end a long and crowded journey in the Shanghai camp."

She was echoing an equally cruel, though more nuanced, pronouncement Sir Victor had made about the refugees. The ones who made it to Shanghai, he'd told her, were

the sweepings of the country. They didn't have the guts or the brains to get out when they should have. They hung on as long as possible. Naturally they're not as likeable as the others. This doesn't go for the old people or the very young relatives, but if you look at the young men in this crowd you'll see what I mean.

Sir Victor, whatever his private opinions, gave the refugees material support, and even sat down with them for lunch in the canteen of the Embankment Building. And, as Mickey reported, he went at the relief work with energy and optimism, even while he suspected time was running out for his Far Eastern empire.

Mickey's uneasy relationship with the refugees was undoubtedly connected to her growing sense of existential unease. She had more in common with them than she liked to admit. Her world, like theirs, had shrunk. It had been two years, she realized, since she had been more than a couple of hundred miles away from Shanghai.

Restless, she began looking for her next story – the one that would get her off the Solitary Island.

美

Mickey had been of two minds about John Gunther's arrival in China.

On one hand, she was happy to see her old Chicago friend. They had first met when he was a cub reporter for the *Chicago*

Daily News. A big-boned, fair-haired lug, famous for his remarkable memory, Gunther had energetically courted her older sister. When Helen spurned him, Gunther had fled to Europe, where, through moxie and hard work, he had transformed himself into a famous foreign correspondent while still in his twenties. When *Inside Europe* was published in 1936, it perfectly filled a niche in the market. For Americans hungry for insight into the chaos on the continent, it provided a one-volume, 600-page overview of the big issues. While Mickey chuckled at Gunther's masculine penchant for making grand pronouncements based on the most glancing on-the-ground experience, she had to admit that he had a real talent for making big geopolitical issues immediately comprehensible to the general public. Now, she learned, he was going to do the same for the East, travelling with his wife from Palestine to the Philippines to research *Inside Asia.*[*]

"The Gunthers," Mickey wrote her family in the spring of 1938, "are horribly almost here; stopping for a time, I think, in Hankow, where John can learn all about China and how to end the war, with his usual speed and precision, in a week."

When the couple arrived in Shanghai, Mickey invited them to dinner with Sinmay. Gunther was amused to discover that one of Sinmay's colleagues was responsible for publishing the bootlegged Chinese edition of *Inside Europe*, which cost him thousands in royalties. He refrained from comment, probably because another of Sinmay's friends was helping to arrange a crucial interview with Chiang Kai-shek.

Gunther considered himself one of Mickey's biggest fans; in Chicago, he had been the first to suggest she make a living by writing for the newspapers. Over dinner that night, he argued she

---

[*] Gunther's first four "Inside" books would sell 2.7 million copies. The title Mickey would later choose for her memoirs about her adventures in the Far East, *China to Me*, was a pointed response to the presumption of authority of the "Inside" books. Unlike Gunther, she was suggesting, she offered only her flawed, subjective – but probably more truthful – account of what she'd seen, and felt, and heard. She would title later non-fiction memoirs *England to Me* and *Africa to Me*.

was ideally placed to write a book New York publishers had been clamouring for: a biography of the Soong sisters, the modern dynasty whose story seemed to symbolize China's struggle.

At the time, Mickey had conceded the point, but in the months that followed she allowed herself to succumb to torpor and shelved the idea. Then a letter arrived from her agent, with the offer of a substantial cash advance from Macmillan. Back in New York, the loose-lipped Gunther had been telling people that Mickey was hard at work on the authorized biography of the Soong sisters.

In truth, Mickey was *very* interested. The Soongs were one of the most famous families in China. The father, Charlie Soong, had adopted Christianity as a teenager after being sent to Boston to help at his uncle's tea and silk shop. His missionary hosts, delighted to have gained a Chinese convert, paid for him to study theology at Vanderbilt University. Soong's connections to the nationalists dated to 1894, when he met Sun Yat-sen at a Sunday service in Shanghai. The two men had much in common: both were Methodists, both shared connections with the Triads, and both grew up hating the Manchu rulers of China. Soong, taking advantage of the Boxer indemnity that funded the education of Chinese students in the United States, sent his three daughters to Wesleyan in Georgia, the world's oldest chartered women's college.

The family's enduring alliance with the nationalists was cemented when – to Charlie Soong's displeasure – his second daughter Qing-ling married the much older Sun Yat-sen, for whom she worked as a secretary. A small woman who favoured simple black silk dresses and detested the public spotlight, Qing-ling was the sister who leaned furthest to the left. After her husband's death in 1925, "Madame Sun," as she was known, became a torch-bearer for the early, idealistic days of the Kuomin-tang, when it had looked to Soviet Russia for inspiration. Ai-ling, the eldest Soong sister, married the Yale-educated banker H.H. Kung, who traced his ancestry back to Confucius. "Madame Kung," as she became known, was said to be obsessed with getting her riches into American banks. The youngest and most stylish of the sisters, Mei-ling, was also the most feared. As "Madame Chiang," the wife of Chiang Kai-shek took personal responsibility for the Kuomintang's air force, and oversaw the petty rules of the New Life Movement.

Together with their brother, the Harvard-educated T.V. Soong – who, as director of China's leading banks and finance minister, was the economic brains behind the nationalists – the American-educated Soong sisters represented China's strong connections to the West. They were also valued as a bulwark against the militarist clique in the Kuomintang that favoured cooperation with the Japanese. The fact that Chiang Kai-shek, under the influence of Mei-ling, had become a Christian boosted his credibility in the United States. ("There's Methodism in his madness," John Gunther's wife Frances quipped about Chiang.) Even the leftist Madame Sun, who had yet to formally endorse Mao Tse-tung and the Chinese communists, was palatable to American politicians. Gunther, in whose prose metaphors proliferated, went farther, calling Madame Sun "a hidden flower; a beautifully luminous bit of porcelain; a source of spiritual continuity and power; a shadow with flame behind it."

The Chinese, Mickey knew, had a saying to distinguish Mesdames Sun, Kung, and Chiang: "One loves China, one loves money, and one loves power." After three years in China, she had also heard the rumours about nationalist corruption. "The whole family," she'd been informed on her arrival in Shanghai, "was simply coining money by various illegal means to be placed in foreign banks where it would be waiting for them when their evil practices had caught up with them and forced them to flee."

The offer to write about them, Mickey had to admit, was tempting. None of the half-dozen attempts at reportage she'd penned since Black Saturday had been accepted; the *New Yorker* only seemed interested in publishing more of the misadventures of "Mr. Pan." Devoting herself to an ambitious work of non-fiction would not only help her shake off her sense of aimlessness; it could also establish her reputation as a serious author.

After all, it had worked for another Midwestern writer who

lived in Shanghai. Mickey was well acquainted with Edgar Snow – he was part of the Missouri Mafia – and was friends with his wife, Helen Foster Snow, who wrote under the name Nym Wales. Snow became an international celebrity after he'd landed the most coveted interview in China: a protracted *tête-à-tête* with Mao Tse-tung.

Two years earlier, Snow, then just twenty-nine, had quietly packed up a carton of Camel cigarettes, a can of Maxwell House coffee, and some Gillette razor blades and left the International Settlement on a daring mission. Bearing a letter of introduction from Madame Sun, and with the help of the Young Marshal – the Manchurian warlord who orchestrated the kidnapping of Chiang Kai-shek – he crossed the nationalist lines in the company of a bandit guide and a mule. When he arrived in Pao-an, near the communists' wartime capital of Yenan, he was greeted, in perfect English, by Chou En-lai, the communists' second-in-command. For four months Snow lived alongside the Red Army and recorded, for the first time in English, the life stories of its leaders and the gripping details of the Long March.

"I was uncommitted for or against the Reds," Snow would later write of his attitude before meeting Mao. "I was genuinely curious to know whether the Reds might be better or worse – a journalist after a story."

Snow came back to Shanghai deeply impressed. The people he met in Pao-an, he wrote, seemed the freest and happiest Chinese he had ever met. He witnessed no armed coercion in their inter-actions with the peasants, only "persuasion and gradualism" – in stark contrast to the Kuomintang's "White Terror." Mao in particular struck him as a complex, articulate man committed to charting a distinctly Chinese course for the future.

When his impressions were published in *Red Star over China* – which became a book-club selection in England, and the decade's bestselling non-fiction book on China in the United States – they caused a revolution in Western attitudes towards the communists. "The 'Red bandits' bear a close resemblance," wrote a *New York Times* reviewer, "to people whom we used to call patriots." It helped that Snow was an excellent writer, with a no-nonsense, down-to-earth style and an eye for the telling detail. President Roosevelt was a fan of the book, and would rely on Snow as one of his unofficial sources on the politics of the Far East during the war. The most negative reactions came from American communists, who were scandalized by Snow's "Trotskyist slanders" against what he called Stalin's "dictatorship."

Snow, in making himself Mao's Boswell, had also turned himself into the most famous journalist in the Far East. Mickey hoped that writing about the Soong sisters could do the same for her.

Sinmay encouraged her to take on the project: if his partner in publishing wrote a bestselling biography, he reasoned, it would help them both. Moreover, Sinmay had connections with the Soongs. His favourite aunt was a childhood friend of the eldest of the Soong sisters. Madame Kung was also on the board of *T'ien Hsia*, an English-language magazine devoted to Chinese culture, to which both he and Mickey contributed. Since the editorial staff of the magazine had relocated to Hong Kong, and Madame Kung herself lived there, he suggested they make an excursion to the British colony. In preparation, Mickey mailed off tactfully worded letters to each of the Soong sisters.

"I believe you are a seeker after truth," Madame Kung replied. "I do want to meet you."

In the first week of June, 1939, Mickey and Sinmay left Shanghai on a small boat, whose circuitous route, the captain admitted to her, was due to the fact he was running ammunition to Chinese guerrillas. They checked into the Hongkong Hotel, on the Victoria Harbour waterfront. Founded in 1863, it was as close as the colony came at the time to having a rival to the Cathay Hotel; its restaurant, Gripps, was a famous meeting place for Hong Kong's leading citizens. Sinmay immediately felt ill at ease in this resort of Peakites, as the residents of Hong Kong's exclusive hilltop neighbourhood were known. With his long scholar's robes, whiskers, and the pallor of the habitual opium smoker, he stopped conversations each time he appeared in the lobby.

The ambient stuffiness and bigotry made Sinmay sulky. The

colony served as the Royal Navy's official station in China, and was ruled by a governor who was the King's plenipotentiary in China. (A seat on the often-crowded Peak Tram was permanently reserved for him, despite the fact that he might ride it only once a year.) In Hong Kong's nightclubs – where gimlets, rather than Shanghai's signature gin slings, were served – the bands still struck up "God Save the King" to signal closing time at the unheard-of hour, for a Shanghainese, of midnight. Most of the educated Chinese in Hong Kong didn't appear in public in traditional clothing; Sinmay's friends at the offices of *T'ien Hsia* all wore suits and ties.

"These young Chinese, these children of compradors!" he complained to Mickey about his Westernized compatriots. "They have money and no brains. At least their fathers have brains enough to make that money out of the foreigners."

Most of all, he was incensed by the British in Hong Kong, who lived lives completely cut off from the Chinese – and the fact that Mickey, while she waited for an invitation to Madame Kung's house, was spending so much time with them.

The one British citizen Sinmay liked was a handsome young army captain named Charles Boxer. Impressed by Mickey's articles in *T'ien Hsia*, Boxer had once shown up at Mickey's house in Shanghai with a letter of introduction. After being faced with an enormous ape wearing a red cap on its head, as well as the beautiful Lorraine Murray, who stared at him in silence while he struggled to make small talk with Mickey, he'd left under the impression that Mickey and Sinmay "were actors in one of the great love stories of the world" and that the entire household was quite mad.

Since that visit, Mickey learned, Boxer had married one of the colony's greatest beauties. He invited Sinmay and Mickey to lunch. Already drunk on gimlets when his guests showed up, he impressed Mickey as being a "brilliant, amusing, mad man." Sinmay was equally charmed; Boxer turned out to be a scholar of Far Eastern colonial history.

"Now there is a real gentleman," he commented to Mickey. "They say he has wonderful books."

By the time the summons finally came for Mickey to meet Madame Kung, on July 15, 1939, she was a nervous wreck. Sinmay found her on her bed at the Hongkong Hotel, shaking and clenching her teeth. Her writing and teaching up until then, she told him, had been "make-believe." She was terrified because she was finally "about to dive into China, into the war and into real life."

Yet when Mickey met the dignified Madame Kung at her small house – appropriately, on Sassoon Road, so named in 1924, probably in tribute to Sir Victor, who that year became a baronet – the interview went swimmingly. She had agreed to the meeting, she told Mickey, because of something John Gunther had written. In *Inside Asia*, he had described her as "a hard-willed creature, possessed of demonic energy and great will-power, violently able, cunning, and ambitious," before adding: "her passionate interest is money."

Madame Kung, who had never met Gunther, wanted to set the record straight. If Mickey could promise to tell the truth, Madame would agree to help her with her project. The first step, she suggested, would be a visit to Chungking to interview her youngest sister, Madame Chiang.

Mickey left the meeting aglow. For her, it marked the beginning of a long relationship with Madame Kung, and a new phase in her career.

The trip to Hong Kong also marked a subtle alteration in the way she looked at both Shanghai and Sinmay.

They returned to Shanghai in melodramatic style. Aboard the *Maréchal Joffre*, Sinmay, convinced he would be detained in Japanese-occupied territory, dressed himself in tweeds and dark spectacles, shaved his whiskers, and posed as a Westernized businessman named "Mr. Tsu."

"He looked perfectly terrible," Mickey recalled. "I had never noticed before that his legs were too short."

The disguise got them past the cordon of spies on the Customs Jetty, but when Mickey got back to the French Concession, something troubled her.

I returned to Shanghai with the eagerness of a lover, and that reminded me of the first time I arrived, bored and sulky and frowning, counting the days before I could sail away again. Yet it was a very different city now. It stood alone and beleaguered, surrounded on all sides by a greedy, watchful enemy.

If she was looking at the city that had become her home with new eyes, it was because part of her knew what was coming. Her relationship with Sinmay – and with it, her beloved Shanghai – was about to end.

19: Waking from the Doze

It had been a hundred years since the outbreak of the First Opium War, which allowed the triumphant Western powers to open Treaty Ports up and down the China coast. The greatest of them remained Shanghai, that "model for the internationalization of the whole world."

What kind of a city had foreign enterprise, given free rein to exploit the world's single largest market, built?

In 1939, Shanghai presented the world with a glorious facade: the "billion-dollar skyline" of the Bund, whose centrepiece was, of course, the streamlined Cathay Hotel. Washed up against the rusticated cornerstones of the banks and shipping companies, however, was an awesome display of human wreckage: serried ranks of Chinese beggars displaying stunted limbs, gouged-out eyes, and festering sores, who were left to die public deaths of hunger and exposure.

Behind the Bund lurked squalor to which all citizens – coolies and taipans – were in some way subjected. Raw sewage leaked into the ground water, which could make ordering a salad a lethal decision. The chimney stacks of the foreign-run power company spewed black coal smoke into the air, sending those who lived nearby to the hospital with eye and lung infections. Typhoid, dysentery, cholera, and bubonic plague took a steady toll; until the Second World War, Shanghai had a leper colony.

For working-class foreigners, especially poorly-paid British soldiers, policemen, and civil servants, life in Shanghai was difficult. The burden of taxation fell on tenants rather than landlords, and their low salaries put the pleasures of a night at Ciro's or the Tower Night Club out of reach. For leisure, many were forced to resort to Blood Alley cabarets, movie theatres, or brothels. For those Chinese who were forced to pull rickshaws, sleep in straw shacks, sweat in silk filatures, or beg on the streets for coppers, life could be well-nigh unbearable.

In this city of skyscrapers built on the mud, *yangtu* – "foreign mud," or opium – was the one sure solace for aching backs and broken dreams. Ironically, it was also the item of trade that had opened China to foreign occupation.

It was also a substance to which Zau Sinmay and Mickey Hahn had developed a serious addiction. For Shanghai to overcome its subjugation, it would have to banish the symbol of that sub-jugation; and if Mickey was to escape from a Shanghai on its way to becoming a trap for Westerners, she would first have to kick opium.

美

On February 3, 1919, on the Pudong side of the Whangpoo River, representatives of the new nationalist government had burned the last stocks of Indian opium to be legally imported into China. Twenty years later, opiates were more widely available and easier to find than aspirin, a medication China had only gotten around to manufacturing in 1934.

Shanghai's wealthiest families – among them the Zaus – pre-ferred Indian-grown opium, still available on the black market, to the native product, which came from the poppy fields of Yunnan and Szechwan and was often adulterated with pork rinds, dried pig's blood, and sesame seed cake. Servants in rich households collected opium dregs and broken pieces of residue-caked pipes and sold them to opium dens, where they were thrown into pots of boiling water. Three or four copper coins were enough to buy a rickshaw puller, a wharf coolie, or a beggar a wine pot full of the resulting "faucet water," potent enough to provide a few hours in dreamland.

Opium, an effective remedy for diarrhea and a powerful pain-killer and anxiolytic, is not a particularly vicious drug. In Shanghai, old-style doctors continued to prescribe it – it remained legal as a medicine – as a cure-all. Compared to alcohol or barbiturates, opium is positively benign: overdoses have always been rare, and addicts often live long (if underachieving) lives.

"The moderate Chinese opium smokers," the American radio announcer Carroll Alcott wrote in his memoirs, "and I know many of them, take a pipe after dinner much as Occidentals drink a liqueur or smoke a pipe of tobacco. They may have a pipe after their lunch, followed by a short nap and, of course, the advertised pleasant dreams."

Graham Greene wrote that of four winters he spent in the Far East, smoking opium in the fumeries of Saigon "left the happiest memory."

Westerners who dabbled with opium, and romanticized it in their writing, were unlikely to become aware of one of its most salient properties. While stifling pain, it also – like tobacco – engendered *yan*, the Chinese word for addiction (which, transformed into "yen," has entered the English lexicon as a synonym for a strong craving). This made it the most formidable of commodities. A consumer product that neutralizes hunger, while inducing euphoria and a strong craving for more, doesn't even have to be advertised: once exposed to its effects, a significant proportion of users will make repeating the experience a priority.

Opium isn't evil, any more than alcohol is evil. There was evil, however, in introducing an addictive narcotic to an impoverished society at a time of extreme social distress. Like the sale of rum and whisky that had such lethal effects on aboriginal cultures, the wholesaling of opium to China was a crime of empire – and one of modern history's lesser known crimes against humanity.

Yangtu had been part of Chinese society long enough – for at least two centuries, when the palace eunuchs in Peking became the first aficionados – that its use had been ritualized among the upper classes, who looked at it as little more than a strong tipple. Opium pipes were offered at weddings, and among businessmen "let's light the lamps" was a synonym for "let's talk business." (The cabin boys on many steamers on the Yangtze offered passengers a choice of tea or opium.) For China as a whole, though, it acted as a slow poison. Opium made a once self-sufficient civilization, facing overpopulation and underemployment, dependent – economically as well as physically – on a product imported from abroad. For the poor (and most Chinese at the time were unimaginably poor), it extended the cycle of poverty to infinity. When the only relief from back-breaking and demeaning labour engenders sloth and further impoverishes the wage-earner, as well as his or her extended family, a citizenry has been transformed into a mass of helpless victims.

By the thirties, the victimizers were no longer Westerners but Asians. Echoing Sun Yat-sen, Chiang Kai-shek had early on pledged his nationalist government would get "not one cent" from opium. The New Life Movement, overseen by Madame Chiang, had made addiction punishable by death. In reality, though, opium was too lucrative a product for the nationalists to ban.* Opium revenues by the mid-thirties had reached $2 billion a year – equivalent to 5.2 per cent of the gross domestic product. By one estimate, 9 per cent of the population – fifty million people – were addicted. While the leaders of Republican China publicly railed against opium, their war machine was powered by the revenues from its sales.

In Shanghai, Chiang Kai-shek appointed the fiercely nationalistic gangster "Big-Eared" Du Yuesheng head of the Bureau of Opium Suppression. This was convenient, as Du also controlled the city's opium trade, which by the thirties had moved to the French Concession with the tacit approval of the Frenchtown gendarmerie. Opium was available in sixty retail shops; through Du, who collected thirty cents for every pipe smoked, a never-ending stream of silver flowed into the nationalist coffers.

Since the Japanese had invaded in 1931, the opium trade had entered a far more vicious phase. The American broadcaster Carroll Alcott was just one of many Westerners to discover that opium

---

* The same was true for the communists, who in the early forties secretly cultivated poppies in the north-west, and referred to opium as "soap" or "special product."

was being refined into morphine and heroin in labs in Japanese-occupied Manchuria, joining the cheap manufactured goods being smuggled through mountain passes to flood the Chinese market.

These more powerful and addictive opiates were instruments of war: since the yen was not recognized by the British or American as foreign exchange, the sale of heroin and morphine brought the Japanese the Chinese currency they needed to buy arms on the international market. At the same time, their availability vitiated the occupied population more quickly and irrevocably than opium ever had. In the late thirties, Alcott paid a visit to the Japanese-run Tai Chong Cigarette and Exchange Shop, just outside the International Settlement. A package of heroin there cost only ten cents, and three packs were enough to supply a hard-core addict for a day. At the same time, the cost of a pipe of opium had risen to forty cents. By retailing industrial-strength opiates, the Japanese had brought imperialism into the twentieth century. Soon enough, they would take over the Shanghai drug traffic, driving "Big-Eared" Du to an early retirement in Hong Kong.

By the summer of 1939, Mickey Hahn had been an opium addict for four years. She didn't regret trying the drug. Without it, she might never have come to know Sinmay and his family, and through them, the Chinese side of Shanghai. Besides, the prejudice against opium among foreigners, who saw it as a sign of "going native," made it irresistible to a woman for whom iconoclasm was a point of pride.

In the early days, it had felt like a harmless indulgence. In an essay entitled "The Price of Poppies," which was rejected by the editor of *The American Mercury* for its telling lack of organization, she wrote: "It gives a good warm feeling that is suspended halfway between body and mind . . . one is in a voluptuous mood, a luxurious mood, a mood in which it is enough to lie beside the opium-tray and make plans." There was nothing sexual about it, but, after smoking enough pipes, one might attain a state of euphoria. Sometimes, too, she entered a half-sleep, in which dream-like visions – as opposed to hallucinations – paraded before her eyes. Mickey called this the "opium doze."

"Once I was retiring," she wrote in the essay,

and had taken off one shoe, sitting on the edge of the bed, when the doze came over me. I had beautiful visions that evening, of which I remember a well-nigh endless procession of, it seemed to me, some Emperor of Peking. I saw the great gates opened, and the marching hundreds; I saw the sedan-chairs with golden satin curtains; I saw the finest detail embroidered of dragons and roses upon the costumes of the attendants, and the prancing ponies. Peking was as clear to me as though I had seen it . . . but I had never seen Peking, and when at last I did the reality was cold and colourless in comparison with my dreams.

I awoke suddenly, and began hastily to take off the other shoe. It was two hours since the first one had fallen to the floor.

When the article was finally published – thirty years later in the *New Yorker*, in much altered form – the above passage was omitted. In 1969, the year after LSD had been made illegal, this would have sounded too much like alluring propaganda for drug use. But it reflected Mickey's growing ambivalence about opium: for all the pleasure it had brought her in the past, by 1939 it had become a source of pain. By the summer of that year she had become sallow and gaunt, and had to be treated for jaundice. Though she revelled in her slimmer figure, the fact that she was no longer eating regular meals meant that she had stopped menstruating. Photos from those days show her with alarmingly dark pouches under her eyes. When she finally visited a doctor, he told her that her addiction meant she was unlikely ever to have children. Yet she couldn't stop. She smoked twelve pipes a day, and had to run home two or three times a day to "refuel." Her forefinger was stained with an oily smudge from testing opium pellets as they cooled. When she smoked alone, as she often did, she kept her left arm crooked around the tray, "affectionately and protectively." She had spent two years, she realized, putting off the last pipe of all.

Now she would have to quit. Writing a book on the Soong sisters meant spending a significant amount of time in nationalist-controlled territory. To escape Japanese bombs, Chiang Kai-shek had moved the capital first from Nanking to Hankow, and finally, in 1938, to Chungking in the heart of China – trading, in his words, "space for time." Making a show of opium suppression, the Kuomintang had already carried out mass executions of addicts in central China. The penalty for those caught in possession there, Mickey knew, was death by beheading.

One evening late in the summer of 1939, after smoking six pipes of opium in rapid succession, Mickey checked herself into a hospital. An ambitious young German doctor had promised he could permanently cure her through hypnosis. After giving her a pill, he asked if he could psychoanalyze her after she'd been hypnotized. When she came out of the trance, seven hours later, the last thing she could remember was the doctor saying, "You will sleep. In a few minutes . . ." She'd been talking, he told her, ever since. When he asked her if she felt any desire to smoke, she shook her head.

The week she spent in the hospital was hell. Rheumatic pains shot through her body, finally settling in her legs. A friend who visited was alarmed: she looked like "yellow death," and couldn't control her limbs, which jerked constantly. Sleep only came for what seemed like a few minutes, usually at dawn; she came to know and hate every knot in her straw mattress. Every day, though, was slightly better than the previous one. Thanks, she thought, to the hypnosis, she never considered smoking a pipe to end her pain. The doctor's pills – they turned out to be potent barbiturates – helped.

Eight days after she'd been hypnotized, Mickey checked out. She felt weak, but reality seemed to have regained a long-lost vividness. She noticed that her sense of smell had returned. In odoriferous Shanghai, of course, this was both a blessing and a curse.

Sinmay had asked if he could take the cure with her. "It's always easier with somebody else," he'd argued. She had declined. Now, when she saw him again, he told her that he had tried to quit on his own, but had only lasted thirty-six hours. She noticed how stained his teeth were, how vague and cloudy his eyes looked. It called to mind the brown scrim that obscured the gaze of the diabolical Dr. Fu-Manchu, whom she'd read about as a girl in St. Louis. That was how she had looked to others, she realized, just over a week before.

Now that she was cured, she was free to leave Shanghai without fear. She arranged for the yoga instructor Indra Devi to look after her Frenchtown house. Sinmay and his family would take care of Mr. Mills while she was gone; she was expecting the delivery of a pair of gibbons, and left him with instructions on caring for them until her return. She told him not to bother seeing her off. She expected to be away for no more than three months.

In October 1939, a month after Hitler had invaded Poland, Mickey left Shanghai much as she'd arrived: in a little steamer, travelling second class. Her cook, the cantankerous Chin Lien – who had earned enough "squeeze" skimming small sums from the household budget to open his own glass-making factory – was the only one to see her off at the wharf.

美

The timing was unfortunate. At a time when Mickey and other members of the foreign community were giving up on Shanghai, the city's profile abroad had never been so high.

The books written by Westerners who had visited the city in the mid-thirties were starting to find a wide readership. Eric Linklater's *Juan in China* had been published in 1937. Set in the midst of the Japanese invasion five years earlier, the picaresque romp featured the hero's vaguely erotic adventures with the Sisters Karamazov (beautiful Russian conjoined twins), visits to the Long Bar of the Shanghai Club, and run-ins with the "Two-Gun" Cohen surrogate, the arms-running Rocco. In spite of Linklater's exposure to Sinmay, the novel lacked a cosmopolitan Chinese poet. Instead, an unbearably chatty bohemian, who rattles with jade necklaces, was transparently modelled on Bernardine Szold-Fritz. ("Beatrice Fanny-Brown" annoys the hero by taking him to her boudoir and trying to sell him a paperweight.)

After reading *Juan in China*, Mickey wrote to Helen, "Don't bother." This was perhaps a matter of self-defense: the book features a portrait of an author named Harriet who lives in a "stuffy and tawdrily over-furnished" apartment off Nanking Road. Harriet, according to the narrator, walked across the Congo at the age of twenty-eight, and though she would rather be a scientist, has a "taste for reckless experiment and distant scenery":

Her hands were slim and finely shaped; good. Her hair was brown and bright as hazel-nut; excellent. Her eyes were candid and sea-gull grey, her mouth wide and well-shaped, her breasts as round and seeming-firm as demi-oranges . . . and who had ever seen a more agreeable waist, an ankle more trimly turned, a neater nose?

Linklater was clearly describing Mickey Hahn. His hero awakes the next morning in a dressing gown in Harriet's flat, where she makes him coffee in a percolator. The implication, of course, was that Juan – and, the reader is led to imagine, Linklater himself – had added the free-thinking American journalist to his list of conquests. It was the behaviour of a cad, and Linklater's writing in *Juan in China*, which leaned heavily on sesquipedalian puns and baroque turns of phrase, was suitably forgettable.

A far more accomplished account of Shanghai was the book that came out of Vicki Baum's two sojourns in the city. *Hotel Shanghai* (which was published as *Shanghai '37* in English) is a sophisticated piece of work. It features an opium-addicted rickshaw coolie named Lung Yen, who borrows money to impress his long-lost son, and a decadent British lord who goes on a binge in the opium dens of Hongkew. One of the most vivid characters is the poet Liu, who was educated at Oxford, lives on the north side of Soochow Creek, and, though he comes from a rich, eminent family, prefers to dress in a dirty brown robe. Liu has a playful sense of humour. The facetious speech he makes over dinner to the bigoted lord is a perfect example of the way Sinmay liked to "kid the ocean people":

"We Chinese are, all told, a fairly inventive people, only we never know what to do with our inventions. For example, as you know of course, we invented gunpowder – and what did we do with it? We made rockets and shot off fireworks for thousands of years. It simply did not occur to us how useful it was for murdering people. Or take the

invention of printing. We printed nothing but poems, sentimental discourses, history, philosophy, poetry. We are a ridiculous race . . ."

The bulky novel's interwoven plotlines come to a conclusion on a Saturday afternoon in August 1937, when the main characters are blown to pieces by bombers. The "Shanghai Hotel" in which the action concludes is an amalgam of the Cathay and the Park Hotel (it features an eighteenth-floor rooftop terrace), though the description of the carnage on Nanking Road and the Bund is a transparent retelling of the events of Black Saturday. The Liu character, who survives the bombing, was directly inspired by Zau Sinmay, who Mickey introduced to Baum during her second stay in Shanghai.

Even Tintin, the boyish cartoon reporter, made a stop in decadent Shanghai. In *The Blue Lotus*, Tintin and his faithful dog Snowy visit the Palace Hotel, across the street from the Cathay, and the Occidental Private Club, recognizable as the Shanghai Club. The 1936 adventure marked an evolution in its creator's attitude towards non-Europeans: Hergé, who became friends with a young Shanghainese artist in Brussels, has Tintin save a young Chinese orphan, Chang Chong-chen, from drowning. Chang is shown laughing heartily when Tintin tells him Europeans think "all Chinese are cunning and cruel and wear pigtails, and are always inventing tortures." (An image of a sallow-hued character in Fu-Manchu-like robes and whiskers illustrates the point.) For a generation of young readers, Tintin's adventures with Chang in Shanghai humanized the Chinese, and brought sympathy for their fight against the Japanese.

It was an image out of real life, not fiction, that won the most hearts to the Chinese cause. After Black Saturday, the Hearst syndicate photographer Wong Hai-sheng (a Chinese-American whose passport officially identified him as "Newsreel" Wong), snapped a black-and-white photograph of a baby sitting alone on the railway tracks of Shanghai's South Station, as smoke rose from fires set by Japanese bombs. Blackened but alive, clothes in shreds, mouth open wide, the image elicited one reaction in all who saw it: a burning desire to pick up the abandoned Chinese baby and bundle it off to safety.

1. Grave of Zau Sinmay (Shao Xunmei) and his wife Sheng Peiyu, First Row, Subdivision A1, Eastern Division, Gui Yuan cemetery, Zhujiajiao, Shanghai Municipality.

2. Opium smoker with pipe and lamp, Shanghai, 1898.

3. The hong of E.D. Sassoon & Co. (right), traders in cotton and opium, corner of Nanking Road and the Bund, 1887. This was the original Sassoon House, and the future site of the Cathay Hotel. The Central Hotel (left) would be replaced by the Palace Hotel, which opened in 1907.

4. A teenaged Emily "Mickey" Hahn, probably taken shortly after her family moved to Chicago, 1920.

5. Mickey Hahn, Manhattan flapper, with her capuchin monkey Punk, 1929.

6. The second Sassoon House (and lower floors of the Cathay Hotel) under construction on the Bund, 1928.

7. Bird's-eye view of Shanghai and its foreign concessions at the time of the January 28 Incident, 1932, from the *Illustrated London News.*

8. Sir Victor Sassoon with professional ballroom dancer Dorothy Wardell (left) and two unidentified women, at Ciro's Night Club, 1936.

9. View of sampans and barges on Soochow Creek, seen from Broadway Mansions. Sir Victor Sassoon's S-shaped Embankment House, center, was the largest building in Asia when it was completed in 1932.

10. Reception desk of the Cathay Hotel, 1929.

11. Lobby of the Cathay Hotel, grand staircase facing the Bund entrance, 1929.

12. The Cathay Hotel's lobby lounge, 1929.

13. Guest room of the Cathay Hotel, 1929.

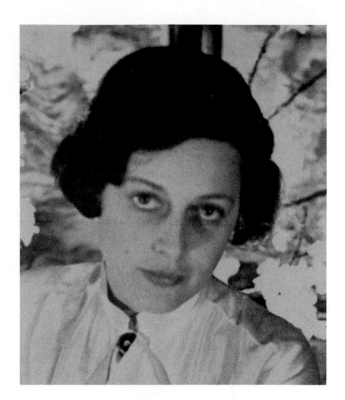

14. Portrait of
Mickey Hahn by
Sir Victor Sassoon,
Shanghai, 1935.

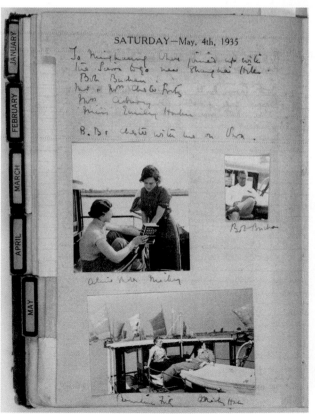

15. Page from one of
Sir Victor Sassoon's
journals recording a
weekend spent on his
houseboat *Vera* with
Bernardine Szold-Fritz,
her sister Aline Sholes,
and Mickey Hahn,
then newly arrived
in Shanghai.

16. Zau Sinmay at home in Shanghai, 1927.

17. Zau Sinmay in 1935, around the time he met Mickey Hahn.

18. Zau Sinmay as seen by Mexican cartoonist, and Mickey Hahn's friend, Miguel Covarrubias.

19. Portrait of the extravagant socialite Bernardine Szold-Fritz,
who found Mickey Hahn a reporting job at the *North-China Daily News*,
by Carl Van Vechten, 1934.

20. View of the Bund, with First World War cenotaph in the foreground
and peaked roof of the Cathay Hotel (center), ca. 1930.

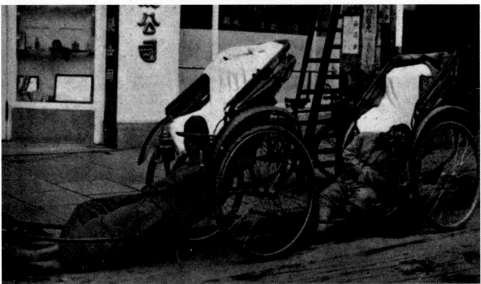

21. Three of the estimated 23,000 rickshaws registered in Shanghai's International Settlement in 1925; the pullers, who made a living "plowing the pavement," were frequently addicted to opium.

22. Buck Clayton and His Harlem Gentlemen, at Shanghai's Canidrome (ca. 1934) playing for a cosmopolitan crowd of Chinese, American, and European couples.

23. "Generalissimo" Chiang Kai-shek, leader of the Nationalists, and his wife Soong Mei-ling, the youngest of the American-educated Soong sisters.

24. This photo, known as "Bloody Saturday," by Chinese-American photographer "Newsreel" Wong, was seen by an estimated 136 million people in 1937, and drew worldwide attention to the Japanese invasion of China and the aerial bombing of Shanghai.

25. The scene on Nanking Road, after two bombs were dropped by Chinese planes on "Black Saturday," August 14, 1937. The ruined canopy of the Cathay Hotel can be seen on the upper right.

26. Japanese infantry manning a barricade on North Sichuan Road,
late in the summer of 1937.

27. Chinese civilians being frisked by Japanese soldiers at an
International Settlement checkpoint, 1937; photo by Sir Victor Sassoon.

28. Refugees crowd one of the gates that separated Chinese districts and Shanghai's foreign settlements, 1937.

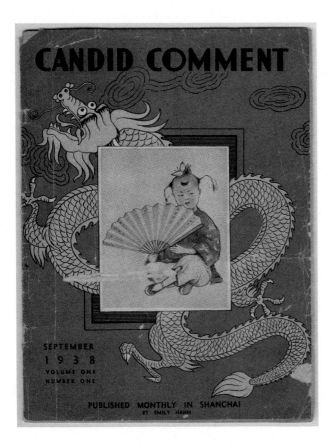

29. Cover of the first issue of *Candid Comment*, edited (and largely written) by Mickey Hahn. It was published in tandem with Zau Sinmay's *Ziyou Tan* (*Free Speech*).

30. "Big-Eared" Du Yuesheng, the gangster who controlled Shanghai's lucrative opium trade, was also appointed head of the Opium Suppression Bureau by Chiang Kai-shek.

31. Trebitsch Lincoln, a Hungarian Jew who transformed himself into the legendary triple agent Chao Kung, the "Abbot of Shanghai."

32. Morris "Two-Gun" Cohen, a Cockney-Canadian who rose to the rank of general serving as Dr. Sun Yat-sen's bodyguard; he would be repatriated on the same ship as Mickey Hahn in 1943.

33. "Princess" Sumaire, of the Punjab, who would become the consort of some of the Far East's shadiest Axis spies, checked in to the Cathay Hotel in 1940 and announced her intention to marry Shanghai's richest bachelor. Photo by Sir Victor Sassoon.

34. Mickey Hahn's lover, and future husband, the scholarly Charles Boxer, who was head of military intelligence in Hong Kong until he was interned by the Japanese in 1941.

35. The document, covered with typewritten messages from Allied internees for friends in the West, smuggled by Mickey Hahn into New York aboard the M/S *Gripsholm*. FBI agents discovered the piece of white silk sewn into the sleeve of her daughter Carola's dress.

Madeleine Fredureau du Chaillou,c/o A.S.Kouya, 195 Beckett St.,PRETORIA, S.A.
                        or c/o Barclay's Bank, PRETORIA.   Betty
Mrs.H.G.Dudley, 37 Castlebar Road, EALING, LONDON,W.5.(Mother of Mrs.Fidoe)
            (Apply to London Red Cross to have me put on repatriation list.Urgent)
Miss Edith Furniss,c/o Texas Oil Co.,CEYLON.
Miss Margaret Turner,c/o E.Hammond & Sons Ltd.,823 Clarke Drive,VANCOUVER,B.C.
Mrs.G.D.Wilson (Betty),544 Melrose Way, LONG BEACH, California.
Mr.Costy Efimoff,P.O.Box 470,BRYTE,California(Would he be able to take me next
  (repatriation or help me financially. Through Red Cross).
Mrs.M.Cario,c/o H.K.Evacuation Committee,SYDNEY.(Harry,Leo interned. Mannie,Esther
  interned Shanghai. Kids Shanghai. Tell Micky my Cousin her husband well,out on
  Spanish pass in same house Kowloon,very fit.Sophie family out on French pass.)
M.J.Durren,24 Northgate,Unler Park, ADELAIDE,Australia.
Jack Odell,Warner Bros.Film Co.,CALCUTTA.
Albert Odell, 17 Sze Chan Sze, CHENGTU.
Mrs.M.C.Hawkins,74 Tenth Avenue,Parktown North,JOHANNESBURG.
Mrs.Ernest Haskell (Ritchie's sister),20 Eastbury Court,LONDON,W.14 (About son's death

Mrs.Mary M.Fenolose,Cismont,Albemarle County,Virginia. (We are standing on a firm
  foundation - one solid undistructive mass of structure, which no hands of modern
  inventions could destroy.) (The family all well,each doing the best for the
  country. As for me,I am out in the southern regions - 71 years old age does not
  count. I am feeling just like a young spring bird, for I know that behind clouds
  sun shines.)
Mr.Galen M.Fisher,Institute of Social & Religious Research,230 Park Ave,NEW YORK.
  (Some day you will hear that D.L.Moody is gone.Don't believe a word of it. These
  were the words uttered in his dying bed. Yes,his spirit lives and should live.
  Nothing shakes my belief of the truth.)
Drs.David Fairchild & W.T.Swingle, U.S.Department of Agriculture,WASHINGTON.
  (The rumour had it that those beautiful Sakura trees on the Potomac were butchered
  I cannit believe it and live in the hope and dream of that beautiful sight. The
  only regret is that the White House had failed to come under the trees and ask
  them what is the spirit and sould of Nippon. The mute messenger would surely have
  enlightened them with Motoori's
      "Shiki shima no -   Yamato gokoro wo - Hito towaba, Asahini niho
  Our Sakura are in a splendid condition throughout the Country,so the spirit and
  sould of the nation.
Dr.& Mrs.H.C.Cutler, Mt.Herman, Mas.
  (Hearty greetings! There is a big difference between white washed and washed
  white. I still remember clearly these words of our dear "D.L." Yes there is a
  big difference. In the ignoble note Washington sent to Japan, the authority, -
  not the people, had sadly failed to see what stuff Japan is made of.
  The family well, doing his and her shares for the country. I am in the Southern
  regions, as there is so much to be done. I am in the best of health and spirit.)

36. Mickey Hahn and her daughter Carola, New York, 1944.

37. An anti-Communist parade outside Sir Victor Sassoon's Gothic Art Deco-style Metropole Hotel on Foochow Road, May 16, 1946.

38. A careworn Zau Sinmay, ca. 1957, at home on Huaihai Road (Avenue Joffre) in Shanghai. In the early years of communism, he made an exiguous living translating the works of Mark Twain, Shelley, and Tagore into Chinese.

39. Contemporary view of the roof of the Peace Hotel (formerly the Cathay), looking across the Huangpu River towards the Oriental Pearl Tower in Pudong.

The photograph, which became known as "Bloody Saturday," was seen by more than 136 million people in the month that followed. Harold Isaacs, *Newsweek*'s man in China, called it "one of the most successful 'propaganda' pieces of all time"; it ranks alongside the images of the naked eight-year-old girl running from a napalm attack in Vietnam, and the three-year-old Syrian boy found dead on a Turkish beach, as one of the most indelible works of photojournalism in modern times. More than any eyewitness testimony, it helped sway public sympathy worldwide towards the Chinese.

By then, however, the Japanese were in control, and nothing the writers and photographers who had come to love China could produce would change what was in store for Shanghai.

美

Late one night in the second week of December 1939, Mickey Hahn, travelling under the name "Mrs. Wang," waddled across the runway at Hong Kong's Kai Tak airfield towards a China National Aviation Corporation DC-3 bound for Chungking. Passengers were limited to a few pieces of baggage, so she wore so many layers that she looked, and walked – in her sheepskin stadium boots – like a deep-sea diver. Flying at night to avoid Japanese fighters, the American pilot crossed 600 miles of hostile airspace before touching down on a sand-spit landing field next to steep cliffs that rose from the Yangtze River.

Mickey's first adventure in the wartime capital of Free China involved getting lost. Though the coolies who carried her in her sedan chair were able to scale the nearly 500 granite steps that rose from the waterfront like mountain goats, they had no idea where her hostel was. When they turned back towards the river, she began to panic. Finally, an Englishman wearing plus-fours and walking his Scottie pointed her in the right direction.

Chungking, the capital of Szechwan Province, had been chosen as the nationalist base because of its near-impregnability to attack. A wedge-shaped peninsula that rises from the confluence of the Yangtze and the Chialing Rivers, it is socked in by fog from

October to April. This, along with the area's geology – to which Mickey's training at the University of Wisconsin made her attentive – meant that Chungking was an ideal refuge from Japanese bombers. The rock-cored hills honeycombed the local topography with natural air-raid shelters.

Mickey would get to know those shelters well. Between 1939 and 1941, the Japanese launched 268 bombing raids on Chungking in an attempt to pound the nationalists into submission. When the watchmen rang gongs on the hillsides in double-time it meant incoming planes had been spotted, and it was time to run for shelter. On bad days, the gongs might sound half a dozen times.

Mickey's first visit lasted ten weeks. She was invited to Chiang Kai-shek's villa, where, as she chatted with Madame Chiang, the Generalissimo, who spoke no English, made a brief appearance – wearing slippers, and without his false teeth. After he excused himself, Mei-ling invited her to accompany her on visits to girls' schools and experimental farms in the area. Mickey, in other words, had been approved: she would be given the access she needed to write her book.

Between long hours in the shelters, she consorted with the strange cast of characters who had made Chungking their temporary home. One was the Living Buddha of Outer Mongolia, waylaid by war on his trip to Tibet – a place he'd only known, he said, in a previous life. In his fifties and suffering from gout, he had decided to travel incognito, which, because his religion required him to wear yellow, meant wearing primrose tweeds and a golden Homburg. Instead of being allowed to complete his trip to the yak ranch that awaited him in Tibet, he was being held as a near-prisoner by the nationalists. Mickey and the Buddha spent an evening trying to soothe each other's homesickness: Mickey sang him the American cowboy songs she'd learned in New Mexico, while he responded with the keening verses of Mongolian shepherd songs.

Most of all, Mickey tapped away on her Hermes Featherweight – the typewriter she'd brought with her from Hong Kong, one of the first true portables, weighing only eight pounds – working harder than she ever had before. She sent the first chapters to Sir Victor Sassoon, who replied, on Cathay Hotel letterhead:

It does not live. We are interested only in the girls . . . we want to know what they thought of each other . . . we want to know what [Ai-ling] felt when walking down Nanking Road for the first time in her American tailor-made and ostrich feather hat.

All the historical background, he complained, put him to sleep in his bed.

Mickey was grateful for the criticism. She'd torn up the first draft, and now she was typing furiously on her battered portable, trying to make the prose sing.

Only one of the Soong sisters had an objection to the manuscript. Madame Sun dispatched Morris "Two-Gun" Cohen – who was working as her bodyguard, and whom Mickey noticed the Soongs treated as a sort of family pet – with a message: "Mme. Sun is disturbed because you say she is a *Commmuuniist*. She ain't no *Commmuniist*." She was, of course – and would later become a key official in the communist regime – but it wasn't the time to show her cards. Mickey dutifully changed the wording to suggest Soong Qing-ling was more "pink" than "red."

On a brief return to the south, she had two crucial encounters at the Hongkong Hotel. One night, she was delighted to witness the three Soong sisters together at Gripps, the hotel's restaurant, laughing like the best of friends. It was the first time they had been seen together in public for a decade; the union of Mmes. Sun, Kung, and Chiang – of Left, Centre, and Right – not only boded well for the future of a China united against the Japanese, but also provided a suitably dramatic resolution for Mickey's book.

On the eve of her return to Chungking, she found herself sitting down to an after-dinner poker game in the hotel's lobby. Fortunately, Cohen, who had followed Madame Sun to Hong Kong, noticed her advanced state of intoxication.

"The general was playing his role of Picturesque Old China Hand in those days," Mickey would write in her memoirs. "He would sit in the lobby of the Grips [sic] day after day, slightly drunk, cheerfully ready to fasten on anyone who came by."

Mickey herself had been nervously overdrinking "ox's blood," a potent mix of brandy, champagne, and sparkling burgundy. "I wasn't sober enough to refuse to play, and I solemnly took my seat with the best sharks in the Far East. It was then that Morris Cohen won my everlasting gratitude. He let me play just one minute before he said, 'Get out of that chair and go upstairs, Mickey.' I meekly obeyed him."

Back in Chungking – after a bombing raid almost incinerated her work – she typed the last page of *The Soong Sisters*. On August 24, 1940, she sent her agent a triumphant letter, written from the depths of a hangover.

I'm waiting here for the last air-raid before I rush for the field and take a plane down to Hongkong. It has been a hell of a week. Here are the final chapters . . . This is not a very sensible letter, but there was a farewell party for me up until this morning, because a new man arrived with SUPPLIES – real whiskey and medicines and things like that – and we used the whiskey first and now we are using the medicine.

She enclosed a "pitiful attempt at a bibliography," a single page of book titles and articles, scrawled in pencil in a shaky hand.

The final passage of *The Soong Sisters* was a lyrical evocation of the deserted streets of Chungking as they came to life after an air raid. After the planes have done their work, people climb out of the shelters, and the dead city is transformed by a throb of human voices and activity carrying over the river – the "dead city is transformed; there is life and color and noise everywhere, particularly noise." It is "the undefeatable din of China." One is left with the image of a nation united like the Soong sisters, and bound to overcome the depredations of the Japanese imperialists. China's resilience in a time of crisis, Mickey was implying, could serve as an inspiration for the West.

What Mickey didn't know was that while China was showing signs of waking from the long nightmare of its history, history was about to close in on Westerners in the Far East.

PART SIX

"Years ago a speck was torn away from the mystery of China and became Shanghai. A distorted mirror of problems that beset the world today, it grew into a refuge for people who wished to live between the lines of laws and customs – a modern tower of Babel."

– Title card from
Josef von Sternberg's film
The Shanghai Gesture, 1941.

20: Shanghai, August 1, 1941

Sir Victor knew that Lucien Ovadia was right: the time had come
to quit Shanghai. His cousin had always prided himself on being
the voice of reason. When he thought back on it, Ovadia's caution
had almost always been justified. It could be damned annoying.

He had spent the afternoon pacing the penthouse of the
Cathay, assailed by visions from the past, while trying hard to
picture some plausible future for the Sassoon dynasty. It was the
Royal Air Force Association tiffin, held that afternoon beneath
the dome of the Hongkong and Shanghai Bank building, that had
thrown him into this blue study. To thank him for his years of
service, the boys had presented him with an inscribed mug. After
all the snubs, it was a true vindication: it had taken many years,
but Shanghai had accepted him. Now it looked as if he would have
to leave everything he had built behind. Standing to make his
speech at the podium, he had felt tears welling in his eyes.

He knew, to the minute, when Shanghai's glitter had begun to
fade: it was the afternoon in 1937 when the bomb had exploded
on Nanking Road, stopping the Cathay's clock at 4:27. Since then,
every passing hour seemed to bring a new sign that the city's star
was setting. Only a year after he'd opened Ciro's it had fallen into
the hands of Chinese gangsters, who'd turned it into a cabaret for
taxi dancers. Shortly after that, a gunfight had occurred in the
lobby of the Cathay: a pro-Japanese official whom the Chinese
considered a traitor was shot in the shoulder, and crumpled to the
floor amidst the stacks of trunks. It had been witnessed, and written up, by Isherwood and Auden – exactly the kind of publicity
the hotel *didn't* need.

Oddly enough, his realty firms were reporting unprecedented

profits. Thanks to the flood of refugees from Germany and Austria, the city was now more populous than ever. For the first two years it had been cheering to see Hongkew become a Little Vienna, filled with cafes and cobblers' shops. But Hongkew was also Japanese territory, and Shanghai's new military rulers apparently foresaw a useful role for the Jewish race, whom they considered fellow Orientals and members of the "Asiatic Co-Prosperity Sphere."

Since the spring of 1939, Sir Victor had been taking meetings with a navy captain named Koreshige Inuzuka, who had been given responsibility for Jewish affairs in Shanghai. The Japanese favoured Jewish immigration – which, given the reputation of the fascists in Europe, was a little surprising. Inuzuka seemed to have dreams of setting up enclaves on the Asian mainland, where the vaunted economic prowess of the Jews would foster economic development. (Their high opinion of the race's financial ability dated, some old Shanghailanders said, from the Russo-Japanese War, when Jacob Schiff, a Jewish financier, helped them find backing for arms purchases from banks in New York.) When a committee had approached him with the suggestion that they set up an Anglo-Japanese property combine to safeguard foreign real estate, Sir Victor and Ellis Hayim had spent months stringing them along with promises of cooperation. When he was finally put on the spot, Sir Victor offered them a few bedbug-infested tenements. Captain Inuzuka had taken it as a grievous insult.

At a dinner party at the Cathay, one of his junior officers had leaned over and asked: "Why exactly are you so anti-Japanese?"

Clipping a fresh cigar, he had replied, slowly and very deliberately: "I am not anti-Japanese at all. I am simply pro-Sassoon and very pro-British."

Antagonistic remarks like that, he knew, were causing his fellow Jews to bristle. While in New York in the summer of 1939, he had opined to newspapermen that Japan had overextended itself with its invasion of China and its economy was bound to crumble. Representatives of the 6,000-strong Ashkenazi Jewish Communal Association had immediately issued a statement distancing themselves from Sir Victor, and expressing gratitude to the

Japanese government for its "humanitarian and unprejudiced attitude." When he'd returned to Shanghai that September, Ellis Hayim and Michele Speelman had been quick to tell him what a difficult position he put the Jewish community in every time he publicly lambasted the Japanese.

Since then, of course, the refugees had stopped coming. A month before Hitler invaded Poland, the Municipal Council had voted to close the International Settlement and the French Concession to any further immigration from Europe. Just twelve days before the outbreak of the Second World War, the Japanese had followed suit by ending immigration to Hongkew. It was the first time that Shanghai had restricted immigration since its founding as a Treaty Port. The evidence of overflowing *shikumen* and sanitary services strained to the limit had led the Committee for the Assistance of European Jewish Refugees to conclude that, to protect the health and safety of those already in Shanghai, the doors would have to close. Closing the world's "port of last resort" for Jews was not a decision they took lightly.

Already, something inside Sir Victor had given up on Shanghai. Since the Japanese invasion, he had slowly been moving his capital to New York. In 1938 he had logged 6,000 miles, aboard Pan American Clippers and Douglas DC-3s, looking at the potential for making clothes with such new synthetic fibres as polyester in the Caribbean and South America. (Unknown to all but his closest business associates was the fact that Sir Victor had purchased ten thousand square miles of land in the Amazon, which he hoped would become a colony for refugees from Nazi Germany. The Brazilian government, however, was willing to accept only trained colonists.) It was on this trip that he discovered the Bahamas, which offered almost as many tax advantages as Shanghai. He set up two companies in Nassau, one of which would look after his racing interests.

The death of Nunky – the old roué had left instructions to be buried in a casket of gold and crystal – seemed to have left Sir Victor even more willing to provoke his enemies. As the Japanese tightened their noose, his criticism of fascist outrages had become ever more emphatic. From Berlin, Hermann Göring had denounced him over the Nazi airwaves as a "mischievous Hollywood playboy."

He was, it was true, spending more time in Los Angeles. When he passed through in February, 1940, the gossip columnist Hedda Hopper had alerted her readers to the presence of "one of the world's wealthiest bachelors." He'd visited the Samuel Goldwyn studio, and the newspapers had printed photos of him using his new 16 mm movie camera to film a few minutes of Bette Davis's acting. At an executive lunch, he'd argued what he saw as common sense: to stop Hitler, "England and the United States must operate under one government." Though the studio bosses had dutifully applauded, his notion of a federal alliance of the two democracies had been greeted with derision elsewhere. A cartoonist had cuttingly portrayed Roosevelt following a pin-striped Sir Victor's urging, becoming the "First Third-Term President of Anglamerica."

By the first months of 1941, Shanghai had already lost its best and brightest. Mickey Hahn was in Hong Kong. Her friend, the fascinating white geisha Lorraine Murray, had moved to Australia. The previous summer, the Seaforth Highlanders had left for Singapore, marking the complete withdrawal of British troops from Chinese soil. There were rumours that the US 4th Marines, already much reduced, would follow. Soon there would be nothing to stop the Japanese from gaining complete control of the settlements.

Their latest efforts centred on dominating the Municipal Council, using methods both legal and underhanded. For months they had packed elections with docile voters from Hongkew, exploiting a loophole that allowed even long-term hotel guests to vote. The Council fought back by creating votes out of thin air by subdividing British- and American-owned properties, legal ballot-box stuffing that enraged the Japanese. At a ratepayers' meeting in January, 1941, a seventy-year-old Japanese man had risen and, yelling "Banzai!" fired four shots at Tony Keswick, a leading taipan at Jardine, Matheson & Co. Keswick recovered, and after a show trial in Nagasaki the Japanese gunman was seen walking the streets of Shanghai, a free man. Since then, Sir Victor had always kept his service revolver handy and was sure to wear his old Royal Flying Corps tie in public.

Ovadia had been telling him since the spring of 1940 that he should quit Shanghai and return to Bombay. Yet even in these dark days, the Cathay Hotel acted like catnip for some of the world's most attractive and outlandish characters. In May he'd met Princess Sumaire when she checked into a suite at the Cathay claiming to be one of the twenty-three daughters of the Maharaja of Patiala, the wealthiest man in the Punjab. Though short, round-faced, and snub-nosed, Sumaire had a hypnotic effect on men. The Japanese had her pegged as a British spy; the Special Branch thought she might be working for the Germans (in their files, she was described as a bisexual nymphomaniac who wasn't above taking Chinese bell-hops back to her room). She claimed to have worked as a fashion model in Paris for Elsa Schiaparelli, Coco Chanel's rival. Even though Sir Victor had already caught her in a half-dozen lies – she may have been one of the Maharaja's nieces, but she was certainly not his daughter, and had never received £2,000 per annum from him – he couldn't help but be flattered by her attentions. From the first time he met her in the Cathay ballroom, she had announced her intention to become his wife. Sumaire reminded Sir Victor of his early days in Shanghai, when the China coast seemed to abound with such fantastic shape-shifters and adventurers as "Two-Gun" Cohen and Trebitsch Lincoln. After Shanghai, even life in a snake-pit would seem dull.

Though his next birthday would be his sixtieth, he was feeling better than he had in years. Though he'd discovered that his Italian masseur, Valvasone, had been involved in an abortion ring in Los Angeles, the man had worked wonders on his legs. There were even nights when he was able to do a turn on the dance floor without his walking sticks.

This afternoon, he found himself thinking about a young woman in Albuquerque. He had met Sandy Tittman in Shanghai, where she had come to stay with her uncle, a judge on the American court. Sir Victor had been charmed by her conversation and beauty one evening in 1936 at the Tower Night Club; it was only when she had risen and walked away with a pronounced limp, the result of her struggle with polio as a child, that he had realized how much they had in common. Since then, he'd visited her in New Mexico and entrusted her with furnishing "El Refugio", a little vacation house of adobe in the desert, across the road from her family's home. He'd given her a walking stick, which she always used. He longed now to place a trunk call to Sandy in Albuquerque; but it was three in the morning in the States.

Tonight, he would attend the Moonlight Follies, one of the fundraisers being organized by Ellis Hayim in the garden of his house on Avenue Haig. Hayim's parties were risky to attend: he made no secret that he intended to donate the proceeds to the Allied war effort. The Japanese always paid close attention to the list of invitees.

Before the dance, though, he would dine with his cousin. That night, he was going to tell Ovadia that he'd booked passage to Bombay, by way of Hong Kong. It seemed he would, after all, be forced to sit out the war in India, a prospect that frankly depressed him. Nor was he looking forward to seeing the look on Ovadia's face when he announced he was taking his advice and leaving Shanghai. The man had a tendency to gloat.

21: The Last Light in a Dark World

The day after Mickey Hahn returned to Hong Kong from Chung-king, early in September, 1940, she went out for a much-anticipated dinner with Charles Boxer. As they knelt on tatami mats over sukiyaki at the Tokyo Hotel on Connaught Road, their romance began. The handsome young officer told her he had always been more interested in Oriental history than military life. At the age of seventeen, he'd read a paper to the Royal Asiatic Society; he'd arrived in the Far East in 1936, a year after Mickey, by way of the pre-revolutionary rolling stock of the Trans-Siberian Railroad. He admitted to having picked up his fluent Japanese on the pillow of a housekeeper-concubine from Hokkaido. Time, Charles said, was running out for Westerners in the Far East – even those, like himself, who fancied themselves expertly versed in Asian ways.

Ursula, Charles's beautiful wife, had been evacuated to Singapore. He dismissed Mickey's fears about not being able to have children, and told her that he wouldn't mind sharing a home with gibbons. He wondered, though, whether her Chinese husband would object.

Sinmay, as it happened, was under the impression that they were still man and wife. A year earlier Mickey had left him in charge of Mr. Mills and the house on Avenue Joffre, with the promise she would be back in three months' time. In a series of passionate letters sent across enemy lines to Chungking, Sinmay's dismay had been obvious.

"Couldn't you love me as much as I do you and write me as often? . . . How could a human being forget a human being so easily and quickly? According to Chinese language, then, you *don't* love me at all. Haven't I told you that Love in Chinese is called Hsiang Shi, which means 'Mutual Non-stop Thinking'?"

On Christmas Eve, finding another day had passed without news from her, he wrote, "God save me, Mickey, my love! I'm in such a state again! Only this afternoon, I found myself asking people how to get a pass to go to the 'captured areas' and I was figuring the ways to get money, enough money to get out of Shanghai and the memories . . . Oh, I MISS YOU SO!"

For Mickey, Sinmay was a habit she'd broken, like opium. His memory engendered warm feelings, but no passionate longing. In Hong Kong, she started to build a new life. She rented a flat on May Road, then the uppermost street in the Mid-Levels district, and hired a new cook, a dignified Cantonese man named Ah King. Mr. Mills had been shipped down the coast, chaperoned by an Australian woman. Soon enough he was joined by four other simians, who spent their time happily raiding Mickey's neighbours' fruit trees and kitchens, watched carefully by the colonel across the street, who kept a spyglass trained on the house. And, as the New Year came, she was able to tell Charles she was pregnant.

The Hong Kong of 1941, Charles knew better than most, was no place to start a family. As it happened, he was more than just a scholar in khaki; he was also the head of military intelligence in Hong Kong. The British had decided that the colony, like Shanghai, was indefensible in the face of the Japanese war machine. The garrison was pitifully small, and in the event of a siege its water supply could be almost instantly choked off. British women and children had been ordered to evacuate the city (though many found pretexts to remain) while Americans were permitted to stay. Charles feared that he, like the British navy in the Far East, would be ordered to move on to Singapore. Mickey, in preparation for such a move, signed a contract to write a biography of Stamford Raffles, the founder of the settlement – who, she'd been delighted to learn, also enjoyed the company of gibbons.

As her pregnancy advanced, Mickey discovered that many of the characters she'd known in Shanghai had also sought refuge in Hong Kong. Rewi Alley, the redheaded factory inspector from

New Zealand, was there. So was Agnes Smedley, who Mickey discovered was an unofficial member of the Missouri Mafia: born into a Quaker farmstead in a village in Osgood, Missouri, near the Iowa border, Smedley had written for the *Manchester Guardian* and the *Frankfurter Zeitung* before her extensive travels with Chinese communist armies.

Mickey also spent time that year with Ernest Hemingway and his new wife, Martha Gellhorn. Though they were on their honeymoon trip, Gellhorn also had an assignment to cover the war for *Collier's* magazine. Hemingway, exhausted after two years of writing and promoting *For Whom the Bell Tolls*, had a contract to do a series of dispatches for the left-wing *PM* newspaper in New York. After arriving from Honolulu in a luxurious Pan Am flying boat, Gellhorn proceeded to Chungking, while Hemingway made the Hongkong Hotel lobby his headquarters.

"U.C.," as Gellhorn called Hemingway (for "Unwilling Companion"), also became great friends with, in her words, "a huge polite thug from Chicago named Cohen whom U.C. believed to be a hit man for some Chinese warlord." The thug in question was actually the Canadian "Two-Gun" Cohen. "He was born on the wrong side of the tracks, and addresses me as Moddom and I love him," she wrote to the *New Yorker*'s Alexander Woolcott. Hemingway was so impressed by Cohen's extravagant stories of defending Sun Yat-sen that he talked about writing an entire book on his life story.[*]

Cohen arranged for the couple to meet the left-leaning Madame Sun – Hemingway privately described her as the only "decent" Soong sister – and, though in private he referred to Chiang Kai-shek as a "tuches," advised them to spend time with the nationalist army. They soon came to resent their role as embedded journalists in what was clearly a corruption-ridden army. In Chungking, a secret meeting was arranged with Chou En-lai. Led

---

[*] Much later, Hemingway would boast that while Gellhorn was away on a side trip to Java he had spent the night with three beautiful Chinese women that Cohen had sent to his suite.

blindfolded to a small, whitewashed room, they listened to Mao Tse-tung's right-hand man until they were "punch-drunk."

"We thought Chou a winner," Gellhorn wrote in her memoirs. "The one really good man we'd met in China; and if he was a sample of Chinese communists, then the future was theirs."

The St. Louis-born Gellhorn was another unofficial member of the Missouri Mafia. (On a twenty-five-hour train ride through Canton Province, Gellhorn bet her new husband that the only other Caucasian on the train was from St. Louis. Hemingway took the bet, and lost twenty Chinese dollars.) By her own admission, she didn't get along with other women; but Mickey, three years her senior, was an exception. Hemingway wrote to her mother: "M. is very happy, treating the men like brothers and the women like dogs." In her memoirs, Gellhorn countered, "I remember only Emily Hahn with cigar and highly savvy on the Orient and I was never foolish enough to be disdainful of her."

One afternoon Mickey had a *tête-à-tête* with Hemingway, who was sitting outside the Hongkong Hotel drinking a Bloody Mary.* He'd heard that she was pregnant.

"What's going to happen to Charles about this baby?" he asked. "Won't they kick him out of the army?"

"They daren't," replied Mickey, "because he's the only man they have who can speak Japanese."

Hemingway, apparently, didn't buy it. "Tell you what," he said. "You can tell 'em it's mine."

Interviewed on his return to the United States in June, Hemingway reported the colony was "excellently defended." Privately, he confided to a fellow veteran of the Spanish Civil War that the British garrison was doomed. "They'll die trapped like rats."

Events didn't take long to confirm Hemingway's prediction. On October 17, 1941, Mickey's first child was delivered by caesar-

---

* Hemingway claimed to have introduced Bloody Marys to Hong Kong. Years later, he told a friend that he believed the drink, more than any other factor, "except perhaps the Japanese army," brought about the fall of the colony.

ean. (Mickey, not surprisingly, insisted on remaining conscious, if heavily dosed with morphine, to watch the entire operation.) Carola Boxer was a small but healthy baby, with enormous eyes. After a month-long stay at the hospital, they had only three weeks at home before the news reached Hong Kong, on December 8, 1941, that the Japanese had bombed Pearl Harbor.

"The balloon's gone up," Charles told Mickey over the phone. "It's come. War."

Twelve days later he was lying in a ravine, bleeding heavily, with a Japanese sniper's bullet through his chest.

The end, when it finally came for the enclaves of the West in the Orient, was anticlimactic.

On December 10, the torpedo bombers of the Japanese navy sank the battleship *Prince of Wales* and the battlecruiser *Repulse*, Britain's most powerful ships in the Far East. Singapore, the "Gibraltar of the East," fell after only a day's fighting, which meant a long and brutal internment for the 120,000 British, Indian, and Australian troops captured by the Japanese.

Without having first declared war on Britain, Japan sent a dozen bombers to destroy the five antiquated airplanes still on the ground at Kai Tak airfield in Hong Kong. On December 2, Mmes. Kung and Sun had been escorted by "Two-Gun" Cohen to a Clipper specially flown in from Chungking; Cohen watched from the airstrip as they were evacuated on the second-last plane to escape from Hong Kong.* The 14,000 British forces, outnumbered four to one by the Japanese, resisted as long as they could. On "Black Christmas," the colony's governor lifted the needle from the Beethoven gramophone record he'd been listening to at Government House and made his way to the third floor of the Peninsula

---

* Cohen, uncharacteristically finding himself tongue-tied as he made his goodbyes, blurted out: "We'll fight to the bitter end, anyway!" Madame Sun reportedly replied: "We'll fight to the end, too, Morris, but not to the *bitter* end. When the end comes, it will be sweet!"

Hotel, where he surrendered in person to the Japanese commander.

In Shanghai, supine and resigned to its fate, barely a shot was fired. Late in November – twelve days before Pearl Harbor, and after fifteen years of service in Shanghai – the remaining members of the US 4th Marine regiment paraded down Nanking Road to the tune of "Stars and Stripes Forever" before being evacuated to Manila. When they passed Jimmy's Kitchen, famous for its burgers and corned-beef hash, an orchestra of American cooks and waiters joined the end of the parade, playing swing music as they marched. The members of the multinational Shanghai Volunteer Corps, founded in 1853 to defend the Settlements against Taiping-inspired rebels, had been given instructions to stand down.

Shortly before four in the morning on December 8, the crew of the one American gunboat on the Whangpoo River was overpowered by Japanese boarders (making the USS *Wake* the only American naval vessel in the Second World War to be captured intact). The sailors aboard its British counterpart, HMS *Peterel*, put up a stiff fight. When a party of Japanese army officers carrying samurai swords climbed on deck, its captain yelled, "Get off my bloody ship!" Trying to buy time to burn the ship's code books in the boiler, its skeleton crew began to machine-gun the *Izumo* – still moored outside the Japanese Consulate – until shells from the cruiser caused the *Peterel* to explode and keel over. (One petty officer escaped, and would hide out in the International Settlement for the remainder of the war under the alias "Mr. Trees.")

A force of Japanese marines in light tanks and armoured cars crossed the Garden Bridge and drove down the Bund unopposed. By ten in the morning, the Rising Sun flag was flying beneath the dome of the Palmer & Turner-designed Hongkong and Shanghai Bank. The army's headquarters were established on the Race Course, next to the Park Hotel. "News Dissemination Trucks" drove up and down Nanking Road, loudspeakers blaring, as soldiers distributed leaflets with caricatures of Roosevelt and Churchill clinging to each other in terror as Japanese bombs fell.

Sir Victor Sassoon's grandest buildings were singled out for special attention. At the Metropole Hotel, where Rotarians had long held their Saturday-night meetings, British and American consular staff were put under a house arrest that would last several months, their bills paid by the Japanese government. The navy turned Sir Victor's Tudor-style hunting lodge into one of their command centres (earlier in the year, Sir Victor had cannily arranged to unload Eve's onto a flamboyant tycoon from Ningpo). On December 9, British and American citizens were told to report to Hamilton House, Sir Victor's luxury apartment complex on Foochow Road. It was turned into the headquarters of the *kempeitai* – the Japanese equivalent of the Gestapo – where foreigners were issued with bright red armbands, to be worn in public at all times. "A" stood for Americans, "B" for Britishers, and "N" for Netherlanders.

The Cathay Hotel became an administrative and social centre for Shanghai's new rulers. Only three months earlier, Chinese saboteurs had set off a time-bomb in Sassoon House, destroying valuable Japanese radio equipment. Now the same officer who had been so insulted when Sir Victor and other Jewish leaders refused to cooperate in the founding of a joint Anglo-Japanese real estate company was able to take his revenge. Captain Inuzuka set up his offices at the Cathay, and waited for Shanghai's wealthiest Sephardim to call on him.

The media was muzzled: that December, eleven Chinese and English-language newspapers were ordered to cease publication. The *Evening Post and Mercury* had long since relocated; wartime editions were published out of Chungking and New York. Carroll Alcott, known for his baiting of the Japanese on radio station XMHA – he called the "New Order" in the Far East the "New Odour" – and travelling with tommy-gun-wielding bodyguards, made the last Pacific crossing on the *President Harrison* before it was seized. The *Shanghai Times*, an English-language outlet for Imperial propaganda, became the city's major daily, and Alcott's foghorn voice was replaced on the airwaves by the sibilant hiss of the alcoholic Herbert Erasmus Moy, a Chinese-American Nazi sympathizer.

At the end of the month, prominent foreigners were told to convene in the Metropole Hotel, where their most pressing questions would be answered. One journalist wondered aloud if they would be thrown into camps.

"The International Settlement is itself a sort of concentration camp," was the chilling response given by a Japanese army spokesman.

All too soon, it became clear exactly what Shanghai's new rulers had in mind.

Bridge House, an eight-storey Chinese hotel at 478 North Szechuen Road on the north side of Soochow Creek, quickly became the most feared address in Shanghai. The officers of the *kempeitai*, perhaps inspired by the insomnia-inducing techniques of their Gestapo counterparts, awakened their victims with a knock on the door in the early hours of the morning and dragged them off to Bridge House. There, they were imprisoned in cages, behind wooden bars, where they were fed on rice gruel and forced to sit cross-legged on lice-infested blankets, with only occasional breaks to shuffle around a cold concrete floor. Those who spoke were beaten or tortured, their chests burned with cigarettes, their nostrils filled by hose with cold water, or their fingernails split with bamboo splinters.

The name of John B. Powell, the amiable Missouri-born editor of the anti-Japanese *China Weekly Review*, turned out to be at the top of the Japanese blacklist. After being tortured at Bridge House, he contracted beriberi. It was only when he'd lost half his body weight and the flesh was peeling off his toes that a doctor was called in.

Luck alone kept Sir Victor Sassoon's right-hand man, Lucien Ovadia, out of Bridge House. In August, Ovadia went to New York to arrange the sale of the Metropole Hotel to the American Consulate. After the deal fell through, he was returning to Shanghai when the radio announced the bombing of Pearl Harbor. Ovadia turned back, joining his boss in New York, where Sir Victor was trying to negotiate supplies of cotton for his mills in India. It would prove to be one of the few times in his career that Ovadia – the man who had been blown across his Sassoon House office when the Black Saturday bombs fell – didn't find himself in the wrong place at the wrong time.

Had Sir Victor been caught in Shanghai when the Japanese invaded, he would certainly have been singled out for special punishment. (One of his chief executives, Harry Arnhold, was caught; and was imprisoned and ruthlessly interrogated.) A 1942 *Collier's* magazine article entitled "Slow Death in a Jap Cage" provided a graphic account of what happened to those who remained behind. Its author, American war correspondent M.C. Ford, who was also imprisoned at Bridge House, wrote that, "in one corner a Baghdad millionaire lay sick and unattended." The sick man told Ford:

"I stood up under these hardships sixty days, but am now breaking up after eighty-two days. For days I have been trying to get a doctor to attend to my fever, but they won't move a hand. A lot of good all my money does me. I never dreamed I would be reduced to living like the filthiest coolie."

Sir Victor was horrified to learn from Ford, who wrote to him after the article was published, that his friend Ellis Hayim was the "Baghdad millionaire" in question. After the Japanese invasion, Hayim and other leaders of the Jewish community had gone to Captain Inuzuka's new offices in the Cathay Hotel to inform him that the relief funds for the refugees in Hongkew were almost exhausted. Recalling how Sir Victor and Hayim had insulted him by offering to sell the Japanese their worst, most rat-infested tenements, Inuzuka "virtually threw the men out of his office." Immediately after the meeting, Hayim was dragged off to Bridge House.

In 1939, Hayim had been the first to tell Sir Victor that his offhand comments about Japanese militarism to the world's press were causing serious repercussions for Jewish refugees in Shanghai. Hayim, Sir Victor was shocked to learn, had been arrested for organizing the Moonlight Follies party in support of the Allies – one of the last social events Sassoon had attended before leaving Shanghai.

"Hyam [sic] was inclined to blame you for his miserable lot,"

Ford wrote to Sir Victor. "I'll never forget one day when two others in the cage carried Ellis over to the can in the corner, one holding his arms and the other his head while he did his stuff . . . He was down with what he said was malaria and his limbs were cramped from lying in his corner so long." The Japanese, Ford continued, seemed to believe Hayim was a British spy.

Those who managed to escape the attentions of the *kempeitai* faced entirely new challenges. White Shanghailanders, accustomed to occupying the top tiers of the Treaty Port's racial hierarchy, had suddenly become enemy aliens under the sword of the Mikado, in an empire whose slogan was "Asia for the Asiatics."

It was a delayed reaction to the perceived insults of the previous century, when Commodore Perry's Black Ships had fired their guns in Tokyo's harbour. By 1942, the Japanese were the rulers of 405 million people – one fifth of the world's population. From the eastern borders of India to the Philippines, they had come close to achieving their goal of chasing the Westerners out of Asia.

Those who remained in Shanghai would have to survive in a city utterly transformed.

美

From castaways on a "solitary island," the people of Shanghai under Japanese rule became residents of what the Chinese call a *heian shijie*, a "dark world." Physically, the foreign settlements, taken without shelling or aerial bombing, remained virtually unchanged. The new occupiers of Shanghai used the same stage and furnishings to enact a sinister shadow play.

Though the hands that moved the strings were in Tokyo, China was nominally ruled by a Nanking-based puppet regime. Its president was the baby-faced Wang Jing-wei, who, after the death of Sun Yat-sen, had vied for control of the Nationalist Party with Chiang Kai-shek. From bomb-throwing anti-Manchu radical, Wang had become China's most notorious traitor. As head of the Reorganized National Government of China – its flag was the white sun of the nationalists topped with a triangular yellow pennant emblazoned with the Chinese characters for "Peace, Anti-

Communism, National Construction" – Wang set up a secret service dedicated to kidnapping and settling scores. A house surrounded by barbed wire and high walls at No. 76 Jessfield Road, in the Western Roads district, became the Bridge House of the Chinese population – with the difference that few who entered left alive.

The French Concession, which had become an outpost of the collaborationist regime of Vichy France, was officially handed over to Wang Jing-wei's government. On August 2, 1943, the Japanese chairman of the Municipal Council gave control of the International Settlement to the mayor of the puppet municipal government. One century after Western enclaves had been established on the Chinese mainland, the bizarre institution of extraterritoriality – which allowed foreigners to commit crimes on Chinese soil with impunity from Chinese law – came to an end. The new government, however, was unable to claim the moral high ground: a year earlier, President Roosevelt had pre-empted Wang by announcing the abrogation of all American privileges in China. Even so, the powerless puppet regime in Nanking officially declared war on the United States.

Meanwhile, the Japanese, after decades of being excluded from power, were busy remaking Shanghai in their own image. Clocks throughout the city were set to Tokyo time. The few public monuments Shanghailanders had gotten around to erecting were dismantled, among them the bronze statue of Sir Robert Hart, the Irish-born founder of China's Maritime Custom Service, on the Bund.* The world's largest prison, the Ward Road Gaol – named after the American adventurer who had fought off the Small Swords rebels – was renamed Tilanqiao, or "Bamboo Basket Bridge," after a nearby landmark. Avenue Édouard VII, once the dividing line between Frenchtown and the International Settlement, was redubbed "Great Shanghai Road."

---

* Hart, a passionate Sinologist who had earned the genuine admiration of the Chinese, had predicted: "The day will come when China will repay with interest all the injuries and insults she has suffered at the hands of the European powers."

In the first week of the occupation, a Japanese naval officer walked into the Shanghai Club – from which the Chinese, but not the Japanese, were excluded – and announced to members they had half an hour to finish their drinks; a frantic binge of chit-signing ensued. The Japanese then set to work with handsaws to shorten the legs of the billiards table, finally resolving a long-standing complaint of the club's most diminutive members.

At the Paramount cabaret, one of the first to hire Chinese hostesses, a Japanese soldier swaggered into the middle of the dance floor and asked the popular taxi dancer Chen Manli for a dance. When she refused, he shot her dead on the dance floor, sending clients fleeing out the door in terror. It was a clear signal that Shanghai's dancing days had come to an end.

The neon lights of the cabarets of Blood Alley – that favoured stomping ground of American sailors on leave – were switched off, and Ciro's began to close its doors at the unheard-of hour of 10:30. What nightlife remained took on a sinister cast. The Badlands, as the Western Roads were known, had long been lawless, but under the Japanese occupation they became truly dangerous, a netherworld where a night on the town meant the possibility of a shoot-out or a kidnapping. Nazis dominated the Masquée Bar, beating those who wouldn't join them in drunken choruses of "The Horst Wessel Song." The once-grand villas of British and American taipans were turned into pleasure palaces and casinos, patrolled by guards with drawn guns, where morphine and heroin were openly sold.

As wartime shortages started to bite, new vehicles appeared in the streets of Shanghai. The diesel-burning double-deckers oper-ated by Sir Victor Sassoon's transit company disappeared, and in Frenchtown the buses that remained were converted to run on coal. The "one-horsepower motorcar" made its début – old fliv-vers drawn by a single horse – and gas stations were replaced by bicycle stands. Inflation meant a single grape went for thirty cents, rickshaw rides that had never exceeded a dollar soon cost fifteen, and a pair of shoes – soled with car-tire rubber – went for $900 in Chinese currency. People sipped groundnut "coffee" with soya-bean milk by the light of ten-watt bulbs.

In the first months of the occupation, some Shanghailanders hoped they would be able to lead a more or less normal life under their new masters. Many of the British and Allied staff of the Municipal Police and Council, charged with overseeing the efficient handover of services, would continue to show up for work, in some cases for months after the Japanese invasion. At Sassoon House, employees – who had been caught in the act of destroying documents by Japanese marines – were told to assemble in a boardroom and informed they were expected to continue showing up for work until further notice.

Such hopes ended in 1943, when the mass internments began. American civilians, ordered to report to the old British American Tobacco godown in Pudong, marched towards the Bund, weighed down with hand luggage to which they'd strapped tennis rackets and fishing rods. In total, 7,600 British, American, Belgian, Canadian, Dutch, and other Allied nationals were gathered in eight "civilian assembly centres" – concentration camps by another name. Though conditions were spartan and internees suffered from overcrowding and disease, the brutality that marked the treatment of Allied soldiers in Japanese prisoner-of-war camps was absent. Families were allowed to remain together. The British author J.G. Ballard, who was then twelve, was interned with his parents and infant sister at a former training college for Chinese teachers five miles south of Shanghai.* Though the Ballards spent their internment picking weevils out of rice gruel, their living conditions were actually better than those of many of the Chinese on the outside.

---

* Thanks to Ballard's explorations of the war-ravaged city, Shanghai became the template for two of the Atomic Age's more memorable science-fiction dystopias. His visits to hastily abandoned villas and ballrooms and Chinese rowhouse districts that had been endlessly subdivided under the influx of refugees inspired both the novel *The Drowned World* and the short story "Concentration City." Ballard would document his internment in his memoirs, *Miracles of Life*, and the novel *The Empire of the Sun*.

By the end of the war, starving peasants were pressed up against the camp's barbed wire, begging for scraps of food.

Shanghai's Jews were not interned in camps. The Japanese, who rightly suspected that only expediency excluded them from the racist theories of their German allies, had balked when prominent Nazis urged them to implement a Far Eastern version of the Final Solution. As of March 1943, all stateless persons who had arrived after 1937 – a category disproportionately made up of German and Austrian Jews – were confined to a one-square-mile area of Hongkew. Passes to leave "Little Vienna" could only be obtained by applying to a sadistic tyrant named Ghoya, notorious for slapping faces and flying into petulant rages.

With Jews confined to a new ghetto and civilian Shanghailanders interned in camps, the city came into its own as a "dark world." Amidst the brilliant wayfarers who had tried their luck on the China Coast, Shanghai had always attracted an unusually large share of "bad hats," as spies, turncoats, and dope-dealers were referred to in the files of the Municipal Police's Special Branch. As the Japanese occupation progressed, and the glamorous and talented left the stage, all that remained in Shanghai were the amoral, the mad, and the desperate.

A fixture on the streets of occupied Shanghai was the abbot Chao Kung, a Buddhist monk whose white skin, long black Chinese robes, and shaven, star-tattooed skull made heads turn as he walked down Nanking Road. Since 1932, when Sir Victor Sassoon had pegged him for a "charlatan," he'd slipped even deeper into eccentricity. For those who knew his story, though, Trebitsch Lincoln was a legend. Like "Two-Gun" Cohen, he had been born to a Central European Jewish family, and had a career in petty theft in England and Canada. Unlike Cohen, though, Trebitsch – who was born Ignácz Trebitsch, in a small Hungarian town on the banks of the Danube – was prey to genuine bouts of mental illness. Before coming to China he had converted to Christianity and worked as a country curate in Kent, and then as a missionary to the Jews in Montreal's port. After serving as a Liberal Member of the British Parliament who campaigned on a free-trade ticket, he worked as a German triple agent in the First World War, outwitted and outran J. Edgar Hoover's agents in the United States, and shook hands with a young Adolf Hitler, who had joined him and other conspirators in a right-wing putsch to overthrow the Weimar Republic.

Trebitsch arrived in China under the unlikely alias "Patrick Keelan." While "Two-Gun" Cohen was brokering arms deals for Sun Yat-sen's nationalists in Canton, Trebitsch was selling guns to the warlords who opposed them in Manchuria. In 1925, though, Trebitsch underwent an epiphany, and, after days of fasting, chanting, and painful tattooing in a monastery, emerged as the venerable abbot Chao Kung, the founder of the League of Truth. Dedicated to the overthrow of British power through mystical means, the League had a mirror-image of a Nazi swastika super-imposed on the globe as its logo. Trebitsch spent his days trying to gain access to Tibet (he believed that the soul of his late friend, the Panchen Lama, second in the Tibetan monkish hierarchy to the Dalai Lama, had transmigrated into his body upon death) and arrange an audience with Hitler. He told German embassy repre-sentatives in Shanghai that when he met the Führer, three Tibetan wise men would materialize out of the wall, and their supernatural powers would help the Nazis end the war.*

By the forties Chao Kung was a familiar figure in the Public Gardens on the Bund, where he took a daily stroll. One day, Ralph Shaw, a reporter for the *North-China Daily News* who had been left unemployed by the Japanese occupation, was sitting on a bench, speculating to a friend about how long it would take for the British to win the war.

"I hate the British," the abbot interrupted. "You, young man, should be ashamed of your race. You will not win the war."

Shaw was left speechless by the anti-English tirade, delivered

---

* Amazingly, the chief SS man in the Far East, Josef Meisinger – "the butcher of Warsaw" – was so impressed by Trebitsch that he recommended the Jewish-born Buddhist be allowed to make the trip to Berlin. It wasn't to be: Meisinger's message arrived shortly after Hitler launched a crackdown on mystics.

with monkish solemnity, that ensued. Trebitsch's favourite son, Shaw would later learn, had been hanged in England after accidentally murdering a man in a drunken robbery.

"One day I will walk in the ruins of London," he concluded. "I will see you a conquered race. You deserve all that the future is going to heap on you."

The man known as the "Olympian of Scoundrelism" spent his last months in a tiny room in the YMCA on Bubbling Well Road, dying in 1943 after an operation for an intestinal complaint.

Eventually, even the Cathay Hotel began to succumb to the ravages of occupation. In his letter to Sir Victor, the American newspaperman M.C. Ford reported that the Cathay's head chef had also been thrown into a cage in Bridge House. The Japanese had apparently discovered that, with an accomplice, he'd squirrelled away $150,000 in a linen room in Cathay Mansions. (Ford added, "Don't know whether it was for themselves or for you they did this brave deed.")

"That crazy 'Rumanian' manager of your hotels," Ford continued, "went all Japanesey, and kept his job." Half of the Cathay's eighth-floor dining room was curtained off so Japanese officials could throw private dinner parties, but otherwise the hotel remained open to the public. "And, yes, the Japs amused themselves in that studio-attelier [sic] of yours, pouring [sic] over the things you'd left behind." Sir Victor was not greatly surprised to learn that his penthouse photo studio, where he stored nude photos of Mickey Hahn and other women, had been ransacked.

The other Sassoon hotels were put under Japanese management, and many of the Cathay's guest rooms were redecorated with tatami mats and wood panelling to suit Japanese tastes.

The quality of the clientele at the Cathay during the Japanese occupation left much to be desired. Room 741 became the headquarters of Captain Eugene Pick, head of a spy ring that terrorized Shanghai's foreign community with shakedowns and kidnappings. Pick, the epitome of the shifty apolitical scoundrel, was able to thrive in Shanghai's netherworld as never before. Born in Latvia to a Cossack army colonel, he was well known in the Treaty Port's

Russian theatre community as a stage manager, opera singer, and ballet dancer, who worked under the name Eugene Hovans. All the while, he was selling secrets to any intelligence agency he could get on the hook. Before the war, a typical job involved blackmailing an American judge for being homosexual (the man's body was subsequently found floating in the Whangpoo). After working for the Soviet Comintern, Pick supplied the British with information about the inner workings of the Communist Party, before settling into more steady work with the Japanese Naval Intelligence Bureau. Pick's ring of forty spies included his muscle-man Paul Lojnikoff, a handsome Russian boxer whose side job as a "purchasing agent" for the Japanese allowed him to maintain a suite at the Cathay. Together, they set up a criminal smuggling ring to run cigarettes, guns, and liquor to war-straitened Shanghai.

As the tide of the Pacific war started to turn, the already dim lights of this "dark world" began to flicker out. In 1944, squadrons of B-29 Superfortresses started their high-altitude bombing raids of Japan's major cities. Work crews began to dig air-raid tunnels under the streets of the former French Concession. Rationing was extended to salt, soap, and even matches.

"Even the most luxurious hotels like the Cathay have been without heat most of the winter," reported the *New York Times* correspondent in China in February 1944, "and have had hot water only a few hours in the morning."

Early in May 1945 an American plane traced the letters "V.E." in the sky over the Lunghwa camp, where J.G. Ballard's family was living, signalling to the internees that the war in Europe was over. On the night of June 9, the keen of sirens foretold yet another air raid. This time, the survivors in the camps rejoiced when they realized that Shanghai was being bombed by American planes.

Eugene Pick and his cronies held a melancholy farewell dinner in his suite at the Cathay, attended by the Japanese naval attaché. Even Pick could see that the time had come to check out. The hotel's storerooms had been turned into warehouses for loot, its once plush carpets were threadbare and dirty, and its radiators had long since been ripped out to be used as scrap metal. The Cathay's glamour, like Shanghai's, was fading fast.

Two weeks before the first atomic bomb was dropped on Hiroshima, Pick sailed across the East China Sea. Soon enough, he would be picked up by American military police as he dined with a companion at the Takahashi Hotel, with whom he was discussing plans to open a Russian nightclub in Tokyo.

When Captain Pick left the Cathay Hotel, it marked the end of an era for Shanghai. Never again would the likes of Morris "Two-Gun" Cohen, Trebitsch Lincoln, or Princess Sumaire appear at the front desk to sign the registry book under an assumed name. Nor, for that matter, would a Lorraine "Miss Jill" Murray, a Bernardine Szold-Fritz, or an Emily "Mickey" Hahn boldly stride into the ballroom. The time had passed when a person could step off a ship and talk his or her way into a garden party or a brand new career, bluffing the world with a convincing manner and a compelling cover story. Shanghai continued to exist, but in name only. Never again would it be the world's most fabulous haven for fabulists.

What the world gained in probity, it lost in romance.

22: Check-Out Time

At first, Mickey didn't recognize Charles, he was so pale from loss of blood. The bullet that had pierced his chest had narrowly missed a lung, and his left arm dangled, semi-paralyzed, in a sling. As he lay on a camp cot at Queen Mary's Hospital, Mickey learned what had happened in the two days since she'd last seen him. While trying to lead a company of Indian troops on a counterattack against the advancing Japanese on Shouson Hill, Charles had been targeted by a sniper as he was climbing out of a ravine. Hours had passed, with blood flowing from his chest wound, before the medics discovered him. Fearing he was close to death, he kept insisting to the stretcher-bearers that the mother of his child should get the $112 in his wallet.

Mickey was able to find work at the hospital, leaving her infant daughter Carola with a Cantonese amah at the house on May Road.

Soon enough, the Japanese introduced mass internment to Hong Kong, as they had in Shanghai. Signs were posted with orders for American, Canadian, Dutch, British, and other enemy nationals to report to the Murray Parade Ground in downtown Victoria. Overwhelmed by the turnout, the occupiers told Eurasians with American or European nationality to go home; thanks to their Asian blood, they would not be interned. The rest, carrying blankets, clothes, and whatever possessions they could pack into suitcases, were loaded onto small boats and ferried to a fishing village on the island's south coast. Stanley would become the largest of the Hong Kong camps, in which a total of 13,390 Allied civilians and soldiers were held for the duration of the war.

Mickey vowed she would not be interned. The camps for

Jewish refugees she had visited in Shanghai had convinced her they were no place to raise an infant. But Charles refused to use his influence as head of military intelligence to keep Mickey and his daughter out of a camp; he thought they would be better off with other Allied non-combatants in Stanley. Noticing that hospital patients had not been included in the round-up, she had herself admitted to Queen Mary, complaining of complications from her caesarean. Then the Japanese began to evacuate the hospital, sometimes tearing off bandages to verify that they hid actual wounds. Charles was sent to the officers' camp on Argyle Street in Kowloon.

Racking her brains for ways to erase the scarlet letter of her American nationality, Mickey told a friend, "I did have a Chinese husband once . . ."

Five years earlier, she had attested in a law office to being Zau Sinmay's wife; possessing the notarized papers had allowed her to rescue his printing press. According to Japanese and Chinese custom, a woman was but a man's chattel – which meant a wife's nationality was automatically the same as her husband's. Mickey's status as Sinmay's wife officially made her Chinese – and in occupied China, where the slogan was now "Asia for the Asiatics," being Chinese was far better than being American. As she lay in her hospital bed, a Japanese medical officer listened to her story, nodded his head, and stamped a pass that gave her two more days of freedom.

At the Foreign Office, the Japanese Consul confirmed that she would not be interned. The man turned out to be an acquaintance; before Pearl Harbor, she and Charles had spent a night drinking Scotch with him at the Tokyo Hotel. In fact, he told her, because she was a Chinese woman in the eyes of the law, she *could* not be interned – he should know, as he was the one who had drafted the law. She was given another pass, this one covered with even more official stamps. Its validity would only be guaranteed, however, if she could provide proof of her marriage.

Soon after, she ran into one of Sinmay's nephews on a crowded Hong Kong street.

"Hello, Freddie," Mickey said to the young student. "Will you come to the Foreign Affairs Office and bear me out when I tell them that I'm your auntie? I'm getting a Chinese pass as Sinmay's wife."

Freddie agreed, and she was issued a Chinese passport. Once again, her relationship with Sinmay had proved invaluable, this time by saving her from the privations of wartime internment.

As she had done so many times before, Mickey translated her experiences into the written word, a series of vignettes that would be collected in the ironically-titled book *Hong Kong Holiday*. Unlike the light-hearted adventures of Pan Heh-ven, they dealt with the business of survival, in a Hong Kong turned upside down by the Japanese occupation.

The Gloucester – the main competition to the Hongkong Hotel – had, she discovered, been renamed the Matsubara. For a time, coolies dressed in cotton pyjamas, newly enriched after looting homes on the Peak, could be seen struggling with knives and forks at Gripps, the hotel's restaurant. Queen's Road, the colony's most venerable promenade, was renamed Meiji-dori, after the 122nd Emperor of Japan.

News of Mickey's "marriage" to Sinmay spread among the Japanese, who took it as a sign that she was open-minded about relationships with Asians. When romantically ambitious officers began to appear at her house, she gave them English lessons in exchange for food, but warded off their more importunate demands. One night, she escaped the drunken pawing of an amorous colonel who had ordered her into his car by dashing into the Kam Loong restaurant, whose manager happened to be the brother of Ah King, her cook. Waiters hid her in a pantry, whisking her out the back door when the coast was clear.

The fact that she'd avoided internment, Mickey believed, saved her daughter's life. In the early days Carola refused to take the breast, and the fact that Mickey had access to black-market jam, milk, and sugar, which were hard to get in the camps, kept her healthy and growing. Terrified that Carola's first language would be the Cantonese pidgin that Mickey spoke with her amah, she made a point of using grammatical Mandarin around her daughter. Carola soon developed a preference for salt fish and bean curd over Jell-O and cereal.

Mickey spent her days walking or hitchhiking to the Stanley Street market, where looted goods were sold, in search of food for Charles and his co-detainees. She gradually sold off her jewellery, and traded a beloved Scottie dog for a few turnip cakes.

Conditions continued to deteriorate. For the Japanese, Hong Kong's value was strictly symbolic; it served no military purpose, and they had neither the desire nor the ability to feed the resident population. Over the course of the war Hong Kong's population would shrink from 1.5 million to half a million, as hungry residents left to try for a better life in "Free China." The Japanese hastened the process by rounding up civilians on the streets and setting them adrift on junks (some actually did reach the plague-ridden coast of Canton via this grotesque parody of "repatriation"). Lawlessness increased. One morning, a thief with a firm grip tried to tear the watch right off Mickey's wrist as she walked through an old part of town. Her house was looted by Chinese thugs who tied her up for two hours, stamping off in frustration when they found no valuables.

"It often looked as if the Japanese had grabbed Hong Kong," Mickey noted in *Hong Kong Holiday*, "only in order to kick the Chinese around more thoroughly than the British had ever thought of doing."

In spite of all the horrors she'd experienced, however, she continued to see the Japanese as individuals. "My attitude towards the Japanese was rapidly becoming one of wary, wondering curiosity, and there it remains to this day. I must admit that I also feel maternal to some of them." They had, she felt, the same prickly volatility as the gibbons she'd cared for. (No insult was intended: for Mickey, who had the highest regard for apes, comparing a human to a simian was a compliment.)

After the Battle of Midway in June 1942, the vastly over-expanded Empire of the Sun, pierced on all sides by Allied attacks, showed the first signs of deflating. The first American bombers appeared in the skies above Hong Kong in July 1943. Mickey learned that, thanks to her sister Helen's energetic hounding of State Department officials, she would be sent home on a repatriation ship – a plan which Charles, preoccupied by his daughter's health, heartily approved.

A few days before her scheduled departure Mickey took Carola on a visit to the Argyle Street camp, where every Monday relatives were permitted to parade in front of the internees. Communication between prisoners and family members was limited to one fifty-word postcard a month. Wives were not allowed to look their husbands in the eyes; the guards had been known to shoot visitors who dared to speak.

To Mickey's surprise, as their rickshaw driver pulled them along the curb close to the barbed wire, her twenty-month-old daughter stood up in the seat and shouted, "Daddy, bye-bye! Daddy, bye-bye!" The guards scowled, but held fire. Her daughter's amah, she learned, had spent the week teaching Carola how to say the words.

Mickey and Carola steamed out of Hong Kong on September 23, 1943, aboard the *Teia Maru*. Theirs was one of only two repatriation voyages to be permitted out of Japanese-occupied China. Mickey was assigned to a three-bunk cabin, which turned out to be infested with red ants. The ship, a captured French vessel with its original cellar of vintage wine, was built for 700, but carried over twice that number. Half of the passenger list was made up of missionaries and their families, creating a culture clash when they picked up a dozen American ex-marines and beachcombers in the Philippines. The rough-living drifters, quickly nicknamed the "Dead End Kids," devoted their energy to draining the ship's stocks of liquor.

Among the repatriates, Mickey recognized a familiar face. Morris "Two-Gun" Cohen, who had first come to China in 1922, was finally going home. Mickey was shocked at his wretched appearance. An old suit jacket, now three sizes too big, hung in folds off his once bulky frame, and he wore crimson shorts fashioned from window curtains. After living on "Stanley Pudding" – a mush of peanut oil, rice, water, and sugar – he'd shed

eighty pounds, and the skin hung in folds off his bones. Over
glasses of champagne and late-night snacks of onion sandwiches,
Cohen had plenty of time to tell her about his last adventure in
China.

Cohen told her that when the internment call came, it had felt
like Judgment Day: all his past life in China – civil-war friends and
foes, poker-playing buddies from the Victoria Hotel in Canton's
Shameen and the Astor House in Shanghai – seemed to have been
assembled on the Murray Parade Ground. When the *kempeitai*
realized that Cohen had been some kind of nationalist "general"
he was sent to a makeshift jail, a building that Cohen was amused
to recognize as a former brothel. After being starved and beaten
with bamboo rods, he was made to sign a paper confessing to his
involvement with the "so-called Chinese National Government."
One morning he was marched out into the yard, and told to kneel
and lower his head. As he muttered the prayer "*Shema Yisrael*,"
– "Hear O Israel" – an officer jerked a two-handed samurai sword
out of its scabbard. Instead of being decapitated, though, Cohen
was given a kick in the ribs and sent to Stanley Camp. There, he
was surprised to receive a summons to the head office, where he
received an apology for the *kempeitai*'s brutal treatment. The civilian overseer, Cohen told Mickey with delight, was an old friend:
none other than Mr. Yamashita, the little Japanese barber at the
Hongkong Hotel, where Cohen had been a long-time resident.
Cohen became a popular figure in the camp: when the internees
were allowed a one-time chance to buy groceries, Cohen spent his
entire $75 allowance on brown sugar – which he then distributed
to the camp's children.

After three weeks at sea the *Teia Maru* docked at the Portuguese colony of Goa on the west coast of India, where the prisoner
exchange was to take place. Hundreds of Japanese nationals who
had been ejected from the United States were herded into the
cramped, filthy ship, while Mickey and her fellow passengers were
welcomed aboard the spick and span Swedish motorship *Gripsholm*.
They were delighted to discover spacious cabins, laundry facilities,
and blond Scandinavian stewards; the new ship even had a hair-

dresser. The "Dead End Kids," finally able to escape the scolding of the missionaries, occupied a corridor which became known – in tribute to Shanghai's most notorious strip of cabarets – as Blood Alley. Mickey hired a Eurasian amah to take care of Carola, who celebrated her second birthday at sea between South Africa and Brazil.

On December 1, 1943, tugboats guided the *Gripsholm* to a Jersey City pier. Cohen and the other Canadians aboard were escorted onto buses and delivered to Grand Central Station, where they were met by Mounties who accompanied them on the train ride north. Mickey, however, was not allowed to disembark. The FBI agents who awaited her were intrigued by her eight-year absence from the United States. They were even more curious when she told them she had smuggled a document home containing messages from Japanese friends and Allied internees.* After a day's interrogation, during which the agents learned much that was interesting – though nothing actually incriminating – Mickey was allowed to leave the ship. She spent the night in Herbert Asbury's apartment, where Helen and their mother Hannah, then eighty-seven but still in good health, were waiting to greet her. A bawling Carola spent her first night in the United States hiding behind furniture.

The royalties that had accumulated since the publication of *The Soong Sisters* and *Mr. Pan*, her collected stories about Sinmay, meant Mickey had no immediate money worries. She rented an apartment on East 95th Street, and Carola was sent to nursery school. When Mickey consulted Benjamin Spock about her

---

* The piece of white silk, which was sewn into the sleeve of the dress Carola was wearing, is filed among the Emily Hahn papers at the University of Indiana's Lilly Library. Typewritten and single-spaced, it lists a dozen or so names and addresses given to her by internees in Hong Kong who had asked her to pass on news to their loved ones. It also contains cryptic phrases that must have troubled the FBI agents: "There is a big difference between white washed and washed white," reads one. Another, after some lines of Japanese verse, has an allusion to flowering cherry trees: "Our Sakura are in a splendid condition throughout the Country, so the spirit and sould [sic] of the nation."

daughter's timidity and size, the pediatrician and psychiatrist told her not to worry: as her diet improved, Carola would develop normally. He advised Mickey to spoil her, within reason.

Mickey had come home to discover she was notorious. The first American publisher of James Joyce's *Ulysses* (and future *What's My Line?* regular) Bennett Cerf wrote a nasty item in the *Saturday Review* about the "publicity-wise Emily Hahn, who, not content with holding her two-year-old, half-Chinese baby Carola in her arms, sported a long black stogie to boot."* On a visit to her sister Rose's house in Winnetka, Mickey agreed to give an interview to a local reporter. The next day, her picture appeared alongside Carola's in the *Chicago Sun* under the headline "I was the concubine of a Chinese!"

Mickey set to work writing an account of her eight years in Shanghai, Chungking, and Hong Kong. *China to Me* was one of the first of a flood of books by Shanghai residents forced by war to return to the United States. There was something comical about the way the old China hands jostled for seniority in the titles of their books. Hallett Abend, the *New York Times*'s man in the Far East, published his memoirs under the title *My Life in China 1926–1941*. John B. Powell, the founder of the *China Weekly Review* – who, as a consequence of his torture in Bridge House, would die shortly after his return – penned *My Twenty-Five Years in China*. In *My War with Japan*, the Axis-baiting broadcaster Carroll Alcott would repeatedly mention the fact that he'd first arrived in Shanghai in 1928.† While Randall Gould's *China in the Sun* abjured personal credentials, it prominently featured an anecdote in which Mickey Hahn's gibbon Mr. Mills, on a visit to the *Evening Post and Mercury* offices, ran into the publisher's black

---

* Mickey regretted sending a letter of complaint: Cerf's retraction emphasized that Carola's father was not Chinese; he was, in fact, a British prisoner-of-war, and still married.

† The winner, surely, in the Old China Hand competition was Sam Ginsbourg, a Russian Jew raised in Harbin and Shanghai, and author of *My First Sixty Years in China*.

spaniel. "The ensuing melee," wrote Gould, "was almost as destructive as the blasts to which we were becoming accustomed."

Written while Charles's fate was still unknown, Mickey's intensely readable account was racy without being scurrilous. She named the right names, and made China's complex politics easy to understand. Eventually the book sold almost three-quarters of a million copies, outselling her previous bestseller, *The Soong Sisters* (whose cover had first appeared with the Chinese character for Soong embossed upside down).

The publication of *China to Me* caused "Two-Gun" Cohen to emerge from retirement. One day, Mickey received a typewritten letter headed by the words "WITHOUT PREJUDICE," heavily underscored. After his return to Canada, Cohen had married a Jewish divorcée named Ida Judith Clark, who owned an upscale dress shop next door to Montreal's Ritz-Carlton. In his newly respectable role, Cohen objected to Mickey's portrayal of him as a drunken regular in the lobby of the Hongkong Hotel.

"I was not a 'hanger-on,'" he wrote. "Again, you know perfectly well that I was not a drinking man and was therefore never drunk . . . the general picture that you conjure up of a tipsy lounge-lizard, living on an unearned stipend and by his wits at cards, is as distasteful as it is untrue."

When Cohen came to New York with his new wife, Hahn was able to mollify him with the promise that passage would be changed in future editions of *China to Me*. The new version read: "The general, plump and cheerful, was one of the landmarks of the Hongkong Hotel."*

For Mickey, the story told in *China to Me* wouldn't be over until she knew Charles was safe. Deprived of news, she succumbed to anxiety. She'd hired Willy, a friend of one of the repatriation ship's "Dead End Kids," to look after her apartment; thanks to his knowledge of the black market he was able to supply her with

---

* An unpublished and undated fragment in the Emily Hahn papers at the University of Indiana reads: "I was rather surprised that he had read it, or, rather, that he could read at all: anyway, I explained what I had said and he was at last satisfied that I had not traduced him, so we parted friends."

morphine, which kept the worst of the worry at bay. A collaboration with her friend, *Grand Hotel* author Vicki Baum, on a Broadway play about the *Gripsholm* – sketched out but never completed – also kept her mind occupied. Meanwhile, friends returning from China kept bringing rumours about Charles's execution. The Japanese, apparently, had discovered a transmitter in the Argyle Street camp, and punished the guilty parties.

On September 14, 1945, the tail end of a *United Press* item made Mickey cry with joy. "LIBERATED BRITISH PRISONERS," read the Hong Kong-datelined dispatch, "TODAY TOLD HOW THEY SHUT THEIR EYES AND SOBBED WHEN A JAPANESE FIRING SQUAD RUTHLESSLY EXECUTED AN AMERICAN AIRMAN. MAJ. CHARLES BOXER OF DORSET, ENGLAND – WHO PLANS TO RETURN TO THE US AND MARRY MANHATTAN WRITER MISS EMILY HAHN AS SOON AS POSSIBLE – TOLD THE STORY." Congratulations poured in from around the world, among them Vicki Baum's jocular telegram from Pasadena:

DEAREST MICKY [*sic*] AWFULLY GLAD ABOUT YOUR GOOD NEWS WISHING AND HOPING FERVENTLY THAT EVEN THE HAPPIEST MARRIAGE WONT MAKE AN HONEST WOMAN OUT OF YOU.

The December 3 edition of *Life* magazine featured a photo of Charles Boxer, grinning broadly as he gave a piggyback ride to Carola – dressed in a plaid skirt and looking plump and healthy – in Mickey's Upper East Side apartment. The following week, Mickey Hahn and Charles Boxer drove up to Connecticut, where they slipped a justice of the peace a hundred-dollar bribe to marry them.

No mention was made of the bride's prior engagement – to a Chinese poet, who still believed that his American concubine would one day lie next to him in the family grave.

美

There were hopes, in the months and years that followed VJ Day, that the old Shanghai would be reborn in all its pre-war glamour.

The settlements built by the British and the French had adapted quickly enough to their new Japanese masters. Surely the new rider in town wouldn't take long to settle into the saddle.

On September 19, 1945, the American flagship *Rocky Mount* was given pride of place at the Number One Buoy on the Whangpoo River – a position that, since the earliest days of the Treaty Port, had been accorded to British vessels. The US naval headquarters were established in the Glen Line Building at No. 28, the Bund, a British-owned building only recently vacated by the German embassy. Sailors poured ashore from ships laden with stores intended for the projected invasion of Japan, throwing bottles of Coca-Cola to Chinese crowds that – for the moment – proclaimed the United States *dinghao*, the best. GIs drunk on Sir Victor Sassoon's U.B. Pilsner astonished the crowds by putting coolies in the back seats of rickshaws and pulling them down Nanking Road.

One of the first orders of business of the new Shanghai Council was to switch the flow of traffic from the left to the right-hand side of the road. The Argentina Nite Club, until recently the favoured redoubt of Nazi agents and Japanese gendarmes, took out ads proclaiming itself "Shanghai's Only American-Run Night-Club and Cocktail Lounge." Hollywood movies returned to the Nanking Theatre, beginning with the already four-year-old *Aloma of the South Seas*, starring Dorothy Lamour, projected from reels just flown in from Chungking. The billiard tables at the Shanghai Club that had been foreshortened for the convenience of Japanese players were raised to their previous height on platforms. Randall Gould returned from the United States to relaunch the *Evening Post and Mercury*, which, now that Shanghai was Chinese territory and subject to oversight by the nationalists, was published under the motto "All the News That's Fit to Print (passed by censor)."

Returned from his exile in Chungking, opium kingpin "Big-Eared" Du set about recreating his pre-war gangster empire, this time with the aid of American military surplus and United Nations Relief and Rehabilitation Administration funds. Food, clothing, and medicine intended for war victims were sold at public auction or diverted to the black market. All told, three billion dollars' worth of material aid authorized by Congress went into the pockets of the nationalists and their cronies. Companies seized by the Japanese, instead of being returned to their rightful owners, were put in the hands of new Kuomintang monopolies. Those who had collaborated with the Japanese occupiers were given light sentences, or even new positions in the resurrected government.

It soon became clear that Shanghai's days as the cosmopolitan Paris of the Orient were behind it. The long-suffering White Russian community decamped for Hawaii, Canada, and South America, many by way of Tubabao, an island offered to the refugees by the Philippine government. Some, seduced by promises of amnesty for non-communists, even braved life in the Soviet Union. The Jewish community moved on – the rich Sephardic families to Hong Kong, while refugees from Europe left to start new lives in the New World and, eventually, Israel. Over 2,600 actually returned to Austria and Germany.* The foreign communities that had made Shanghai a "Cosmopolis-on-the-Whangpoo" were vacating the premises.

At the same time, the influx of internal migrants never stopped: as the city's population approached 5.5 million, never-before-seen levels of crowding came to the *shikumen* houses and shanty towns. Overpopulation was accompanied by hyperinflation. The price index, 100 before the war, had leaped to 627,000 by 1947.† In an attempt to deal with the problem, Chiang Kai-shek's eldest son was brought in to replace the old currency with a new "gold *yuan*," and instituted a crackdown on the black market. The upright, Soviet-educated official had some success cracking down on speculators

---

* By 1953, only 404 Jews would remain in Shanghai, among them the honorary treasurer of the Council of the Jewish Community, one Ezra S. Hardoon – one of Silas Hardoon's many adopted sons.

† On a 1947 round-the-world tour with cartoonist Al Hirschfeld, the Marx Brothers scriptwriter and *New Yorker* writer S.J. Perelman stayed at the Cathay Hotel. He was charged $14,000 for breakfast, and $120,000 for a room lacking radiators, and thus, heat. "Just to indicate how cold it was," Perelman quipped, "I left a tumbler of water at my bedside and when I woke up, it was gone. Hirschfeld had drunk it and also eaten the glass. That was one cold night."

– until he announced he was going to arrest a relation of Madame Kung, the eldest of the Soong sisters. After his stepmother, Madame Chiang, personally flew to Shanghai to slap him in the face, he was pulled off the job. By 1948, a single American dollar – which bought three Chinese dollars when Mickey arrived – was worth 1.2 million. By then, the rich were paying for butter with wheelbarrows full of bills, and restaurants charged millions for a cup of coffee.

The United States never had any intention of setting up a new American Settlement in Shanghai. At best, the "China Lobby" in Washington, DC – epitomized by the China-born publisher of *Life*, Henry Luce – hoped the nationalist government would keep the Reds out of power. By the end of the war, the United Front that had brought the nationalists and the communists together had devolved into the merest facade. All through the war, Chiang had accepted military aid from the United States, but refused to commit his troops and equipment to major battles against the Japanese. It was no secret that the Generalissimo and Madame Chiang had cordially despised the American advisers with whom they'd been forced to work (particularly General "Vinegar Joe" Stilwell, who had gone so far as discussing with Roosevelt a plan to have Chiang assassinated). With the war over, Chiang, who had reserved his best soldiers and materiel for a final showdown, had the resources to attack the real focus of his hatred: the Reds.

After the bombing of Hiroshima and Nagasaki, the panicked Japanese occupiers of Manchukuo laid down their arms. Fortuitously, Mao's communists were able to reach Manchuria from their base in Yenan more quickly than Chiang's nationalists. There, aided by the Soviets, they seized the stockpiles of Japanese aircraft, machine guns, and artillery pieces that would provide the People's Liberation Army with real military might. Starting in 1947, they began a nationwide counteroffensive, smashing out of Manchuria into Kuomintang-held areas. As the Reds advanced, the collapse of nationalist military morale, combined with civilian disgust at corruption, overtaxation, and hyperinflation, made it increasingly clear that Chiang's days were numbered.

It was against this background that Sir Victor Sassoon prepared for his return to Shanghai. During the war, he had never
given up on China. The Eurasian doctor and author Han Suyin
met him aboard the motorship *Tjiluwah*, a ship that sailed from
Bombay to New York early in 1942. "He came on board with a
limp, a monocle, and that Shanghai brand of arrogance that now
seemed almost a parody," and offended her by walking out after
only twenty minutes of an amateur play in which she had a role.
When Han noticed him contemplating the shipboard bulletin one
day with "monocled haughtiness," he said to her peremptorily,
"We'll be back in Shanghai next year."

He spent much of the war living in the Taj Mahal Hotel in
Bombay. With its dusty marble pillars and its army of attendants
in scarlet and white, it had an inimitable Victorian charm, but it
was a poor replacement for the amenities of the Cathay. Though
Gandhi had been jailed after his speech exhorting the British to
"Quit India," and the Sassoon mills performed well supplying the
Allies with cotton, Sir Victor remained pessimistic about his prospects in a heavily-taxed India. Very early one morning in 1943, he
sold his factories to Marwari traders from Rajasthan for £4 million
(their superstitions required the contract be signed at exactly 2:47
a.m.). Sassoon turned his energies, and hopes, to Shanghai, where
his remaining properties were valued at £7.5 million – of which
the Cathay Hotel and Sassoon House accounted for one million.

But after the war, the reports that Lucien Ovadia had been
sending from Shanghai (where Sir Victor's cousin had returned
early in 1946) were dispiriting. Stilwell's replacement, General
Wedemeyer, had taken over Sir Victor's penthouse – to be followed by General Marshall, who had hoped to bring about a
rapprochement between nationalists and communists. Though the
American brass was eventually dislodged from his suite in the
Cathay, it was proving well-nigh impossible to do business in a city
racked by inflation, profiteering, and hoarding. Ovadia was doing
his best to dispose of the remaining Sassoon properties, but finding few takers.

When Sir Victor landed at the airfield in Shanghai on December 16, 1947, it was the first time he had seen the city in six years. The joy of realizing that much of the old crowd was still in town – he attended dinners with the McBains and the Liddells, the Kadoories and the Keswicks – was soon overshadowed by the realization that the place was going to the dogs. When he was delivering a friend to the wharf at Hongkew in the early hours of the morning, a thug tore the platinum watch he was wearing right off his wrist.

It was around this time that, echoing Louis XV's presentiment about the French Revolution, he'd started muttering "*Après moi, le déluge*," under his breath.

Working people, including the staff of the Cathay, were finding day-to-day life close to impossible. The currency fluctuated so wildly that the staff at Sassoon House were asking to receive part of their pay in rice, pots and pans, rubber boots, or anything edible or wearable. (Footware and cookware, laid on towels on the Bund at night, were some of the only things farmers who'd made the trek to the city would accept in payment for produce.) One evening, Sir Victor, unaware that he was plundering the following day's payroll, gallantly emptied the hotel's night safe to buy passage on a ship to Buenos Aires for a Frenchwoman, Jeanne de Monet, and her two children. When rumours that the offices had been robbed spread, an emergency meeting of the Chinese staff was held in the eighth-floor ballroom. Ovadia was forced to wait on the orchestra platform, with hotel chefs armed with meat cleavers on either side of him; the revolt was only quelled when the bank delivered fresh stacks of bills.

Negotiations began for the final liquidation of E.D. Sassoon & Co., the trading company his grandfather had founded in 1867. The best offer for the Cathay Mansions, the exclusive apartment house in the former Concession, came from the Soviet government – a development Sir Victor saw as further evidence of a coming Red tide. By the end of the summer, he had disposed of most of his luxury apartment buildings. He was unable to sell Hamilton House, the brewery that made Shanghai's beloved

U.B. Pilsner, or the former cornerstone of his empire, the Cathay Hotel.

Sir Victor left Shanghai for the last time at eight o'clock in the morning on November 27, 1948. For his previous departures he'd always reserved a first-class cabin on the most luxurious ocean liner in port, being sure to lay in a stock of some of the best vintage wines from his cellars in the hold. This time, he occupied a single seat on a Hong Kong Airways flying boat. In his suitcase, though, was one of his most precious possessions – something he would never let the Chinese get their hands on. It was the leather-bound journal in whose pages he'd kept a meticulous record of his life. He had twenty-one more like it: pages filled with his cramped script, newspaper clippings, dinner-party seating plans, and black-and-white snapshots going back to 1927.

The day would come, he knew, when people would have difficulty believing a city as fantastic as Shanghai had ever existed. Events might erase the old Shanghai from the globe; at least he was leaving with evidence of all that he'd built.

En route to Hong Kong, Sir Victor sat next to a reporter for the *Los Angeles Times*. Sir Victor was clearly in a dark mood. During the four-hour flight, he told Waldo Drake:

Remember, the Chinese don't like foreigners and they never have. They'll do business with us but only to the extent that it suits their purpose. The most unpopular person in China today is the American. That's because the Chinese is like a woman. The more you give her, the more she expects. And if something she does against your advice turns out wrong she says, 'Why didn't you stop me?' I need hardly tell you I'm an old bachelor.

Sir Victor clearly hadn't lost his wryly self-aware sense of humour. He offered the reporter a "tremendous commission" if he could dispose of the remaining Sassoon assets in Shanghai.

Drake further reported that "the venerable British industrialist wizard of prewar Asia" had made a prediction:

His last sojourn in Shanghai confirmed his conviction that Chiang Kai-shek and the Kuomintang regime have by an endless procession of ineptitudes lost any chance of regaining the support of

*the Chinese people, who are now ready to welcome the Communists as
the lesser of two evils.*

As it happened, Sir Victor was right on both counts.

On the night of December 2, 1948, while Mao Tse-tung's
forces were approaching the north bank of the Yangtze River, a
freighter disguised as a coastal tramp and carrying a crew dressed
in rags tied up in front of the Cathay Hotel, at the corner of the
Bund and Nanking Road.

From the *North-China Daily News* building, where Mickey
Hahn had presented herself for her first job in Shanghai thirteen
years before, George Vine, an assistant editor who had stayed
behind to work late, witnessed an amazing scene.

The newspaper's fifth-floor office offered a good view of the
Bank of China, the building next to the Cathay. Despite the late
hour, the bank's doors were opened wide onto the Bund. On
street corners, nationalist troops had appeared, cordoning off an
area of several blocks around the bank that held China's greatest
reserves of bullion. Then, a file of dock labourers, dressed in
indigo tunics and short baggy trousers, emerged from the bank.
Each carried a bamboo pole, from which dangled parcels containing bars of gold. The newsman heard the soft *pad, pad, pad* of
their feet, and watched in awe as the riches of the Middle Kingdom were carried to the ship the traditional way – on the shoulders
of coolies. They were soon followed by the bank's executives, who,
in return for their cooperation and silence, had been promised safe
passage to Taiwan, the new Republic of China.

It had all been arranged by Chiang Kai-shek, whose final coup
was a masterful one: he had taken the money – or more precisely,
half a million ounces of gold bullion – and run, leaving China
broke.

On April 20, 1949, thousands of little boats, some no bigger
than sampans, poured out of creeks and inlets and crossed the
mighty Yangtze in ragged formations. Nanking, Chinkiang, and
the other major cities south of the river fell to the communists
with only minor skirmishes.

Shanghai steeled herself for the new conquerors. Vine, who

had witnessed the plundering of the Bank of China, happened to be in the lobby of the Cathay Hotel when fifty nationalist troops arrived. Their commanding officer informed the manager they needed a dozen riverfront rooms in which to set up their machine guns. The soldiers, wearing full packs and German-style helmets, carried pots, pans, and firewood through the lobby and spread straw sleeping mats on the polished floors. Vine even heard one of them ask, "Where can we billet our mules?" The manager hurriedly set about removing the grand piano and the best furniture from the Tower Night Club, and took the hand-carved dragons and silk lanterns down from the walls of the restaurant, so only the gilded Buddhas in their niches remained. But there were no Reds on the horizon that day, and the nationalist soldiers, abandoned by their leadership, began to melt into the backstreets.

On May 14, 1949, the first communist troops reached Hungjao Road, where foreign villas like Eve's, Sir Victor's former hunting lodge, were located. For the first time since he'd arrived in Shanghai, Vine saw that Soochow Creek was barren of sampans; the poor families who made its waters their home had fled upriver, apparently alerted by an extremely efficient riverine grapevine.

A few days later, the soldiers of the Red Army, wearing shoes of felted cloth made for them by female supporters, walked two abreast down the old Avenue Édouard VII. They were saluted by local policemen who had put red armbands over the sleeves of their uniforms; female street vendors offered them cups of tea and rice cakes.

The only fighting, which most foreign witnesses described as desultory and purely intended to save face, happened around the Garden Bridge. For two days, the retreating nationalist army put up cover fire to allow its officers to make their evacuation to Taiwan by way of the Bund. Nationalist snipers occupied the Broadway Mansions until foreign residents, fearing the skyscraper would be shelled, convinced the one hundred occupiers to lay down their arms in exchange for a feast cooked by the apartment building's excellent chef. After a sumptuous meal, the soldiers were handed red armbands as they left the building. Soon after, the streets of Hongkew were littered with discarded nationalist uniforms.

In the lobby of the Cathay, the staff awaited the new occupiers anxiously. Some wondered if the hotel, the Bund's most towering symbol of Western capital, would be looted.

But the tectonic clash that rocked Shanghai 117 years before – on the day an opium trader and a missionary ordered the wooden doors of the Taotai's Yamen to be splintered – would end not with a violent seism, but with the soft padding of feet in cotton shoes.

The first to arrive was a skinny young man, the commander of one hundred Red Army troops. After pushing through the revolving door he walked cautiously across the marble floor, gazing in wonder at the sumptuous lobby.

At the front desk he enquired, politely but firmly, if there were any rooms available for the night.

23: Settling the Bill

Mickey's reunion with Charles Boxer brought to a singularly sat-
isfying conclusion one of the Second World War's better-known
love stories. The woman who had left the United States a cigar-
chomping flapper, and had kept her lover and infant daughter alive
in Japanese-occupied Hong Kong, was now back home, a happily
married woman.

Things, of course, were more complex than that. Charles and
Mickey hadn't been given much time to get to know one another
before his internment. They had a passionate physical bond – the
bookish Charles, schooled in love by a concubine-housekeeper in
Tokyo, was, in his own words, "lusty as an eagle" – but they were
very different people. Though his friends were bemused by his
occasional outbursts of barrack-room doggerel, Charles was a
savant by nature, not a warrior, and lived mentally in the seventeenth century: he was obsessed with adding to his collection of
rare books, and his contributions to the historiography of the
Portuguese and Dutch colonial presence in the Far East would
make him one of the most respected scholars in his field.

The worldly Mickey sometimes found his single-mindedness
maddening: "Anything later than 1750 in painting or architecture
annoys him," she would observe of her husband later, "and he
never reads anything at all unless it has some connection to his
favourite historical period."

Both had already lived full and complex lives, and Charles was
not emotionally forthcoming – arguably a sound defensive position, as he had fallen in love with a woman who made her living
through public confession. Perhaps for this reason, Mickey didn't
feel it necessary to share every detail of her life with him. On his

return to the United States she quit morphine cold turkey and fired Willy, the cook who had been obtaining it for her. She never, she would tell her biographer many years later, talked to Charles about the relapse. At the time, he was under the impression she was suffering from a bad flu.

Mickey and Charles settled into an unconventional relationship that befitted two independent personalities. Mickey tried living on the Boxer family's farmhouse in Dorset, but after her experience with privation in Hong Kong she found the post-war rationing, and life in a drafty manor, maddening. The *New Yorker*'s Harold Ross, who by then was paying his star correspondent $2,000 an article, offered her an office of her own at 25 West Forty-third Street, a privilege she would continue to enjoy for four decades under four different editors. Charles, though he lacked a university degree, was appointed to a prestigious chair at King's College in London. (He got the job, he always said, because there was no real competition. "It's like the duck-billed platypus. I'm the only one of my kind.") They decided on an "open marriage" – while remaining sexually exclusive, they would enjoy complete freedom of movement. Based on shared adventure and mutual respect, their relationship was marked by long absences and passionate reunions. They had a second daughter, Amanda, who would grow up to be an accomplished stage and movie actress.

Mickey continued to have adventures. Her travels as a correspondent for the *New Yorker* took her to Brazil, Malaysia, Turkey, India and Pakistan, Nigeria and South Africa, and books such as *England to Me* and *Africa to Me* brought an intimate and idiosyncratic twist to the genre of the travelogue. She indulged her love of non-human primates in dozens of articles in popular and academic journals, as well as books such as *Look Who's Talking*, *Animal Gardens*, and *On the Side of the Apes* (her last book, *Eve and the Apes*, was a charming attempt to fathom why female primatologists such as Dian Fossey, Jane Goodall, and herself established such deep relationships with chimps, gorillas, and gibbons).

Mickey's China years, though, were the ones that marked her most deeply. For better and for worse, they also defined her politically. Like so many other foreigners in pre-war Shanghai, she had identified Chiang Kai-shek and his nationalists as the best hope for China's salvation. At the time, it was a reasonable position. When Mickey arrived in Shanghai, the horrific nationalist purge of communists, abetted by the foreign-controlled Municipal Council, was not well known: "Big-Eared" Du and the other gangsters who enacted the "White Terror" were regarded as patriots who had saved the International Settlement from chaos. For foreigners sympathetic to Chinese aspirations for independence, the real struggle was against Japanese aggression. The communists in their mountain hideaways were widely considered bandits; only such extraordinary characters as Agnes Smedley and Edgar Snow had the temerity to leave behind urban comforts and risk their lives to discover what the dreaded Reds were fighting for. The nationalists, who could still convincingly cite the idealistic founding principles of their founder Sun Yat-sen, seemed to offer the most realistic hope against Japanese occupation.

At the time even Han Suyin, the Eurasian author of *A Many Splendoured Thing* whose embrace of Mao's China would eventually extend to her supporting the Cultural Revolution, sided with the Generalissimo. In 1938, returning from Belgium determined to join the Chinese war of liberation, she married a Blueshirt, one of Chiang's secret and elite paramilitaries. Even when she realized that he embodied the worst traits of the nationalists – her husband was an authority-obsessed chauvinist who beat her for daring to defy tradition – Han continued to support his party. It was only in 1941, when Chiang Kai-shek's troops slaughtered the communists' New Fourth Army as it crossed the Yangtze River, that Han began to question her own support of the nationalists. By then, Mickey Hahn was trapped in Hong Kong, where the Japanese occupiers cut her off from news about Chiang's betrayal of the United Front.

After leaving China, Mickey was denounced by prominent American leftists as an apologist for the nationalists. Her book *The Soong Sisters* was seen as cutting the corrupt Generalissimo a blank cheque, and in the mid-fifties, critics complained that her unauthorized biography of Chiang Kai-shek passed over the issue of nationalist corruption. In 1945, Agnes Smedley, with whom she'd struggled to find food on Hong Kong's black market, ran into her at a backstage reception for a panel about China on an NBC radio program. "The bitch Emily Hahn came," Smedley wrote to a friend, "and of course we [did] not speak." (The accusation that the "picturesque Agnes Smedley," as Mickey liked to refer to her, was a Soviet spy was long considered an ill-founded McCarthyite smear. However, the author of Smedley's most recent biography has turned up extensive evidence in the Shanghai Municipal Police archives that Smedley had been paid to spy for the Comintern all through her time in China.) When Pearl Buck, whose novel *The Good Earth* had won early sympathy for the Chinese peasantry, publicly declared that the Soongs "had paid her to write" their biography, Mickey asked for, and was given, an apology.

In Mickey's voluminous writing about China, published and unpublished, the communists emerge as sincerely motivated but over-promoted guerrillas with little chance of liberating the country from oppression, let alone running it. Mickey believed that Chiang Kai-shek, in spite of his shortcomings, should be taken seriously as the leader of Republican China. As for Mao Tse-tung, she didn't know enough about the man or his beliefs to offer an informed opinion.[*]

On May 1, 1945, a week before the war in Europe ended, Mickey used *New Yorker* stationery to write a letter to Randall Gould, the editor of the *Shanghai Evening Post and Mercury*, accusing him of shifting the paper's policy towards support of the communists while privately spreading rumours that she had been "working under cover for the Soongs." Gould replied, "the most

---

[*] Edgar Snow, Mao's biographer, considered *China to Me* one of the best books on China written by an American. "I was looking through my small library the other day," he wrote to her in 1956, "and the thought occurred to me that only half a dozen books in it were worth reading from the viewpoint of understanding what is happening in China or Asia generally today; all or nearly all this past comment is irrelevant; it was written from minor elevations now all wiped out."

I have ever heard about you, and that very casually, was the suggestion that your friendship with Madame Kung might be influencing you toward closing your eyes to certain aspects of the present Nationalist government."

Gould had hit on something. Mickey *was* guilty of closing her eyes. The same could be said, though, of anybody who had enjoyed a privileged life in Shanghai before the Second World War. Closing one's eyes to the nationalists' venality and corruption went along with accepting the conditions that had allowed the growth and prosperity of Shanghai's foreign settlements.

The Nationalist Party, as it was run by Chiang Kai-shek, was a pure manifestation of the culture that had been born with the Treaty Ports themselves. From the start, foreign traders, unable to speak the language or navigate a culture utterly alien to them, had engaged local proxies to help them prosper in the opium, cotton, oil, tobacco, and tea trades. These proxies, the compradors, were able to exploit the fact that they were the only mediators between West and East for personal advancement. The institution of "squeeze," in which the compradors skimmed expenses and exacted commissions while their employers turned a blind eye, became enshrined in a culture of corruption, in which those closest to the foreigners gained the most profit and power.

The sons and daughters of the compradors, who dressed in Western clothes and spoke with accents picked up at Oxford, Yale or, in the case of the Soong sisters, Wesleyan, became the new proxies. In the hands of the nationalists, the party that was the political manifestation of this comprador culture, "squeeze" became the basis of a national economy, in which the proxy elite in closest proximity to foreign exchange, aid, or munitions profited the most. By periodically threatening to negotiate a separate peace with the Japanese, and then portraying himself as a bulwark against communism, Chiang Kai-shek was able to squeeze more military aid and recovery money out of the United States. The nationalists had no interest in changing the living conditions of the workers in Shanghai's mills and factories. Under their leadership, the chronic impoverishment of China's peasantry had come to be accepted as an inherent component of the eternal pageant of life in the flowery kingdom.

In China it was inevitable that revolution, when it did come, would originate from outside the urban comprador class. It was entirely fitting that the man who initiated it was the son of a peasant from a Hunanese village, who had never travelled outside of China and for whom "squeeze" was a foreign concept. One of the tragedies of the Maoist revolution – apart from the twenty million or more who would die prematurely under communism, and the reign of terror that attempted to eradicate some of the greatest art and traditions of an ancient culture – was that it would eventually empower a new bureaucracy for whom the age-old practice of "squeeze" once again became a standard operating procedure.

One man who was able to see through the veneer of comprador culture was Zau Sinmay, that Cambridge-educated decadent poet who wore the robes of a Confucian scholar. He had nothing but disdain for the "returned students" who, after a sojourn abroad, affected worsted tweed and Westernized their names. His love affair with a like-minded free spirit from America subverted the commercialized conventions that had always muddied and corrupted relations between West and East in Shanghai. Mickey and Sinmay met as equals and cultivated a relationship filled with humour, mutual respect, and genuine affection. Simply put, they fell in love, and that changed everything.

For a time, at least. The sharper edges of their relationship – the fact that Sinmay was married, and the head of a large household – were hidden behind a fug of opium smoke. Mickey, who since her youth had made a habit of turning her life into written anecdote, made the complex reality of her lover's life into charming, and saleable, caricature. When Mickey gave up the "Big Smoke" in which their union had been born, she left Sinmay behind. It was clear, to her and to others, that the Shanghai that had fostered complex cultural exchanges and brought together strange bedfellows was doomed. By then, Mickey herself was moving on to new places and a new phase in her career.

Sinmay, feeling abandoned during Shanghai's "solitary island" phase when the city was surrounded by Japanese, sent a series of yearning letters to Mickey as she worked on *The Soong Sisters* in Chungking. (Mickey generally replied with brief telegrams enquiring about the health of her gibbon, Mr. Mills.) After Pearl Harbor, the occupation ended communication between them for the duration of the war. Finally, after Mickey had been repatriated to New York, a handwritten letter from Shanghai arrived at the *New Yorker*.

"It's about time that we should try to get to know each other again," Sinmay began. "For more than 5 yrs I have been hit with disasters, but [I've had] nobody to tell them to. I do miss the famous author of the Pan Heh-ven stories, you know. And how much I have changed! . . . Once I even looked more than 60, people were asking when was my birthday . . . Lord knows they were kind: I could kiss any young girl without fearing that a slap might be delivered on my cheek, but there would always be a smile or two which meant 'I am sorry for you, old rascal.'" He begged Mickey to send him a copy of *China to Me*, and added, with a sardonic nod to the inflation besetting the city, "Oh I'd give 1 million gold (do you know what's the rate now?) to hear your voice!" His closing salutation was wistful: "Love from your ever Platonic Sinmay."

The tone of Mickey's reply, to "Dearest Sinmay," was affectionate but formal. She congratulated Sinmay and Peiyu on their l atest child, a boy. "I wonder if you know how much I owe to you," she went on. "I claimed to be your wife and took out a Chinese passport under the Japanese government as such. For two years I was Mrs. Zau, American-born Chinese . . . I am sure you saved Carola's life, if not mine." After informing him that she and Charles had been married, she signed the letter, "Love to all the family from Mickey."

The message was clear: for Mickey, their love affair had become a fond memory.

As the situation in Shanghai became more desperate, however, Sinmay pinned his hopes on his former lover. He came up with a plan to use his printing press to put out a Chinese edition of *Life* magazine, and hoped Mickey would put him in touch with its publisher, Henry Luce. He wrote asking for her to send him a movie camera, a gold Rolex wristwatch, and a Parker pen. In 1948 he flew to Los Angeles in a bid to land work making movies for the nationalists. Nothing came of it, but he was able to visit Mickey in New York, and they lunched at the Algonquin Hotel, where they talked of old times.

Mickey found him a much changed man. The exquisite symmetry of the poet's face had been ruined by an attack of palsy, which gave him a drooping eyelid, and his features had been coarsened by years of opium addiction. Her young nephew, who Sinmay took to lunch one day, would remember the novelty of a meal at a Chinese restaurant better than Sinmay himself, and wonder what his aunt could ever have seen in this "small Chinese man."

When, the following year, the bamboo curtain came down separating China from the West, Mickey lost all contact with Sinmay. When she visited Taiwan in 1953 to research an article on the nationalists, she tried unsuccessfully to obtain a visa to visit him in Shanghai. As the years passed, she heard rumours that he'd been imprisoned by the communists and forced to take the cure for his opium addiction.

Life went on for Mickey, full of challenges, joys, and sorrows. From time to time, when visitors with connections to the Far East came to England, she would get out an old opium pipe and enjoy a few puffs of the "Big Smoke." Once, after her *New Yorker* feature on smoking opium with Sinmay had made her old habit common knowledge, she ran into the cartoonist Charles Addams in a crowded elevator. Silently, he lifted a tiny box with the word "Opium" clearly lettered on its top from his coat pocket, and flashed her a theatrical wink. Invited to the home of Canadian businessman Edgar Bronfman in 1969, she appeared in black leather boots and pulled out a huge cigar. To a female guest who gaped at her effrontery, she said in a stage whisper: "Can't smoke opium here, you know."

Gradually, though, even her memories of pre-war Shanghai, that most vivid of cities, began to fade. When she thought of Sinmay, she remembered his dark eyes, fine hands, and the mischievous smile that used to play on the full lips beneath the thin, Fu-Manchu-like moustache.

美

There were mornings when Sir Victor would awake in a daze at Eve's, the pink-and-white Nassau beach house he'd built on the grounds of an old Colonial estate surrounded by traveller's palm trees. For a few moments he would believe he was in his bed in the penthouse of the Cathay, with the most exciting city in the world at his feet.

As the present came back into focus, it was a consolation to him that the building itself, that ferroconcrete Art Deco skyrocket he'd erected on the mud, continued to stand in Shanghai.

The news of the communist takeover had come while he was sitting in an office in New York. By then, he was resigned to never seeing Shanghai again. "Well, there it is," he'd said quietly to his lawyer. "I gave up India and China gave me up."

He was troubled by the fact that his cousin Lucien Ovadia had been forced to remain behind, a hostage to the unsold Sassoon real estate. At first, Ovadia would later tell him, the communists had made a virtue of courtesy. Before their arrival, the nationalist troops had had a bad reputation: they crowded onto the trams without paying, turned nightclubs and hotels into barracks, and drove locals out of movie theatres by filling reserved seats. The communists, instructed by Mao not to take "even a sweet potato" from the local population, purchased their own tram tickets and refused offers of tea and cigarettes from the people of Shanghai.

Since then, however, the situation had deteriorated. As a new cadre of politicians settled into power, new laws were passed. There were a total of forty real-estate companies remaining in Shanghai, managing 9,965 buildings, and the Sassoon group, which included the Cathay Land Company, the Far Eastern

Investment Company, San Sin Properties, and five other companies, was by far the largest single property owner. Ovadia was required to guarantee the income of over 14,000 staff members; he had no power to dismiss them. He tried his best to sell the Cathay Hotel, but the government, who saw it as a useful source of foreign exchange, preferred to lease it. They squeezed him by increasing the taxes from year to year, and told him to import foreign funds to cover the bills. It was clear that the communists were milking Sir Victor, forcing him to pay a huge sum to hand his own Cathay over to the state. For three years Ovadia had been kept under virtual house arrest in Grosvenor House, Sir Victor's exclusive apartment building in the old French Concession. There, he was importuned at all hours of the night with absurd requests from officious little men. They went so far as to deny him a visa based on trumped-up charges brought by former employees. Finally, late in the spring of 1952, he was handed a one-way train ticket to Hong Kong and given forty-eight hours to leave the country.

Ovadia flew to London, where, over lunch at the Ritz, his first order of business was to personally hand in his letter of resignation to Sir Victor. Ovadia had survived the Black Saturday bombing, narrowly missed the Japanese invasion after Pearl Harbor, and lived through communist revolution. He settled into a quiet, well-earned retirement in the south of France. When Sir Victor's remaining holdings in Shanghai were finally written off in 1958, he ironized gently to a reporter: "The Communists are funny. They don't just like to take things; they want to be given them instead."

For his part, Sir Victor now looked at his life as being divided into two phases: Shanghai, and after Shanghai. In Shanghai, he had been the master of a world of his own building. After Shanghai, he was just the occupant of a world with a bewildering proliferation of new masters.

But then, the world had changed. The little people had taken over. He had known it would come, and said as much to a *New*

York Times reporter after Pearl Harbor. "Most people don't understand this is a revolution," he had told the newsman. "There will be no more rich men. The power to make decisions on commerce and trade, which heretofore has been in the hands of a few men, will be spread out."

Whether this was an improvement, he still couldn't say. But one thing was certain: the world would never be as gay a place as it had been for people like himself. There would be no more Shanghais, no playgrounds where anything in the world was possible.

He had turned his energy to raising thoroughbreds; he owned two hundred, liveried in the Sassoon colours of old gold and peacock blue. Their victories, at Ascot and Epsom, brought him his most intense moments of joy. After a stumble on a chair in 1950, he'd torn a ligament, and he had increasing recourse to a wheelchair. When he walked, it was now painfully, and almost always with sticks. Tom Slick, an eccentric Texan famous for tracking the yeti and the Sasquatch, gave him canes with hollowed-out tops from which he could sip cognac.

Sandy Tittman, the young woman from Albuquerque he had thought he loved, had eventually married a man closer to her age. But after years of warding off gold-diggers, Sir Victor had finally ended his membership in the bachelors' club and married a woman he could trust: his nurse. Evelyn Barnes was a petite blonde from Dallas and thirty years his junior. She shared his love for horses as well as his interest in photography. He'd wed "Barnesie" on the first of April 1959 in a simple ceremony at Eve's. He chose the date not as a Fool's Day joke at his own long bachelorhood, but because the Royal Air Force had been founded on the same day, forty-one years earlier.

He kept in touch with some of the crowd from the Shanghai days. He'd learned that "Tug" Wilson, the architect of the Cathay, had only left Shanghai with great reluctance in 1938. After lingering too long in the Far East (in Singapore, Tug complained of "living in a wretched hotel called Raffles – supposed to be first class!!"), he had finally managed to book passage to England. His vessel was bombed en route, and he survived the shipwreck on a small island near Sumatra. Apparently he was enjoying retirement in an old farmhouse in Hampshire which he'd filled with jades, porcelains, and other souvenirs of livelier days in the Orient.

When he passed through Los Angeles, Sir Victor popped in on Bernardine Szold-Fritz and visited the nightclubs on the Sunset Strip with Charlie Chaplin.

Letters from Mickey Hahn, who continued to have adventures, kept him amused. A note she sent after a trip to Taiwan offered small hope that either of them would ever return to Shanghai.

"The Chinese are hating the Communists more every day," he'd replied to her, "but are not loving Chiang Kai-shek whom they seem to dislike for all the graft that his regime enjoyed during the time he was in power. I think what they are looking for is somebody who can bring back the old days impartially without a bad background."

Mickey had mentioned that she'd run into "Two-Gun" Cohen, who seemed to be under the impression that Sir Victor wouldn't be allowed into England for tax reasons. Sir Victor replied, "Next time you see General Cohen you might ask him from me, could he expand his remarks and let me know why I'm not allowed in England because it really would rather interest me. Of course he may have been mixing it up with China."

He saw Mickey from time to time, lunching with her when he and Barnesie flew up to New York to see a Broadway show. Gradually, though, as his health declined, he wasn't able to keep up with his correspondence. A bout of pneumonia led to recurring asthma attacks, and after the wedding he was frequently confined to an oxygen tent.

Nassau, for all its beauty, would never be Shanghai. He was generally content with his life, if almost never excited at being alive. One ritual from the old days had remained: now in his eighties, he prided himself on still being able to digest a tiffin whose centrepiece was vegetable curry, the kind they had served every Thursday at the Cathay. He still had it made according to the old recipe, with plenty of turmeric and Worcestershire sauce, served with chutney and chow-chow relish on the side, to be washed down with a bottle of ice-cold Bass ale.

He found himself looking forward to the next one.

美

Towards the end of her life, which would span all but eight years of the twentieth century, Mickey Hahn lived with Helen in an apartment in lower Manhattan. She liked the company of her older sister, and the fact that they could share a maid, Hyacinth, to look after the housework. It reminded her of the family home on Fountain Avenue in St. Louis.

Sixty years earlier, she'd had a premonition that she and Helen would spend their final years together. Mickey had written to Helen, then recovering from a hysterectomy, from her Kiangse Road apartment in the International Settlement: "We must end our lives quietly widowed, sitting in little lace caps one each side of a fireplace, rocking and knitting and quarrelling over men."

Helen's ex-husband, the author Herbert Asbury, had passed away in 1963. "The Major," as Mickey called Charles, was very much alive, though hardly a constant presence in her life; when he came to visit his wife, he preferred to check into the Yale Club behind Grand Central Station. Though the octogenarian sisters bickered – as they had ever since Mickey stole Helen's French boyfriend away in St. Louis – they did so lovingly.

One by one, people were falling out of Mickey's life. Sir Victor, the man who had so charmingly ushered her into Shanghai's social swirl, died in his oxygen tent – after eating one last vegetable curry – with his nursemaid-wife Barnesie by his side, in 1961. Though a rabbi conducted the memorial service, it took place at Christ Church Cathedral. The end of a thousand-year-old dynasty is marked not by a tombstone, but a simple marble plaque set in the earth in Nassau's Western Cemetery. It bears the names of Sir Victor and Lady Sassoon and the family crest, which reads *Candide et Constanter*; its Hebrew equivalent, *Emeth ve Emunah* (truth and faith), is inscribed above.

Morris "Two-Gun" Cohen's marriage to the Canadian dressmaker had ended after only twelve years. Even jazzy Montreal wasn't fast enough to cure Cohen's chronically itchy feet, and in the fifties he'd returned to China, where he was welcomed as a former protégé of Madame Sun. Retained as a consultant by Rolls-Royce, he helped broker the West's first sale of civilian aircraft to Red China. During the Great Leap Forward, "Five Percent Cohen," as he became known, could be seen haunting the lobbies of the grand hotels of the China coast – a stout, bald figure, carrying a malacca cane and puffing on a King Edward cigar, his bills picked up by the communist government. His final moment of glory came in 1966, at the beginning of the Cultural Revolution, when he was invited to Peking to attend the centenary of the birth of the man he'd most admired, Sun Yat-sen. He died four years later, leaving a gravestone in a Manchester cemetery inscribed by Madame Sun and bearing his Chinese name, Ma Kun.

Bernardine Szold-Fritz had lived on in her Hollywood mansion surrounded by mementoes of her glory days in the Far East, like an Orientalist version of *Sunset Boulevard*'s Norma Desmond, until 1982.

In 1988, Mickey received a letter from the People's Republic of China. It was from "Little Red," one of Sinmay's daughters, who was then fifty-six and a retired dentist in Nanjing. "Dad died in 1968 from heart disease together with complications," Shao Xiaohong, as she now spelled her name, informed Mickey. "Before his death he told me that he had written a letter to you, most likely he mailed it to Hong Kong. I don't know whether you have received it or not."

Mickey had never received that letter, or any other. China had been a closed book to her for four decades, and the events in Tiananmen Square that would soon follow made a visit even less likely. Even had she been permitted to visit the Zau family, her health would not have allowed it.

After Helen's death from cancer in 1990, Mickey suffered a bad fall and had to use a walker – she called it a "birdcage" – to reach her office at the *New Yorker*. Her recovery was slow, and in the last years of her life this most independent of women found her inability to walk, and eventually to type, maddening. After breaking her leg as she rose from her bed one morning, she was taken to the hospital. Her heart was too weak to recover from the strain of an operation on her femur.

Mickey Hahn died on February 18, 1997, at the age of ninety-two, with her daughters Carola and Amanda at her side. Charles, who was too ill to cross the Atlantic to see her off, died at a nursing home in St. Albans three years later.

美

Hidden among the hundreds of linear feet of writing in Emily Hahn's papers is an undated piece of juvenilia written with a fountain pen in a lined Chante Clair notebook, from her teenage years in Chicago.

It is a piece of soul-searching, in which an adolescent Mickey agonizes about a nascent streak of exhibitionism. She has already, she writes, become known for her witty conversation. She recalls her satisfaction with keeping a young couple from St. Louis – "they were starved for something exterior" – amused:

I kept things going without trying . . . I met people who would invite me to more parties, more and more – I'm so amusing. And always less young men alone. Why keep me hidden? I'm not so much fun in concentrated form. In a crowd everyone has a chance, even when I'm there. Not that I ever notice individuals in a crowd: enough for me that there are lights, voices, ears – most certainly ears.

She then describes a dream in which she is lying upon a table, offered up like a meal; as if by common accord, the couples who have been seated around her abandon her. The piece ends, "Oh, what shall I do? What shall I do?"

All through her life, Mickey would suffer from her critics' suggestions that her penchant for showiness and talent for self-promotion detracted from her full potential as a writer. Privately, she was haunted by the idea that her need to be at the centre of attention would leave her isolated and miserable.

It was this same streak of exhibitionism, though, that brought Mickey a life of adventure, and into contact with such like-minded exhibitionists as Bernardine Szold-Fritz, Harold Acton, "Two-Gun" Cohen, and Sir Victor Sassoon. At her best, Mickey's talent for observation overcame all that was meretricious in her writing. She excelled when she was lovingly describing a genuine object of her affection – whether that happened to be a mischievous gibbon or a mercurial Chinese poet. In the case of Zau Sinmay, she triumphed over narcissism by creating an enduring, fully-fleshed portrait of a complex and beloved friend – one that, despite the passing of decades, retains its power to charm readers.

Over the course of her life Mickey Hahn wrote fifty-two books and contributed 181 articles to the *New Yorker*. Had she known one detail of Sinmay's life after she left China, and had circumstances allowed her to follow the lead, I like to think she would have returned to Shanghai to discover, and write about, what had happened to her long-ago lover.

The letter that Sinmay's daughter Xiaohong mentioned, the one that Mickey never received, fell into the hands of the communist authorities. It was, in fact, for sending this message to his old lover – not for opium addiction, as Mickey would believe until the end of her life – that Sinmay was jailed during the Great Leap Forward. He died not long after he was released, his health and spirit broken by the malnutrition he suffered in jail.

Zau Sinmay's "marriage" to Mickey had saved her daughter Carola's life – and quite possibly her own, and that of Charles – by keeping her out of a Japanese prison in Hong Kong. I wanted to know whether Mickey had unwittingly helped to end Sinmay's life. After Shanghai, Mickey and Sir Victor Sassoon lived out the final acts of their lives in a climate of openness in the West, while the fate of Sinmay – the maddening, whimsical Pan Heh-ven beloved by so many *New Yorker* readers – has never been revealed.

I knew that the end of his story, like so many of the legends of the lost world of Shanghai, remained to be told.

Epilogue

Eight decades ago, the first real impression world travellers, after days or weeks at sea, had of China came in the form of the Cathay Hotel. As their luggage was inspected at the Customs Jetty, its tower loomed over them, a streamlined monolith that could have been transplanted from Chicago's Loop or Los Angeles's Bunker Hill.

On my first trip to Shanghai, the building barely registered. After eleven hours in the air I arrived at the gleaming Shanghai-Pudong International Airport, where I boarded a magnetic-levitation train that whisked me along elevated tracks at a third of the speed of sound to Pudong, the new commercial centre of the megacity. As late as the eighties, Pudong was a low-rise industrial suburb; it now bristles with "supertalls" and even "megatalls," towers that by definition are at least 600 metres tall, twice the height of New York's Chrysler Building. Shanghai, the third most populous city on the planet, is now home to more skyscrapers than the entire west coast of the United States.

On one of my first nights in the city, I rode a series of three express elevators to the Cloud 9 Bar of the pagoda-tiered Jin Mao Tower, on the eighty-seventh floor of the Park Hyatt Hotel in Pudong. There I sipped an exquisitely mixed cocktail while taking in the vertiginous view. Beneath me was a building whose bulbous nodes, pulsing with red and blue lights, called to mind an atomic-age spacecraft from the cover of a Fifties pulp science-fiction magazine. At the beginning of the twenty-first century, the Oriental Pearl Tower – erected on the exact site where Jardine, Matheson & Co. once warehoused opium to be shipped down the Yangtze River – was the tallest structure in China. It has since been dwarfed by the 121-storey Shanghai Tower and the World Financial Center, a megatall shaped like a bottle-opener whose observation deck is said to be the world's highest.

From 1,148 feet above street level, the "Five-Star Red Flags" of the People's Republic, which fly from every major building, were mere specks of scarlet and gold. What lit up the night were the glowing logos of international enterprise: "Nestle," "Nikon," "Wynn," and, atop a shopping mall in what had long ago been the American Settlement, the emblem of China's largest real-estate company, "CapitaLand."

That night, altitude reduced the floodlit stone facades of the buildings along the Bund, the "billion-dollar skyline" of the old Treaty Port, to a small band of white light on the opposite bank of the river, like a thumb-smear of paint in a horizon-to-horizon panorama. I felt like a player looking down on a Monopoly board. It was only later that I realized that one of the buildings I was looking at was the once-great Cathay Hotel.

Viewed from the lofty heights of the new China, it looked no grander than a die-cast hotel on Park Lane.

For most of its modern history, Shanghai has done double duty as a symbol and a real, fully-functioning city. The competing ideologies that forged modern Asia – the unrestrained capitalism of the opium merchants, the nationalism of the comprador class, the Pan-Asiatic imperialism of Japan, Mao's interpretation of Marxism – played out in its narrow streets. What astonished me, on my first visit, was how much of the old stage set remained. The heart of foreign Shanghai was spared the sustained shelling and bombing that levelled the city's Chinese districts. In 1949, the communists had taken the city almost without a fight. For four decades, old Shanghai stood like the mothballed set of some silent-era Hollywood epic that had been left miraculously intact on a back lot. Because so much survived, the city served as an urban palimpsest, on which traces of previous writings by hands long since stilled could still be discerned in the living manuscript of the city.

Such is the pace of development in modern China that, even in the seven years that separated my visits, much had changed. I found that the Shanghai Metro, which didn't exist in 1992, had added another nine lines, to beat out New York's subway as the single largest system in the world. The city had added 5.65 million residents, bringing its population to twenty-four million. This made Shanghai – the most populous city in the world's most populous nation – the largest concentration of human beings under a single municipal administration on the planet. Poverty still exists, but the squalor that once cohabited so visibly with splendour has largely been eliminated. Following the 1978 market reforms which culminated in the creation of the Shanghai Free-Trade Zone, it has become by far the nation's richest city. In the former "Paris of the East," more households can claim membership in the middle class than in Paris itself.

Breakneck growth has brought with it the worst problems of modernity. The odour of opium smoke that used to permeate the backstreets is long gone (authoritarian states tend to excel at drug interdiction), to be replaced by a new scourge: pollution. Even on a good day, the entire city can smell like a cheaply renovated condominium that has been finished with a particularly noxious brand of carpet glue. On the worst days, the smog from coal-fired plants makes drawing a breath a dangerous activity. I talked to a British executive – eighty years ago, he would have been called a taipan – at the advertising firm Ogilvy's, who remembered a winter day when the count of deadly $PM_{2.5}$ particles per cubic metre neared 600 – on an index of 500. (A count of over 300 officially qualifies as "hazardous.") Visibility on the Bund, he told me, was reduced to twenty yards, and his employees came to the office wearing mouth filters and gas masks. The fact that the Chinese Communist Party has declared war on pollution, and is making unprecedented investments in green technology, is small consolation for those who have to survive China's modern-day pea-soupers.

As the city unscrolled for me again, the ironies written into its streets seemed intensely legible. The place names had changed, of course; the Wade–Giles system of transcribing Chinese names, common in Mickey Hahn's day, has been replaced by the system known as pinyin. The Whangpoo is now the Huangpu River, Soochow is Suzhou Creek, and the Chapei district, bombed so exhaustively by the Japanese, is Zhabei. The Bund, now officially Zhongshan East Number One Road (after the Chinese name for Sun Yat-sen) has become a ten-lane boulevard, crowded with trucks and racing taxis, and Nanking Road is now Nanjing East. Outside the Hongkong and Shanghai Bank building, now the Pudong Development Bank, replicas of the lions representing protection and security are still stroked by Chinese passers-by. Before the old Custom House, a bronze of a crimson-hued bull paws the pavement. The Bund Bull is the same size as the one on Wall Street, but its snout is turned upwards. It is also, in the words of its sculptor, "redder, younger and stronger."

The building at No. 2, the Bund, from whose confines all Chinese were once excluded, has once again become an exclusive address. When Mao was in power the Shanghai Club was made into the headquarters of the Seamen's Union, and the famous Long Bar, segmented by dividers, served only near-beer and soft drinks. After Deng Xiaoping launched his market reforms, it became an outlet for Kentucky Fried Chicken, one of the first Western chains to penetrate Red China. Since 2011, it has been the bar of the Waldorf Astoria. In its softly lit interior, ceiling fans turn slowly, black-vested Chinese bartenders make a creditable whisky sour, and all 111 feet of linearity have been restored to the Long Bar.

Yet much of old Shanghai has vanished, or is about to. The *shikumen* alleyway complex, once ubiquitous, is now an endangered species. The population of Shanghai's signature architectural form, those mazes of rowhouses where proximity bred sociability, is being shifted into twenty- to forty-storey residential towers that stretch far beyond the old city's limits. With Lydia, my interpreter, I visited one such complex in Hongkew – or Hongkou, as it is now known. We were invited into the three-storey house of a fifty-seven-year-old taxi driver, whose family was one of only seven left in a block that was once home to 200. It was in this *shikumen*, he told us, that he'd gone to primary school. He'd married a woman from the block; in the evenings, families had gathered at night to play mah-jong and eat won-ton while their children did homework together. Within a few months, the complex was scheduled to be razed and the land, purchased by Hong Kong billionaire Li Ka-shing, was to be replaced by a skyscraper. The community, our host told us, was destined to be split up and scattered.

We walked up steep stairs into empty flats, where hygiene posters still hung on the walls and strainers and plastic utensils lay scattered beneath dripping faucets. I was reminded of the boyhood trespassing of J.G. Ballard, who, after the Japanese invasion, lingered in hastily abandoned mansions on Avenue Joffre.

One of the few remaining *shikumen* complexes is Xintiandi, preserved in part because it was a meeting place for the First Congress of the Communist Party. It is now a museum, peopled with wax dummies of Mao Tse-tung and Chou En-lai; the adjoining rowhouses feature outlets of Starbucks and Shanghai Tang, an upscale fashion chain that retails modern interpretations of body-hugging *qipaos* and Manchu-era silks.

Most of the old Sassoon buildings are intact. In 1958 – six years after the communists gave Lucien Ovadia a one-way ticket to Hong Kong – fifty-seven buildings belonging to the Sassoon group, representing just under six million square feet of real estate, were transferred to the state-owned China Enterprise Company. Ciro's, Sir Victor Sassoon's elegant nightclub, was made into a puppet theatre. In the fifties, the best apartments in Embankment House (the "S" in the signature Sir Victor stitched into the city) were handed over to high-ranking party members. Foreigners have since trickled back, renovating the high-ceilinged suites, some of whose balconies offer spectacular views over a Suzhou Creek whose waters are no longer fetid with effluent and untreated sewage. Elegant neon still glows on the marquee of the Cathay Theatre, now a multiplex. On some nights movies are projected for the visually impaired, with in-house narrators describing the action on the screen.

While the original décor of Cathay Mansions has been effaced by its graceless transformation into a mid-range business hotel, Grosvenor House (now Grosvenor Mansions) has retained its charm. Its "apartements de-luxe," complete with servants' quarters, still come with curvaceous niches, polished parquet floors, and claw-foot bathtubs. Both buildings are part of the Jinjiang Hotel complex, named after a popular restaurant in Grosvenor House once managed by Dong Zhujun, the mistress of a Szechuanese officer. With the coming of communism, she took over as director and turned the Jinjiang buildings into Shanghai's most famous state guest house. In 1972, Richard Nixon stayed at Grosvenor House when he signed the Shanghai Communiqué, the first step towards détente in Sino-American relations. Mao Tse-tung liked to use the tunnels that link the complex to the building across the street, the Cercle Sportif Français, to go swimming in the old French Club's pool.

Eve's, where Sir Victor entertained Mickey and her friends, is hidden behind high stone walls and razor wire on a lot adjoining the Shanghai Zoo. (In 2004, the Tudor-style hunting lodge, which had served as a private villa for the Gang of Four during the Cultural Revolution, briefly went on the market for $15 million; it remains in private hands.) Another of Sir Victor's retreats, the more modestly scaled Rubicon Gardens, can still be seen from Hongqiao Road. Its half-timbered walls and red-tiled roof, now overgrown with vines, suggest a Sleeping Beauty's castle mysteriously marooned amidst modern apartment towers. When I saw it, it was unoccupied; a sign on a brick wall warned trespassers to beware of guard dogs.

One afternoon, I explored the twin fourteen-storey skyscrapers that continue to square off across a curved intersection three blocks south of Sassoon House. The Metropole is still a hotel catering to businesspeople; its setting, in a backstreet off the Bund, means that after sundown foreign visitors tend to be plagued by touts offering counterfeit Rolexes and "lady massage." ("We'd like to remind gently when you approached by strangers on the street at night," reads a sign in the lobby, "please remember not to go to the place they led to just in case to cause any unnecessary property and spiritual loss.") Hamilton House, the Metropole's mirror image across Fuzhou Road, has been left in a state of picturesque decay. It was here that the *kempeitai* established its headquarters, and foreigners were issued armbands with letters that identified them by nationality. In the fifties, its luxurious triplex apartments and doctors' offices were relentlessly subdivided; it is now home to 1,300 residents.

Beneath red-and-gold Lunar New Year decorations, a glassed-in directory board in the lobby still lists the names of long-gone tenants including Viola Smith, who became American Consul to Shanghai in 1939. On my way to the upper floors, a silver-haired man surprised me by driving his scooter – which had an infant balanced on the seat behind him – directly into the elevator behind me. Walking down a dark corridor redolent with frying garlic and chiles, I emerged onto the eleventh-floor roof, over which loomed the dark bricks of the uppermost storeys of the building's stepped Gothic Art Deco tower. Hamilton House's new tenants had made what were once private rooftop terraces reserved for rich Westerners into a community garden. An elderly man sprinkled fish food into an aquarium filled with iridescent carp, and an arrangement of miniature *penjing* trees, Chinese bonsai, shared a panoramic view of the Huangpu River with a three-foot-tall statue of Chairman Mao.

In the early years of Mao's rule it was Shanghai's people, not its buildings, that were singled out for special attention. The Chinese Communist Party officially classified Shanghai as "not a productive city, rather . . . a model consumerist city that served the bureaucrat, comprador, landlord and imperialist." Their long-term goal was to make the parasitic, non-productive middle class a thing of the past. As China's bourgeois centre, and former beach-head of foreign domination, Shanghai became a target and pet project. During the "Five-Antis" Campaign of 1952, loudspeakers blared outside shops and offices urging bosses to confess to tax evasion, bribery, the stealing of state property, and other instances of corruption. At the time, visitors were urged to stay off the side-walks to avoid being hit by the bodies of former business leaders hurling themselves from high buildings. Gradually, the old kinship ties of large families were dismantled, to be replaced by the "big family" of school, commune, and work unit. The "bourgeois" concept of privacy itself became intensely suspect. (One of the slogans of the day was "struggle ruthlessly against the flash of the private self.") It was a time of symbolic, sometimes even poetic, justice. The newspapers printed photos of former Green Gang boss "Pock-Marked" Huang Jinrong sweeping the sidewalks outside the Great World, the entertainment centre he once owned on the former Avenue Édouard VII.

It was certainly not a good time to have built a reputation as a decadent poet, whose art was predicated on a Baudelairean cult of the private self. Especially not one educated at the best foreign schools, with long-standing connections to the former nationalist government in Nanking, a wife who came from one of the wealthiest families in old Cathay, and complicated ties to one notoriously outspoken American wayfarer.

Given all the changes overtaking Shanghai, there were times I despaired of finding any trace of Zau Sinmay or his legacy.

But China had a knack for surprising me. Though the wood and bricks of old houses and buildings disappear, often the original names and traditions cling to the same spot on the map. One evening, I tracked down the vegetarian restaurant where Sinmay entertained George Bernard Shaw. While the original building is long gone, a restaurant called Gongdelin – popularly known as "Godly" – occupies the same corner of what was once Bubbling Well Road – now Nanjing Road West, just across the street from Ciro's Plaza. (Since 2002, a misshapen thirty-nine-storey office tower has risen on the site of Sir Victor Sassoon's old cabaret.) Over a plate of vegetarian barbecue duck, molded out of seitan into a remarkable simulation of the real thing, I read the brief history of the establishment on the menu, whose list of former clients included the left-wing author Lu Xun. There was no mention of

Zau Sinmay, who had picked up the bill for both Shaw and Lu Xun back in 1933.

A few days later I rode an elevator to another Shanghai institution, Sun Ya, where Sinmay and other Shanghainese writers had met to discuss European literature. Once a teahouse on North Szechuen Road, it moved in 1932 to a new location across from the Sun Sun department store. Its site on Nanking Road became a Cantonese restaurant whose soda fountain and reputation for cleanliness made it a favourite stop for Western visitors.

After passing through an anteroom where Chinese patrons lined up to be seated, I approached an alcove in a brightly-lit room where a middle-aged woman and an elderly couple were drinking tea. I introduced myself, bowed deeply, and sat down next to Zau Sinmay's fifth daughter, Xiao Duo. She had been joined by her husband, Wu Lilan, a retired professor of psychology, and her daughter, Pearl, an electrical engineer employed by a printed-circuit-board manufacturer. As we picked apart a "squirrel fish," the house specialty of crisp-fried perch in a sweet-and-sour sauce, I began to learn what had happened to the Zau family after 1949.*

I had to remind myself not to use the name Zau Sinmay, but the modern Chinese rendering, Shao Xunmei. His daughter's name had also changed. In a playful spirit, he had called the seventh of his nine children Xiao Duo, meaning "too many." She'd wearied of the joke as a young woman, she told me, and changed her name to Shao Yang. She was a distinguished-looking woman with a heavily-lidded gaze, high cheekbones and a bee-stung smile set in a face that was a near-perfect oval. When I mentioned that

---

* I got in touch with the Shao family after finding a ten-year-old Associated Press article about a chance meeting between the reporter and an elderly English-speaking Chinese man in a downtown cafe. The article described the experiences of retired elementary school teacher Shao Zucheng, adding he was the son of "Shao Xunmei, a noted poet." This, I realized, was Sinmay's firstborn, Xiao Mei – the boy who struck Mickey Hahn, the first time she saw him, as being a miniature version of Sinmay. Xiao Mei died in 2005, at the age of seventy-seven.

I saw a resemblance to her father, especially around the mouth, she wasn't pleased; she liked to think she took after her mother.

In the days that followed, Wu Lilan, Shao Yang, and Pearl graciously helped me track down the addresses associated with the family history. Only one had been completely erased from the map. After we pulled up in a taxi at a busy intersection west of People's Square – formerly the corner of Love Lane and Bubbling Well Road – Shao Yang pointed out the former site of Sinmay's bookstore. The Maison d'Or had been a tiny space, she said: less than 200 square feet, its shelves stacked high with poetry books and journals published by her father. In its place stood a medium-rise office building whose facade was obscured by scaffolding.

"My grandfather," Pearl said, in halting but grammatical English, "helped a lot of people who wanted to publish. Lots of famous writers had their first books published there." Across the street, she explained, was Truth-Beauty-Goodness, the bookstore on which Sinmay had modelled his. It had been run by a Francophile father-and-son team whose exposure to Europe was limited to walking the streets of Frenchtown. The son, Zeng Xubai, Pearl told me, had followed Chiang Kai-shek to Taiwan, where he would serve as culture minister for the nationalists.

Sinmay's office and the old family home, I was pleased to learn, were still standing. One Sunday morning I met Shao Yang's husband Wu Lilan, nattily dressed in a tweed blazer, long scarf, and black beret, at the Yangshupu Road metro station, and we walked up busy Pingliang Road to the offices of Sinmay's old publishing house. As we entered a *shikumen*-like complex, a young woman, gnawing on a piece of peeled sugar cane, emerged from a doorway. Wu Lilan led me up a steep wooden staircase to the old office of the Modern Press, on the second floor. The single room was now occupied by an entire family. Sinmay chose the location, Wu Lilan told me, because it was just a few hundred yards from the docks, where his rotogravure press had arrived from Germany. Its waterfront location meant that after 1937 the district was overrun by Japanese marines. (It was from here that Mickey moved the press to a garage on Avenue Joffre.) One of the residents, a Mr.

Shu, pointed out a trapdoor in the stone floor of the entranceway that led to a cellar used as a bomb shelter. During the war, the complex was taken over by a captain in the Japanese military police and his family. Later, Mr. Shu told us, the building was turned into a button factory.

We entered a courtyard, and then walked through an alleyway that led to Sinmay's home. Along the way, Wu pointed to *shiku-men* walls: many of the bricks, stained grey with the coal dust of decades, bore prominent Chinese characters embossed with the names of their makers. Similar marks can be found in the stones of the Great Wall; in Shanghai, their presence usually suggests a structure was built before the 1911 overthrow of the Qing dynasty. (These days, the bricks are often stencilled over with the cell phone numbers of companies offering water bottle delivery.)

We emerged onto Yulin Road, paralleling Pingliang Road one block to the north, to face a row of three-storey red-brick houses that wouldn't have looked out of place in Victorian Manchester. Pushing through a metal gate, we entered a front yard where sheets hung from clotheslines. Indulging in a little light trespassing, I entered through the front door of No. 47 and walked down a hallway lined with bicycles and lit by bare bulbs over creaking floorboards. A broad wooden staircase, its newel post rubbed bare of paint by generations of hands, led upwards into obscurity. These were the stairs where Mickey, after meeting Peiyu and her first-born son, followed Sinmay and his friends to smoke her first pipe of opium. The doors upstairs, to what were now separate and private residences, were closed. Returning to the sunlit yard, I noticed some of the houses in the row were boarded up; Wu Lilan told me Sinmay's old home was owned by a family from Taiwan who couldn't afford the cost of renovations.

In the former French Concession, the house to which Sinmay and his family had moved after the Japanese invasion of 1937 also continued to stand. A municipal government plaque on the stone gatehouse at the entrance to the complex identified it as a "Terrace house on Avenue Joffre. Built in 1930s. Masonry structure. Modern style." A row of three-storey detached houses was separated from the busy street, once the main drag of the French Concession, by a tall stone wall. A guard in a little wooden booth at the front gate refused to allow me to enter, but through the iron bars I could see the front yard of Mickey's house – whose lawn was now guarded by a crouching Chinese lion – which was two doors away from Sinmay's. This was where, to her neighbour's disgust, Mickey had once let Mr. Mills and her other simian companions run free.

As I spent time with Shao Yang, Wu Lilan, and Pearl, I learned what had happened to Sinmay after the communists took power. In May 1949 he was ordered to stop publishing his longest-running magazine, the satirical journal *Analects*. When the party requisitioned his printing press, he oversaw its delivery to Beijing, where it was put to use printing four-colour propaganda magazines. With Peiyu and five of their children, Sinmay relocated to the capital, where he hoped to find work with the new regime. In preparation, he applied himself to the study of Marxism. A photo from that period shows him alone on the edge of a sofa, an unlit cigarette in his right hand. Gone is his floor-length brown robe; instead, he wears an ill-cut Mao suit of rough cotton. Gone, too, is any hint of ease or languor. There is a vague smile on his lips, but his face is careworn, his eyes tired. No longer the young master with all of Shanghai at his feet, in the new China he was officially classified a "petty urbanite," one of millions.

When his connections in Beijing failed to pan out, Sinmay returned to Shanghai. With a friend who'd become a chemistry professor at Fudan University, he rented a house and invested in equipment to make phenol, a chemical with a wide variety of pharmaceutical and industrial uses. The experiments worked, but he found it impossible to scale up production in a home laboratory; he ended up selling the equipment. Returning to literature, he concentrated on translating works by Percy Shelley, Mark Twain, and his old idol Rabindranath Tagore. Though an edition of *Tom Sawyer* sold well, his literary work no longer brought in enough money to support his family, and he began to sell off his beloved stamp collection. The death of their eldest daughter, who succumbed to pulmonary emphysema at the age of twenty-five, devastated him. It was only later that the family discovered Xiao Yu had visited several doctors, but opted not to use the more expensive drugs that might have improved her condition. In penance, Sinmay swore off cigarettes; his daughter had long complained they had troubled her breathing.

His wife, more successful at adapting to life under communism, supplanted him as head of the household. When the party announced its Four Pests campaign, Peiyu became a hygiene supervisor for their alleyway, in charge of exterminating flies, mosquitoes, rats, and cockroaches. She oversaw the spraying of basements with DDT, and created a game in which children were rewarded with a red flag for every hundred flies they killed. When their block became a people's commune, Peiyu agreed to turn the ground floor of the house into a neighbourhood canteen. She, Sinmay, and the two children still at home moved into the upstairs rooms.

Then the worst happened. As part of his attempt to modernize the economy through the traumatic shock therapy of the Great Leap Forward, Mao launched a Campaign to Suppress Counter-revolutionaries. Peiyu came back from Nanjing in 1958 to find Sinmay had been taken away to the old Ward Road Gaol. At the Tilanqiao Detention Centre, as it was now known, family members were forbidden to visit detainees or send them food.

Sinmay shared his cell with Jia Zhifang, a literature professor from Fudan University. Pearl helped me track down the article that Jia wrote about his prison experiences. He had first met Sinmay in the early fifties, at a gathering of writers at Sun Ya Restaurant. At that time, recalled Jia, "Sinmay had a head of messy hair, and an old bronze colored Chinese silk wedding jacket, which he'd left unbuttoned. He looked very uninhibited."

At first, Jia didn't recognize the weak old man with whom he shared a cell. Sinmay, after two years in jail, was a wraith who spent his days curled up in a corner. They shared the cell with a Belarusian editor and a Taiwanese scientist who had worked in Unit 731, the covert biological and chemical weapons lab the Japanese ran in Manchuria, where horrific experiments were carried out on Chinese subjects.

As China experienced widespread famine brought on by the excesses of the Great Leap Forward and a series of natural disasters, prisoners were put on a near-starvation diet. Sinmay received just 600 cubic centimetres of vegetables and porridge a day. The only exercise he got was scrubbing the cell floor on hands and knees.

Fearing death, Sinmay risked punishment – speaking was forbidden in the cells – and whispered to Jia that, should he die in jail, he wanted the world to know two things.

"The first concerns the visit of George Bernard Shaw in nineteen thirty-three," he told his cellmate.

"Since Shaw was a vegetarian, we treated him at the Godly restaurant, at my expense. The bill was forty-six dollars. Madame Sun, Lin Yu-tang, and Lu Xun were all there. But in the end, the newspapers did not mention my name. I felt upset about that. The second matter concerns my articles. Lu Xun said I hired other people to write in my own name. Though I respected Lu Xun, I found it regrettable that he believed such false rumors. As poorly written as he may have believed my articles to be, they were all my own work."

Jia gradually learned the rest of Sinmay's story. Contrary to what Mickey Hahn believed, his arrest was not for opium addiction: poverty had forced him to give up the habit, along with drinking, long before. Sinmay had asked a friend of the family who was going to Hong Kong to mail a letter for him to the United States. ("He was not a good friend," Pearl told me, "more of an acquaintance.") The letter was addressed to Emily Hahn; in it, he asked if she could send him $1,000, an amount he'd remembered loaning her before her final departure from Shanghai in 1939. His youngest brother, who was then living in Hong Kong, was seriously ill and needed money for his treatment.

The letter was never mailed; instead, the family friend turned it in to the authorities. After his arrest, his interrogators wanted to know why, if he was the author, it had been signed by one "Pan Heh-ven." His convoluted explanations about the true identity of Mr. Pan led to more questions – particularly about his early association with leading members of the Nationalist Party. The fact that one of Sinmay's brothers had been a communist guerrilla, and that he and Mickey had published the first English translation of Chairman Mao's speeches about "Prolonged War," counted for little.

Sinmay, in the end, was not jailed for counter-revolutionary activity, but for his "complicated relationships."

Sinmay survived his three years in Tilanqiao, but barely. Peiyu remembered him looking like a skeleton on his release, with skin "pale like a Westerner's." He was so weak that the pedicab driver who brought him back to the house had to carry him on his back up to the second floor.

"We had to be thankful he'd come back at all," Peiyu wrote on his release. "We had no one to blame but ourselves, of not knowing the norms and the right sides to take."

At first, Sinmay was allowed to do some translating work, for which he was given a government income of fifty yuan a month (less than what a recent university graduate was allotted). With the beginning of the Cultural Revolution in 1966, even this work dried up. Worse still, intellectuals were subject to violence and public humiliation. His eldest son, Xiao Mei, a schoolteacher, was ordered to stand in a corner as they threw his clothes, books, and mattress into the street, before being put to work digging air-raid shelters while teenagers called him "snake" and "devil." Sinmay's age and frailty may have spared him similar abuse, but the confiscation of his few remaining books must have been torture. (Two precious objects were spared the wrath of the Red Guards: a peach-shaped brush cleaner, made out of porcelain and dating from the Song dynasty, and the painting by Jean-Auguste Dominique Ingres that Sinmay had bought as a student in Paris.)

After Peiyu urged him in a letter to forget about his old poems, he replied to her: "You were in effect saying my old-fashioned poetry was useless. But didn't even Chairman Mao write old-fashioned poems? Perhaps my work should be preserved to show the next generation how the world once was."

In the final two years of his life, as he witnessed the nightmare of a China undertaking an anti-intellectual purge of millennia of culture, Sinmay's already shaky health went into a final downward spiral. The last months of his life, Peiyu wrote in her memoirs, were miserable. He had trouble breathing, and a hellish stay at a crowded local hospital worsened his condition. He returned home, but all that remained for him was a single room in what used to be the garage of the Avenue Joffre house that Mickey Hahn had found for him. Like Mickey, who lived in a Manhattan apartment with sister Helen in her later years, he shared a room with one of his brothers.

After a stomach hemorrhage, Sinmay died on May 5, 1968, at the age of sixty-two. His widow, who would live to be eighty-four, saw the beginning of a new era: she died in 1989, four months after the violent suppression of the protests in Tiananmen Square.

Peiyu also lived long enough to see the beginning of Sinmay's redemption. In 1985, the original allegation against him was quashed by the Shanghai police. Since then, his literary reputation has been growing. After being dismissed by critics, influenced by Lu Xun's opinion, as a plagiarist who churned out erotic and detective fiction for money, he has come to be regarded in mainland Chinese literary circles as a sophisticated exemplar of the blending of modern European verse and traditional poetry during the Republican period. (The academics I spoke to also emphasized Sinmay's sociability and generosity, and the sheer number of artists and writers he put into print through his many magazines.) For younger Chinese, he is even the object of some fascination. In 2005, the last moments of his life were used as the basis of *Decadent Love*, a twelve-scene multimedia play staged by a Hong Kong rock musician. Though there are no monuments to him – unlike Lu Xun, whose *shikumen* house has been turned into a museum – his complete works, in nine volumes, are in print, and his eldest daughter Xiao Hong is writing a biography. Its working title, after the poem on the back of his tomb in Zhujiajiao, is *A Natural-Born Poet*.

It is no longer dangerous to express an interest in Shanghai's bad old days. In a China negotiating the twenty-first century on its own terms, the Treaty Port years are remote enough that they are no longer considered a threat to the present. Shao Yang and her husband, eager to share details of Sinmay's life, invited me to their apartment in the south-west part of the city. As we got out of the cab, Shao Yang quietly mentioned that her grandfather, the industrialist Sheng Xuanhuai – whose household included one hundred horses and 350 servants – used to own *all* the territory we had just covered. We had driven from the Jing'An Temple to the west end of Line One of the Metro – a distance of nine miles. The land that belonged to a single family in 1905 is now home to hundreds of thousands, stacked vertically in residential towers.

We rode an elevator to their apartment, where the couple live modestly behind a door protected by a thick and heavily pad-locked metal gate.

As we sipped white tea, Shao Yang showed me her father's ivory-handled fountain pen and matching inkwell, and his tobacco pipes (the opium pipes had long since been discarded). On one wall hung an original Miguel Covarrubias cartoon that depicted her father in happier days, wearing a floor-length brown robe and an inscrutable smile. They showed me pages of notebooks covered with brown ink in his exquisite hand, and albums filled with black-and-white photos from a time long gone. Sinmay in a Western car-coat and beret standing in front of ruined columns at Pompeii; Sinmay looking rakish with his friends in the Celestial Hound Society on the Left Bank in Paris; Sinmay in wedding robes with his young bride Peiyu.

There were no images, I noticed, of his old American lover. I asked whether the family had ever resented Mickey Hahn. After all, she had left Shanghai just when things were getting bad. As the intended recipient of the letter from "Pan Heh-ven," she had also been the indirect cause of his imprisonment.

A smile spread serenely over Shao Yang's full lips, and she said, simply, "No."

Pearl amplified: it had not been Mickey's fault that her grand-father had tried to send her a letter, and the family never blamed her for his imprisonment. Sinmay's children had only good memories of their "Aunt Mickey."

I was relieved. I hadn't wanted the old love story to end in bitterness.

Sinmay, after all, was not imprisoned simply because he was caught trying to send a letter abroad. In the end, the gravamen of the charge against him was for "complicated relationships." It was a charge that could also have been levelled against Mickey Hahn, or Sir Victor Sassoon. In fact, it could have been applied to the entire city of Shanghai in the thirties – not to mention *fin-de-siècle* Paris, Berlin in the twenties, New York in the late forties, or any other place where intense cultural ferment and the coming together of races and the meeting of civilizations has made for strange, wonderful bedfellows. From "complicated relationships" come new ways of making art and new ideas, and a heightened sense of empathy and understanding. When all-levelling, all-simplifying ideologies win the day, complexity, along with irony and whimsy, are the first things to get steamrollered. In the case of the Treaty Port of Shanghai, that semi-colony of the West, the ferment was accompanied by inequity so egregious that some kind of levelling was inevitable; "Pan Heh-ven" got caught in the crush.

As we continued to chat, I stole the occasional glance out the window. The sun by then was lowering in the sky, making the smog glow a hepatitic yellow. The outskirts of Shanghai extended to the horizon, residential towers interlaced with elevated expressways dominating the foreground and middle distance.

This was where it had all led, for Shanghai and for the Shao family. The confoundingly crowded Zau household where Mickey had first encountered the clan – on any given day filled with old jockeys and superannuated chauffeurs, cooks and amahs, innumerable offspring and cousins, reprobate brothers, and one rakish old father – now amounted to a couple in their seventies who shared a few rooms on the twenty-third floor of one of the countless towers of the megacity. By the time Sinmay's children had come of age, China had entered the era of its single-child policy; Pearl, his granddaughter, had no children of her own.

In Shanghai's long transition from Treaty Port to "non-consumerist city" of the fifties to modern Free-Trade Zone, much had been gained for many. For the select few – characters like Sinmay – all had been lost.

There were times when the new Shanghai felt exciting, fast-paced, never-resting. But it never felt as vivid or alive to me, as people remembered it feeling to them in the thirties. One thing was certain: never again would it produce a character as improbably complicated as Zau Sinmay.

On my last night at the hotel, I sat at a table in the lobby Jazz Bar, which had been known so many years ago as the Horse and Hounds. On the table before me, a glass of chilled gin, Cointreau, and vermouth, spiked with a shot of crème de menthe, seemed to glow green from within. Raising slender arms, a chanteuse in a *qipao* – scarlet, tight-fitting, and sleeveless – stilled a babble of Mandarin, German, and Japanese voices as she trilled the first tones of "Ye Shang Hai," an aching lullaby of the lost nightlife of the China coast. If I squinted, and let the alcohol do its job, it felt almost like old times. The crowd was cosmopolitan, the playlist pre-revolutionary, the drinks divine. Part of me hoped that a tall man sporting a monocle and a top hat would emerge from the shadows to make the rounds of the tables with proprietorial ease.

That night, I'd helped matters along by slipping the bartender the recipe for the Conte Verde, the cocktail Sir Victor Sassoon had named in honour of the ocean liner on which he'd enjoyed so many fancy-dress parties. The fact that it was served in a martini glass – rather than a Collins glass, as it should have been – caused the spell to lift a little; as did the music, which was provided not by Henry Nathan and His Orchestra, but by a sextet of septuagenarian Chinese jazz musicians. Through the bad years of the Cultural Revolution, the Old Jazz Band had kept the old standards alive by doggedly rehearsing "Begin the Beguine" and "Slow Boat to China" in clandestine jam sessions.

It was all very nostalgic, and rather charming, but not quite *quite*, as Mickey Hahn was fond of saying.

Since 1956, the Cathay Hotel has been officially known as Heping Fandian, which is Mandarin for "Peace Hotel." (A name that came, prosaically enough, from the Asia and Pacific Rim Peace Conference held in Beijing four years earlier.) In the fifties, it was the favoured guest house for delegations from socialist countries; across Nanjing Road, the Palace Hotel, which had suffered such extensive damage during the Black Saturday bombings, was turned into the south wing of the Peace. Sir Victor's penthouse became a restaurant, where guests from Albania, Cuba, and North Korea were served by Chinese waiters who had been required to study Russian. Sassoon House was made the headquarters of the portly Chen Yi, Shanghai's first communist mayor.

One of the hotel's oldest employees, a tall and saturnine Northerner named Ma Yongzhang, told me what happened to the hotel in the sixties. Ma began working as a bellhop in 1964, when he was a teenager. With other employees, he slept in a bunk bed in a dormitory on the third floor. With the beginning of the Cultural Revolution, the most zealous staff members began plastering the lobby with "Big Character" posters that denounced capitalist backsliders. The former grillroom's gilded dragons and phoenixes, symbols of the bad old Manchus, were covered with paper and paint (another hotel that failed to take this precaution, Ma said, saw its décor destroyed by the Red Guards). Behind the scenes, a campaign of intimidation was launched to wrest control from the original management team. The general manager was forced to move his offices to the boiler room. One waiter, known to have worked with the nationalists, was harassed by other staff members to suicide; he was found hanging from a tap in the staff bathroom. By the late sixties, Ma recalled, the Peace was barely operating; at one point, the hotel's solitary foreign guest had seventy staff members waiting on him. Ma was given English lessons by one of the hotel's long-term residents, a black American trade unionist named Vicki Garvin, who came to China after a coup in Ghana ended her hopes of helping to found a socialist state in Africa. Shanghai's six leading hotels were put under the control of the municipal garrison. By the end of the Cultural Revolution, the Peace Hotel was officially managed by the People's Liberation Army.

In the Peace Gallery – the hotel's small museum, tucked away in a mezzanine room – I talked to a history teacher from Texas now based in Hong Kong, who had stayed at the hotel a dozen times in the last thirty years.

"It was not nice at *all*," she told me of her first visit, in the eighties. "It was like walking into a back alley. There were these false dropped ceilings, and the only shop in the lobby was a government travel agency. The staff was completely unhelpful; they'd just shuffle around and look at the ground. The rooms had single beds with thin mattresses. The bedcovers were obviously high quality once, but they looked like they hadn't been replaced in sixty years."

In 2007, the hotel closed its doors and a complete restoration was launched. Tang Yu-en, a distinguished female architect, was put in charge of the project; the celebrated conservationist Ruan Yisan, responsible for saving Shanghai's Little Vienna and many Yangtze Valley water towns from destruction, ensured its architectural integrity was respected. When the hotel reopened three years later under the management of the Toronto-based, Qatari-owned Fairmont Hotels and Resorts group, much of the Cathay's old glamour had been resurrected. Priceless Lalique sconces were returned to the corridor that led to the eighth-floor ballroom. The décor of the Nine Nations suites was recreated from old photos, and the Indian Room made resplendent with filigreed plasterwork and peacock-hued cupolas; a semicircular moon gate was restored to the Chinese Room. In the ground-floor Arcade, a hideous spiral staircase made of poured concrete was removed, allowing the rotunda to regain pride of place. Marble reliefs of the stylized greyhounds that remain the hotel's insignia now undergird the rotunda ceiling's soaring webwork of leaded glass.

Some of the changes, had he been alive to see them, would have caused Sir Victor to arch an eyebrow. Elevators now skip directly from the third to the fifth floor: the number four sounds like the word for "death" in Cantonese. The revolving door on the

Bund is now chained shut with a heavy padlock, as it is bad *feng shui* for a building's main door to face water. Chinese geomancers, however, credit the Sassoons with wisdom for choosing to site their headquarters at a bend in the Huangpu, at the exact spot where the river is said to deposit all its metaphorical gold.

In what is now Room 888, or Sassoon's Presidential Suite – formerly Sir Victor's aerie – side-by-side portraits of a grinning Sir Victor and a bejewelled Barnesie greet guests. Though the presence of twin bathtubs would have pleased the penthouse's former occupant, the view from the king-sized bed in the master bedroom, which looks out over the skyscrapers of Pudong, would have confounded him. The five-star Peace Hotel is now dwarfed by the Shanghai Tower, atop which sits the seven-star J-Hotel, the tallest hotel in the world. Like the Peace itself, the J-Hotel is owned by Jinjiang International group – a state-run enterprise founded by the woman who used to run the kitchens at Sir Victor's Grosvenor House.

During the renovations of Sir Victor's penthouse, workers uncovered a framed mosaic of what appeared to be Poseidon – or perhaps some Phoenician god of the sea – hidden behind the boards in the corridor leading to the master bedroom. Among the staff, the speculation was that the deity was to Baghdadi Jews as Siddhartha was to many Asian Buddhists. It had undoubtedly been put there to ensure good fortune; and the hotel's longevity, in spite of invasion and revolution, was clear proof of its efficacy. After being allowed one peek at the brave new world of sparkling and flashing mega-tall skyscrapers, the ancient sea god was hidden away again behind the wooden panelling.

Perhaps it was the Sassoons' tutelary spirit at work, but my stay at the Cathay Hotel – it will always be the Cathay to me – was a time of unusual calm and contentment. In my fifth-floor suite overlooking Nanking Road, my thought processes were unusually lucid, and I worked with application and wrote with fluidity. I understood how Noël Coward, after a long voyage by ocean liner and train, had found the serenity of spirit to write the first draft of a play in just four days. The sensation of being swaddled in luxury, while at the same time being at the centre of the action, is unique. There were times I felt like I was in the calm eye of a storm, watching, as in an opium reverie, visions of the world and all its marvels swirl around me. At the Cathay, I was exactly where I needed to be. Sir Victor, I imagined, in his moments of greatest felicity, must have felt the same.

The genius of Sir Victor Sassoon was that he built his great hotel at the exact point where far Cathay met the West. It was here that a stubborn Chinese woman spat in the face of the official who was trying to convince her to sell her ancestral property to one of the outer barbarians. And it was at this exact spot that the bomb blasts signalling the end of Shanghai's era of glorious, ill-founded glamour came, one very Black Saturday in 1937, at exactly 4:27 p.m.

It is here, too, that history continues to happen; here that China continues to demonstrate its complicity in the good and bad that emerges from her ambivalent relationship with the outside world; here that the future of a civilization, and thus our planet, can be descried. Eight months after I checked out of the hotel, on the eve of 2015, people poured down Nanjing Road East in the direction of the Bund, in numbers unprecedented even for Shanghai. As the officials in charge of the area were enjoying a banquet of sushi and sake at a nearby luxury restaurant, the forces assigned to keep order were inadequate to deal with the mob, which grew to 300,000. The crowding was most intense near the point where Chiang Kai-shek had made off with all the gold in the vaults of the Bank of China, and in the part of the Bund in front of the Peace Hotel. Revellers on the rooftop of the hotel watched with growing alarm as every square foot of the riverfront became concentrated with humanity. At twenty-five minutes before midnight, a sudden onrush in front of a building on the Bund – two doors from the Peace Hotel, and next door to the old *North-China Daily News* building where Mickey Hahn found the job that allowed her adventures in China to begin – caused a wave of panic through the crowd.

The stampede began when coupons for a nightclub, printed to

look like green-and-white banknotes, showered from an upper window of the building at No. 18, the Bund. As the crowd lunged to grab them, hundreds were trampled underfoot. Thirty-six people died, and forty-nine were seriously injured after being suffocated or crushed against walls and security barriers.

A few hours after the tragedy, a photographer snapped a photo of the coupons that had provoked the stampede. It was only by looking closely that you could tell they weren't real American one-hundred-dollar bills, but convincing imitations. Outside the old Cathay Hotel, at the spot where China has always met the world, the pavement was littered with them.

Acknowledgements

Every book is a journey. Though this one involved covering less actual distance than my previous books, it allowed me to travel farther in time. Without the timely assistance of some inspired guides, the journey would never have begun.

On my first journey to Shanghai, I was fortunate to have landed well. I'm especially grateful to Peter Hibbard, an independent scholar and author of *The Bund*, *Peace at the Cathay* and other excellent books on the city's foreign architectural heritage, for introducing me to the Peace, as well as the former Astor House Hotel and the Hongkong and Shanghai Bank building, on my first walking tour of the Bund. The charming Tess Johnston, author of fifteen books on the expatriate experience in China, introduced me to the surviving homes and haunts of Shanghailanders (and, thanks to her knowledge of Shanghainese, helped me retrieve a camera forgotten in the back seat of a taxi).

In Montreal, Shirley Zhu of Vanier College put me in touch with Meng Ou, who – with grace, intelligence, and endless patience – helped me establish my first contacts with the Shao family in China. I'd like to thank Martin Fackler of the *New York Times* for putting me in touch with Ellen Zhu, who went into her files and helped me track down the last known address of Shao Xunmei's oldest son.

The best journeys bring one into contact with the best people: namely the archivists, amateur historians and librarians whose passion keeps the past alive. At Yale, Lisa Conathan of the Beinecke Rare Book and Manuscript Library went out of her way to help me track down Bernardine Szold-Fritz's correspondence with Harold Acton, Shao Xunmei, and many others. In Bloomington, Zach Downey and Jody Mitchell helped me find some evocative photos; Rebecca Baumann showed me how to navigate the fantastic collections of the University of Indiana's Lilly Library, and her colleagues directed me to the Charles Boxer papers (and, as a bonus, allowed me to hold one of John Ford's Oscar statuettes). In Dallas, Anne Peterson guided me through Sir Victor Sassoon's journals, letters, and photographs at the Southern Methodist University's DeGolyer Library, and Terre Heydari provided help with photographs with grace and charm. Steven Pieragastini provided invaluable advice on negotiating the Shanghai Municipal Archives; I would also like to thank Jon Howlett, Grace Wang, Chang Qing at Tongji University, and Ryan Morden of *National Geographic*. Heyward Parker James, who shared his thesis on Sir Victor Sassoon and other research with me, exemplifies the spirit of openness that is always a pleasure (if often a surprise) to find in the academy. I would also like to thank Yuping Wang at Fudan University, Lian Duan at Concordia, and Christian Henriot, whose website virtualshanghai.net is an endlessly fascinating, and incredibly useful, repository of images and texts about Shanghai's Treaty Port years.

Evelyn Cox welcomed me to Dallas and generously showed me around her uncle's mansion, sharing with me what remains of Sir Victor Sassoon's photos, letters, and ivories. Both she and R.E. Barnes, Sir Victor's nephew, were patient and generous in answering my questions.

Special thanks to Carola Vecchio, Emily Hahn's oldest daughter, who welcomed my interest in her mother's life in China, and enthusiastically consented to allow unpublished material from the Lilly Library to be used in this book.

On my most recent trip to Shanghai, Andrew David Field, chronicler of Shanghai's dancing days, took me on a jazz-themed tour of the Bund, and introduced me to the scholars at the Royal Asiatic Society. I'm particularly grateful to the distinguished scholar Ruan Yisan, responsible for preserving so much of China's historical architecture, for taking the time to talk about the Bund and the *shikumen* of Shanghai. Chen Zishan, a professor of literature at East China Normal University, talked to me frankly about Shao Xunmei's standing in contemporary Chinese letters.

I was made to feel at home at the Cathay Hotel (all right, the

Peace, if you must) by manager George Wee and his highly profes-sional staff, among them Belle Bai, who gave me an extended tour of the hotel's hidden corners. Special thanks to Robert Cousins, who followed up with crucial information, and to Ma Yongzhang (Martin), who went out of his way to provide me with historical photos and fascinating stories about his experiences at the hotel from the 1960s on. The accomplished architect Tang Yu-en shared insights into her work preserving and restoring the hotel; Ian Carr of HBA also took the time to talk to me about his experiences working on the most recent renewal of the Peace.

I was fortunate to work with some talented, and highly cultured, interpreters in Shanghai, among them Liu Xiao and Guo Xiaohan. Lydia She in particular went above the call of duty and became a key support, helping me land on my feet – and stay on them – during my time in Shanghai and Hangzhou. The well-informed and diligent Chan Wing Shuen (Donna) of Hong Kong was always reliable and thorough in the translating work she did for me. Lu Yichao, who smoothly welcomed me to Shanghai, also used his own time to guide me through the *shikumen* of Hongkou. Charlie Macpherson gave me insight into expat life in Shanghai, as well as a memorable night out on the Bund that I don't fully remember.

Sincere thanks to Edward Denison, author of *Building Shanghai*, and Bernard Wasserstein, author of the exhaustively researched and very engaging books *Secret War in Shanghai* and *The Secret Lives of Trebitsch Lincoln*, for crucial advice that early on helped orient me in my research. I owe a debt of gratitude to Mickey Hahn's biographer Ken Cuthbertson, whose book *Nobody Said* Not *to Go* so thoroughly documented a woman whose writing and adventures deserve to be celebrated in the twenty-first century.

The heart of this journey brought me into the heart of Shanghai, but also into the heart of the Shao family. I wasn't astonished by their hospitality and warmth – they are, after all, the direct descendants of the extraordinary Zau Sinmay – but I was certainly grateful for it. I'd like to thank Shao Yang and her husband Wulin for all the time they took helping me to discover homes and haunts of Sinmay and Mickey, and Xiaohong, Shao's oldest daughter, for her willingness to answer my endless questions. Wuxin (Pearl) and her husband Hubert Driller were especially generous in acting as a liaison with the family. The Canada Council of the Arts provided a much needed, and much appreciated, grant, which funded a trip to Shanghai and gave me the peace of mind to focus on writing for several months.

I'd be remiss if I didn't thank Joe at St. Viateur Bagels for material support (in the form of at least five all-dressed per week), and to Patrizia, Pino, Eugenio, Pascuale, Antonio, Franco, and all the other members of the extended Lucifero family at Montreal's Club Social. Without their unswervingly impeccable dry macchiatos I wouldn't have been able to *sgobbare come un mazzatu*, and this book would have taken much longer to write.

Nor would it have been as readable or accurate a volume without the sharp eye, musical ear, and fine mind of Scott Chernoff, who read the manuscript, in instalments, on various lines of Tokyo transit over the summer of 2015, and whose insightful comments helped me refine the second draft. Audrey Grescoe, my mother, came out of retirement as the "Spotted Retriever" to fetch the often all-too-far-flung and recondite facts that have helped enliven so many parts of this story. Paul, my father, was one of the most enthusiastic readers (and perceptive editors) of *Shanghai Grand*, in its all various iterations. My parents are unflagging in their support; without their innate enthusiasm, I would never have become a writer.

My agent, Michelle Tessler, was closely involved in the book's early development, and provided key guidance when it came to time to narrow the story's focus; if it hadn't been for her, bucking me up from the start, *Shanghai Grand* would still be a vague idea. At Harper Collins, Jim Gifford's genuine enthusiasm for this project convinced me I was on the right track; at St. Martin's, Charles Spicer's unstinting support helped me through the research and early drafts; and at Macmillan, Georgina Morley's clear affinity for the project was a constant inspiration. Their restrained yet exacting editorial advice turned sprawling early drafts into a coherent book.

All of my journeys end at home – and home for me is not so much a place as the proximity of my lovely, generous, and patient wife Erin Churchill, and our constantly astonishing son Desmond, whose life to this date coincides with the conception and writing of *Shanghai Grand*. Having the two of you in my life has made me a better person, and for that I'm very grateful indeed.

Notes

Abbreviations

BNL Beneicke Rare Book Library, Yale University (New Haven, Connecticut)

DGL DeGolyer Library, Southern Methodist University (Dallas, Texas)

FOC Foreign Office Files for China, The National Archives (London, England)

LLB Lilly Library, University of Indiana (Bloomington, Indiana)

SMA Shanghai Municipal Archives (Shanghai, China)

SMP Shanghai Municipal Police records, U.S. National Archives (College Park, Maryland)

XJL Xujiahui branch of the Shanghai Municipal Library (Shanghai, China)

Prologue

page

1. "After you enter the cemetery": email from "Pearl" (Shao Wuxin), granddaughter of Shao Xunmei, March 25, 2014.

3. speakers of the Hu dialect: see Lu Hanchao, *Beyond the Neon Lights*, p. 54.

3. sweeping the heroine: Emily Hahn, *Steps of the Sun*, p. 11.

3. he was Mr. Zinmay Zau: see W.H. Auden and Christopher Isherwood, *Journey to a War*, p. 6.

3. pioneering publisher of *manhua*: see Ellen Johnston Laing, "Shanghai Manhua," *Modern Chinese Literature and Culture*.

3. in *Mr. Wang*: see Hung Chang-tai, *War and Popular Culture*, p. 32.

4. wrote a contemporary: the passage appears in Zhang Ruogu's *Urban Symphonies*. Cited in Jonathan Hutt, "Monstre Sacré," *China Heritage Quarterly*, June 2010, p. 11.

4. Ingres canvas: see Jonathan Hutt, "Monstre Sacré," *China Heritage Quarterly*, p. 12.

5. swan song of Pan Heh-ven: see Emily Hahn, "Heh-Ven, Pawnbroker", the *New Yorker*, March 9, 1940, p. 79. The last Pan Heh-ven story, "Brother in Japan," appeared in the issue dated March 30, 1940.

7. niece of the wealthiest Maharajah: see Bernard Wasserstein, *Secret War in Shanghai*, p. 41.

8. travelogue about walking across the Congo: Emily Hahn, *Congo Solo*.

8. recollections of defying sexism: see Emily Hahn, *Times and Places*, p. 59.

8. essay about living on D.H. Lawrence's ranch: see Emily Hahn, *Times and Places*, p. 105.

8. follow a muleteer into the remote mountains: see Edgar Snow, *Red Star over China*, p. 57.

9. to read and write Mandarin: on Emily Hahn's linguistic skills, see Ken Cuthbertson, *Nobody Said Not to Go*. Towards the end of her life, she told her biographer she could still swear in Chinese.

10. the route of an ancient creek: see Edward Denison, *Building Shanghai*, p. 222.

10. renamed Great Shanghai Road: see Bernard Wasserstein, *Secret War in Shanghai*, p. 234.

10. inventor of a bestselling brain tonic: see Pan Ling, *In Search of Old Shanghai*, p. 93.

10. true beginning of the Second World War in Asia: for a discussion of historians' attitudes to the significance of Black Saturday, see Peter Harmsen, *Shanghai 1937*, p. 9.

12. "in Room 536 or thereabouts": see Emily Hahn, *Steps of the Sun*, p. 13.

12. "a natural-born poet": I'm grateful to Chan Wing Shuen (Donna) for translating this and other texts by and about Zau Sinmay. The date of the poem is provided in the article (also translated by Chan Wing Shuen) by Zhang Wei, "The Publishing Career of an Intellectual," *New Citizen Evening Post*, December 24, 2006.

13. 10,000 plus items: see www.indiana.edu/~liblilly/lilly/mss/index.php?p=hahn (last accessed October 18, 2015).

13. Sir Victor Sassoon's thirty-five journals: see www.lib.utexas.edu/taro/smu/00208/smu-00208.html (last accessed October 18, 2015).

13. his love of velocity and novelty: author's interview with Evelyn Cox, Sir Victor Sassoon's niece, Dallas, TX, July 22, 2013.

14. sons of impoverished peasants: I refer to "Big-Eared" Du Yuesheng;

many other examples of the extraordinary characters that peopled the Shanghai underworld can be found in Lynn Pan's *Old Shanghai: Gangsters in Paradise*.

15. played the Westminster Quarters: see Peter Hibbard, *The Bund*, p. 160.

1: Shanghai, January 28, 1932

page

19. room boy had just cleared Sir Victor Sassoon's desk: my reconstruction of Sir Victor's experiences during the January 28 Incident are based on the account he gave to biographer Stanley Jackson (*The Sassoons*, pp. 230–1), as well as his journal entries from the Sassoon Journal, January 28–9, 1932, DGL. In addition, the *North-China Daily News* published a day-by-day account of the events in a Sunday magazine supplement published on February 21, 1932.

19. not fifty yards from the *Izumo*: see Stanley Jackson, *The Sassoons*, p. 230.

20. Chinese boycott of Japanese-made goods: see Peter Harmsen, *Shanghai 1937*, p. 20.

20. trespassing on the neutrality of the International Settlement: Sassoon Journal, January 29, 1932, DGL.

20. a dozen Japanese destroyers: "A Shanghai War Diary Jan. 18–Feb. 17, 1932," *North-China Sunday News*, February 21, 1932.

20. "The political situation in India": "Fearing Indian Unrest, Sassoon Goes to China," *New York Times*, July 18, 1931.

21. thousands of mechanized spools: see Stanley Jackson, *The Sassoons*, p. 201.

21. life in India had become tiresome: on Sir Victor's preference for Shanghai, see Stanley Jackson, *The Sassoons*, p. 211.

21. transferred sixty lakhs of silver taels: "The Shanghai Boom," *Fortune*, January 1935, p. 31.

22. "Claridge's of the Far East": "Opening of Cathay Hotel," *North-China Herald*, August 3, 1929, p. 174.

22. he'd written an entire play: see Graham Payn, ed., *The Noël Coward Diaries*, pp. 167–70.

22. He had known love once: see Stanley Jackson, *The Sassoons*, p. 136.

23. a ringer for . . . Adolphe Menjou: from author's interview with Evelyn Cox, Dallas, TX, July 22, 2013.

23. 215 rooms and suites on five floors: *North-China Herald*, August 3, 1929, p. 174.

23. spotters of the Shanghai Fire Brigade: see Peter Hibbard, *Peace at the Cathay*, p. 64.

24. straighten out the dog-legged Nanking Road: see Edward Denison, *Modernism in China*, p. 148.

24. a fitting emblem: among historians of Shanghai's Western architecture, there are persistent rumours that Sir Victor deliberately built the Cathay Hotel and the Embankment Building in the shapes of a "V" and an "S." His journals, though they don't confirm this, do record his penchant for initialling: his racing dogs all bear the initials V.S., and fourteen godchildren listed in a 1941 entry have either the initials "V.S." or the middle names "Eve" or "Evelyn." When he finally brought his bachelorhood to an end, he married a woman named Evelyn.

24. a composite of concrete and Douglas fir: "Shanghai's New Billion-Dollar Skyline," *Far Eastern Review*, June 1927, p. 260.

24. Sir Victor could detect no cracks: see Stanley Jackson, *The Sassoons*, p. 230.

25. uninterrupted torrent of humanity: see Harriet Sergeant, *Shanghai: Collision Point of Cultures*, p. 190.

25. a windowpane shattered: see Stanley Jackson, *The Sassoons*, p. 230, and Sassoon Journal, January 28, 1932, DGL.

26. and chatting with the soldiers: Sassoon Journal, January 28, 1932, DGL.

26. playing at being soldiers: quoted from Sassoon Journal, January 28, 1932, DGL.

26. take him to the Carlton Theatre: Sassoon Journal, January 28, 1932, DGL; *Dawn Patrol* playing at the Carlton: *The China Press*, January 27, 1932, p. 5.

27. pitched battle with the Japanese: "A Shanghai War Diary Jan. 18–Feb. 17, 1932," *North-China Sunday News*, February 21, 1932.

27. put chains on the tires of the Studebaker: Sassoon Journal, January 29, 1932, DGL.

27. Entire blocks of rowhouses: "Only Ghosts of Ruined City Remain Where Chapei Stood," *Shanghai Evening Post*, February 12, 1932.

27. photograph of the North Station: snapshot of North Station in Sassoon Journal, January 29, 1932, DGL.

28. mounting sense of despair: Sir Victor's fears in the wake of the January 28 Incident are recorded in Stanley Jackson, *The Sassoons*, p. 231.

28. "It really is a war": Sassoon Journal, January 29, 1932, DGL.

2: *Where China Meets the World*

page

29. where marshbirds stilt-walked: Lu Hanchao, *Beyond the Neon Lights*, p. 30.

29. landside-prone plateaux of Tibet: see Simon Winchester, *The River at the Center of the World*, p. 13.

29. temperature variations of 130 degrees: see Edward Denison, *Building Shanghai*, p. 85.

30. alluvial soil goes down 1,000 feet: "Is Shanghai Outgrowing Itself?" *Far Eastern Review*, October 1927, p. 445.

30. even coffins have to be ballasted: see Heyward Parker James's thesis, *Victor Sassoon and the Twilight of Foreign Shanghai*, p. 63.

30. travelled to Imperial Rome: see Peter Harmsen, *Shanghai 1937*, p. 252.

30. earliest known name: see Edward Denison, *Building Shanghai*, p. 18.

30. a fishing contraption: see Pan Ling, *In Search of Old Shanghai*, p. 93.

31. (footnote) meaning "above the Pacific Ocean": see Edward Denison, *Building Shanghai*, p. 18.

31. sacked the Shanghai region five times in 1553: see Edward Denison, *Building Shanghai*, p. 20.

31. ranked Shanghai a "third-class county seat": see Lu Hanchao, *Beyond the Neon Lights*, p. 26.

31. one in five of the world's inhabitants: based on estimate of 198 million population in Yangtse watershed, 1843, in Susan Naquin, *Chinese Society in the Eighteenth Century*, p. 213.

32. physically knock that doorway down: the account of the *Lord Amherst*'s mission to Shanghai is taken from Hugh Lindsay's report to H. Lang, in the lecture "Shanghai Considered Socially," pp. 11–12.

32. "may gradually be opened to British commerce": further details of the *Lord Amherst*'s mission come from Immanuel C.Y. Hsü, "The Secret Mission of the *Lord Amherst* on the China Coast, 1832."

32. "two vigorous charges at the centre door": see H. Lang, "Shanghai Considered Socially," p. 11.

33. to keep out drafts: see Julia Lovell, *The Opium War*, p. 28.

33. monopoly on its import: see Maurice Collis, *Foreign Mud*, p. 8.

34. they reported to the Company: see Immanuel C.Y. Hsü, "The Secret Mission of the *Lord Amherst* on the China Coast, 1832," p. 252.

34. harvesting of rice and millet: see Martin Jacques, *When China Rules the World*, p. 75.

34. Zheng He was mapping the coast of Africa: see Martin Jacques, *When China Rules the World*, p. 78.

34. "We have never valued ingenious articles": quoted in Jonathan Spence, *The Search for Modern China*, p. 122.

34. spinning machines and steam engines: for a list of Chinese inventions, see Simon Winchester, *The Man Who Loved China*, pp. 267–77.

35. as urbanized as France or England: see Martin Jacques, *When China Rules the World*, p. 75.

35. weak, divided, and poor in rare periods: see Odd Arne Westad, *Restless Empire*, p. 1.

35. was succeeded by the Qings: see Jonathan Spence, *The Search for Modern China*, p. 26.

35. lacquered with elephant dung: see Julia Lovell, *The Opium War*, p. 46.

35. Qing power was at its peak: see Odd Arne Westad, *Restless Empire*, p. 9.

35. astonished to find a palace: see Odd Arne Westad, *Restless Empire*, p. 12.

36. Silk Road city of Kaifeng: see Maisie J. Meyer's thesis, *The Sephardi Jewish Community of Shanghai 1845–1939 and the Question of Identity*, p. 60.

36. would ride into battle: see Odd Arne Westad, *Restless Empire*, p. 34.

36. allowed Portuguese middlemen . . . to occupy Macao: see Jonathan Spence, *The Search for Modern China*, p. 19.

36. white-walled warehouses: see Maurice Collis, *Foreign Mud*, p. 16.

37. more as cultural interpreters: see Odd Arne Westad, *Restless Empire*, p. 34.

37. wandered the Forbidden City in patched robes: see Julia Lovell, *The Opium War*, p. 49.

37. "an old, crazy, first rate man-of-war": quoted in Jonathan Spence, *The Search for Modern China*, p. 123.

37. struck simultaneously by floods: see Julia Lovell, *The Opium War*, p. 49.

37. "leaving them outside": quoted in Odd Arne Westad, *Restless Empire*, p. 31.

37. shells from their stern guns popping: see Immanuel C.Y. Hsü, "The Secret Mission of the *Lord Amherst* on the China Coast, 1832," p. 245.

3: The Sassoon Gamble

39. the special Jubilee edition: much of the account of the events around the fiftieth anniversary of the Treaty Port is contained in "The Shanghai Jubilee (1843–1893)," published as a special edition of the *North-China Daily News*, datelined November 17, 1893.

39. the English-language banners: I am grateful to Christian Henriot and the team at www.virtualshanghai.net for their archive of dated photos of Shanghai in its Treaty Port period. My reconstruction of Silas Hardoon's stroll along the Bund is based on the site's photos of buildings from the 1890s.

39. climbed to the rooftops: from "The Day's Rejoicings," special edition of the *North-China Daily News*, datelined November 17, 1893, p. 33.

40. "We have steamers": the full text of Reverend Muirhead's speech is taken from "The Day's Rejoicings," special edition of the *North-China Daily News*, datelined November 17, 1893, pp. 38–40.

41. a thick Arabic accent: see Maisie J. Meyer's thesis, *The Sephardi Jewish Community of Shanghai 1845–1939 and the Question of Identity*, p. 29.

41. waistcoat and pocket watch: see Chiara Betta's thesis, *Silas Aaron Hardoon (1815–1931): Marginality and Adaptation in Shanghai*.

41. Sheikh Sason Ben Saleh: details of the Sassoon family's years in Baghdad and Bombay are taken from Stanley Jackson, *The Sassoons*, pp. 1–30.

42. the argument that led to his sudden dismissal: the nature of the dispute was never disclosed, according to Chiara Betta, *Silas Aaron Hardoon (1815–1931): Marginality and Adaptation in Shanghai*.

42. the profile of St. Andrew: see "The Day's Rejoicings," special edition of the *North-China Daily News*, datelined November 17, 1893, p. 43.

43. *kau*, or "old" Sassoon: see Stanley Jackson, *The Sassoons*, p. 51.

43. his meagre salary of twelve: see Maisie J. Meyer's thesis, *The Sephardi Jewish Community of Shanghai*, p. 32.

43–44. minted from silver from Mexican mines: from Warren Bailey, "Familiarity, Convenience, and Commodity Money: Spanish and Mexican Silver Dollars in Qing and Republican China," p. 1.

44. habit spread to palace eunuchs: see Jonathan Spence, *The Search for Modern China*, p. 130.

44. "scrambling dragons": see Maurice Collis, *Foreign Mud*, p. 25.

44. as much as £100: see Stanley Jackson, *The Sassoons*, p. 22.

44. two million addicts: see Alan Baumler, *The Chinese and Opium under the Republic*, p. 29.

44. When his letter went unanswered: see Jonathan Spence, *The Search for Modern China*, p. 151.

45. "perhaps the least pleasant residence": quoted in Julia Lovell, *The Opium War*, p. 1.

45. "Iron-Headed Old Rat": see Julia Lovell, *The Opium War*, p. 25.

45. the iron-sided paddle-wheeler: see Jonathan Spence, *The Search for Modern China*, p. 157.

46. experiencing imperial overreach: see Julia Lovell, *The Opium War*, p. 2.

46. opened five Chinese coastal cities: see Jonathan Spence, *The Search for Modern China*, p. 120.

46. after noticing his competitors: see Stella Dong, *Shanghai: The Rise and Fall of a Decadent City*, p. 57.

46. one later Eurasian commentator: see Han Suyin, *Birdless Summer*, p. 220.

46. "witnessed the obstinacy and determination": see Captain W.H. Hall, *The Nemesis in China*, p. 328.

47. sold the finest pickings: see Edward Denison, *Building Shanghai*, p. 33.

47. twenty-three "Land Regulations": see Edward Denison, *Building Shanghai*, p. 34.

47. 470 acres of foreshore: see Lu Hanchao, *Beyond the Neon Lights*, p. 26.

47. one speechifier had exulted: see "The Shanghai Jubilee (1843–1893)," *North-China Daily News*, datelined November 17, 1893, p. 3.

47. (footnote) Mandarin pronunciation meant "bitter strength": see Stella Dong, *Shanghai: The Rise and Fall of a Decadent City*, p. 162.

48. within thirty feet of the Whangpoo River: see Edward Denison, *Building Shanghai*, p. 47.

48. "It consisted largely of burying grounds": see "The Shanghai Jubilee (1843–1893)," *North-China Daily News*, datelined November 17, 1893, p. 5.

48. followed the course of a creek: see H. Lang, "Shanghai Considered Socially," p. 23.

48. "*spat in the Taotai's face*": see H. Lang, "Shanghai Considered Socially," p. 22.

48. buildings of Augustine Heard & Co: see Eric Politzer, "The Changing Face of the Shanghai Bund," *Arts of Asia*, pp. 64–81.

49. where coolies smoked: see "View of the Bund at Dawn," 1880–1889, at http://www.virtualshanghai.net/Photos/Images?ID=165 (last accessed October 18, 2015).

49. a village schoolteacher named Hong Xiuquan: see Jonathan Spence, *The Search for Modern China*, p. 171.

49. the rebels were driven away: see Edward Denison, *Building Shanghai*, p. 36.

49. caused twenty million deaths: see Odd Arne Westad, *Restless Empire*, p. 48.

50. soared to $12,000 an acre: see Edward Denison, *Building Shanghai*, p. 64.

50. only 5,274 of whom: see "Report for the Year Ended 31st December 1891," Municipal Council, Shanghai, p. 86.

50. a French Jewish policeman: see Sarah Abrevaya Stein, "Protected Persons?" *American Historical Review*, 2011, p. 81.

50. simultaneously repeated "*hareath*": see Chiara Betta's thesis, *Silas Aaron Hardoon (1815–1931): Marginality and Adaptation in Shanghai*, p. 69.

51. named a councillor: see Chiara Betta's thesis, *Silas Aaron Hardoon (1815–1931): Marginality and Adaptation in Shanghai*, p. 75.

51. Shanghai's next Jubilee in 1943: see "The Shanghai Jubilee," p. 4.

52. chasing after actresses and dancers: see Stanley Jackson, *The Sassoons*, p. 99; Jackson refers to David Sassoon as "Nunkie"; I've opted to follow the spelling favoured by Sir Victor in his journals, "Nunky."

4: St. Louis, May 27, 1916

page

55. one of those late spring days: reconstruction based on author's visit to Emily Hahn's family home in St. Louis, Hahn's recollections of her childhood in "The Escape," *Times and Places*, pp. 1–14, and a return visit to her childhood home when she was in her seventies, chronicled in "Special City," in *St. Louis Magazine*, June 1982.

55. all the words she'd looked up: see Emily Hahn, *Times and Places*, p. 31.

55. a chummy Irish saloonkeeper: see Ken Cuthbertson, *Nobody Said Not to Go*, p. 15.

55. cleft of the peach tree: see Emily Hahn, *Times and Places*, p. 3.

56. she'd read *The Wallet of Kai Lung*: a record of Hahn's childhood reading about Asia is found in an untitled, undated (1979 or later) document that begins "As a child," Box 15, Hahn mss. III, LLB.

A Hahn article entitled "The China Boom," published in *T'ien Hsia*, 1938, also records her childhood reading of Sax Rohmer's Fu-Manchu series.

56. "In his long, yellow robe": see Sax Rohmer, *The Insidious Fu-Manchu*, Chapter XVII.

57. "an indescribable gait": see Sax Rohmer, *The Insidious Fu-Manchu*, Chapter XIII.

57. only Oriental person: see Emily Hahn, "The China Boom," *T'ien Hsia*, 1938.

5: The Flapper's Progress

page

58. stood and fought: the 19th Route Army's resistance to the Japanese is well chronicled in Harriet Sergeant's interviews with surviving soldiers, *Shanghai: Collision Point of Cultures*, pp. 185–205.

58. heroes to the ordinary people: see Han Suyin, *A Mortal Flower*, p. 179.

58. killed 10,000 Chinese civilians: see Peter Harmsen, *Shanghai 1937*, p. 21.

58. (footnote) the fascists bombed Guernica: see Peter Harmsen, *Shanghai 1937*, p. 62.

59. appearances at the Horse and Hounds: see Stanley Jackson, *The Sassoons*, p. 231.

59. sweating aide-de-camp: see Stanley Jackson, *The Sassoons*, p. 231.

59. his confidence in Shanghai's future: see Sassoon Journal, March 17, 1932, DGL.

59. foiled an attempted assassination: dispatch from J.P. Brenan to Chargé d'affaires, Peking, November 8, 1932, FO 371/17060/1485, FOL.

59. inviolability of the foreign settlements: see Heyward Parker James's thesis, *Victor Sassoon and the Twilight of Foreign Shanghai*, p. 85.

59. "kept its place": see Stanley Jackson, *The Sassoons*, p. 230.

60. the "world-girdlers": see Peter Hibbard, *Peace at the Cathay*, p. 97.

60. arriving from Trieste: list of ships arriving from *North-China Herald*, April 10, 1935, p. 84.

60. a fancy-dress cocktail concert: recipe for cocktail from Conte Verde pamphlet in Sassoon Journal, November 16, 1934, DGL.

61. Chinese acrobats: see "Personal Notes," *North-China Herald*, January 30, 1935, p. 178.

61. proceeded to defecate: see Harriet Sergeant, *Shanghai: Collision Point of Cultures*, p. 133.

61. hire a young woman: see Sassoon Journal, January 24, 1935, DGL.

61. introduced to Sun Fo: see Sassoon Journal, December 7, 1934, DGL.

62. purchased from one of the partners: the partner was Lt. Col M.H. Logan of Palmer & Turner; see Peter Hibbard, *Peace at the Cathay*, p. 37.

63. they were both nursing broken hearts: see Sassoon Journal, April 12, 1935, DGL.

63. born in the middle of a St. Louis cold snap: I have taken details of Emily Hahn's early years in St. Louis from Ken Cuthbertson's excellent biography, *Nobody Said Not to Go*, pp. 9–30.

64. "crushing mass of girls": see Emily Hahn, *Times and Places*, p. 28.

64. on Saturday mornings: see Emily Hahn, *Times and Places*, p. 33.

64. the Hahn home still stands: author's visit to Emily Hahn home at 4858 Fountain Avenue, St. Louis, MO, July 21, 2013.

65. home to the Midwestern elite: see Albert Montesi, *Central West End St. Louis*, p. 7.

66. "my private opinion": see Emily Hahn, *Times and Places*, p. 20.

66. When Helen broke his heart: see Ken Cuthbertson, *Nobody Said Not to Go*, p. 27.

66. "the female mind is incapable": see Emily Hahn, *Times and Places*, p. 59.

67. packed up a Model T Ford: see Ken Cuthbertson, *Nobody Said Not to Go*, p. 37.

67. "My parents complained": see Emily Hahn, *Times and Places*, p. 82.

67. At her first job: see Emily Hahn, *Times and Places*, p. 45.

67. drinking near-beer: see Emily Hahn, *Times and Places*, pp. 94–6.

68. Mickey lit out for the West: see Emily Hahn, *Times and Places*, pp. 97–111.

68. rented a room on Forty-fifth Street: Emily Hahn's experiences in Manhattan from *Times and Places*, pp. 112–124.

69. "a series of paintings": from untitled, undated document that begins "My career as a mining engineer," p. 62, Box 15, Hahn mss. III, LLB.

69. glimpsed Benito Mussolini: see *Love, Mickey*, p. 11.

69. always to a seat in Aisle K: see Emily Hahn, *Times and Places*, pp. 125–37.

70. "Lisbon is built entirely": see *Love, Mickey*, p. 9.

70. I mentioned Ursula Greville: see *Love, Mickey,* p. 17.

70. Without Mickey's knowledge: see Ken Cuthbertson, *Nobody Said Not to Go,* p. 67.

70. literary editor, Katherine Angell, rejected them: see Ken Cuthbertson, *Nobody Said Not to Go,* p. 67.

70. "'you're a funny person'": in "Lovely Lady," the *New Yorker,* May 25, 1929, pp. 78–9. (Hahn also contributed an unsigned, two-paragraph item about a tipsy sailor on the subway to the "Talk of the Town" section in 1928.)

71. a daughter of Bilitis: see Gore Vidal, *The Last Empire, Essays 1992–2000,* p. 209.

71. "bitchier than anyone": see Ken Cuthbertson, *Nobody Said Not to Go,* p. 73.

71. sealed by alcohol and tears: see Ken Cuthbertson, *Nobody Said Not to Go,* p. 73.

71. she'd lost her virginity: letter to Ken Cuthbertson, March 8, 1995, Cuthbertson mss, LLB.

72. "long twisted streamers of men": in "Women without Work," *The New Republic,* May 31, 1933, p. 63.

72. a bottle of sleeping pills: see Emily Hahn, *Times and Places,* pp. 119–21.

73. on Christmas Day: see Emily Hahn, *Congo Solo,* p. 3.

73. watch Al Jolson amaze an audience: see Emily Hahn, *Times and Places,* p. 200.

73. "dull as the ditchwater it did not resemble": see Ken Cuthbertson, *Nobody Said Not to Go,* p. 117.

74. an injection of morphine: from Ken Cuthbertson interview with Emily Hahn, October 22, 1992, p. 4, in Cuthbertson mss, LLB.

74. work as a cook for six dollars: in "Women without Work," *The New Republic,* May 31, 1933, p. 64.

74. "He was drunk at the time": Emily Hahn letter to Ken Cuthbertson, September 15, 1994, in Cuthbertson mss, LLB.

74. Mickey studied anthropology: see Ken Cuthbertson, *Nobody Said Not to Go,* p. 126.

74. glimpse of a red silk curtain: see Emily Hahn, *Steps of the Sun,* p. 16.

76. On March 5, 1935: though Hahn writes she sailed out of San Francisco "just after New Year's Day, 1935," in *Times and Places* (p. 205), the *Chichibu Maru* actually sailed from Los Angeles on March 4 and left San Francisco the following day, arriving in Honolulu on March 13. See *Los Angeles Times,* "Shipping News," March 5, 1935, p. 9.

6: Shanghai Grand

page

77. 35 miles of wharves: see Bernard Wasserstein, *Secret War in Shanghai*, p. 3.

77. population had almost doubled: it had increased from 1.7 million to approximately 3.5 million in the mid-1930s, according to Lu Hanchao, *Beyond the Neon Lights*, p. 248.

77. one of the world's first cities: see Lu Hanchao, *Beyond the Neon Lights*, p. 249.

77. American-owned diesel generating plant: "Shanghai Boasts World's Largest Diesel Generating Plant," *Far Eastern Review*, January 1938, p. 23.

77. whose pilots tended to hail from Indiana or Missouri: see "The Shanghai Boom," *Fortune*, January 1935, p. 120.

78. Jimmy James insisted: see Helen Foster, *My China Years*, p. 73.

78. bowling alley at the Country Club: see Carl Crow, *Foreign Devils in the Flowery Kingdom*, p. 205.

78. maintained by attendants: see "The Shanghai Boom," *Fortune*, January 1935, p. 104.

78. "dense, rank, richly clotted life": see Aldous Huxley, *Jesting Pilate*, p. 241.

78. "crushing throngs spilling": see Edgar Snow, *Journey to the Beginning*, p. 16.

79. (footnote) strict divisions were maintained: see Bernard Wasserstein, *Secret War in Shanghai*, pp. 9–10.

79. cracked quarterstaffs: see Lu Hanchao, *Beyond the Neon Lights*, p. 39.

79. La Donna Silk Salon Modernique: see Peter Hibbard, *Peace at the Cathay*, p. 47.

80. vomit up a rich meal: anecdote from documentary *The Man Who Changed Shanghai*; trailer at https://vimeo.com/83718691 (last accessed October 18, 2015).

80. drop a bowl of rice: see Carroll Alcott, *My War with Japan*, p. 71.

80. a single candle burning: from Irene Corbally Kuhn, "Shanghai: the Vintage Years," in *Endless Feasts*, p. 79.

80. "No Mama, No Papa": see J.G. Ballard, *Miracles of Life*, p. 15.

80. 20,000 professional beggars: see Lu Hanchao, *Beyond the Neon Lights*, p. 136.

81. 5,950 cadavers: see Harriet Sergeant, *Shanghai: Collision Point of Cultures*, p. 66.

81. amounted to a mere 8.94 square miles: see Edward Denison, *Building Shanghai*, p. 75.

81. occupied just twenty-seven square miles: see Lu Hanchao, *Beyond the Neon Lights*, p. 26.

81. 3 per cent of the total population: see Lu Hanchao, *Beyond the Neon Lights*, p. 2.

81. 2,342 of the half-million residents: figure for 1936; 2,648 were British. See chart in Christian Henriot, ed., *In the Shadow of the Rising Sun*, p. 261.

82. just 3,852 non-Chinese voters: see Edgar Snow, *Journey to the Beginning*, p. 21.

82. (footnote) was the pet project of Henry Luce: see Alan Brinkley, *The Publisher*, p. 149.

82. "dedicated to safety": see "The Shanghai Boom," *Fortune*, January 1935, p. 31.

83. "Charity: a small item": see "Appendix III: Extract from a Taipan's Budget," *Fortune*, January 1935, p. 120.

83. "and he is great": "The Shanghai Boom," *Fortune*, January 1935, p. 38.

83. first become aware of Shanghai's potential: see Stanley Jackson, *The Sassoons*, p. 137.

84–85. founding member of the Royal Aero Club: see Stanley Jackson, *The Sassoons*, p. 144.

85. the crash broke both of his legs: see Stanley Jackson, *The Sassoons*, p. 153.

85. dispatched to Bombay: see Stanley Jackson, *The Sassoons*, p. 214.

86. the third Baronet of Bombay: see Heyward Parker James's thesis, *Victor Sassoon and the Twilight of Foreign Shanghai*, p. 41.

86. "natural dignity of a lion": Victor Sheean, *Personal History*, p. 203.

86. workers took to the streets: see Stella Dong, *Shanghai: The Rise and Fall of a Decadent City*, p. 179.

87. notoriously feckless man: see Lynn Pan, *Gangsters in Paradise*, p. 56.

87. leader of the Green Gang: see Frederic Wakeman, Jr., *Policing Shanghai 1927–1937*, p. 31.

87. "one of the leading financiers": see George F. Nellist, *Men of Shanghai and North China*, p. 111.

87. dried monkey's head: see Ralph Shaw, *Sin City*, p. 123.

88. reportedly $3 million: see Lynn Pan, *Gangsters in Paradise*, p. 56.

88. (footnote) was changed to Peiping: see Carl Crow, *Foreign Devils in the Flowery Kingdom*, p. 185.

88. checking into Suite 104: see Sassoon Journal, April 27, 1928, DGL.

89. "Ziegfeld of Shanghai": see Andrew David Field, *Shanghai's Dancing World*, p. 41.

89. caused a stir: see Andrew David Field, *Shanghai's Dancing World*, p. 64.

89. "Definitely decided on Hotel": the gestation of the Cathay Hotel can thus be precisely dated, see Sassoon Journal, April 29, 1928, DGL.

89. Palmer & Turner: the firm's archives were lost during the Second World War.

89. weighed 50,000 tons: see Peter Hibbard, *The Bund*, p. 137.

90. the first propeller manufactured: see Peter Hibbard, *The Bund*, p. 141.

90. enjoyed steeple-chasing: see Peter Hibbard, *The Bund*, pp. 74–76.

90. since the Han dynasty: see Heyward Parker James's thesis, *Victor Sassoon and the Twilight of Foreign Shanghai*, p. 56.

91. at the Massachusetts Institute of Technology: see Malcolm Purvis, *Tall Storeys*, p. 55.

91. to a depth of sixty-two feet: see Peter Hibbard, *Peace at the Cathay*, p. 42.

91. Partway through construction: see Sassoon Journals, April 29, 1928, DGL.

91. a new company: see Peter Hibbard, *Peace at the Cathay*, p. 42.

91. enjoying the nightlife: see Sassoon Journal, months of July and August 1929, DGL.

91. the first name: "Cathay Hotel, Monarch of Far Eastern Hostelries, Observes Second Birthday," *China Press*, August 2, 1931.

91. "Arrived S'hai 6:30": see Sassoon Journal, March 31, 1930, DGL.

92. mirror-image Hamilton House: see Peter Hibbard, *Peace at the Cathay*, p. 67.

92. flagons of UB Beer: see Peter Hibbard, *Peace at the Cathay*, p. 69.

92. largest building in Asia: see Francesco Constenino, *Shanghai: from Modernism to Modernity*, p. 123.

92. Aerocrete Company: see Peter Hibbard, *Peace at the Cathay*, p. 75.

92. 22,000 new buildings: see Peter Hibbard, *Peace at the Cathay*, p. 22.

93. featured a portrait of Hardoon: see Rena Krasno, *Strangers Always*, p. 160.

93. modelled on a building: see Maisie J. Meyer's thesis, *The Sephardi Jewish Community of Shanghai*, p. 34.

93. (footnote) "rich store of Shanghai memories": see Emily Hahn, "Paradise Found," unpublished prose piece, c. 1937, p. 11, LLB.

93. clumsily planed pine desk: see Carl Crow, *Foreign Devils in the Flowery Kingdom*, p. 54.

94. confounded the world's press: see "Mixed Rituals Mark Funeral," *Los Angeles Times*, July 19, 1931, p. C13.

94. recorded several meetings: see Sassoon Journal, April 14 and 19, 1931, DGL.

94. valued at $150 million: see Maisie J. Meyer's thesis, *The Sephardi Jewish Community of Shanghai*, p. 34.

94. in the Streamline Moderne style: see Heyward Parker James's thesis, *Victor Sassoon and the Twilight of Foreign Shanghai*, p. 75.

94. French Tramway Company: see "Grosvenor House Is Opened Today," *Shanghai Evening Post and Mercury*, May 1935.

94–95. "a very large block of flats": Sir Victor letter to Princess Ottoboni, undated, c. 1935, DGL.

95. toilet buckets emptied: see Dora Sanders Carney, *Foreign Devils Had Light Eyes*, p. 21.

95. washed in a spray of atomized water: see "Opening of Cathay Hotel," *North-China Herald*, August 3, 1929, p. 174.

95. an antiquated pile: allusion to "Tug" Wilson, see Malcolm Purvis, *Tall Storeys*, p. 65.

95. Louis Suter stolen away: see "Louis Suter" obituary, *New York Times*, January 3, 1945, p. 17.

95. hard-drinking White Russian: see Peter Hibbard, *Peace at the Cathay*, p. 50.

96. shaving mirrors: see "Opening of Cathay Hotel," *North-China Herald*, August 3, 1929, p. 174.

96. New York jazzman: see "Cathay Hotel is Now Popular With Shanghai Public," *China Press*, November 22, 1929.

96. statuesque White Russians: see Brooks Atkinson, "Through China's Open Door," *New York Times*, June 18, 1933, p X1.

96. "apartements de-luxe": see Peter Hibbard, *Peace at the Cathay*, p. 60.

96. butter from Australia: see Peter Hibbard, *Peace at the Cathay*, p. 78.

96. soaring gilded bats: see "Grill Room of Cathay Hotel Opens Tuesday," see *China Press*, August 13, 1933, p. 16.

96. flamboyant Jewish stage actor: see Andrew David Field, *Shanghai's Dancing World*, p. 91.

97. in just four days: see Noël Coward, *Present Indicative*, p. 296. Upon his return, seven years later, Coward would write to a friend: "Shanghai gay as bedamned, Cathay gave me a resplendent suite filled with flowers."

98. "sugar with our coffee": see "Mr. Rogers Hears of Things He Missed in the Far East," *New York Times*, April 14, 1932, p. 23.

98. chided the foreigners: "A Slap at Modern Architects," *North-China Herald*, May 1, 1935, p. 182.

98. plans would be rejected: see Peter Hibbard, *The Bund*, p. 277.

98. five-year cycles: see Peter Harmsen, *Shanghai 1937*, p. 253.

7: Mickey Checks In

page

100. rusty steamer: see Emily Hahn, *China to Me*, p. 3. Mickey crossed the Pacific on the *Chichibu Maru*, but came to Shanghai from Nagasaki on the overnight mail steamer also operated by NYK lines. She arrived on April 10, 1935.

100. ceded to oil tank farms: description taken from contemporary photos (1935) from virtualshanghai.net, description of banks of Whangpoo from Carl Crow, *Foreign Devils in the Flowery Kingdom*, p. 202, and US Army Map of International Settlement, based on drawings from 1933 Municipal Plan.

100. the temperature . . . far from clement: weather reports taken from *North-China Herald*, April 7, 1935.

101. a weekend might suffice: see Emily Hahn, *China to Me*, p. 5.

101. the sink was too low: see Emily Hahn, *Times and Places*, p. 206.

102. so much "applesauce": see Emily Hahn, *Times and Places*, p. 207.

102. increasingly frustrated with Helen: see Emily Hahn, *China to Me*, p. 2.

103. "China is red and gold and big": see Emily Hahn, *China to Me*, p. 2.

103. address of Hung Fah Loh: see "Chester Fritzes Give Dinner For Visitors," see *China Press*, April 12, 1935.

103. upper-middle-class family: see Jack Slater, "Social Catalyst of a Golden Era," *Los Angeles Times*, June 12, 1977, p. J1.

104. wed a taciturn Englishman: "Bernadine [sic] Szold Weds in China," *Chicago Daily Tribune*, June 26, 1929.

104. had a brokerage office: see Stanley Jackson, *The Sassoons*, p. 233.

104. "soul of manganese dioxide": see Emily Hahn, *Steps of the Sun*, p. 31.

104. (footnote) "Take two tins Heinz pork": see Lady Maze, *Bon Appétit*, p. 73 XJL.

104. three trunks of jewellery: see "Front Views and Profiles," *Chicago Daily Tribune*, November 9, 1934, p. 21.

104. absurdly long cord: see Harold Acton, *Memoirs of an Aesthete*, pp. 286–8.

105. "Trebitsch gives impression": in Sassoon Journal, March 13, 1932, DGL.

105. anticipated her arrival: see "Local News Brevities", *China Press*, March 28, 1935, p. 7.

105. "her love for travel": see "Teatime Chats," *China Press*, April 14, 1935, p. 11.

105. dinner for Pearl White: see "I.A.T.G. To Sponsor Reception for Two," *China Press*, April 12, 1935.

105. worked for a summer: see Ken Cuthbertson, *Nobody Said Not to Go*, p. 121.

106. "plays were damn good": see Emily Hahn, *China to Me*, p. 6.

106. "back at the Cathay Mansions": Helen Asbury and Emily Hahn letter to Hannah Hahn, April 25, 1935, LLB.

107. "chatting with Mrs. Asbury": in *Town and Sportsman*, May 1935, p. 26, LLB.

107. known Bernardine for over three years: Sir Victor's first meeting with her recorded in Sassoon Journal, March 13, 1935, DGL.

107. "M. seduced at 23": see Sassoon Journal, May 13, 1935, DGL.

107. was being coy: letter to Ken Cuthbertson, March 8, 1995, Cuthbertson mss, LLB.

107. "liked girls with broken hearts": Emily Hahn interview by Ken Cuthbertson, November 16, 1993, Cuthbertson mss, LLB.

108. "such a nice *nature*": Emily Hahn interview by Ken Cuthbertson, November 16, 1993, Cuthbertson mss, LLB.

108. bottle of crème de menthe: see Harriet Sergeant, *Shanghai: Collision Points of Culture*, p. 132.

109. concoction like the Cobra's Kiss: see Sassoon Journal, 1937 (opening page), DGL.

109. horribly jealous of them: see Stanley Jackson, *The Sassoons*, p. 203.

109. he liked sharing his bed: see *Shanghai: Collision Points of Culture*, p. 132.

109. "monkeyglands into millionaires": see *The Journal of the E.E. Cummings Society*, October 2000, pp. 44–5.

109. (footnote) "might necessitate rejuvenation": see "Monkey Glands and Youth," *North-China Herald*, April 29, 1930, p. 179.

109. the equivalent of $350: or $1,000 in Mexican silver; see Sassoon Journal, April 17, 1935.

110. "unusually quick and witty": Emily Hahn interview by Ken Cuthbertson, November 16, 1993, Cuthbertson mss, LLB.

110. "leave their friends lamenting": see "Here and There," *North-China Herald*, June 12, 1935, p. 455.

110. "It's cheap, did you say?": see Emily Hahn, *China to Me*, p. 7.

111. "The Shanghai Summer has set in": Emily Hahn to Hannah Hahn, June 12, 1935, LLB.

111. "I am naturally a creative person": Eddie Mayer to Emily Hahn, postdated March 6, 1935, LLB.

8: On the Shanghai Beat

page

112. "COMMERCE, TRUTH, PRINTING": see Peter Hibbard, *The Bund*, p. 175.

112. American insurance magnate: see "The Shanghai Boom," *Fortune*, January 1935, p. 105.

112. a young reporter: Mickey replaced Phyllida Gowing, "a cute little grig," letter to Ken Cuthbertson, March 21, 1994, Cuthbertson mss, LLB.

112. wrote a letter: Helen Asbury and Emily Hahn, letter to Hannah Hahn, April 25, 1935, LLB.

112. half-smoked Ruby Queen cigarette: see Ralph Shaw, *Sin City*, p. 50.

113. no more populous than Muskogee: see Lu Hanchao, *Beyond the Neon Lights*, p. 2.

113. the powerful XCDN: see Bernard Wasserstein, *Secret War in Shanghai*, p. 66.

113. subsidized by the French Consul-General: see Bernard Wasserstein, *Secret War in Shanghai*, p. 66.

114. bankrolled by the Yokohama Specie Bank: see Hallett Abend, *My Life in China*, p. 39.

114. Hitler's speeches on XGRS: see Bernard Wasserstein, *Secret War in Shanghai*, p. 68.

114. First to come was Thomas Millard: see Paul French, *Through the Looking Glass*, p. 102.

114. thirty-year-old Missourian: see Edgar Snow, *Journey to the Beginning*, p. 24.

114. room in "steerage" for $60 a month: see John B. Powell, *My 25 Years in China*, p. 9.

115. "you will see all the crooks": see John B. Powell, *My 25 Years in China*, p. 7.

115. "The largest English-reading group": see John B. Powell, *My 25 Years in China*, p. 12.

115. a bitingly sarcastic essay: see "The Americans in Shanghai," *American Mercury*, August 1930, pp. 437–45.

115. wrote a panegyric: see Arthur Ransome, "The Shanghai Mind," *Manchester Guardian*, May 2, 1927.

116. saw human flesh being sold: see Edgar Snow, *Journey to the Beginning*, p. 4.

116. gave up his job: see Paul French, *Through the Looking Glass*, p. 105.

116. rotund curmudgeon: see Paul French, *Through the Looking Glass*, pp. 103–7.

116. Minnesota-born Randall Gould: see Randall Gould, *China in the Sun*, p. 7.

116. ads for the latest talkies: back issues of *Shanghai Evening Post and Mercury* from the 1930s are available, and were consulted by the author, at XJL, Shanghai.

117. hated by the nationalists: see Hallett Abend, *My Life in China*, p. 111.

117. early voices warning: see Hallett Abend, *My Life in China*, p. 200.

117. family of Utah Mormons: see Paul French, *Through the Looking Glass*, pp. 178–9.

117. famous for scooping: see Paul French, *Through the Looking Glass*, pp. 147–8.

117. purest expression: for Emily Hahn's attitude towards the *North-China Daily News*, see *China to Me*, p. 8.

117. horses . . . competed at the Racecourse: see Ralph Shaw, *Sin City*, p. 51.

117. today a guest house: based on author's 2007 stay at the former Morriss mansion, now the Ruijin Hotel.

118. bespectacled former lieutenant: see Ralph Shaw, *Sin City*, p. 52. His pen-name also earned Mickey's respect: "Sapajou" was another name for a capuchin monkey, like the one she'd had in Manhattan. He would later provide Mickey with illustrations for an unpublished children's book about primates.

118. kept up to date: see Bernard Wasserstein, *Secret War in Shanghai*, p. 63.

118. "very much indeed": see Emily Hahn, *China to Me*, p. 8.

118. "I was all right": see Emily Hahn, *China to Me*, p. 11.

119. "Shanghai is debauched!": see "Writer Finds City Disappointing," *North-China Herald*, May 1, 1935, p. 183.

119. signed "Noblesse Oblige": Letters, *North-China Herald*, May 1, 1935.

119. squib on the editorial page: "Emily Hahn's Newest Novel," *Shanghai Evening Post and Mercury*, May 13, 1935.

119. "lunch at the Cathay": see Emily Hahn, *China to Me*, p. 11.

119. "Room 536 or thereabouts": see Emily Hahn, *Steps of the Sun*, p. 13.
120. extricating themselves from mudbanks: Sir Victor letter to Princess Ottoboni, undated, c. 1935, DGL.
120. snapshots from . . . 1935: see Sassoon Journal, May 4, 1935.
121. first time that native Shanghainese: see Emily Hahn, *China to Me*, p. 3.
121. key figure in bridging the worlds: see Lu Hanchao, *Beyond the Neon Lights*, p. 57.
121. hardly social equals: see Carl Crow, *Foreign Devils in the Flowery Kingdom*, p. 38.
121. purported Chinese pronunciation: see Carl Crow, *Foreign Devils in the Flowery Kingdom*, p. 30.
121. "contact vernacular": see Nessa Wolfson, ed., *Language of Inequality*, p. 256.
121. *Kumshaw* meant "tip": examples taken from Carl Crow, *Foreign Devils in the Flowery Kingdom*, p. xiii.
122. 1935 newsletter . . . Cathay Hotel: reprinted in Peter Hibbard, *Peace at the Cathay*, p. 183.
122. Compradors acquired fortunes: see Lu Hanchao, *Beyond the Neon Lights*, p. 57.
122. instrumental in creating a business class: see Edward Denison, *Building Shanghai*, p. 81.
123. "We were all much too physical": see Harold Acton, *Memoirs of an Aesthete*, p. 288.
123. partial inspiration for the wicked dandy: see Paula Byrne, *Mad World: Evelyn Waugh and the Secrets of Brideshead*, p. 303.

9: Shanghai, April 12, 1935

page
127. when she walked in: reconstruction of Zau Sinmay's first meeting with Emily Hahn based on *Steps of the Sun*, pp. 48–9; Emily Hahn, *Mr. Pan*, p. 36. The date of their first meeting is almost certainly a lecture on D.H. Lawrence organized by the International Arts Theatre, recorded in Sassoon Journal, April 12, 1935.
127. "kidding the ocean people": see Emily Hahn, *Mr. Pan*, p. 8.
128. "Come to me, my Sinmay!": see Jonathan Hutt, "Monstre Sacré," *China Heritage Quarterly*, p. 4.
128. depicted standing beside a man: the so-called Sappho portrait in the Museo Archeologico Nazionale is actually a "Portrait of a Young

Woman," depicted with a stylus to show that she is literate, from Pompeii. In the same room can be found the portrait of the baker Terentius Neo, also from Pompeii, and his wife, who is portrayed in a manner similar to the so-called Sappho. From author's visit to Museo Archeologico Nazionale, Naples, June 19, 2015.

10: Cathay and the Muse

page

129. "His body was slight": see Emily Hahn, *Steps of the Sun*, p. 8.

129. Sinmay's "milk name": see Jonathan Hutt, "Monstre Sacré," *China Heritage Quarterly*, p. 9.

129. affectionate but temporary: on naming in Chinese culture, see Han Suyin's *A Mortal Flower*, p. 50.

130. spat sunflower seeds onto the ground: see Emily Hahn, *Steps of the Sun*, p. 48.

130. the hot night of the Chinese city: the episode is described in Emily Hahn's "The Big Smoke," the *New Yorker*, February 15, 1969, p. 35.

130. discovery of gold: see Jennifer 8. Lee, *The Fortune Cookie Chronicles*, p. 51.

130. the "pig trade": see Stella Dong, *Shanghai: The Rise and Fall of a Decadent City*, p. 62.

130. horrifically crowded ships to Peru: see Odd Arne Westad, *Restless Empire*, p. 27.

130. came from the hinterland of Canton: see Jonathan Spence, *The Search for Modern China*, p. 211.

131. "Celestials": see Jennifer 8. Lee, *The Fortune Cookie Chronicles*, p. 52.

131. the Chinese Exclusion Act: see Jonathan Spence, *The Search for Modern China*, pp. 237–8.

131. a "Head Tax" of up to $500: see Arlene Chan, *Righting Canada's Wrong*, p. 7.

131. after the pastoral nomads: see J.A.G. Roberts, *A History of China*, p. 60.

131. Cathay was just another name: see Nicolas Trigault, *China in the Sixteenth Century*, p. 7.

131. poem in praise of the Qianlong: see Jonathan Spence, *The Search for Modern China*, pp. 133–4.

131. The tea the Sons of Liberty: see Carl Crow, *Foreign Devils in the Flowery Kingdom*, p. 14.

131. famous *mei foo* lamps: see Carl Crow, *Foreign Devils in the Flowery Kingdom*, p. 42.

132. learned to love chop suey: see Jennifer 8. Lee, *The Fortune Cookie Chronicles*, p. 49.

132. (footnote) edited the lavishly illustrated *Asia*: see Edgar Snow, *Journey to the Beginning*, p. 133.

133. never set foot in China: the first time Malraux came to Shanghai was in 1931, as part of a worldwide tour. See Oliver Todd, *Malraux: A Life*, p. 200.

133. friend of Sir Victor's: see Sassoon Journal. Sir Victor records first seeing Mei Lan-fang on December 23, 1932.

133. Westerners were held hostage: see John B. Powell, *My 25 Years in China*, p. 92.

133. prototype for Ming the Merciless: for a comprehensive discussion of the theme, see Christopher Frayling, *The Yellow Peril: Dr Fu Manchu and the Rise of Chinaphobia*.

133. congenial fictional antithesis: see Huang Yuante, *Charlie Chan: The Unknown Story*.

134. "Cold omelette, like fish out of sea": from author's viewing of *Charlie Chan in Shanghai*.

134. mocked the stilted dialogue: in "The China Boom," *T'ien Hsia Quarterly*, October 1935, p. 198.

134. deemed Oland's accent: Emily Hahn, letter to Hannah Hahn, May 3, 1936.

134. "always wanted to be an opium addict": see "The Big Smoke", the *New Yorker*, February 15, 1969, p. 35.

135. reclined on flat couches: the account is taken from Emily Hahn, "The Big Smoke," the *New Yorker*, February 15, 1969, p. 36.

135. long tube of polished bamboo: additional details of the smoking of opium come from Emily Hahn's unpublished manuscript, "The Price of Poppies," LLB.

136. product of a strategic alliance: Zau Sinmay's biography is taken from Jonathan Hutt, "Monstre Sacré," *China Heritage Quarterly*, Zau Sinmay's "My Triangle of Grandfathers" (translated by Emily Hahn), Shao Xiaohong, *Wo de ba ba Shao Xunmei* (My Father Sinmay Zau) and Sheng Peiyu, *Sheng shi jia zu, Shao Xunmei yu wo* (translation commissioned by author).

137. "the first fortune-teller in China": see Zau Sinmay's "My Triangle of Grandfathers," p. 3.

137. "small white elephant": see Jonathan Hutt, "Monstre Sacré," *China Heritage Quarterly*, p. 8.

137. popular comic strip: see John A. Lent, ed., *Illustrating Asia*, p. 114.
138. voracious "mosquito press": see Randall Gould, *China in the Sun*, p. 316.
138. *femme fatale* named Prudence: see Emily Hahn, *Mr. Pan*, p. 156.
138. surreptitious snapshot: see Shao Xiaohong, *Wo de ba ba Shao Xunmei* (My Father Sinmay Zau), p. 21.
138. knitted him a white sweater: see Sheng Peiyu, *Sheng shi jia zu, Shao Xunmei yu wo*, p. 54.
139. thought he was a circus performer: see Emily Hahn, *Mr. Pan*, p. 87.
139. fringe of silky white hair: Robert I. Crine, "News of the Profession," (Moule obituary), *Journal of Asian Studies*, November 1957, p. 173.
139. introduced Sinmay to a professor: the professor was J.C. Edmonds; see Jonathan Hutt, "Monstre Sacré," *China Heritage Quarterly*, p. 5.
139. farmer's daughter named Lucy: see Emily Hahn, *Mr. Pan*, p. 88.
139. slouch hats and old clothes: see Emily Hahn, *Steps of the Sun*, p. 72.
140. photo from the summer of 1925: album shown to the author by daughter Shao Yang, Shanghai, March 14, 2014.
140. became "sworn brothers": see Sheng Peiyu, *Sheng shi jia zu, Shao Xunmei yu wo*, p. 67.
140. "The women liked me *so* much": see Emily Hahn, *Mr. Pan*, p. 88.
140. properties had burned down: see Sheng Peiyu, *Sheng shi jia zu, Shao Xunmei yu wo*, p. 70.
140. in a short memoir: see Zau Sinmay, "My Triangle of Grandfathers," p. 14, LLB.
141. picked up a copy of . . . Sphinx: see Leo Ou-fan Lee, *Shanghai Modern*, p. 247.
141. "From a flower bed": the translations are taken, with the author's permission, from Leo Ou-fan Lee, *Shanghai Modern*, pp. 250–3.
142. "China has a new poet": attributed to Xu Zhimo; quoted in Jonathan Hutt, "Monstre Sacré," *China Heritage Quarterly*, p. 2.
142. another of his literary idols: see Leo Ou-fan Lee, *Shanghai Modern*, p. 248.
142. an impeccable *duilian* poem: see Lee Leo Ou-fan, *Shanghai Modern*, p. 251.
142. every character is counterweighted: see Hubert Delahaye, "Les phrases parallèles et convergentes," *Extrême-Orient Extrême Occident* No. 11, 1989.
142. hiring as editor Lin Yu-tang: see Emily Hahn, *China to Me*, p. 16.
143. leading venue for the creators of *manhua*: see Chang-tai Hung, *War and Popular Culture*, pp. 28–39.

143. father–son team of Francophiles: namely Zeng Pu and Zeng Xubai, see Zhang Yinde, "Le Cas de Shao Xunmei," p. 620.

143. caricaturist Miguel Covarrubias: see "Chinese Poet Gives Praise to Noted Mexican Artist," *China Press*, October 25, 1933.

143. welcomed Rabindranath Tagore: see Sheng Peiyu, *Sheng shi jia zu, Shao Xunmei yu wo*, p. 108.

143. organizing a feast: account of Shaw's visit taken from "Students 'Welcome' Shaw" in *North-China Herald*, February 22, 1933, p. 294.

144. Lu Xun looked on in disgust: see Jonathan Hutt, "Monstre Sacré," *China Heritage Quarterly*, June 2010, p. 19.

144. Shaw's visit in 1933: see letter from Zau Sinmay to Mrs. Chester Fritz dated April 4, 1933, in Bernardine Szold-Fritz correspondence, BNL.

144. passionate tone of her letters: see Emily Hahn letter to Helen Asbury, June 23, 1936, LLB.

144. "so many stunned Romeos": Zau Sinmay to Bernardine, undated, BNL.

11: The Fantastic Mr. Pan

page

145. autumn of 1935: the first Mr. Pan story, "Cathay and the Muse," appeared in the March 14, 1936 issue of the *New Yorker*, pp. 80–1.

145. "pale and wraithlike": see Emily Hahn, *Mr. Pan*, p. 9.

146. once his jockey: see Emily Hahn, *Mr. Pan*, p. 51.

146. the Traitor Brother: see Emily Hahn, *Mr. Pan*, p. 128.

146. the patriarch claims: see Emily Hahn, *Mr. Pan*, p. 23.

146. crossed a street in Shanghai: see Emily Hahn, *Mr. Pan*, p. 36.

147. "refuse to take this house": see Emily Hahn, "Wind and Water," unpublished manuscript, LLB.

148. (footnote) "Here lies Mrs. Buck": see Ken Cuthbertson, *Nobody Said Not to Go*, p. 140.

148. more than 171,000 copies per issue: see Ben Yagoda, *About Town*, p. 96.

149. "when I first saw you": see Emily Hahn, *Steps of the Sun*, pp. 50–1.

149. "statuette of glazed porcelain": see Emily Hahn, *Steps of the Sun*, pp. 42–3.

149. (footnote) "had a big bottom": see Sheng Peiyu, *Sheng shi jia zu, Shao Xunmei yu wo*, p. 182.

150. "collecting the Chinese language": Emily Hahn letter to Helen Asbury, December 27, 1935, LLB.

150. in a letter to Helen: Emily Hahn signs her name in Chinese in letter to Helen Asbury, July 24, 1935, LLB.

151. "fresh and wonderful that way": see Emily Hahn, *China to Me*, p. 10.

151. over two dozen times: see Sassoon Journal, 1935, DGL.

151. "ride the smallest horses": Emily Hahn letter to Hannah Hahn, February 20, 1936, LLB.

152. "her sex life to the town": undated Bernardine Szold-Fritz letter headed "Dear Sir V." in Bernardine correspondence, BNL.

152. "it seems a little strange": see Sir Victor letter to "My Dear Bernadine," April 30, 1936, Bernardine correspondence, BNL.

152. night on his houseboat: see Sassoon Journal, April 25–6, 1936, DGL.

152. "His name is Herr *Gamaling*!": see Ken Cuthbertson, *Nobody Said Not to Go*, p. 152.

153. "once a week in the Tower": Emily Hahn letter to Helen Asbury, November 27, 1935, LLB.

153. "almost wet my pants": Emily Hahn letter to Helen Asbury, November 27, 1935, LLB.

153. "I walked out in the middle": the woman in question was Enid Saunders Candlin; see Harriet Sergeant, *Shanghai: Collision Point of Cultures*, p. 292.

154. "weak attempt to stage the fruity old comedy": "Lysistrata," *North-China Herald*, December 25, 1935, p. 520.

154. "very much in love with me": Emily Hahn letter to Helen Asbury, December 27, 1935, LLB.

154. "wasting a lot of time": "Canons of Taste," Letter to the Editor, *North-China Herald*, December 25, 1935, p. 520.

154. "something going on in North China": Emily Hahn letter to Helen Asbury, November 30, 1935, LLB.

154. "small bomb under Al Capone": Emily Hahn letter to Helen Asbury, December 27, 1935, LLB.

155. "Japanese across the creek": see Emily Hahn, *China to Me*, p. 12.

12: Cosmopolis-on-the-Whangpoo

page

156. a five-storey commercial complex: description of Shanghai's Jiangxi Middle Road based on author's visit, March 13, 2014.

157. the Shanghai city directory: Shanghai City Directory 1936, p. 544, XJL.

157. lacquered "pheasant" rickshaws: see Lu Hanchao, *Beyond the Neon Lights*, p. 85.

158. piggyback passengers to their door: see Lu Hanchao, *Beyond the Neon Lights*, p. 85.

158. fast and manoeuvrable: see Lu Hanchao, *Beyond the Neon Lights*, p. 69.

158. pants pulled above the knees: see Dora Sanders Carney, *Foreign Devils Had Light Eyes*, p. 144.

158. mixed with heroin and arsenic: see Carroll Alcott, *My War with Japan*, p. 222.

158. "eating foreign ham": see Lu Hanchao, *Beyond the Neon Lights*, p. 311.

159. "plowing the pavement": see Lu Hanchao, *Beyond the Neon Lights*, p. 76.

159. "Not As Hard As It Looks": see *North-China Herald*, August 18, 1937, p. 281.

159. "carried it for a hundred paces": see Lu Hanchao, *Beyond the Neon Lights*, p. 95.

159. feed 340,000 mouths: all figures from Lu Hanchao, *Beyond the Neon Lights*, p. 73.

159. refusing on principle: see Edgar Snow, *Journey to the Beginning*, p. 75.

160. "Why balk at a ricksha": see Emily Hahn, *China to Me*, p. 113.

160. main alleys . . . were thirteen feet wide: see Lu Hanchao, *Beyond the Neon Lights*, p. 152.

161. known as a *kumen*: see Lu Hanchao, *Beyond the Neon Lights*, p. 143.

161. Municipal Council surveyors: see Lu Hanchao, *Beyond the Neon Lights*, pp. 156-7.

162. a large *shikumen* complex the Zau family owned: see Jonathan Hutt, "Monstre Sacré," *China Heritage Quarterly*, p. 16.

162. shacks known as *gundilong*: see Lu Hanchao, *Beyond the Neon Lights*, p. 119.

163. "legs developing chromium-holes": see W.H. Auden and Christopher Isherwood, *Journey to a War*, p. 236.

163. the world's lowest industrial wages: see Heyward Parker James's thesis, *Victor Sassoon and the Twilight of Foreign Shanghai*, p. 27.

163. Sassoon reputation for generous paternalism: see Stanley Jackson, *The Sassoons*, p. 205.

163. "I know where *I* should start": see W.H. Auden and Christopher

Isherwood, *Journey to a War*, p. 243. In the years that followed, Alley set up Indusco, a network of industrial cooperatives to encourage a homegrown, and Chinese-managed, economic revival and counter the spread of cheap Japanese-manufactured goods during the Second World War.

164. (footnote) replaced by a luxury mall: see "Chairman Mao's old home to reopen inside luxury mall," *Telegraph*, December 26, 2013.

164. delivering clothes to customers: see Philip Short, *Mao: A Life*, p. 114.

164. Working at Peking University: see Jonathan Spence, *Mao Zedong: A Life*, p. 33.

164. appeared only that spring: see Philip Short, *Mao: A Life*, p. 114.

165. founded the Chinese Communist Party: see Jonathan Spence, *Mao Zedong: A Life*, p. 56.

165. delegates fled to Hangchow: see Lynn Pan, *Gangsters in Paradise*, p. 41.

165. "like a lemon": see Lynn Pan, *Gangsters in Paradise*, p. 41.

165. "May Thirtieth Movement": see Stella Dong, *Shanghai: The Rise and Fall of a Decadent City*, pp. 166–8.

166. "men from a Shanghai *tingzijian*": see Lu Hanchao, *Beyond the Neon Lights*, p. 61.

166. "the barrel of a gun": see Jonathan Spence, *Mao Zedong: A Life*, p. 75.

166. slender, dark-eyed movie star: see Stella Dong, *Shanghai: The Rise and Fall of a Decadent City*, p. 147.

166. discovered a mailbox: see Bernard Wasserstein, *Secret War in Shanghai*, p. 84.

166. handing over alleged "subversives": see Bernard Wasserstein, *Secret War in Shanghai*, p. 84.

166. slogging through a . . . swamp: see Jonathan Spence, *Mao Zedong: A Life*, p. 86.

167. "We are Chinese": see Philip Short, *Mao: A Life*, pp. 337–9.

167. bandits and rural brigands: see Emily Hahn, *China to Me*, p. 8.

168. cost only $6: see Edgar Snow, *Journey to the Beginning*, p. 18.

168. afford to pay room boys: see Ralph Shaw, *Sin City*, p. 24.

168. "I'm in the middle of China!": Emily Hahn letter to Helen Hahn, February 11, 1936, LLB.

168. "giddy structure rested on rice": see Emily Hahn, *China to Me*, p. 12.

13: *Shanghai, November 3, 1936*

173. the U.B. brewery on Gordon Road: for a discussion of Sir Victor Sassoon's various businesses, see Stanley Jackson, *The Sassoons*, p. 234; they are also listed in the *Comacrib Industrial & Commercial Manual, 1935*, pp. 362–3, consulted in XJL.

173. the licence plate "EVE 1": see Stanley Jackson, *The Sassoons*, p. 250.

174. Wing On was beyond his grasp: see Edward Denison, *Building Shanghai*, p. 92.

174. nibbled dried duck gizzards: see Maurine Karns, *Shanghai: High Lights, Low Lights, Tael Lights*, p. 17.

174. "which rather surprised me": Sir Victor letter to Princess Ottoboni, May 1, 1936, DGL.

175. Mickey Hahn had met him: see Sassoon Journal, March 22, 1936, DGL.

175. a press conference in the Cathay Suite: see "Chaplin Likes China," *China Press*, March 10, 1936, p. 1.

175. "though not young is childish": see Sassoon Journal, April 4, 1936, DGL.

175. written 8,000 words: see "Chaplin Writes Scenario with Orient Locale," *China Press*, May 13, 1936, p. 1.

175. table . . . awash with champagne: see photos in Sassoon Journal, May 24, 1936, DGL.

176. circumnavigating the face of the globe: chronicled in Jean Cocteau, *Mon premier voyage*.

176. "It seems you're writing": Cocteau's reaction to the meeting, recorded in *Mon premier voyage*, is worth adding here: "If I ended up writing about Victor Sassoon, it certainly wouldn't be anything amusing – rather it would be thrilling, because this significant character, who seems to be motivated by something like vengeance, who drives China like it was a Rolls-Royce, whose cane (he limps thanks to a war wound) reveals treasures and whose eye undertakes calculations behind an icy monocle, is worth far more than a few simple notes in a newspaper column." (Author's translation.)

176. with stops in Reno: see Sassoon Journal, June 4, 1936, DGL.

176. Princess Ottoboni's villa: see Sassoon Journal, July 29, 1936, DGL.

176. yacht he'd had built in Norway: see "Sassoon's Eve Wins 100-Mile Yacht Event," *China Press*, August 4, 1936, p. 6.

177. beaten out the Cathay . . . by fully seventy-two feet: see Lenore Hietkamp, "The Park Hotel in Shanghai," in Jason C. Kuo, *Visual Culture in Shanghai*, p. 300.

177. chosen to stay at the Park: see "Anna May Wong Arrives in Port Today," *China Press*, February 11, 1936, p. 9.

177. had not been easy: Anna May Wong's experiences in China are recounted in Graham Hodges's *Anna May Wong*, pp. 146–50.

177. barred from . . . Columbia Country Club: see Emily Hahn, *China to Me*, p. 38.

178. white-washed walls: see "Ciro's Night Club Opens Next Month," *China Press*, October 27, 1936, p. 9. The original Ciro's was opened in Monte Carlo in 1897 by an Italian-born Egyptian. An English syndicate bought the brand in 1911, and the distinctive Ciro's logo became associated with restaurants and nightclubs in Paris, London, Berlin, Biarritz, and, after 1940, a famous branch on Los Angeles's Sunset Strip.

178. five Chinese dollars: see ad in *China Press*, November 1, 1936, p. 3.

178. incident at the Paramount Ballroom: recounted in Andrew David Field's *Shanghai's Dancing World*, p. 104.

179. rather flirtatious: see Sassoon Journal, November 5, 1936, DGL.

179. elderly *marchese* to shop: the Marchese Visconti-Vanosta, Emily Hahn letter to Helen Asbury, December 27, 1935.

180. "where he met Sinmay": Emily Hahn letter to Hannah Hahn, September 16, 1936.

180. ignoring the screams: see John Baxter, *Von Sternberg*, p. 203.

180. checking into the Cathay Hotel: see "Von Sternberg Tells Interviewer Hollywood No Place, Only an Idea," *China Press*, September 12, 1936, p. 9.

180. "a pregnant girl of six!": see Stella Dong, *Shanghai: The Rise and Fall of a Decadent City*, p. 206.

180. "jumping from the roof": see Josef von Sternberg, *Fun in a Chinese Laundry*, p. 82. Thanks to such excursions, von Sternberg's next Chinese-themed film would be a far more precise reflection of the city's actual geography. In 1941's *The Shanghai Gesture*, Gene Tierney's character falls for a gigolo who works in an International Settlement cabaret run by a Madame – with the memorable name "Mother" Gin Sling – forced to move her business across Soochow Creek to Chapei.

181. grateful for an introduction: Emily Hahn to Helen Asbury, March 6, 1936, LLB.

181. came to China in the spring of 1936: see "Juan Arrives in Shanghai," *North-China Herald*, February 19, 1936, p. 311.

181. "full of champagne": Emily Hahn letter to Hannah Hahn, February 20, 1936, LLB.

182. "simply called off classes": Emily Hahn to Helen Asbury, June 23, 1936, LLB.

182. "fine poet in everything": Harold Acton letter to Bernardine Szold-Fritz, June 20, 1936, BNL.

182. "The Great Bernardine War": see Emily Hahn to Helen Asbury, March 11, 1936, LLB.

182. by a Turkish prize-fighter: see Vicki Baum, *It Was All Quite Different*, p. 281.

183. "a first-rate second-rate writer": see Vicki Baum, *It Was All Quite Different*, p. 288.

183. a suite at the Cathay Hotel: see "Vicki Baum Returns to Shanghai from North China Visit," *China Press*, May 21, 1936, p. 9.

183. "Vicki Baum came back": Emily Hahn to Helen Asbury, May 15, 1936, LLB.

184. "the great Chinese novel": see "Vicki Baum to Pen No 'Grand Hotel' of City", *China Press*, May 6, 1936, p. 9.

184. "it gets incredibly dull": Emily Hahn to Helen Asbury, April 20, 1936, LLB.

184. "outlook is brighter too": Emily Hahn to Helen Asbury, August 12, 1936, LLB.

184. "something like an idiot": Emily Hahn to Helen Asbury, December 27, 1935, LLB.

185. "should stay away from writers": see Emily Hahn, *China to Me*, p. 65.

186. "never speaks of Mussolini": Emily Hahn to Helen Asbury, May 15, 1936, LLB.

186. raised a toast to Wallis Simpson: Emily Hahn to Helen Asbury, December 5, 1936, LLB.

186. "Esquimeaux and Negroes": Emily Hahn letter to Helen Asbury, November 27, 1935, LLB.

186. "always thought of marrying": Emily Hahn letter to Helen Asbury, August 12, 1936, LLB. The mystery about the identity of Sir Victor's "Rosebud" will probably never be solved. However, there are clues in his journals, including records of phone calls and repeated meetings with a woman named Peg, who lived in London. During his lifetime, a journalist in Nassau printed the rumour that he had been in love with a beautiful woman named "Eve", who died before they could marry.

187. *Twenty-five Poems*: see Jonathan Hutt, "Monstre Sacré," *China Heritage Quarterly*, June 2010, p. 15.

188. educated abroad: see Pankaj Mishra, *From the Ruins of Empire*, pp. 167–8.
188. "pale face and long gown": see Emily Hahn, *China to Me*, p. 12.
188. visited a British friend at the Cathay Hotel: see Lu Hanchao, *Beyond the Neon Lights*, p. 348.
188. bullies those weaker than him: see Edgar Snow, *Journey to the Beginning*, p. 132.
188. "their bodies to bedbugs": see Lu Hanchao, *Beyond the Neon Lights*, p. 253.
189. Ba Jin, Yu Dafu, and Mao Dun: see Lu Hanchao, *Beyond the Neon Lights*, p. 60.
189. League of Left-Wing Writers: see David E. Pollard, *The True Story of Lu Xun*, p. 135.
189. Crescent Moon Society: see Kai-yu Hsu, *Twentieth-Century Chinese Poetry*, p. xx.
189. executed Shanghai's leading leftist authors: see Pan Ling, *In Search of Old Shanghai*, p. 113.
189. "his ivory-topped cane": quoted in Jonathan Hutt, "Monstre Sacré," *China Heritage Quarterly*, June 2010, p. 8.
189. his renown grew: see Yu Hua's discussion of Lu Xun's influence in *China in Ten Words*, pp. 95–112.
190. "You are disappointed?": see Emily Hahn, *Steps of the Sun*, p. 62.
190. doomed most of his enterprises: see Jonathan Hutt, "Monstre Sacré," *China Heritage Quarterly*, June 2010, p. 18.
190. "Shanghai was a bilingual city": see Emily Hahn, *China to Me*, p. 27.
191. "the whole apple cart": Emily Hahn to Helen Asbury, December 14, 1936, LLB.
191. "man in a cage with a gorilla": Emily Hahn to Helen Asbury, December 22, 1936, LLB.

14: The Rise of the Dwarf Bandits

page
193. tea sipped from the finest porcelain: see Emily Hahn, *Times and Places*, p. 213.
193. "behind the delicate landscape": see Emily Hahn, *China to Me*, p. 2.
194. "the more scared you are": Emily Hahn to Hannah Hahn, October 18, 1936, LLB.
194. "official policy of *sakoku*": see Michael S. Laver, *The Sakoku Edicts and the Politics of Tokugawa Hegemony*, p. 14.

194. crucified Franciscan and Jesuit missionaries: see H. Paul Varley, *Japanese Culture*, p. 166.

194. artificial island of Dejima: see Andrew Gordon, *A Modern History of Japan*, p. 17.

195. "extend from sea to sea": see Pankaj Mishra, *From the Ruins of Empire*, p. 130.

195. teenage Emperor Meiji to the throne: see Andrew Gordon, *A Modern History of Japan*, pp. 58–9.

195. a landless military nobility: see Pankaj Mishra, *From the Ruins of Empire*, p. 132.

195. organized on American lines: see Martin Jacques, *When China Rules the World*, p. 53.

196. Japan in 1894 invaded Korea: see Jonathan Spence, *The Search for Modern China*, pp. 222–3.

196. waters of the Yalu River: see Stella Dong, *Shanghai: The Rise and Fall of a Decadent City*, p. 71.

196. ceded the island of Formosa: see Jonathan Spence, *The Search for Modern China*, p. 223.

196. narrow waters of Tsushima Strait: see Andrew Gordon, *A Modern History of Japan*, p. 17.

197. "a slap in the face": see Pankaj Mishra, *From the Ruins of Empire*, p. 4.

197. imports . . . from the Middle Kingdom: see Martin Jacques, *When China Rules the World*, p. 48.

197. around the port of Tsingtao: see Pankaj Mishra, *From the Ruins of Empire*, p. 179. Shantung's main harbour was the Treaty Port of Tsingtao, now Qingdao, where the Anglo-German Brewery Co., makers of China's signature pilsner, Tsingtao, became the property of the Dai-Nippon Brewery.

197. watermarked with battleships: see Pankaj Mishra, *From the Ruins of Empire*, p. 179.

198. "Asia as her ultimate goal": see Hallett Abend, *My Life in China*, p. 225.

198. "I had never heard of it": see Emily Hahn, *China to Me*, p. 4.

199. there were 30,000: see Harriet Sergeant, *Shanghai: Collision Point of Cultures*, p. 181.

199. which promoted cleanliness: see Randall Gould, "A Foreigner Looks at the New Life Movement," *T'ien Hsia*, pp. 341–7.

200. resting on a sword hilt: see Han Suyin, *A Mortal Flower*, p. 47.

200. The Generalissimo: from the Italian word for "utmost general," the term "generalissimo" has been applied to, among other

authoritarians, Joseph Stalin, Spain's Francisco Franco, and North Korea's Kim Il-sung.

200. participant in the Taiping: see Carl Crow, *Foreign Devils in the Flowery Kingdom*, p. 155.

200. Manchu assassins in pursuit: see Stella Dong, *Shanghai: The Rise and Fall of a Decadent City*, p. 85.

200. read a headline: see Emily Hahn, *The Soong Sisters*, p. 78.

200. meeting hall in Hankow: see Jonathan Spence, *Mao Zedong: A Life*, p. 12.

200. sixteen years of wandering: see Emily Hahn, *The Soong Sisters*, p. 79.

201. general named Yuan Shi-kai: see Stella Dong, *Shanghai: The Rise and Fall of a Decadent City*, p. 89.

201. secret societies as the Triads: see Jonathan Spence, *The Search for Modern China*, pp. 169.

201. the Chinese coast as Ma Kun: see Sara Jo Ben Zvi, "The Extraordinary Adventures of Two-Gun Cohen," *Asian Jewish Life*, No. 12, June 2010, p. 2.

201. Sir Victor Sassoon first met him: see Sassoon Journal, December 7, 1934, DGL.

201. "might very easily have invented him": see "Dr. Sun's No. 1 Boy," *New York Times*, June 27, 1954, BR10.

201. "Fat Moisha": see Daniel Levy, *Two-Gun Cohen*.

202. "told him to beat it": see Charles Drage, *Two-Gun Cohen*, p. 26.

203. the nickname "Two-Gun": see Daniel Levy, *Two-Gun Cohen*.

203. "the Blarney Stone": see Randall Gould, *China in the Sun*, p. 354.

203. "Cohen was a faithful watchdog": see John B. Powell, *My 25 Years in China*, p. 33.

204. set up the Whampoa Military Academy: see Jay Taylor, *The Generalissimo*, pp. 45–7.

204. bodyguard for his son and his widow: see Daniel Levy, *Two-Gun Cohen*.

204. "Baby-Faced Wang": see Lynn Pan, *Gangsters in Paradise*, pp. 64–5.

204. expected to forage: see Dora Sanders Carney, *Foreign Devils Had Light Eyes*, p. 178.

204. Chiang became leader: see Jay Taylor, *The Generalissimo*, p. 3.

204. tea-producing hamlet: see Jay Taylor, *The Generalissimo*, p. 10.

204. broker on the Chartered Stock: see Lynn Pan, *Gangsters in Paradise*, p. 42.

204. anarchist art dealer: see Stella Dong, *Shanghai: The Rise and Fall of a Decadent City*, p. 92.

205. whom he called "Peanut": see Jay Taylor, *The Generalissimo*, pp. 196–8.

205. planting maple trees: see Han Suyin, *A Mortal Flower*, p. 304.

205. resemblance to the German Gestapo: see Edgar Snow, *Journey to the Beginning*, p. 123.

205. "prevention of change": see Edgar Snow, *Journey to the Beginning*, p. 137.

206. "don't gossip on idle subjects": see Randall Gould, "A Foreigner Looks at the New Life Movement," *T'ien Hsia*, pp. 341–7.

206. "a towel round their shoulders": see Han Suyin, *A Mortal Flower*, p. 297.

206. for personal honesty: see Jay Taylor, *The Generalissimo*, p. 21.

207. "ham actor in melodrama": see Eric Linklater, *Juan in China*, p. 40.

207. "what he considers the limit": Emily Hahn to Helen Asbury, November 30, 1935, LLB.

207. Comintern's "Third Period": see Morris Dickstein, *Dancing in the Dark*, p. 37.

208. introducing onerous new taxes: see Han Suyin, *A Mortal Flower*, p. 99. For example, until 1949, peasants in the province of Kansu were required to pay forty-four separate taxes, including the "soldier reward tax," the "kindling wood tax," the "kettle tax," and the "extraordinary tax." In some provinces, corrupt officials found pretexts to extract taxes ninety-nine years in advance.

208. under the supreme command: see Edgar Snow, *Journey to the Beginning*, p. 226.

208. easily-manipulated puppet: see Jay Taylor, *The Generalissimo*, pp. 84–5.

208. sent him to Europe to be cured: see Emily Hahn, *The Soong Sisters*, p. 180.

209. shivering in a cave: see Hallett Abend, *My Life in China*, p. 233.

209. the united front . . . had been achieved: for his effrontery, Chiang Kai-shek's kidnapper was placed under house arrest in Nanking. Though he would only be freed – thirty-eight years later, and in Taipei – on the Generalissimo's death, the "Young Marshal" lived to be a very old man, dying peacefully in Honolulu at the age of one hundred.

209. On Christmas Day: see Stella Dong, *Shanghai: The Rise and Fall of a Decadent City*, p. 90.

209. "we laughed shrilly": see Emily Hahn, *China to Me*, p. 45.

15: Sweetie Pie Goes to Nanking

210. Nobody said not to go: the line is taken from the opening of Emily Hahn's "Round Trip To Nanking," the *New Yorker*, September 18, 1937, p. 76.

210. occasionally dozed off in class: see Ken Cuthbertson, *Nobody Said Not to Go*, p. 154.

211. shared house off Yuyuen Road: Emily Hahn to Helen Asbury, March 27, 1937, LLB.

211. "I think it's safe": Emily Hahn to Hannah Hahn, March 6, 1937, LLB.

211. three Chinese servants: Emily Hahn to Helen Asbury, June 4, 1937, LLB.

212. "Avoid addicts": see Ken Cuthbertson, *Nobody Said Not to Go*, p. 156.

212. "What a hell you have put me in!": Zau Sinmay letter to Emily Hahn, May 26, 1937, LLB.

212. "hoping for the best": Zau Sinmay letter to Bernardine Szold-Fritz, undated, BNL.

213. suggested she call it *Whirlpool*: Emily Hahn to Helen Asbury, November 12, 1937, LLB.

213. "marbles with quicksilver": Emily Hahn to Helen Asbury, April 1, 1937, LLB.

213. on the Bund for ten cents: see Emily Hahn, "Round Trip To Nanking," the *New Yorker*, September 18, 1937, p. 76.

213. British naval officer: see Ken Cuthbertson, *Nobody Said Not to Go*, p. 156.

213. German named Wally: see Emily Hahn, "Round Trip To Nanking," the *New Yorker*, September 18, 1937, p. 82.

214. "killed in Shanghai that day": see Emily Hahn, "Round Trip To Nanking," the *New Yorker*, September 18, 1937, p. 86.

16: Shanghai, August 14, 1937

217. "cloudy, fine, breezy": *China Press*, August 14, 1937, p. 1.

217. tossed around like leaves: see Rhodes Farmer, *Shanghai Harvest*, p. 39.

218. 3,000 miles away: see Sassoon Journal, month of August 1937, DGL.

218. invest in a molybdenum deposit: see Stanley Jackson, *The Sassoons*, p. 232.

219. "teach China a lesson": see Peter Harmsen, *Shanghai 1937*, p. 23.

219. via the ticker-tape machine: see Stanley Jackson, *The Sassoons*, p. 248.

219. a bullet-ridden sedan: see Peter Harmsen, *Shanghai 1937*, p. 13.

219. There were rumours: see Peter Harmsen, *Shanghai 1937*, p. 37.

219. was a guest: "Mrs. Theodore Roosevelt Jr. Describes Shanghai Events," *New York Times*, August 21, 1937, p. 1.

220. a race weekend in Bombay: see Stanley Jackson, *The Sassoons*, p. 248.

220. unarmed Hawk 75 monoplane: see Claire Chennault, *The Ways of a Fighter*, p. 58.

221. only ninety-one were fit for combat: see Claire Chennault, *The Ways of a Fighter*, p. 38.

221. "always be a princess to me": see Claire Chennault, *The Ways of a Fighter*, p. 35.

221. their target the *Cumberland*: see Claire Chennault, *The Ways of a Fighter*, p. 46.

222. twenty minutes past four: the account of Bloody Saturday, as seen from the Cathay rooftop, is taken from Rhodes Farmer, *Shanghai Harvest*, pp. 44–9.

224. hurled him to the floor: see Stanley Jackson, *The Sassoons*, p. 248.

224. had been blown clean off: Louis Suter's experience of Bloody Saturday recounted in Emily Hahn's unpublished short prose piece, "Shanghai is Picturesque," LLB.

224. two dozen American schoolteachers: see William Verhage, "The Bombing of Shanghai, An Eye-Witness Account," *Sigma Phi Epsilon Journal*, vol. 35, no. 2, 1937, pp. 109–15.

224. witnessed a Chinese mob: see Rhodes Farmer, *Shanghai Harvest*, p. 45 and "Mrs. Theodore Roosevelt Jr. Describes Shanghai Events," *New York Times*, August 21, 1937, p. 1.

225. distributed to refugees: see Peter Harmsen, *Shanghai 1937*, p. 59.

226. death toll . . . would reach 825: see Peter Harmsen, *Shanghai 1937*, p. 62.

226. explained that the bomb racks: see Peter Harmsen, *Shanghai 1937*, p. 64.

227. playing on movie screens around the world: "4:27," *Time Magazine*, August 23, 1937, p. 21.

227. "With nice irony": Barbara Miller, "Shanghai Bombing Declared End of Gay Oriental Era," *Los Angeles Times*, August 17, 1937, p. 2.

17: After Saturday

228. closed to navigation: see "Yangtse is Closed to Navigation," *China Press*, August 14, 1937, p. 1.

228. only restaurant open was Sun Ya: see "City's Amusement Places Are Closed," *China Press*, August 16, 1937, p. 2.

228. turned into vast sickbays: see Emily Hahn, *The Soong Sisters*, p. 249.

228. iron gates . . . were closed: see Emily Hahn, "Shanghai is Picturesque," p. 8, LLB.

229. "a foul charnel house": see Hallett Abend, *My Life in China*, p. 254.

229. ground gave a sickening lurch: see Hallett Abend, *My Life in China*, pp. 258–63.

229. erased from the map: see Hallett Abend, *My Life in China*, p. 265.

230. 40,000 in the first three weeks: see Peter Harmsen, *Shanghai 1937*, p. 247.

230. "peering into the sky": Emily Hahn letter to Helen Asbury, August 24, 1937, LLB.

230. "perceive those Japanese gentlemen": Emily Hahn, "Shanghai is Picturesque," p. 2, LLB.

230. "brief fountains of liquid gold": see Emily Hahn, *Mr. Pan*, p. 135.

231. Girl Guide . . . snuck into the warehouse: see Peter Harmsen, *Shanghai 1937*, p. 205.

231. rushed away in twenty British trucks: dispatch to British Embassy, Tokyo (November 30, 1937), FO 262/1958 Vol. III, p. 6, FOC.

231. "you're all vultures": see Emily Hahn, *China to Me*, p. 51.

231. the battle was Pembroke Stevens: see Edgar Snow, *Journey to the Beginning*, pp. 195–6.

232. ended at 3:34 p.m.: see Peter Harmsen, *Shanghai 1937*, p. 243.

232. prized possessions in a van: see Emily Hahn, *Mr. Pan*, p. 134.

232. Japanese-run opium dens: see Stella Dong, *Shanghai: The Rise and Fall of a Decadent City*, p. 264.

232. almost hit the chimney: see Ken Cuthbertson, *Nobody Said* Not *to Go*, p. 164.

232. 25,000 White Russians: see Harriet Sergeant, *Shanghai: Collision Point of Cultures*, p. 26.

232. "Voluptuous Vampires": see Stella Dong, *Shanghai: The Rise and Fall of a Decadent City*, p. 133.

233. remains to this day: based on author's visit to Shanghai, March 2014.

233. Mickey had found the Zau family: Emily Hahn letter to Helen Asbury, December 9, 1937, LLB.

233. "you must marry me": see Emily Hahn, *China to Me*, p. 56.

234. a gang of twenty White Russian movers: see Ken Cuthbertson, *Nobody Said Not to Go*, p. 164.

234. "I ceased to worry": see Emily Hahn, *China to Me*, p. 57.

234. death of Mary Garrison's duckling: Emily Hahn letter to Helen Asbury, August 24, 1937, LLB.

234. Mickey's constant companion: see Emily Hahn, *China to Me*, p. 103.

235. "such places as the Cathay Hotel bar": see "Gibbons in Interactions with Man in Domestic Settings," in *Gibbon and Siamang*, vol. 1, p. 250.

235. she feared she was infertile: Emily Hahn letter to Hannah Hahn, April 4, 1939, LLB.

235. sent to Manila: see "Refugees Greeted by Manila Quakes," *New York Times*, August 21, 1937, p. 1.

235. an affair with their White Russian maid: see Ken Cuthbertson interview with Mickey Hahn, July 12, 1993, Cuthberson mss, LLB.

236. "WE ARE VERY SAFE": Emily Hahn letter to Hannah Hahn, August 16, 1937, LLB.

236. horseback riding on Keswick Road: described in short prose piece entitled "Keswick Road," LLB.

236. attack . . . on the British ambassador: see Stanley Jackson, *The Sassoons*, p. 249.

236. "Long Live China!": see Peter Harmsen, *Shanghai 1937*, p. 247.

236. brought to a standstill: secret cipher telegram to the War Office, Hong Kong, December 8, 1937, FO 371 / 21020, FOC.

236. sinking of the USS *Panay*: see Hallett Abend, *My Life in China*, pp. 270–5. According to Abend, the *Panay* was sunk when a rogue army colonel, who later became the head of Japan's version of the Hitler Youth, drunkenly ordered his planes to bomb everything moving on the Yangtze River.

237. a campaign of letter-writing: see Simon Winchester, *The Man Who Loved China*, p. 47.

237. perhaps as many as 300,000: see Bob Wakabayashi, ed., *The Nanking Atrocity*, p. 365.

237. "it was three days too late": see Emily Hahn letter to Helen Asbury, December 24, 1937, LLB.

238. and by air from Hong Kong: see Sassoon Journal, November 3, 1937, DGL.

238. "Toy Shop" ball in the Cathay: see Sassoon Journal, February 10, 1937, DGL.

238. "Did dance steps without stick": see Sassoon Journal, July 1, 1937, DGL.

239. her roommate Mary $500 each: see Sassoon Journal, December 19, 1937, DGL.

239. (footnote) "Victor is here": Emily Hahn letter to Hannah Hahn, November 12, 1937, LLB.

239. "Two Japs noisy and insulting": see Sassoon Journal, December 12, 1937, DGL.

240. "how depressed I am": Sir Victor Sassoon letter to Derek FitzGerald, January 1, 1938, DGL.

18: *The Solitary Island*

241. rivalled Berlin: Berlin's population by 1939 was 4.3 million; Shanghai's was estimated to be between 3.5 and 5 million. See Christian Henriot, ed., *In The Shadow of the Rising Sun*, p. 146.

241. constant irritant to the Japanese: see Hallett Abend, *My Life in China*, p. 287.

241. a Solitary Island: Lu Hanchao, *Beyond the Neon Lights*, p. 166.

242. going further than ever: see Emily Hahn letter to Hannah Hahn, November 11, 1938, LLB.

242. "collect all these noise-makers": see Emily Hahn letter to Hannah Hahn, February 12, 1938, LLB.

243. "tried commit suicide fortnight ago": see Sassoon Journal, January 12, 1938, DGL.

243. plausible version: the archives of the Shanghai Municipal Police, which has a file on "Miss Lorraine Murray alias Lorraine Lee," records her arriving in Shanghai on September 25, 1933, on the *Empress of Russia* from Hong Kong. See Memorandum on Miss Lorraine Murray, No. D-5695, March 3, 1934, SMP.

243. Canadian-born Lorraine: Emily Hahn disguised Lorraine's identity in *China to Me*, in which she refers to her as an Australian named Jean. In letters, though, she repeatedly refers to the "little Canadian girl." Emily Hahn letter to Helen Asbury, February 12, 1938, LLB.

243. powerful Tokugawa family: see Emily Hahn, *China to Me*, pp. 70–1.

243. nationalist finance minister: see Sassoon Journal, January 12, 1938, DGL and Emily Hahn, *Miss Jill from Shanghai* (where he's referred to as B.K. Liu), p. 51.

243. "used to be a prostitute": see Emily Hahn, *China to Me*, p. 67.

244. "Of Possible Worlds": see *Candid Comment*, September 1939, p. 2, LLB.

244. Paddy O'Shea: see Emily Hahn, *China to Me*, pp. 30–2.

244. "and peeks in cuspidors": see Emily Hahn, "Return to Nature," *Candid Comment*, October 1938, p. 2.

244. "plenty of advertising": see Emily Hahn, *China to Me*, p. 32.

245. "his love of the bizarre": see Emily Hahn, *China to Me*, p. 79. Indra Devi would go on to other adventures, setting up a yoga studio in Madame Chiang's Frenchtown house, before moving to Hollywood in 1947. There, she taught Greta Garbo and Eva Gabor, and introduced asana yoga to the American public in the best-selling book *Forever Young, Forever Happy*. She died in Buenos Aires in 2002, at the age of a hundred and two.

245. prominent Shanghailanders: see Bernard Wasserstein, *Secret War in Shanghai*, p. 171.

245. (footnote) version of Lord Haw-Haw: see Carroll Alcott, *My War with Japan*, p. 126.

245. "such a patient slut?": see Emily Hahn, *China to Me*, p. 80.

245. unoccupied back room: see Emily Hahn, *China to Me*, p. 62.

245. Yang Gang: see Zhang Yinde, "Le Cas de Shao Xunmei," *Shanghai: Histoire, Promenades, Anthologie et Dictionnaire*, p. 628 and Sheng Peiyu, *Sheng shi jia zu, Shao Xunmei yu wo*, p. 211.

246. could be a cousin: Emily Hahn letter to Helen Hahn, May 12, 1938, LLB.

247. picking up 18,000 cadavers: see "Increase Recorded in Bodies Picked Up on Streets of Shanghai," *China Press*, November 26, 1937, p. 9.

247. 100,000 refugees: see Peter Harmsen, *Shanghai 1937*, p. 241.

247. "standard of the Red Cross": see Marcia Ristaino, *The Jacquinot Safe Zone*, p. 133.

247. bewhiskered Russian "Chief of Police": see "Jacquinot Advances Plan for All Nations," *China Press*, November 20, 1937.

247. failed chemistry experiment: see Peter Harmsen, *Shanghai 1937*, p. 35.

247. model for urban demilitarized zones: see Peter Harmsen, *Shanghai 1937*, p. 241.

248. Johnson-Reed Immigration Act: see Aristide Zolberg, *A Nation by Design*, p. 258.

248. great mass of city-born Jews: see Irving Abella, *None is Too Many*, p. 55.

248. away from Halifax and Havana: see Gordon Thomas, *Voyage of the Damned*, p. 35.

248. 18,000 Jews: see Maisie Meyer, *From the Rivers of Babylon to the Whangpoo*, pp. 208–17.

248. Italian ocean liners at Trieste: see Bernard Wasserstein, *Secret War in Shanghai*, p. 143.

248. with only ten marks: see Stanley Jackson, *The Sassoons*, p. 237.

248. pseudonym "Val Seymour": see Stanley Jackson, *The Sassoons*, p. 251.

248. movie camera to record the throngs: see Sassoon Journal, April 3, 1939.

249. $90,000 would be needed: see "Committee Giving Aid to European Emigres Needs Help Urgently," *China Press*, January 15, 1939.

249. "you're the man to do it": see Harriet Sergeant, *Shanghai: Collision Point of Cultures*, p. 320.

249. donated an expensive iron lung: see Stanley Jackson, *The Sassoons*, p. 253.

249. receiving station for new arrivals: see Marcia Ristaino, *Port of Last Resort*, p. 102.

249. (footnote) on the subject of Zionism: see Stanley Jackson, *The Sassoons*, p. 238.

250. "God will forgive him all his sins": quoted in Maisie Meyer, *From the Rivers of Babylon to the Whangpoo*, p. 212.

250. Sachertorte and strudel: see Harriet Sergeant, *Shanghai: Collision Point of Cultures*, p. 320.

250. "Welcome to Shanghai": see Maisie Meyer, *From the Rivers of Babylon to the Whangpoo*, p. 208.

250. "with the Nazis left out": Emily Hahn letter to Hannah Hahn, May 12, 1938, LLB.

251. "bothering people generally": see Emily Hahn, *China to Me*, p. 77.

251. "putting up at the Cathay": see Emily Hahn, "Shanghai, Land of Plenty," unpublished short prose, LLB.

252. "the sweepings of the country": see Emily Hahn, *China to Me*, p. 78.

253. when Helen spurned him: see Ken Cuthbertson, *Nobody Said Not to Go*, p. 27.

253. published in 1936: see Ken Cuthbertson, *Inside: The Biography of John Gunther*, p. 132.

253. "usual speed and precision": see Emily Hahn letter to Helen Asbury, April 11, 1938, LLB.

253. dinner with Sinmay: see Ken Cuthbertson, *Inside: The Biography of John Gunther*, p. 171.

253. ideally placed to write a book: see Ken Cuthbertson, *Nobody Said Not to Go*, p. 167.

254. uncle's tea and silk shop: see Han Suyin, *A Mortal Flower*, p. 81.

254. Sunday service in Shanghai: see Emily Hahn, *The Soong Sisters*, p. 24.

254. Wesleyan in Georgia: see Jay Taylor, *The Generalissimo*, p. 27.

254. favoured simple black silk dresses: see Vincent Sheean, *Personal History*, p. 208.

255. bulwark against the militarist clique: see Han Suyin, *A Mortal Flower*, p. 187.

255. "Methodism in his madness": see Ken Cuthbertson, *Inside: The Biography of John Gunther*, p. 172.

255. "a shadow with flame behind it": see John Gunther, *Inside Asia*, p. 204.

255. "one loves power": see Stella Dong, *Shanghai: The Rise and Fall of a Decadent City*, p. 106.

255. "forced them to flee": see Emily Hahn, *China to Me*, p. 5.

256. can of Maxwell House coffee: see Helen Foster Snow, *My China Years*, p. 188.

256. crossed the nationalist lines: see Edgar Snow, *Red Star Over China*, p. 57.

256. "a journalist after a story": see Edgar Snow, *Journey to the Beginning*, p. 156.

256. "persuasion and gradualism": see Edgar Snow, *Journey to the Beginning*, p. 170.

256. "bear a close resemblance": see "A Remarkable Survey of the Red in the Map of China," *New York Times*, June 9, 1938, p. BR3.

256. Mickey hoped that writing: "I haven't a word to say against Edgar Snow," she wrote later. "But when you have read *Red Star Over China* you begin to expect much more of the Reds than you have got . . . though as a symbol the guerrillas are inspiring and invaluable, the great burden of resistance has rested on the regular Army . . . I'm not trying to run them [the Communists] down, Agnes Smedley and Ed Snow and General Carlson and the rest of you; I'm only trying to undo some of the harm you have unwittingly done to your friends." *China to Me*, p. 199.

257. both he and Mickey contributed: see Emily Hahn, *China to Me*, p. 88.

257. "I do want to meet you": Madame Kung letter to Emily Hahn, July 13, 1939, LLB.

257. left Shanghai on a small boat: see Emily Hahn, *China to Me*, p. 83.

257. famous meeting place: see Emily Hahn, *The Soong Sisters*, p. 208.

258. "money and no brains": see Emily Hahn, *China to Me*, p. 42.

258. "one of the great love stories": see Emily Hahn, *China to Me*, p. 70.

258. "he has wonderful books": see Emily Hahn, *China to Me*, p. 88.
259. "his legs were too short": see Emily Hahn, *China to Me*, p. 98.

19: Waking from the Doze

page
261. "internationalization of the whole world": Letters Page, *North-China Herald*, February 23, 1932, p. 292.
261. Typhoid, dysentery, cholera: see Carroll Alcott, *My War with Japan*, p. 34.
262. burned the last stocks of Indian opium: see Alan Baumler, *The Chinese and Opium under the Republic*, p. 1.
262. manufacturing in 1934: see Carroll Alcott, *My War with Japan*, p. 34.
262. adulterated with pork rinds: see Lynn Pan, *Gangsters in Paradise*, p. 29.
262. pot full of . . . "faucet water": see Lu Hanchao, *Beyond the Neon Lights*, p. 215.
262. old-style doctors: see Carroll Alcott, *My War with Japan*, p. 87.
263. "advertised pleasant dreams": see Carroll Alcott, *My War with Japan*, p. 218.
263. "left the happiest memory": see Graham Greene, *Ways of Escape*, p. 166.
263. engendered *yan*: see Alan Baumler, *The Chinese and Opium under the Republic*, p. 36.
264. "not one cent": see Alan Baumler, *The Chinese and Opium under the Republic*, p. 4.
264. (footnote) "soap" or "special product": see Julia Lovell, *The Opium War*, p. 31.
264. reached $2 billion a year: see Alan Baumler, *The Chinese and Opium under the Republic*, p. 29.
264. Du Yuesheng head of the Bureau: see Lynn Pan, *Gangsters in Paradise*, p. 60.
264. thirty cents for every pipe: see Stella Dong, *Shanghai: The Rise and Fall of a Decadent City*, p. 160.
265. refined into morphine and heroin: see Carroll Alcott, *My War with Japan*, p. 210.
265. Tai Chong Cigarette and Exchange Shop: see Carroll Alcott, *My War with Japan*, p. 216.
266. "fallen to the floor": see Emily Hahn, "The Price of Poppies," unpublished, undated short prose, pp. 10–1, LLB.

266. stopped menstruating: Emily Hahn letter to Hannah Hahn, April 4, 1939, LLB.

266. three times a day to "refuel": see Emily Hahn, "The Price of Poppies," unpublished, undated short prose, pp. 16, LLB.

267. "space for time": see Bernard Wasserstein, *Secret War in Shanghai*, zp. 19.

267. mass executions of addicts: see Carroll Alcott, *My War with Japan*, p. 222.

267. "In a few minutes . . .": see Emily Hahn, "The Big Smoke," the *New Yorker*, February 15, 1969, p. 42.

267. "yellow death": see Emily Hahn, "The Price of Poppies," unpublished, undated short prose, pp. 23, LLB.

267. "easier with somebody else": see Emily Hahn, "The Big Smoke," the *New Yorker*, February 15, 1969, p. 40.

268. the cantankerous Chin Lien: see Emily Hahn, *China to Me*, p. 103.

268. "Beatrice Fanny-Brown": see Eric Linklater, *Juan in China*, p. 164.

269. "an ankle more trimly turned": see Eric Linklater, *Juan in China*, p. 173.

270. "we are a ridiculous race": see Vicki Baum, *Shanghai '37*, p. 346.

270. "Shanghai Hotel": see Vicki Baum, *Shanghai '37*, p. 317.

270. Occidental Private Club: see Hergé, *The Blue Lotus*, p. 7.

270. young Shanghainese artist in Brussels: see Tu Thanh Ha, "Is Tintin Racist?" *Globe and Mail*, March 20, 2015.

270. Blackened but alive: see Stella Dong, *Shanghai: The Rise and Fall of a Decadent City*, p. 216.

270. photographer . . . "Newsreel" Wong: see Paul French, *Through the Looking Glass*, p. 119.

271. waddled across the runway: see Emily Hahn, *China to Me*, p. 112.

272. socked in by fog: see Emily Hahn, *The Soong Sisters*, p. 297.

272. 268 bombing raids: see Simon Winchester, *The Man Who Loved China*, p. 74.

272. without his false teeth: see Emily Hahn, *China to Me*, p. 123.

272. Mongolian shepherd songs: see Emily Hahn, *China to Me*, p. 140.

273. "It does not live": Sir Victor Sassoon letter to Emily Hahn, November 20, 1939, LLB.

273. witness the three Soong sisters: see Emily Hahn, *The Soong Sisters*, p. 308.

274. "I meekly obeyed him": see Emily Hahn, *China to Me*, pp. 159–60.

274. "man arrived with SUPPLIES": Emily Hahn letter to Bernice Baumgarten (agent), August 24, 1940, LLB.

274. "undefeatable din of China": see Emily Hahn, *The Soong Sisters*, p. 320.

20: Shanghai, August 1, 1941

page

277. felt tears welling: see Sassoon Journal, August 1, 1941, DGL.

277. the hands of Chinese gangsters: see Andrew David Field, *Shanghai's Dancing World*, p. 186.

277. by Isherwood and Auden: see W.H. Auden and Christopher Isherwood, *Journey to a War*, p. 231.

278. "Asiatic Co-Prosperity Sphere": see Bernard Wasserstein, *Secret War in Shanghai*, p. 73.

278. navy captain named Koreshige Inuzuka: see Maisie Meyer, *From the Rivers of Babylon to the Whangpoo*, p. 214.

278. Jacob Schiff, a Jewish financier: see Naomi W. Cohen, *Jacob H. Schiff*, p. 134.

278. "very pro-British": see Stanley Jackson, *The Sassoons*, p. 256.

279. "humanitarian and unprejudiced attitude": see "Shanghai Jews 'Repudiate' Sassoon Views on Japan," *China Weekly Review*, March 16, 1940, p. 73.

279. ending immigration to Hongkew: see Maisie Meyer, *From the Rivers of Babylon to the Whangpoo*, pp. 214–5.

279. discovered the Bahamas: Sassoon Journal, April 1938, DGL.

279. buried in a casket of gold and crystal: see Stanley Jackson, *The Sassoons*, p. 253.

279. "mischievous Hollywood playboy": see Stanley Jackson, *The Sassoons*, p. 255.

279–80. "one of the world's wealthiest bachelors": see "Hedda Hopper's Hollywood," *Los Angeles Times*, February 6, 1940, p. A11.

280. "must operate under one government": see *San Bernardino County Sun*, June 19, 1941, p. 4.

280. Seaforth Highlanders: see Stanley Jackson, *The Sassoons*, p. 255.

280. yelling "Banzai!": see Bernard Wasserstein, *Secret War in Shanghai*, p. 79.

281. Royal Flying Corps tie: see Stanley Jackson, *The Sassoons*, p. 257.

281. he'd met Princess Sumaire: see Sassoon Journal, May 22, 1940, DGL.

281. checked into a suite at the Cathay: see Confidential Report on Princess Sumaire to Shanghai Municipal Police, No. H-1656c, November 17, 1940, SMP.

281. round-faced, and snub-nosed: see Bernard Wasserstein, *Secret War in Shanghai*, p. 44.

281. worked wonders on his legs: see Sassoon Journal, June 22, 1939, DGL.

281. met Sandy Tittman in Shanghai: see Sassoon Journal, March 22, 1936, DGL.

282. vacation house of adobe in the desert: see *Albuquerque Journal*, March 9, 1941.

282. attend the Moonlight Follies: see Sassoon Journal, August 1, 1941, DGL.

21: The Last Light in a Dying World

page

283. Tokyo Hotel on Connaught Road: see Emily Hahn, *China to Me*, p. 200.

283. paper to the Royal Asiatic Society: see Emily Hahn, *China to Me*, p. 208.

283. pre-revolutionary rolling stock: see "Boxer on Boxer: A Conversation," *Camões Center Quarterly*, p. 12.

283. housekeeper-concubine from Hokkaido: see "Boxer on Boxer: A Conversation," *Camões Center Quarterly*, p. 13.

283. dismissed Mickey's fears: see Emily Hahn, *China to Me*, p. 207.

284. "Mutual Non-stop Thinking?": see Zau Sinmay letter to Emily Hahn, December 22, 1939, LLB. The contemporary pinyin Romanization is Xiang Si, usually translated as "yearning" or "lovesickness."

284. " Oh, I MISS YOU SO!": see Zau Sinmay letter to Emily Hahn, December 24, 1939, LLB.

284. Cantonese man named Ah King: see Emily Hahn, *China to Me*, p. 215.

284. spyglass trained on the house: see Emily Hahn, *Hong Kong Holiday*, p. 25.

284. in the event of a siege: for a summary of Hong Kong's vulnerability to siege, see Hallett Abend, *My Life in China*, p. 243.

284. biography of Stamford Raffles: see Emily Hahn, *China to Me*, p. 242.

285. born into a Quaker farmstead: see Ruth Price, *The Lives of Agnes Smedley*, p. 11.

285. left-wing *PM* newspaper: see Ralph Ingersoll, "Hemingway Interviewed," *PM*, in *Byline: Ernest Hemingway*, p. 304.

285. "a huge polite thug from Chicago": see Caroline Moorhead, ed., *The Letters of Martha Gellhorn*, p. 110.

285. (footnote) three beautiful Chinese women: see Carlos Baker, *Ernest Hemingway: A Life Story*, p. 364.

286. "The one really good man": see Martha Gellhorn, *Travels with Myself and Another*, p. 52.

286. "highly savvy on the Orient": see Martha Gellhorn, *Travels with Myself and Another*, p. 21.

286. (footnote) "except perhaps the Japanese army": see Peter Moreira, *Hemingway on the China Front*, p. 34.

286. "tell 'em it's mine": see Peter Moreira, *Hemingway on the China Front*, p. 58. One night, when Hemingway was drinking in The Grips, one of his companions wondered where Mickey was. Hemingway shot back: "Probably putting down a Boxer uprising." When American pilot Hugh Woods reported the quip to Mickey, she told him: "You can assure I had the situation well in hand."

286. "trapped like rats": see Carlos Baker, *Ernest Hemingway: A Life Story*, p. 364.

287. bombed Pearl Harbor: in a 1989 interview, Charles Boxer said he knew the bombing of Pearl Harbor was coming. As head of military intelligence in Hong Kong, he'd been informed by British army headquarters in Singapore that the Americans had broken the Japanese codes; coded messages were transmitted in routine radio weather reports. Charles and another Japanese-speaking colleague, who monitored the weather reports twenty-four hours a day, had learned of the attack a week before it happened. Boxer suspected that, in order to unify public opinion for a war against Japan, the Americans had decided not to alert the forces at Pearl Harbor and Manila of the upcoming Japanese attack. See "Boxer on Boxer," *Camões Center Quarterly*, p. 15.

287. "balloon's gone up": see Emily Hahn, *China to Me*, p. 258.

287. most powerful ships in the Far East: see Bernard Wasserstein, *Secret War in Shanghai*, p. 109.

287. (footnote) "We'll fight to the bitter end!": see Charles Drage, *Two-Gun Cohen*, p. 231.

287. On "Black Christmas": see Oliver Lindsay, *The Lasting Honour*, p. 146.

288. U.S. 4th Marine regiment paraded: see Bernard Wasserstein, *Secret War in Shanghai*, p. 94.

288. "Get off my bloody ship!": see Bernard Wasserstein, *Secret War in Shanghai*, p. 98.

288. caricatures of Roosevelt: see Bernard Wasserstein, *Secret War in Shanghai*, p. 101.

289. the Metropole Hotel: see Peter Hibbard, *Peace at the Cathay*, p. 151.

289. flamboyant tycoon: James Lee, according to Ling Pan, *In Search of Old Shanghai*, p. 46.

289. "N" for Netherlanders: see Rena Krasno, *Strangers Always*, p. 79. Silas Hardoon's eleven adopted children, because they were considered by the Japanese to be neither stateless, Chinese, nor British, were allowed to live in Aili Gardens throughout the war. The Japanese confiscated Hardoon's collection of pre-1919 Renaults, and the family compound was used to store gasoline.

289. time-bomb in Sassoon House: see "Shanghai Bomb Halts Tokyo Radio Service," *New York Times*, September 17, 1941, p. 3.

289. set up his offices at the Cathay: see Bernard Wasserstein, *Secret War in Shanghai*, p. 144.

289. The media was muzzled: see Bernard Wasserstein, *Secret War in Shanghai*, p. 64.

289. the "New Odour": see Carroll Alcott, *My War with Japan*, p. 333.

289. alcoholic Herbert Erasmus Moy: see Bernard Wasserstein, *Secret War in Shanghai*, p. 263.

290. "a sort of concentration camp": see *Shanghai Times*, December 13, 1941.

290. most feared address in Shanghai: see Stella Dong, *Shanghai: The Rise and Fall of a Decadent City*, pp. 272–6.

290. doctor was called in: see John B. Powell, *My 25 Years in China*, p. 388. Powell's feet had to be amputated after his journey back to the United States. He would die two years after completing his autobiography, one of the liveliest accounts of life in China between the wars. After the Second World War, his son came to Shanghai and briefly published a revived edition of the *China Weekly Review*.

290. arrange the scale of the Metropole: see Stanley Jackson, *The Sassoons*, p. 259.

291. "living like the filthiest coolie": see M.C. Ford, "Slow Death in a Jap Cage," *Collier's*, September 5, 1942, pp. 15.

291. "inclined to blame you": M.C. Ford letter to Sir Victor Sassoon, April 10, 1943, DGL.

292. rulers of 405 million people: see Hallett Abend, *My Life in China*, p. 161.

292. *heian shijie*, a "dark world": see Maisie Meyer, *From the Rivers of Babylon to the Whangpoo*, p. 220.

292. triangular yellow pennant: see Lynn Pan, *Gangsters in Paradise*, p. 128.

293. No. 76 Jessfield Road: see Bernard Wasserstein, *Secret War in Shanghai*, p. 23.

293. abrogation of all American privileges: see Lynn Pan, *Gangsters in Paradise*, p. 166.

293. bronze statue of Sir Robert Hart: see Bernard Wasserstein, *Secret War in Shanghai*, p. 240.

293. (footnote) "the hands of the European powers": quoted in Ralph Shaw, *Sin City*, p. 80.

293. renamed Tilanqiao: see Rena Krasno, *Strangers Always*, p. 120.

293. "Great Shanghai Road": see Bernard Wasserstein, *Secret War in Shanghai*, p. 243.

294. binge of chit-signing ensued: see Hallett Abend, *My Life in China*, p. 72.

294. shorten the legs of the billiards table: see Peter Hibbard, *The Bund*, p 97.

294. popular taxi dancer Chen Manli: see Xi Zhang, "The Paramount Ballroom in the 1930s," Electronic Theses and Dissertations, University of Louisville, 2012, paper 1642.

294. shot her dead on the dance floor: see Geoffrey York, "Dancing the Dreary Decades Away," *Globe and Mail*, December 22, 2006.

294. the Masquée Bar: see Bernard Wasserstein, *Secret War in Shanghai*, p. 129.

294. diesel-burning double-deckers: see Ralph Shaw, *Sin City*, p. 210.

294. soled with car-tire rubber: see Rena Krasno, *Strangers Always*, p. 29.

295. continue to show up for work: see Bernard Wasserstein, *Secret War in Shanghai*, p. 157.

295. 7,600 . . . Allied nationals: see Bernard Wasserstein, *Secret War in Shanghai*, p. 137.

295. (footnote) template for . . . science-fiction dystopias: see J.G. Ballard, *Miracles of Life*, p. 251.

296. sadistic tyrant named Ghoya: see Bernard Wasserstein, *Secret War in Shanghai*, p. 150.

296. born Ignácz Trebitsch: biographical details of Trebitsch Lincoln's life taken from Bernard Wasserstein, *The Secret Lives of Trebitsch Lincoln*.

297. founder of the League of Truth: see Bernard Wasserstein, *The Secret Lives of Trebitsch Lincoln*, p. 261.

297. the Panchen Lama: see Bernard Wasserstein, *The Secret Lives of Trebitsch Lincoln*, p. 230.

297. "I hate the British": see Ralph Shaw, *Sin City*, p. 213.

298. "they did this brave deed": M.C. Ford letter to Sir Victor Sassoon, April 10, 1943, DGL.
298. headquarters of Captain Eugene Pick: see Bernard Wasserstein, *Secret War in Shanghai*, p. 113.
299. B-29 super-fortresses: see Rena Krasno, *Strangers Always*, p. 150.
299. "luxurious hotels like the Cathay": see "Shanghai Gripped By Soaring Prices," *New York Times*, February 15, 1944, p. 7.
299. traced the letters "V.E.": see Bernard Wasserstein, *Secret War in Shanghai*, p. 259.
299. melancholy farewell dinner: see Bernard Wasserstein, *Secret War in Shanghai*, p. 263.

22: Check-Out Time

page
301. didn't recognize Charles: see Emily Hahn, *China to Me*, pp. 268–78.
301. camp cot at Queen Mary's Hospital: see Emily Hahn, *Hong Kong Holiday*, p. 70.
301. report to the Murray Parade Ground: see Emily Hahn, *China to Me*, p. 300.
301. total of 13,390 Allied civilians and soldiers: see Bernice Archer, *The Internment of Western Civilians under the Japanese*, p. 68.
302. had herself admitted to Queen Mary: see Emily Hahn, *Hong Kong Holiday*, p. 79.
302. "a Chinese husband once": see Emily Hahn, *China to Me*, p. 311.
302. she *could* not be interned: according to the Japanese Consul, Mr. Kimura; see Emily Hahn, *China to Me*, p. 321.
303. "Hello, Freddie": see Emily Hahn, *China to Me*, p. 323.
303. renamed Meiji-dori: see Ken Cuthbertson, *Nobody Said Not to Go*, p. 243.
303. dashing into the Kam Loong restaurant: see Emily Hahn, *China to Me*, p. 404.
304. preference for salt fish: see Emily Hahn, *Hong Kong Holiday*, p. 265.
304. Scottie dog for a few turnip cakes: see Emily Hahn, *Hong Kong Holiday*, p. 136.
304. from 1.5 million to half a million: see Philip Snow, *The Fall of Hong Kong*, p. 107.
304. hastened the process: see Philip Snow, *The Fall of Hong Kong*, p. 167.
304. "Japanese had grabbed Hong Kong": see Emily Hahn, *Hong Kong Holiday*, p. 247.

304. "wondering curiosity": see Emily Hahn, *China to Me*, p. 348.

305. State Department officials: see Emily Hahn, *Hong Kong Holiday*, p. 355.

305. "Daddy, bye-bye!": see Emily Hahn, *China to Me*, p. 269.

305. the "Dead End Kids": see "Homeward 1 – The *Teia Maru*," the *New Yorker*, December 18, 1943, p. 31.

306. felt like Judgment Day: see Charles Drage, *Two-Gun Cohen*, p. 234.

306. Mr. Yamashita: see Geoffrey Charles Emerson, *Hong Kong Internment*, 1942–45, p. 56.

306–7. even had a hairdresser: see "Homeward II – The *Gripsholm*," the *New Yorker*, December 25, 1943, p. 24.

307. (footnote) "Our Sakura are in a splendid condition": Hahn mss, LLB.

307. hiding behind furniture: see Ken Cuthbertson, *Nobody Said* Not *to Go*, p. 280.

308. "a long black stogie to boot": see "Trade Winds," *Saturday Review*, January 15, 1944, p. 14.

308. "the concubine of a Chinese!": see Ken Cuthbertson, *Nobody Said* Not *to Go*, p. 285.

309. "the ensuing melee": see Randall Gould, *China in the Sun*, p. 326.

309. three-quarters of a million copies: see Ken Cuthbertson, *Nobody Said* Not *to Go*, p. 286.

309. embossed upside down: see Emily Hahn letter to Helen Asbury, May 13, 1941, LLB.

309. "a tipsy lounge-lizard": see General M.A. Cohen letter to Emily Hahn, December 16, 1944, LLB.

309. (footnote) "I was rather surprised": see Emily Hahn, undated, unpublished fragment beginning, "I first saw Morris Cohen in Shanghai," LLB.

309–10. supply her with morphine: see Ken Cuthbertson interview with Emily Hahn, December 14, 1992, p. 11, LLB.

310. collaboration with her friend: see Vicki Baum letter to Emily Hahn, October 27, 1944, LLB.

310. punished the guilty parties: Kenneth R. Maxwell, "The C.R. Boxer Affaire," Council on Foreign Relations, March 16, 2001. After Charles Boxer's death, a journalist accused him in the *Guardian* of being a Japanese spy and "prolonging" the Second World War. The transmitter in question, according to his biographer Daurel Aldin, was actually a clandestine short-wave receiver being used to keep up the internees' morale.

310. "LIBERATED BRITISH PRISONERS": see United Press dispatch, dateline Hong Kong, September 14, 1945, LLB.

310. "DEAREST MICKY": Vicki Baum to Emily Hahn, Western Union Telegram, from Pasadena, September 15, 1945, LLB.

310. photo of Charles Boxer: see *Life*, December 3, 1945, p. 40.

310. hundred-dollar bribe: see Ken Cuthbertson, *Nobody Said Not to Go*, p. 302.

311. at the Number One Buoy: see Lynn Pan, *Gangsters in Paradise*, p. 297.

311. pulling them down Nanking Road: see Stella Dong, *Shanghai: The Rise and Fall of a Decadent City*, p. 281.

311. "Night-Club and Cocktail Lounge": see Bernard Wasserstein, *Secret War in Shanghai*, p. 265.

311. oversight by the nationalists: see Randall Gould, *China in the Sun*, pp. 303–40.

312. three billion dollars' worth: see Stella Dong, *Shanghai: The Rise and Fall of a Decadent City*, p. 282.

312. White Russian community decamped: see "A Forgotten Episode in Russian History Leaves Links with the Philippines," *Independent*, December 3, 2013.

312. (footnote) only 404 Jews remained: see Maisie J. Meyer, *From the Rivers of Babylon to the Whangpoo*, p. 229.

312. approached 5.5 million: see Lu Hanchao, *Beyond the Neon Lights*, p. 166.

312. leaped to 627,000 by 1947: see Pan Ling, *In Search of Old Shanghai*, p. 47.

312. (footnote) "That was one cold night": see S.J. Perelman, *Westward Ha!*, p. 53.

313. slap him in the face: see Stella Dong, *Shanghai: The Rise and Fall of a Decadent City*, p. 289.

313. millions for a cup of coffee: see Noel Barber, *The Fall of Shanghai*, p. 50.

313. "China Lobby" in Washington: see Noel Barber, *The Fall of Shanghai*, p. 58.

313. have Chiang assassinated: see Bernard Wasserstein, *Secret War in Shanghai*, p. 247.

313. seized the stockpiles of Japanese aircraft: see Jonathan Spence, *Mao Zedong: A Life*, p. 103.

314. "We'll be back in Shanghai next year": see Han Suyin, *Birdless Summer*, pp. 250–1.

314. traders from Rajasthan for £4 million: see Stanley Jackson, *The Sassoons*, p. 265.

314. valued at £7.5 million: see Stanley Jackson, *The Sassoons*, p. 267.

314. taken over Sir Victor's penthouse: see Peter Hibbard, *Peace at the Cathay*, p. 154.

315. dinners with the McBains: see Sassoon Journal, December 17, 1947, DGL.

315. "*Après moi, le déluge*": see Stanley Jackson, *The Sassoons*, p. 264.

315. anything edible or wearable: see Stanley Jackson, *The Sassoons*, p. 268.

315. Jeanne de Monet: see Sassoon Journal, April 12, 1948, DGL.

315. armed with meat cleavers: see Stanley Jackson, *The Sassoons*, p. 268.

315. best offer for the Cathay Mansions: see Sassoon Journal, November 26, 1948, DGL.

315–16. brewery that made . . . U.B. Pilsner: see "Sassoon Sees Dim Future in China Trade," *Los Angeles Times*, September 21, 1948.

316. eight o'clock in the morning: see Sassoon Journal, November 27, 1948.

316. "lesser of two evils": see "China's Army Badly Run, Says Sassoon," *Los Angeles Times*, December 12, 1948.

317. north bank of the Yangtze: Stella Dong, *Shanghai: The Rise and Fall of a Decadent City*, p. 292.

317. tied up in front of the Cathay: see Noel Barber, *The Fall of Shanghai*, pp. 77–8.

318. spread straw sleeping mats: see "Shanghai Troops Occupy Hotels; Man Gun Posts in Skyscrapers," *New York Times*, May 2, 1949, p. 3.

318. "billet our mules?": see Noel Barber, *The Fall of Shanghai*, p. 123.

318. offered them cups of tea: see Noel Barber, *The Fall of Shanghai*, p. 148.

319. discarded nationalist uniforms: see Noel Barber, *The Fall of Shanghai*, p. 152.

23: Settling the Bill

page

320. "lusty as an eagle": see "Boxer on Boxer: A Conversation," *Camões Center Quarterly*, p. 13.

320. "anything later than 1750": see Emily Hahn, *England to Me*, p. 171.

321. suffering from a bad flu: see Ken Cuthberston interview with Emily Hahn, December 14, 1992, pp. 11–3, LLB.

321. farmhouse in Dorset: see Emily Hahn, *England to Me*, p. 25.

321. $2,000 an article: see Ken Cuthbertson, *Nobody Said* Not *to Go*, p. 289.

321. under four different editors: see Ken Cuthbertson, *Nobody Said* Not *to Go*, p. 319.

321. "the duck-billed platypus": quoted in Kenneth R. Maxwell, "The C.R. Boxer Affaire," Council on Foreign Relations, March 16, 2001.

321. freedom of movement: see Ken Cuthbertson, *Nobody Said* Not *to Go*, p. 317.

321. attempt to fathom: see Emily Hahn, *Eve and the Apes*, p. 6.

322. Han began to question her own support: see Han Suyin, *Birdless Summer*, p. 214.

323. the issue of nationalist corruption: see Wilbur Burton, "Generalissimo – Intimate View," *Saturday Review*, March 26, 1955, p. 13.

323. "The bitch Emily Hahn came": see Ruth Price, *Agnes Smedley*, p. 371.

323. extensive evidence: see Ruth Price, *Agnes Smedley*, p. 8.

323. "paid her to write": see Ken Cuthbertson, *Nobody Said* Not *to Go*, p. 328.

323. (footnote) "written from minor elevations": Ed Snow letter to Emily Hahn, April 18, 1956, LLB.

324. "closing your eyes to certain aspects": see Emily Hahn letter to Randall Gould, May 1, 1945, LLB.

324. the proxy elite: for a discussion of the role of "proxies" in Afghanistan and other contemporary societies, see Sarah Chayes, *Thieves of State: Why Corruption Threatens Global Security*.

325. twenty million or more: see Odd Arne Westad, *Restless Empire*, p. 15.

325. disdain for the "returned students": see Emily Hahn, *China to Me*, p. 58.

326. "your ever Platonic Sinmay": Zau Sinmay letter to Emily Hahn, August 1, 1945, LLB.

326. "sure you saved Carola's life": Emily Hahn letter to Zau Sinmay, January 26, 1946, LLB.

327. a gold Rolex wristwatch: Zau Sinmay letter to Emily Hahn, October 11, 1948, LLB.

327. "small Chinese man": Charless Hahn, quoted in Ken Cuthbertson, *Nobody Said* Not *to Go*, p. 330.

327. heard rumours that he'd been imprisoned: see Ken Cuthbertson interview with Emily Hahn, July 12, 1993, p. 4, Cuthbertson mss, LLB.

327. enjoy a few puffs: see Ken Cuthberston interview with Emily Hahn, December 14, 1992, p. 12, LLB.

327. "Can't smoke opium here": see Ken Cuthbertson, *Nobody Said* Not *to Go*, p. 320.

328. an old Colonial residence: see Stanley Jackson, *The Sassoons*, p. 282.

328. "China gave me up": see Stanley Jackson, *The Sassoons*, p. 268.

328. "even a sweet potato": see Han Suyin, *A Mortal Flower*, p. 117.

328. managing 9,965 buildings: see Jonathan J. Howlett, "Creating a New Shanghai," p. 256.

329. house arrest in Grosvenor House: see Stanley Jackson, *The Sassoons*, p. 272.

329. over lunch at the Ritz: see Stanley Jackson, *The Sassoons*, p. 274.

329. "There will be no more rich men": *New York Times*, May 29, 1942, p. 18.

330. canes with hollowed-out tops: see Stanley Jackson, *The Sassoons*, p. 282.

330. married a man closer to her age: see *Albuquerque Journal*, August 20, 1942, p. 9.

330. founded on the same day: see Stanley Jackson, *The Sassoons*, pp. 283–4.

330. "wretched hotel called Raffles": quoted in Malcolm Purvis, *Tall Storeys*, p. 65.

331. "bring back the old days impartially": Sir Victor Sassoon letter to Emily Hahn, January 23, 1953, LLB.

331. "mixing it up with China": Sir Victor Sassoon to Emily Hahn, June 3, 1953, LLB.

331. centrepiece was vegetable curry: see Stanley Jackson, *The Sassoons*, p. 287.

332. "quarrelling over men": Emily Hahn letter to Helen Asbury, January 17, 1937, LLB.

332. glory days in the Far East: see Jack Slater, "Social Catalyst of a Golden Era," *Los Angeles Times*, June 12, 1977, p. J1.

333. "Dad died in 1968": letter to "Aunt Mickey" from Shao Xiaohong, October 18, 1988, LLB.

333. Carola and Amanda at her side: see Ken Cuthbertson, *Nobody Said* Not *to Go*, p. 357.

334. "What shall I do?": Emily Hahn, undated short prose, LLB.

335. fifty-two books: see Ken Cuthbertson, *Nobody Said* Not *to Go*, p. 1.

Epilogue

page

336. more skyscrapers than the entire west coast: see "Where Blade Runner Meets Las Vegas," the *Guardian*, November 8, 2004.

336. the vertiginous view: based on author's visit to Shanghai, February 2007.

336. exact site where Jardine, Matheson: see Simon Winchester, *The River at the Center of the World*, p. 64.

338. largest system in the world: see "How the NYC subway compares to London, Tokyo and Shanghai," *Washington Post*, March 30, 2015.

338. population to twenty-four million: see "Climate change threatens China's booming cities," the *Guardian*, July 25, 2015.

338. middle class than in Paris itself: "Shanghai: Can the Fastest-Growing City in the World Keep it Up?" the *Atlantic*, May 2012.

338. over 300 officially qualifies as "hazardous": from Shanghai Environmental Monitoring site, www.semc.gc.cn.

339. "redder, younger and stronger": see "Shanghai Gets a Bull for its Own Shop," *Wall Street Journal*, April 20, 2010.

339. outlet for Kentucky Fried Chicken: see Peter Hibbard, *The Bund*, p. 91.

339. fifty-seven-year-old taxi driver: author's visit to *shikumen* in Shanghai, March 28, 2014.

340. fifty-seven buildings belonging to the Sassoon group: see Jonathan J. Howlett, "Creating a New Shanghai," p. 260.

341. managed by Dong Zhujun: "Shanghai Loses a Monument to a Cold War Rapprochement," *Wall Street Journal*, February 28, 1997.

341. went on the market for $15 million: "A House for 120 Million Yuan," *Shanghai Daily*, November 27, 2004.

341. the Metropole is still a hotel: author's visit to Metropole and Hamilton House, March 20, 2014.

342. "a model consumerist city": quoted in Jonathan J. Howlett, "Creating a New Shanghai," p. 18.

342. "Five-Antis" Campaign of 1952: see Lynn Pan, *Gangsters in Paradise*, p. 243.

343. hurling themselves from high buildings: notes from W.B. Rae-Smith to John Swire & Sons, Hong Kong, March 7, 1952, FO 371/99283, FOL.

343. "struggle ruthlessly against the flash": see Jie Li, *Shanghai Homes*, p. 17.

343. sweeping the sidewalks: see Lynn Pan, *Gangsters in Paradise*, p. 238.

344. moved in 1932 to a new location: see Paul French, *The Old Shanghai A–Z*, p. 141.

344. soda fountain: see Carl Crow, *Foreign Devils in the Flowery Kingdom*, p. 180.

344. (footnote) a chance meeting between the reporter: see Martin Fackler, "Nation's Oldest Residents See Lifetime of Change," Associated Press, February 16, 2003.

344. changed her name to Shao Yang: author's interview with Shao Yang, March 14, 2014.

345. culture minister for the nationalists: see Jian Wang, ed., *Soft Power in China*, p. 178.

345. walked up busy Pingliang Road: based on author's visit to Pingliang Road with Wu Lilan, March 23, 2014.

346. "Terrace house on Avenue Joffre": based on author's visit, March 29, 2014.

347. The experiments worked: see Sheng Peiyu, *Sheng shi jia zu, Shao Xunmei yu wo*, p. 117.

348. Xiao Yu had visited several doctors: see Sheng Peiyu, *Sheng shi jia zu, Shao Xunmei yu wo*, p. 120.

348. turn the ground floor . . . into a neighbourhood canteen: see Sheng Peiyu, *Sheng shi jia zu, Shao Xunmei yu wo*, p. 291.

348. Sinmay had been taken away: see Sheng Peiyu, *Sheng shi jia zu, Shao Xunmei yu wo*, p. 293.

348. "looked very uninhibited": see Jia Zhifang, *Wo de ren sheng dang an: Jia Zhifang hui yi lu* (translation by Chan Wing Shuen, commissioned by author), pp. 288–94.

350. communist guerrilla: his brother Huan; see Emily Hahn, *China to Me*, p. 64.

350. "pale like a Westerner's": see Sheng Peiyu, *Sheng shi jia zu, Shao Xunmei yu wo*, p. 299.

350. teenagers called him "snake" and "devil": see Martin Fackler, "Nation's Oldest Residents See Lifetime of Change," Associated Press, February 16, 2003.

350. "old-fashioned poetry was useless": see Sheng Peiyu, *Sheng shi jia zu, Shao Xunmei yu wo*, p. 308.

351. last months of his life . . . were miserable: see *Sheng Peiyu, Sheng shi jia zu, Shao Xunmei yu wo*, p. 319.

351. academics I spoke to: interview with Professor Chen Zishan, literature department, East China Normal University, at Peace Hotel, Shanghai, March 17, 2014.

351. twelve-scene multimedia play: see "Dying Moments of a Tragic Poet," *South China Morning Post*, December 26, 2004.

353. "complicated relationships": also translated as "complex connections"; see Zhou Linagpei, ed., *A Compendium of Modern Chinese Poetry*, vol. 4, p. 801.

355. delegations from socialist countries: see Peter Hibbard, *Peace at the Cathay*, p. 164.

355. headquarters of the portly Chen Yi: see Christian Henriot, "The Shanghai Bund in Myth and History," *Journal of Modern Chinese History*, June 2010, p. 25.

355. Northerner named Ma Yongzhang: interview with "Martin" Ma Yongzhng, Peace Hotel, Shanghai, March 13, 2014.

356. Tang Yu-en . . . put in charge of the project: interview with Tang Yu-en, Shanghai, March 20, 2014.

356. conservationist Ruan Yisan: interviewed in Shanghai, March 14, 2014.

357. In what is now Room 888: author's tour of Peace Hotel, March 14, 2014.

357. what appeared to be Poseidon: email to author from Roy Li, assistant front-office manager, Peace Hotel, October 3, 2014.

358. enjoying a banquet of sushi: see Evan Osnos, "Born Red," the *New Yorker*, April 6, 2015.

358. watched with growing alarm: see "36 dead, 47 injured during New Year's stampede in Shanghai," Shanghaiist.com, December 31, 2014, http://shanghaiist.com/2014/12/31/35_dead_42_injured_in_ bund_stampede.php (last accessed October 18, 2015).

Bibliography

Primary sources

All About China and Environs: the 1934–35 Standard Guide Book. Hong Kong: China Economic Review Publishing, 2008.

Abend, Hallett. *My Life in China 1926–1941*. New York: Harcourt, Brace and Company, 1943.

Acton, Harold. *Memoirs of an Aesthete*. London: Methuen, 1948.

Alcott, Carroll. *My War with Japan*. New York: Henry Holt, 1943.

Auden, W.H., and Christopher Isherwood. *Journey to a War*. London: Faber and Faber, 1973.

Ballard, J.G. *Miracles of Life: Shanghai to Shepperton – An Autobiography*. London: Harper Perennial, 2008.

Baum, Vicki. *Shanghai '37*. Oxford: Oxford University Press, 1986.

Buck, Pearl S. *The Good Earth*. New York: Washington Square Press, 2004.

Cocteau, Jean. *Mon premier voyage (tour du monde en 80 jours)*. Paris: Gallimard, 1936.

Coward, Noël. *Present Indicative: The First Autobiography of Noël Coward*. London: Methuen, 2004.

Jia Zhifang. *Wo de ren sheng dang an: Jia Zhifang hui yi lu*. (*Memorial of Jia Zhifang*.) Nanjing: Jaingsu wen yi chu ban she, 2009.

Maze, Lady, and V.G. Bowden. *Bon Appétit: Secrets from Shanghai Kitchens*. Shanghai: privately printed, 1940.

Nellsit, George F. *Men of Shanghai and North China: A Standard Bibliographical Reference Work*. Shanghai: The Oriental Press, 1933.

Zau Sinmay. "My Triangle of Grandfathers," translated by Emily Hahn. Unpublished, undated manuscript in LLB.

Secondary sources

Abella, Irving, and Harold Troper. *None is Too Many: Canada and the Jews of Europe*. Toronto: University of Toronto, 2012.

Archer, Bernice. *The Internment of Western Civilians under the Japanese*. New York: Routledge, 2014.

Baker, Carlos. *Ernest Hemingway: A Life Story*. New York: Charles Scribner's Sons, 1969.

Ballard, J.G. *Empire of the Sun*. New York: Simon & Schuster, 2005.

Barber, Noel. *The Fall of Shanghai*. New York: Coward, McCann & Geoghegan, 1979.

Baum, Vicki. *It Was All Quite Different: The Memoirs of Vicki Baum*. New York: Funk & Wagnalls, 1964.

Baumler, Alan. *The Chinese and Opium Under the Republic: Worse than Floods and Wild Beasts*. Albany: State University of New York Press, 2007.

Baxter, John. *Von Sternberg*. Lexington: University Press of Kentucky, 2010.

Betta, Chiara. *Silas Aaron Hardoon (1815–1931): Marginality and Adaptation in Shanghai*. Ph.D. thesis, University of London, 1997.

Bickers, Robert. *Empire Made Me: An Englishman Adrift in Shanghai*. London: Penguin, 2003.

Bien, Gloria. *Baudelaire in China: A Study in Literary Reception*. Newark, DE: University of Delaware Press, 2013.

Birns, Jack, et al. *Assignment Shanghai: Photographs on the Eve of a Revolution*. Berkeley: University of California Press, 2003.

Brinkley, Alan. *The Publisher: Henry Luce and His American Century*. New York: Alfred A. Knopf, 2010.

Brook, Daniel. *A History of Future Cities*. New York: W.W. Norton, 2013.

Carney, Dora Sanders. *Foreign Devils Had Light Eyes: A Memoir of Shanghai 1933–1939*. Toronto: Virgo Press, 1980.

Chan, Arlene. *Righting Canada's Wrong: The Chinese Head Tax*. Toronto: James Lorimer & Co, 2014.

Chang, Eileen. *Half a Lifelong Romance*. London: Penguin, 2014.

Chang, Jung, and Jon Halliday. *Mao: The Unknown Story*. New York: Anchor Books, 2006.

Chayes, Sarah. *Thieves of State: Why Corruption Threatens Global Security*. New York: W.W. Norton & Co, 2015.

Cheng, Pei-kai, and Michael Lestz, with Jonathan D. Spence. *The Search for Modern China: A Documentary Collection*. New York: W.W. Norton, 1999.

Chennault, Claire Lee. *The Ways of a Fighter: The Memoirs of Claire Lee Chennault*. New York: G.P. Putnam's Sons, 1949.

Clavell, James. *Tai-pan*. New York: Dell, 1986.

Collis, Maurice. *Foreign Mud*. Singapore: Graham Brash, 1980.

Constenino, Francesco. *Shanghai: from Modernism to Modernity.* . Charleston, SC: CreateSpace, 2013.

Cowley, Malcolm. *The Dream of the Golden Mountains: Remembering the 1930s*. New York: Penguin, 1981.

—— *Exile's Return: A Literary Saga of the Nineteen-Twenties*. New York: Compass Books, 1956.

Cranley, Patrick, et al. *Still More Shanghai Walks*. Hong Kong: Old China Hand Press, 2011.

Crouch, Gregory. *China's Wings: War, Intrigue, Romance and Adventure in the Middle Kingdom During the Golden Age of Flight*. New York: Bantam, 2012.

Crow, Carl. *Foreign Devils in the Flowery Kingdom*. Hong Kong: China Economic Review Publishing, 2007.

Cuthbertson, Ken. *Inside: The Biography of John Gunther*. Chicago: Bonus Books, 2005.

—— *Nobody Said* Not *to Go: The Life, Loves, and Adventures of Emily Hahn*. New York: Faber and Faber, 1998.

Denison, Edward, and Guang Yu Ren. *Building Shanghai: The Story of China's Gateway*. Chichester: Wiley-Academy, 2006.

—— *Modernism in China*. Chichester: John Wiley, 2008.

Dickstein, Morris. *Dancing in the Dark: A Cultural History of the Great Depression*. New York: W.W. Norton, 2009.

Dikötter, Frank, et al. *Narcotic Culture: A History of Drugs in China*. Chicago: University of Chicago Press, 2004.

Dong, Stella. *Shanghai: The Rise and Fall of a Decadent City*. New York: Harper Perennial, 2000.

Drage, Charles. *Two-Gun Cohen*. London: Panther, 1956.

Farmer, Rhodes. *Shanghai Harvest: A Diary of Three Years in the China War*. London: Museum Press, 1945.

Fenby, Jonathan. *Tiger Head Snake Tails: China Today, How it Got There and Why it Has to Change*. London: Simon & Schuster, 2012.

Field, Andrew David. *Shanghai's Dancing World: Cabaret Culture and Urban Politics, 1919–1954*. Hong Kong: Chinese University of Hong Kong, 2010.

Frayling, Christopher. *The Yellow Peril: Dr Fu Manchu and the Rise of Chinaphobia*. London: Thames & Hudson, 2014.

French, Paul. *The Old Shanghai A–Z*. Hong Kong: Hong Kong University Press, 2010.

—— *Through the Looking Glass: China's Foreign Journalists from Opium Wars to Mao*. Hong Kong: Hong Kong University Press, 2009.

Gelber, Harry G. *The Dragon and the Foreign Devils: China and the World, 1100 BC to the Present*. New York: Walker & Company, 2007.

Gellhorn, Martha. *Travels with Myself and Another*. New York: Putnam, 2001.

Gordon, Andrew. *A Modern History of Japan: From Tokugawa Times to the Present*. New York: Oxford University Press, 2003.

Gould, Randall. *China in the Sun*. New York: Doubleday, 1946.

Greene, Graham. *Ways of Escape*. London: Vintage, 1999.

Gunther, John. *Inside Asia*. New York: Harper & Brothers, 1939.

Hahn, Emily. *Affair*. New York: Fawcett, 1955.

—— *Chiang Kai-shek: An Unauthorized Biography*. Garden City: Doubleday, 1955.

—— *China Only Yesterday: 1850–1950, A Century of Change*. London: Weidenfeld & Nicholson, 1963.

—— *China to Me*. London: Virago Press, 1987.

—— *Congo Solo: Misadventures Two Degrees North*. Montreal: McGill-Queen's University Press, 2011.

—— *England to Me*. Garden City: Doubleday, 1949.

—— *Eve and the Apes*. New York: Weidenfeld & Nicolson, 1988.

—— *Hong Kong Holiday*. New York: Doubleday, 1946.

—— *Miss Jill from Shanghai*. New York: Avon, 1950.

—— *Mr. Pan*. London: Robert Hale, 1942.

—— *The Soong Sisters*. Garden City: Garden City Publishing, 1941.

—— *Steps of the Sun*. London: Robert Hale, 1945.

—— *Times and Places*. New York: Thomas Y. Crowell, 1970.

Hahn, Emily, and the editors of Time-Life Books. *The Cooking of China*. Alexandria, VA: Time-Life Books, 1981.

Hailey, Arthur. *Hotel*. London: Corgi, 1991.

Hall, Captain W.H. *The Nemesis in China*. London: Henry Colburn, 1847.

Han Bangqing. *The Sing-song Girls of Shanghai*. Translated by Eileen Chang. New York: Columbia University Press, 2005.

Han Suyin. *Birdless Summer*. London: Triad, 1988.

—— *A Mortal Flower*. London: Jonathan Cape, 1969.

Harmsen, Peter. *Shanghai 1937: Stalingrad on the Yangtze*. Havertown: Casemate, 2013.

Hauser, Ernest O. *Shanghai: City for Sale*. New York: Harcourt, Brace and Company, 1940.

Hemingway, Ernest. *Byline: Ernest Hemingway*. New York: Scribner's, 1967.

Henriot, Christian, and Wen-hsin Yeh, eds. *In the Shadow of the Rising Sun: Shanghai under Japanese Occupation*. Cambridge: Cambridge University Press, 2004.

Hergé. *The Blue Lotus*. New York: Little, Brown and Company., 2011.

Hibbard, Peter. *The Bund Shanghai: China Faces West*. Hong Kong: Odyssey, 2007.

—— *Peace at the Cathay*. Hong Kong: Earnshaw Books, 2013.

Hobart, Alice Tisdale. *Oil for the Lamps of China*. New York: Bantam Books, 1945.

Hodges, Graham. *Anna May Wong*. Hong Kong: Hong Kong University Press, 2012.

Honig, Emily. *Sisters and Strangers: Women in the Shanghai Cotton Mills, 1919–1949*. Stanford: Stanford University Press, 1986.

Howlett, Jonathan. *Creating a New Shanghai: the End of the British Presence in China, 1949–57*. Ph.D. thesis, University of Bristol, 2012.

Hsu, Kai-yu. *Twentieth-Century Chinese Poetry, An Anthology*. New York: Doubleday, 1960.

Huang, Yuante. *Charlie Chan: The Unknown Story*. New York: W.W. Norton, 2010.

Hung, Chang-tai. *War and Popular Culture: Resistance in Modern China, 1937–1945*. Berkeley: University of California Press, 1994.

Huxley, Aldous. *Jesting Pilate: An Intellectual Holiday*. New York: George H. Doran Co., 1926.

Ishiguro, Kazuo. *When We Were Orphans*. London: Faber and Faber, 2000.

Jackson, Stanley. *The Sassoons*. New York: E.P. Dutton, 1968.

Jacques, Martin. *When China Rules the World: The End of the Western World and the Birth of a New Global Order*. New York: Penguin Press, 2009.

James, Heyward Parker. *Victor Sassoon and the Twilight of Foreign Shanghai*. M.A. thesis, Tufts University, 1993.

Karns, Maurine, and Pat Patterson. *Shanghai: High Lights, Low Lights, Tael Lights*. Hong Kong: Earnshaw Books, 2009.

Krasno, Rena. *Strangers Always: A Jewish Family in Wartime Shanghai*. Berkeley: Pacific View Press, 1992.

Kuo, Jason C., ed. *Visual Culture in Shanghai, 1850s–1930s*. Washington, DC: New Academia, 2007.

Lampe, David, and Szenasi Laszlo, *The Self Made-Villain: A Biography of I.T. Trebitsch-Lincoln*. London: Cassel & Company, 1961.

Lee, Jennifer 8. *The Fortune Cookie Chronicles: Adventures in the World of Chinese Food*. New York: Grand Central Publishing, 2009.

Lee, Leo Ou-fan. *Shanghai Modern: The Flowering of a New Urban Culture in China, 1930–45*. Cambridge, MA: Harvard University Press, 1999.

Lent, John A., ed. *Illustrating Asia: Comics, Humor, Magazines and Picture Books*. Honolulu: University of Hawai'i Press, 2001.

Levy, Daniel S. *Two-Gun Cohen*. New York: Inkwell Publishing, 1997.

Li, Jie. *Shanghai Homes: Palimpsests of Private Life*. New York: Columbia University Press, 2015.

Lin Qi. *Hai shang cai zi: Shao Xunmei*. Shanghai: Shanghai ren min chu ban she, 2002.

Lin Yutang. *The Vigil of a Nation*. London: William Heinemann, 1946.

Lindsay, Oliver. *The Lasting Honour: The Fall of Hong Kong, 1941*. London: Hamilton, 1978.

Linklater, Eric. *Juan in China*. London: Bloomsbury Reader, 2013.

Lovell, Julia. *The Opium War: Drugs, Dreams and the Making of China*. London: Picador, 2011.

Lu, Hanchao. *Beyond the Neon Lights: Everyday Shanghai in the Early Twentieth Century*. Berkeley: University of California Press, 1999.

Lu Xun. *Silent China: Selected Writings of Lu Xun*. Edited and translated by Gladys Yang. London: Oxford University Press, 1973.

MacKinnon, Janice R., and MacKinnon Stephen R, *Agnes Smedley: Life and Times of an American Radical*. Berkeley: University of Los Angeles Press, 1988.

Malraux, André. *Man's Fate*. London: Vintage, 1990.

Messmer, Matthias. *Jewish Wayfarers in Modern China: Tragedy and Splendor*. Lanham: Lexington Books, 2013.

Meyer, Maisie J. *The Sephardi Jewish Community of Shanghai 1845–1939 and the Question of Identity*. Ph.D. thesis, University of London, 1994.

—— *Shanghai's Baghdadi Jews: A Collection of Biographical Reflections*. Hong Kong: Blacksmith Books, 2015.

Miller, G.E. *Shanghai: The Paradise of Adventurers*. New York: Orsay Publishing House, 1937.

Miller, Michael B. *Shanghai on the Métro: Spies, Intrigue and the French between the Wars*. Berkeley: University of California Press, 1994.

Mishra, Pankaj. *From the Ruins of Empire: The Revolt Against the West and the Remaking of Asia*. London: Penguin, 2013.

Montesi, Albert, and Richard Deposki, *Central West End St. Louis*. Chicago: Arcadia Publishing, 2000.

Moorehead, Caroline, ed. *The Letters of Martha Gellhorn*. London: Chatto & Windus, 2006.

Moreira, Peter. *Hemingway on the China Front: His WWII Spy Mission with Martha Gellhorn*. Washington, DC: Potomac Books, 2007.

Naquin, Susan, and Evelyn S. Rawski. *Chinese Society in the Eighteenth Century*. New Haven: Yale University Press, 1987.

Pan, Lynn. *Old Shanghai: Gangsters in Paradise*. Singapore: Marshall Cavendish, 2011.

—— *Shanghai Style: Art and Design Between the Wars*. San Francisco: Long River Press, 2008.

Pan, Ling. *In Search of Old Shanghai*. Hong Kong: Joint Publishing, 1991.

Payn, Graham, and Sheridan Morley, *The Noël Coward Diaries*. Cambridge, MA: Da Capo Press, 2000.

Perelman, S.J. *Westward Ha!, or Around the World in Eighty Clichés*. New York: Burford Books, 1998.

Pollard, David E. *The True Story of Lu Xun*. Hong Kong: Chinese University Press, 2002.

Polo, Marco. *The Travels*. Transated by R.E. Lantham. London: Penguin, 1959.

Powell, John B. *My Twenty-Five Years in China*. New York: Macmillan, 1945.

Price, Ruth. *The Lives of Agnes Smedley*. Oxford: Oxford University Press, 2005.

Purvis, Malcom. *Tall Storeys: Palmer and Turner, Architects and Engineers – the First 100 Years*. Hong Kong: Palmer and Turner, 1985.

Rand, Peter. *China Hands: The Adventures and Ordeals of the American Journalists Who Joined Forces with the Great Chinese Revolution*. New York: Simon & Schuster, 1995.

Ristaino, Marcia R. *The Jacquinot Safe Zone: Wartime Refugees in Shanghai*. Stanford: Stanford University Press, 2008.

Roberts, J.A.G. *A History of China* (third edition). London: Macmillan-Palgrave, 2011.

Rohmer, Sax. *The Insidious Dr. Fu-Manchu*. Available at www.gutenberg.org/files/173/173-h/173-h.htm#chap01 (last accessed October 18, 2015).

Schirokauer, Conrad. *A Brief History of Chinese Civilization*. New York: Thomson Learning, 1991.

Sergeant, Harriet. *Shanghai: Collision Points of Culture 1918/1939*. New York: Crown Publishers, 1990.

Shao Xiaohong. *Wo de ba ba Shao Xunmei (My Father Sinmay Zau)*. Shanghai: Shanghai shu dian chu ban she, 2005.

Sheng Peiyu. *Sheng shi jia zu, Shao Xunmei yu wo: Sheng Peiyu de hui yi*. Beijing Shi: Ren min wen xue chu ban she, 2004.

Shaw, Ralph. *Sin City*. London: Warner Books, 1997.

Sheean, Vincent. *Personal History*. Garden City: Doubleday, Doran & Co., 1935.

Short, Philip. *Mao: A Life*. New York: Henry Holt, 1999.

Snow, Edgar. *The Battle for Asia*. New York: Random House, 1941.

—— *Journey to the Beginning*. New York: Random House, 1958.

—— *Red Star Over China: First Revised and Enlarged Edition*. New York: Grove Press, 1968.

Snow, Helen Foster. *My China Years: A Memoir by Helen Foster Snow*. Beijing: Foreign Languages Press, 2004.

Spence, Jonathan. *Mao Zedong: A Life*. London: Penguin, 1999.

—— *The Search for Modern China*. New York: W.W. Norton, 1991.

Stansky, Peter. *Sassoon: The Worlds of Philip and Sybil*. New Haven: Yale University Press, 2003.

Sues, Ilona Ralf. *Shark's Fins and Millet*. Boston: Little, Brown and Company, 1944.

Taylor, Saundra. *Love, Mickey: Letters to Family from Emily Hahn*. Bloomington: The Lilly Library, 2005.

Theroux, Paul. *Sailing through China*. Boston: Houghton-Mifflin, 1984.

Tagore, Rabindranath. *The Home and the World*. London: Penguin, 1985.

Taylor, Jay. *The Generalissimo: Chiang Kai-shek and the Struggle for Modern China*. Cambridge, MA: Belknap Press, 2011.

Thomas, Gordon. *Voyage of the Damned*. New York: Stein and Day, 1974.

Thomas, S. Bernard. *Season of High Adventure: Edgar Snow in China*. Berkeley: University of California Press, 1996.

Trigault, Nicolas. *China in the Sixteenth Century*. New York: Random House, 1953.

Tuchman, Barbara W. *Stilwell and the American Experience in China, 1911–45*. New York: Bantam, 1972.

von Sternberg, Josef. *Fun in a Chinese Laundry*. London: Columbus Books, 1987.

Voticky, Anka. *Knocking on Every Door*. Toronto: Azrieli Foundation, 2012.

Wakabayashi, Bob, ed. *The Nanking Atrocity, 1937–38*. Oxford: Berghahn, 2007.

Wakeman, Frederic, Jr. *Policing Shanghai 1927–1937*. Berkeley: University of California Press, 1995.

Wang Jinfang. *Shao Xunmei chu ban jie de Tangjikede*. Guangzhou Shi: Guangdong jiao yu chu ban she, 2012.

Wasserstein, Bernard. *The Secret Lives of Trebitsch Lincoln*. New Haven: Yale University Press, 1988.

—— *Secret War in Shanghai: An Untold Story of Espionage, Intrigue, and Treason*. Boston: Houghton Mifflin, 1999.

Wen, Yuan-ning. *Imperfect Understanding*. Shanghai: Kelly & Walsh, 1935.

Westad, Odd Arne. *Restless Empire: China and the World Since 1750*. New York: Basic, 2012.

Winchester, Simon. *The Man Who Loved China: The Fantastic Story of the Eccentric Scientist Who Unlocked the Mysteries of the Middle Kingdom*. New York: HarperCollins, 2008.

—— *The River at the Center of the World*. New York: Picador, 2004.

Wu Liang. *Old Shanghai: A Lost World*. Beijing: Foreign Languages Press, 2003.

Wu Ying, ed. *The City, the People – Essays by Shanghai Writers*. Shanghai: Shanghai Press and Publishing Development Company, 2006.

Yagoda, Ben. *About Town: The* New Yorker *and the World it Made*. New York: Da Capo Press, 2000.

Yeh, Wen-hsin. *Shanghai Splendor: Economic Sentiments and the Making of Modern China, 1843–1949*. Berkeley: University of California Press, 2007.

Yu Hua. *China in Ten Words*. New York: Anchor, 2012.

Yue Meng. *Shanghai and the Edges of Empire*. Minneapolis: University of Minnesota Press, 2006.

Zolberg, Aristide. *A Nation by Design, Immigration Policy in the Fashioning of America*. Cambridge, MA: Harvard University Press, 2008.

Articles in newspapers, journals, websites, and edited volumes

"Boxer on Boxer: A Conversation," *Camões Center Quarterly*, Vol. 1, No. 2, June 1989.

"Report for the Year Ended 31st December 1891," Municipal Council, Shanghai.

"The Shanghai Boom," *Fortune Magazine*, January 1935.

"The Shanghai Jubilee (1843–1893)," special edition of the *North-China Daily News*, datelined November 17, 1893.

Bailey, Warren, and Zhao Bin. "Familiarity, Convenience, and Commodity Money: Spanish and Mexican Silver Dollars in Qing and Republican China." Based on Zhao's MA thesis at Cornell University, 2006.

Hahn, Emily. "Brother in Japan," the *New Yorker*, March 30, 1940, p. 62.

—— "The China Boom," *T'ien Hsia*, 1938.

—— "Gibbons in Interactions with Man in Domestic Settings," in *Gibbon and Siamang*, vol. 1, pp. 250–60.

—— "Heh-ven, Pawnbroker", the *New Yorker*, March 9, 1940, p. 79.

—— "Special City," in *St. Louis Magazine*, June 1982, p 19.

Henriot, Christian. "The Shanghai Bund in Myth and History," *Journal of Modern Chinese History*, June 2010, pp. 1–27.

Hsü, Immanuel C.Y. "The Secret Mission of the *Lord Amherst* on the China Coast, 1832," *Harvard Journal of Asiatic Studies*, Vol. 17, No. 1–2, June 1954, pp. 231–52.

Hutt, Jonathan. "Monstre Sacré: The Decadent World of Sinmay Zau". *China Heritage Quarterly*, No. 22, June 2010.

Kuhn, Irene Corbally. "Shanghai: the Vintage Years," in *Endless Feasts: Sixty Years of Writing from* Gourmet. New York: Modern Library, 2003.

Laing, Ellen Johnston. "Shanghai Manhua, the Neo-Sensationist School of Literature, and Scenes of Urban Life," *Modern Chinese Literature and Culture*, October 2010.

Lang, H. "Shanghai Considered Socially: A Lecture". Shanghai: American Presbyterian Mission Press, 1875.

Maxwell, Kenneth. "The C.R. Boxer Affaire," *Council on Foreign Relations*, March 16, 2001.

Politzer, Eric. "The Changing Face of the Shanghai Bund, 1849–1879," *Arts of Asia*, 2005, pp. 64–81.

Rigby, Richard. "Sapajou's Shanghai," *China Heritage Quarterly*, No. 22, June 2010.

Stein, Sarah Abrevaya. "Protected Persons? The Baghdadi Jewish Diaspora, the British State, and the Persistence of Empire," *The American Historical Review*, 2011, pp. 80–108.

Zhang Yinde. "Les sociabilités littéraires shanghaiennes des années 1930: le cas de Shao Xunmei," in Nicolas Idier, ed., *Shanghai: Histoire, Promenades, Anthologie et Dictionnaire*. Paris: Boquins, 2010.

Index

Permissions Acknowledgements

The author and publisher are grateful to the following for granting permission to reprint from their materials.

Edgar Snow materials reprinted with permission of Sian and Lois Snow.
Translation of Shao Xunmei's poetry courtesy of Professor Leo Oufan Lee.
Martha Gellhorn materials reprinted with permission of Alexander
   Matthews, literary executor.
Eric Linklater materials reprinted with permission of his estate, represented
   by Peters Fraser & Dunlop, London.
Christopher Isherwood's chapters in *Journey to a War* granted by The
   Christopher Isherwood Foundation, Santa Monica, CA.
Sir Harold Acton materials courtesy of Sir Harold Acton estate,
   represented by Artellus Literary Agency.
Emily Hahn materials reprinted with permission of Carola Vecchio and the
   Lilly Library, University of Indiana, Bloomington, Indiana.
Sir Victor Sassoon papers, held in the DeGolyer Library, Southern
   Methodist University, Dallas, Texas.
Shao Xunmei (Zau Sinmay) materials reprinted with permission of Shao
   Xiao Yang.
Bernardine Szold-Fritz letters, held in the Beinecke Library, Yale, New
   Haven, Connecticut.
S.J. Perelman passage quoted with permission of Harold Ober Associates,
   New York.